Treaty Series

Treaties and international agreements registered or filed and recorded with the Secretariat of the United Nations

VOLUME 3212

Recueil des Traités

Traités et accords internationaux enregistrés ou classés et inscrits au répertoire au Secrétariat de l'Organisation des Nations Unies

United Nations • Nations Unies
New York, 2026

Print ISBN: 978-92-1-003311-4
e-ISBN: 978-92-1-106855-9
ISSN: 0379-8267
e-ISSN: 2412-1495

TABLE OF CONTENTS

I

Treaties and international agreements registered in November 2017 Nos. 54780 to 54790

TABLE DES MATIÈRES

I

Traités et accords internationaux
enregistrés en novembre 2017
N°s 54780 à 54790

NOTE BY THE SECRETARIAT

Under Article 102 of the Charter of the United Nations, every treaty and every international agreement entered into by any Member of the United Nations after the coming into force of the Charter shall, as soon as possible, be registered with the Secretariat and published by it. Furthermore, no party to a treaty or international agreement subject to registration which has not been registered may invoke that treaty or agreement before any organ of the United Nations. The General Assembly, by resolution 97 (I), established regulations to give effect to Article 102 of the Charter (see text of the regulations, vol. 859, p. VIII; https://treaties.un.org/Pages/Resource.aspx?path=Publication/Regulation/Page1_en.xml).

The terms "treaty" and "international agreement" have not been defined either in the Charter or in the regulations, and the Secretariat follows the principle that it acts in accordance with the position of the Member State submitting an instrument for registration that, so far as that party is concerned, the instrument is a treaty or an international agreement within the meaning of Article 102. Registration of an instrument submitted by a Member State, therefore, does not imply a judgement by the Secretariat on the nature of the instrument, the status of a party or any similar question. It is the understanding of the Secretariat that its acceptance for registration of an instrument does not confer on the instrument the status of a treaty or an international agreement if it does not already have that status, and does not confer upon a party a status which it would not otherwise have.

*

* *

NOTE DU SECRÉTARIAT

Aux termes de l'Article 102 de la Charte des Nations Unies, tout traité ou accord international conclu par un Membre des Nations Unies après l'entrée en vigueur de la Charte sera, le plus tôt possible, enregistré au Secrétariat et publié par lui. De plus, aucune partie à un traité ou accord international qui aurait dû être enregistré mais ne l'a pas été ne pourra invoquer ledit traité ou accord devant un organe de l'Organisation des Nations Unies. Par sa résolution 97 (I), l'Assemblée générale a adopté un règlement destiné à mettre en application l'Article 102 de la Charte (voir texte du règlement, vol. 859, p. IX; https://treaties.un.org/Pages/Resource.aspx?path=Publication/Regulation/Page1_fr.xml).

Les termes « traité » et « accord international » n'ont été définis ni dans la Charte ni dans le règlement, et le Secrétariat a pris comme principe de s'en tenir à la position adoptée à cet égard par l'État Membre qui a présenté l'instrument à l'enregistrement, à savoir que, en ce qui concerne cette partie, l'instrument constitue un traité ou un accord international au sens de l'Article 102. Il s'ensuit que l'enregistrement d'un instrument présenté par un État Membre n'implique, de la part du Secrétariat, aucun jugement sur la nature de l'instrument, le statut d'une partie ou toute autre question similaire. Le Secrétariat considère donc que son acceptation pour enregistrement d'un instrument ne confère pas audit instrument la qualité de traité ou d'accord international si ce dernier ne l'a pas déjà, et qu'il ne confère pas à une partie un statut que, par ailleurs, elle ne posséderait pas.

*

* *

I

Treaties and international agreements registered in November 2017 Nos. 54780 to 54790

Traités et accords internationaux enregistrés en novembre 2017 N°s 54780 à 54790

No. 54780

Mexico
and
Saint Lucia

Basic Agreement on technical and scientific cooperation between the United Mexican States and Saint Lucia. Asunción, 4 June 2014

Entry into force: *30 April 2017, in accordance with article XIII*

Authentic texts: *English and Spanish*

Registration with the Secretariat of the United Nations: *Mexico, 22 November 2017*

Mexique
et
Sainte-Lucie

Accord de base relatif à la coopération technique et scientifique entre les États-Unis du Mexique et Sainte-Lucie. Asunción, 4 juin 2014

Entrée en vigueur : *30 avril 2017, conformément à l'article XIII*

Textes authentiques : *anglais et espagnol*

Enregistrement au Secrétariat de l'Organisation des Nations Unies : *Mexique, 22 novembre 2017*

[TEXT IN ENGLISH – TEXTE EN ANGLAIS]

BASIC AGREEMENT ON TECHNICAL AND SCIENTIFIC COOPERATION BETWEEN THE UNITED MEXICAN STATES AND SAINT LUCIA

The United Mexican States and Saint Lucia hereinafter referred to as "the Parties";

AIMED by the desire to strengthening the ties of friendship between both countries, through the promotion of technical and scientific cooperation;

CONVINCED of the importance of updating and strengthen the mechanisms that contribute to their development and of the necessity to execute technical and scientific cooperation programs, that have effective incidence in the economic and social advancement of its respective countries;

ACKNOWLEDGING that the establishment of a broad and consistent frame of reference for cooperation shall be of mutual benefit;

Have agreed as follows:

ARTICLE I
OBJECTIVE

This Agreement has as it objective to promote the technical and scientific cooperation between both Parties, through the joint elaboration of programs and projects in priority areas, in accordance with their respective development policies.

ARTICLE II
SPECIFIC AGREEMENTS

The Parties shall develop and coordinate all the activities of technical and scientific cooperation carried out under the specific agreements signed between agencies and institutions of both countries, in order to facilitate and strengthen their cooperation relations.

ARTICLE III
MODALITIES

For the purposes of this Agreement, the technical and scientific cooperation between the Parties may be developed through the following modalities:

a) exchange of experts;

b) exchange of documents and information;

c) training of human resources;

d) exchange of material and equipment;

e) joint scientific and technological development projects;

f) organization of seminars or conferences, and

g) any other modality agreed upon by the Parties.

The execution of this Agreement shall not be conditional on the establishment by the Parties of projects in all the modalities of cooperation referred to in this Article.

The Parties shall not be obliged to collaborate in those activities which have an internal restriction or any other derived from a law, institutional rule or custom.

ARTICLE IV
MIXED COMMISSION

In order to ensure a proper following-up and coordination mechanism of the cooperation activities carried out under this Agreement and to achieve the best conditions for its execution, the Parties shall establish a Mixed Commission on Technical and Scientific Cooperation Mexico – Saint Lucia, composed of representatives of both countries.

The Mixed Commission shall carry out meetings in person alternatively in the United Mexican States and Saint Lucia or through suitable electronic means on the date agreed upon by the Parties through diplomatic channels. Likewise the Parties may convoke by mutual agreement extraordinary meetings to evaluate specific projects or topics.

The Mixed Commission shall monitor the effective execution of this Agreement, shall prepare the biennial activities program, shall periodically evaluate the program as a whole and shall submit recommendations to Parties as it deems appropriate.

ARTICLE V
RESPONSIBLE AUTHORITIES OF THE COOPERATION

On behalf of the United Mexican States the executing body in charge of coordinating the cooperation activities carried out under this Agreement shall be the Ministry of Foreign Affairs, through the Mexican Agency for International Development Cooperation and on behalf of Saint Lucia shall be the Ministry of External Affairs, International Trade and Civil Aviation.

ARTICLE VI
REPORTS ON SPECIFIC AGREEMENTS

The agencies and institutions in both countries, responsible for the execution of the specific agreements envisaged in Article II of this Agreement, shall inform the Mixed Commission of the results of their cooperation activities, submitting proposals for subsequent development.

ARTICLE VII
PERSONNEL

The personnel assigned by each one of the Parties for the execution of the cooperation activities under this Agreement, shall continue to be under the management and direction of the institution to which it belongs, therefore avoiding the creation of labor relations with the other Party, who in no case shall be considered as a substitute employer.

Each Party shall grant all the necessary facilities that its laws and immigration regulations allows, for the entry, stay and departure of personnel who shall officially take part in the cooperation projects resulting from this Agreement. The personnel shall be subjected to the current laws and migratory, fiscal, customs, sanitary, and security dispositions in force at the receiving country and shall not be able to develop or perform any other activity. The personnel shall leave the receiving country, in accordance with its laws and dispositions.

ARTICLE VIII
ENTRANCE AND EXIT OF EQUIPMENT

The Parties shall grant each other the administrative, fiscal and customs facilities necessary for the entrance under a temporary character and exit from their territory of the equipment and other materials that shall be used in the accomplishment of the projects, in accordance with their national legislation.

ARTICLE IX
INFORMATION

Regard to the exchange of information and its diffusion, the Parties shall observe the effective laws and other provisions in both States, as well as the respective international commitments, national security interests and the rights and obligations that consent in relation to third parties. When the information is provided by one of the Parties, this Party may state, when consider it appropriate, the restrictions to its diffusion.

ARTICLE X
FINANCING

The cooperation activities shall be financed with the resources assigned in the budgets of the agencies and institutions of both Parties responsible of its execution, in conformity to their availability and in accordance with their respective national legislation.

The Parties may request for financing support from external sources such as international organizations and third countries for the execution of programs and projects that are performed in accordance with this Agreement.

ARTICLE XI
SHARED COSTS

The international transportation costs for the personnel referred in Article III of this Agreement shall be supported by the sending Party. The lodging, feeding and local transportation costs, necessary for the execution of their activities under the frame of this Agreement, shall be covered by the receiving Party, unless expressly agreed otherwise or are subject to specific agreements, referred to in Article II.

ARTICLE XII
DISPUTES

Any difference or dispute arising from the interpretation or execution of this Agreement shall be settled for the Parties by mutual agreement.

ARTICLE XIII
ENTRY INTO FORCE AND VALIDITY

This Agreement shall enter into force thirty (30) days after the receipt of the last communication, sent by diplomatic channels, in which the Parties inform each other of the fulfillment of the requirements demanded by its national legislation for such effect.

ARTICLE XIV
AMENDMENTS

This Agreement may be amended by mutual consent of the Parties, by the request of either Party. The modifications shall be formalized in writing and shall enter into force in accordance with the established in the Article XIII.

ARTICLE XV
TERMINATION

This Agreement may be terminated by either Party by written notification addressed to the other Party, through diplomatic channels, six (6) months in advance.

The termination of this Agreement shall not affect the cooperation activities formalized during its validity, unless otherwise agreed upon by the Parties.

Signed in the city of Asuncion, Paraguay, on the fourth day of June of two thousand and fourteen, in two original copies, in the Spanish and English languages, both texts being equally authentic.

FOR THE UNITED MEXICAN STATES	**FOR SAINT LUCIA**
José Antonio Meade Kuribreña **Minister of Foreign Affairs**	**Alva R. Baptiste** **Minister for External Affairs, International Trade and Civil Aviation**

[TEXT IN SPANISH – TEXTE EN ESPAGNOL]

CONVENIO BÁSICO DE COOPERACIÓN TÉCNICA Y CIENTÍFICA ENTRE LOS ESTADOS UNIDOS MEXICANOS Y SANTA LUCÍA

Los Estados Unidos Mexicanos y Santa Lucía, en adelante denominados "las Partes";

ANIMADAS por el deseo de fortalecer los vínculos de amistad entre ambos países, a través de la promoción de la cooperación técnica y científica;

CONVENCIDAS de la importancia de actualizar y fortalecer mecanismos que contribuyan a su desarrollo y de la necesidad de ejecutar programas de cooperación técnica y científica, que tengan efectiva incidencia en el avance económico y social de sus respectivos países;

RECONOCIENDO que el establecimiento de un amplio y consistente marco de referencia para la cooperación será de beneficio mutuo;

Han convenido lo siguiente:

ARTÍCULO I
OBJETIVO

El presente Convenio tiene como objetivo promover la cooperación técnica y científica entre ambas Partes, a través de la elaboración conjunta de programas y proyectos en áreas prioritarias, de conformidad con sus respectivas políticas de desarrollo.

ARTÍCULO II
ACUERDOS ESPECÍFICOS

Las Partes desarrollarán y coordinarán todas las actividades de cooperación técnica y científica que se realicen al amparo de los acuerdos específicos que se celebren entre dependencias e instituciones de ambos países, para facilitar y fortalecer sus relaciones de cooperación.

ARTÍCULO III
MODALIDADES

Para los fines del presente Convenio, la cooperación técnica y científica entre las Partes se podrá desarrollar a través de las modalidades siguientes:

a) intercambio de especialistas;

b) intercambio de documentos e información;

c) capacitación de recursos humanos;

d) intercambio de materiales y equipo;

e) proyectos conjuntos de desarrollo científico y tecnológico;

f) organización de seminarios o conferencias, y

g) cualquier otra modalidad que las Partes convengan.

La operación del presente Convenio no estará condicionada a que las Partes establezcan proyectos en todas las modalidades de cooperación a que se refiere el presente Artículo.

Las Partes no estarán obligadas a colaborar en aquellas actividades respecto de las cuales exista prohibición interna derivada de una ley, normativa institucional o costumbre.

ARTÍCULO IV
COMISIÓN MIXTA

Con el fin de asegurar un adecuado mecanismo de seguimiento y coordinación de las actividades de cooperación en cumplimiento del presente Convenio y de lograr las mejores condiciones para su ejecución, las Partes establecerán una Comisión Mixta de Cooperación Técnica y Científica México – Santa Lucía, integrada por representantes de ambos países.

La Comisión Mixta llevará a cabo reuniones de manera presencial, alternadamente en los Estados Unidos Mexicanos y en Santa Lucía, o a través de medios electrónicos adecuados, en la fecha que acuerden las Partes por vía diplomática. Asimismo, las Partes podrán convocar por mutuo acuerdo a reuniones extraordinarias, para evaluar proyectos o temas específicos.

La Comisión Mixta vigilará el buen funcionamiento del presente Convenio, elaborará el programa bienal de actividades, evaluará periódicamente el programa en su conjunto y formulará a las Partes las recomendaciones que considere pertinentes.

ARTÍCULO V
AUTORIDAD RESPONSABLE DE LA COOPERACIÓN

Por parte de los Estados Unidos Mexicanos el órgano ejecutor encargado de coordinar las actividades de cooperación que se deriven del presente Convenio será la Secretaría de Relaciones Exteriores, a través de la Agencia Mexicana de Cooperación Internacional para el Desarrollo y por parte de Santa Lucía será el Ministerio de Asuntos Exteriores, Comercio Internacional y Aviación Civil.

ARTÍCULO VI
INFORMES DE LOS ACUERDOS ESPECÍFICOS

Las dependencias e instituciones de ambos países, responsables de la ejecución de los acuerdos específicos previstos en el Artículo II del presente Convenio, deberán informar a la Comisión Mixta sobre los resultados de sus actividades de cooperación, sometiendo propuestas para su desarrollo posterior.

ARTÍCULO VII
PERSONAL

El personal comisionado por cada una de las Partes para la ejecución de las actividades de cooperación al amparo del presente Convenio, continuará bajo la dirección y dependencia de la institución a la que pertenezca, por lo que no se crearán relaciones de carácter laboral con la otra Parte, a la que en ningún caso se considerará como patrón sustituto.

Cada Parte otorgará las facilidades necesarias que su legislación y regulaciones migratorias le permitan para la entrada, permanencia y salida del personal que en forma oficial intervenga en los proyectos de cooperación que se deriven del presente Convenio. El personal se someterá a las leyes y disposiciones migratorias, fiscales, aduaneras, sanitarias y de seguridad vigentes en el país receptor y no podrá dedicarse a ninguna actividad ajena a sus funciones. El personal abandonará el país receptor, de conformidad con las leyes y disposiciones del mismo.

ARTÍCULO VIII
ENTRADA Y SALIDA DE EQUIPO

Las Partes se otorgarán las facilidades administrativas, fiscales y aduaneras necesarias para la entrada con carácter temporal y salida de su territorio, del equipo y otros materiales que se utilizarán en la realización de los proyectos, de conformidad con su legislación nacional.

ARTÍCULO IX
INFORMACIÓN

Respecto al intercambio de información y su difusión, las Partes observarán las leyes y demás disposiciones vigentes en ambos Estados, así como los respectivos compromisos internacionales, intereses de seguridad nacional y los derechos y obligaciones que se acuerden en relación con terceros. Cuando la información sea proporcionada por una Parte ésta podrá señalar, cuando lo juzgue conveniente, restricciones para su difusión.

ARTÍCULO X
FINANCIAMIENTO

Las actividades de cooperación serán financiadas con los recursos asignados en los presupuestos de las dependencias e instituciones de ambas Partes, responsables de su ejecución, sujeto a su disponibilidad y lo dispuesto por su legislación nacional.

Las Partes podrán solicitar el apoyo financiero de fuentes externas como organismos internacionales y terceros países, para la ejecución de programas y proyectos que se realicen de conformidad con el presente Convenio.

ARTÍCULO XI
COSTOS COMPARTIDOS

Los costos de transporte internacional del personal a que se refiere el Artículo III del presente Convenio, serán sufragados por la Parte que lo envíe. El costo de hospedaje, alimentación y transporte local, necesarios para la ejecución de sus actividades al amparo del presente Convenio, se cubrirán por la Parte receptora, a menos que expresamente se especifique de otra manera o sean objeto de los acuerdos específicos, a que hace referencia el Artículo II.

ARTÍCULO XII
CONTROVERSIAS

Cualquier diferencia derivada de la interpretación o ejecución del presente Convenio será resuelta por las Partes de común acuerdo.

ARTÍCULO XIII
ENTRADA EN VIGOR Y VIGENCIA

El presente Convenio entrará en vigor treinta (30) días después de la fecha en que se reciba la última notificación, remitida a través de los canales diplomáticos, mediante la cual las Partes se notifiquen del cumplimiento de los requisitos exigidos por su legislación nacional para tal efecto.

ARTÍCULO XIV
MODIFICACIONES

El presente Convenio podrá ser modificado por mutuo consentimiento de las Partes, a solicitud de cualquiera de ellas. Las modificaciones deberán formalizarse por escrito y entrarán en vigor de conformidad con el procedimiento establecido en el Artículo XIII.

ARTÍCULO XV
TERMINACIÓN

El presente Convenio podrá darse por terminado por cualquiera de las Partes mediante notificación escrita, dirigida a la otra Parte a través de la vía diplomática, con seis (6) meses de antelación.

La terminación del presente Convenio no afectará las actividades de cooperación formalizadas durante su vigencia, a menos que las Partes lo acuerden de otra forma.

Firmado en la ciudad de Asunción, Paraguay, el cuatro de junio de dos mil catorce, en dos ejemplares originales en idioma español e inglés, siendo ambos textos igualmente auténticos.

POR LOS ESTADOS UNIDOS MEXICANOS

José Antonio Meade Kuribreña
Secretario de Relaciones Exteriores

POR SANTA LUCÍA

Alva R. Baptiste
Ministro de Asuntos Exteriores, Comercio Internacional y Aviación Civil

[TRANSLATION IN FRENCH – TRADUCTION EN FRANÇAIS]

ACCORD DE BASE RELATIF À LA COOPÉRATION TECHNIQUE ET SCIENTIFIQUE ENTRE LES ÉTATS-UNIS DU MEXIQUE ET SAINTE-LUCIE

Les États-Unis du Mexique et Sainte-Lucie, ci-après dénommés les « Parties »,

Désireux de renforcer les liens d'amitié existant entre les deux pays par la promotion de la coopération technique et scientifique,

Convaincus de l'importance d'actualiser et de renforcer les mécanismes qui contribuent à leur développement, et de la nécessité d'exécuter des programmes de coopération technique et scientifique qui ont une incidence effective sur les progrès économiques et sociaux de leurs pays respectifs,

Reconnaissant que la mise en place d'un cadre de référence large et cohérent en matière de coopération présente un avantage réciproque,

Sont convenus de ce qui suit :

Article premier. Objectif

Le présent Accord a pour objectif de promouvoir la coopération technique et scientifique entre les deux Parties, par l'élaboration conjointe de programmes et de projets dans des domaines prioritaires, conformément à leurs politiques de développement respectives.

Article II. Accords spécifiques

Les Parties conçoivent et coordonnent toutes les activités de coopération technique et scientifique menées dans le cadre des accords spécifiques signés entre les organismes et institutions des deux pays, afin de faciliter et de renforcer leurs relations de coopération.

Article III. Modalités

Aux fins du présent Accord, la coopération technique et scientifique entre les Parties peut être renforcée selon les modalités suivantes :

a) Échange d'experts ;

b) Échange de documents et de renseignements ;

c) Formation des ressources humaines ;

d) Échange de matériel et d'équipement ;

e) Projets communs d'innovations scientifiques et techniques ;

f) Organisation de séminaires et de conférences ; et

g) Toute autre modalité dont les Parties conviennent.

L'exécution du présent Accord n'est pas conditionnée à ce que les Parties établissent des projets pour toutes les modalités de coopération visées au présent article.

Les Parties ne sont pas tenues de collaborer aux activités soumises à une restriction interne ou à toute autre restriction découlant d'une loi, d'une règle institutionnelle ou d'une coutume.

Article IV. Commission mixte

Afin d'assurer un mécanisme adéquat de suivi et de coordination des activités de coopération menées dans le cadre du présent Accord et de réunir les meilleures conditions pour son exécution, les Parties mettent en place une Commission mixte de coopération technique et scientifique Mexique–Sainte-Lucie, composée de représentants des deux pays.

La Commission mixte organise des réunions en personne ou par des moyens électroniques appropriés, alternativement aux États-Unis du Mexique et à Sainte-Lucie, aux dates convenues par les Parties par la voie diplomatique. De même, les Parties peuvent convoquer, d'un commun accord, des réunions extraordinaires pour évaluer des projets ou des thèmes spécifiques.

La Commission mixte surveille la mise en œuvre effective du présent Accord, prépare le programme d'activités biennal, évalue périodiquement le programme dans son ensemble et soumet aux Parties les recommandations qu'elle juge appropriées.

Article V. Autorités responsables de la coopération

L'organe d'exécution chargé de coordonner les activités de coopération menées dans le cadre du présent Accord est, pour les États-Unis du Mexique, le Ministère des affaires étrangères, par l'intermédiaire de l'Agence mexicaine de coopération internationale pour le développement, et, pour Sainte-Lucie, le Ministère des affaires étrangères, du commerce international et de l'aviation civile.

Article VI. Rapports relatifs à des accords spécifiques

Les organismes et institutions des deux pays, chargés de la mise en œuvre des accords spécifiques prévus à l'article II du présent Accord, informent la Commission mixte des résultats de leurs activités de coopération, en soumettant des propositions pour leur amélioration ultérieure.

Article VII. Personnel

Le personnel affecté par chacune des Parties à l'exécution des activités de coopération prévues par le présent Accord reste géré et sous la direction de l'institution à laquelle il appartient, ce qui évite de créer des relations de travail avec l'autre Partie, qui n'est en aucun cas considérée comme un employeur de substitution.

Chaque Partie accorde toutes les facilités nécessaires autorisées par sa législation et sa réglementation en matière d'immigration, pour l'entrée, le séjour et le départ du personnel qui participe officiellement aux projets de coopération découlant du présent Accord. Le personnel est soumis à la législation et aux dispositions migratoires, fiscales, douanières, sanitaires et sécuritaires en vigueur dans le pays d'accueil et ne peut créer ou exercer aucune autre activité. Le personnel quitte le pays d'accueil, conformément aux lois et dispositions de celui-ci.

Article VIII. Entrée et sortie de matériel

Les Parties s'accordent les facilités administratives, fiscales et douanières nécessaires à l'entrée temporaire sur leur territoire et à la sortie de leur territoire des équipements et autres matériels qui sont utilisés dans la réalisation des projets, conformément à leur législation interne.

Article IX. Renseignements

En ce qui concerne l'échange et la diffusion de renseignements, les Parties respectent les lois et autres dispositions en vigueur dans les deux États, ainsi que leurs engagements internationaux respectifs, les intérêts de sécurité nationale et les droits et obligations consentis à l'égard des tiers. Lorsque les renseignements sont fournis par l'une des Parties, celle-ci peut indiquer, lorsqu'elle le juge approprié, les restrictions à sa diffusion.

Article X. Financement

Les activités de coopération sont financées par les ressources prévues dans les budgets des organismes et institutions des deux Parties chargés de leur mise en œuvre, en fonction de leur disponibilité et conformément à leur législation interne respective.

Les Parties peuvent demander un soutien financier à des sources extérieures, telles que des organisations internationales et des pays tiers, pour l'exécution de programmes et de projets réalisés conformément au présent Accord.

Article XI. Coûts partagés

Les frais liés au transport international du personnel visé à l'article III du présent Accord sont pris en charge par la Partie d'envoi. Les frais de logement, d'alimentation et de transport local, nécessaires à l'exécution de leurs activités dans le cadre du présent Accord, sont couverts par la Partie d'accueil, sauf s'il en est expressément convenu autrement ou s'ils font l'objet d'accords spécifiques, visés à l'article II.

Article XII. Différends

Tout différend découlant de l'interprétation ou de l'exécution du présent Accord est réglé par les Parties d'un commun accord.

Article XIII. Entrée en vigueur et validité

Le présent Accord entre en vigueur 30 jours après la réception de la dernière communication, envoyée par voie diplomatique, par laquelle les Parties s'informent de l'accomplissement des exigences requises par leur législation interne à cet effet.

Article XIV. Amendements

À la demande de l'une des Parties, le présent Accord peut être amendé d'un commun accord entre celles-ci. Les modifications sont formalisées par écrit et entrent en vigueur conformément à la procédure prévue à l'article XIII.

Article XV. Dénonciation

Le présent Accord peut être dénoncé par l'une ou l'autre des Parties moyennant notification écrite adressée à l'autre Partie, par la voie diplomatique, en respectant un préavis de six mois.

À moins que les Parties n'en conviennent autrement, la dénonciation du présent Accord n'a pas d'effet sur les activités de coopération établies au cours de sa période de validité.

SIGNÉ à Asunción (République du Paraguay), le 4 juin 2014, en deux exemplaires originaux en langues espagnole et anglaise, les deux textes faisant également foi.

Pour les États-Unis du Mexique :

JOSÉ ANTONIO MEADE KURIBREÑA
Ministre des affaires étrangères

Pour Sainte-Lucie :

ALVA R. BAPTISTE
Ministre des affaires étrangères, du commerce international et de l'aviation civile

No. 54781

Luxembourg and Hungary

Convention between the Grand Duchy of Luxembourg and Hungary for the avoidance of double taxation and the prevention of fiscal evasion with respect to taxes on income and on capital (with protocol). Brussels, 10 March 2015

Entry into force: *26 January 2017, in accordance with article 28*

Authentic texts: *English, French and Hungarian*

Registration with the Secretariat of the United Nations: *Luxembourg, 6 November 2017*

Luxembourg et Hongrie

Convention entre le Grand-Duché de Luxembourg et la Hongrie tendant à éviter les doubles impositions et à prévenir la fraude fiscale en matière d'impôts sur le revenu et sur la fortune (avec protocole). Bruxelles, 10 mars 2015

Entrée en vigueur : *26 janvier 2017, conformément à l'article 28*

Textes authentiques : *anglais, français et hongrois*

Enregistrement au Secrétariat de l'Organisation des Nations Unies : *Luxembourg, 6 novembre 2017*

[TEXT IN ENGLISH – TEXTE EN ANGLAIS]

CONVENTION

BETWEEN

THE GRAND DUCHY OF LUXEMBOURG

AND

HUNGARY

FOR THE AVOIDANCE OF DOUBLE TAXATION

AND THE PREVENTION

OF FISCAL EVASION WITH RESPECT TO TAXES

ON INCOME AND ON CAPITAL

The Grand Duchy of Luxembourg and Hungary, desiring to conclude a Convention for the avoidance of double taxation and the prevention of fiscal evasion with respect to taxes on income and on capital, and to further develop and facilitate their relationship,

Have agreed as follows:

Article 1
PERSONS COVERED

This Convention shall apply to persons who are residents of one or both of the Contracting States.

Article 2
TAXES COVERED

1. This Convention shall apply to taxes on income and on capital imposed on behalf of a Contracting State or of its local authorities, irrespective of the manner in which they are levied.

2. There shall be regarded as taxes on income and on capital all taxes imposed on total income, on total capital or on elements of income or of capital, including taxes on gains from the alienation of movable or immovable property, taxes on the total amount of wages or salaries paid by enterprises, as well as taxes on capital appreciation.

3. The existing taxes to which the Convention shall apply are in particular:

(a) in Hungary:
- (i) the personal income tax (személyi jövedelemadó);
- (ii) the corporate tax (társasági adó);
- (iii) the land parcel tax (telekadó); and
- (iv) the building tax (építményadó);

(hereinafter referred to as "Hungarian tax");

(b) in Luxembourg:
- (i) the income tax on individuals (l'impôt sur le revenu des personnes physiques);
- (ii) the corporation tax (l'impôt sur le revenu des collectivités);
- (iii) the capital tax (l'impôt sur la fortune); and
- (iv) the communal trade tax (l'impôt commercial communal);

(hereinafter referred to as "Luxembourg tax").

4. The Convention shall apply also to any identical or substantially similar taxes that are imposed after the date of signature of the Convention in addition to, or in place of, the existing taxes. The competent authorities of the Contracting States shall notify each other of any significant changes that have been made in their taxation laws.

Article 3
GENERAL DEFINITIONS

1. For the purposes of this Convention, unless the context otherwise requires:

(a) the term "Hungary" means the territory of Hungary as defined by its laws in accordance with international law;

(b) the term "Luxembourg" means the Grand Duchy of Luxembourg and, when used in a geographical sense, it means the territory of the Grand Duchy of Luxembourg;

(c) the terms "a Contracting State" and "the other Contracting State" mean Hungary or Luxembourg, as the context requires;

(d) the term "person" includes an individual, a company and any other body of persons;

(e) the term "company" means any body corporate or any entity that is treated as a body corporate for tax purposes;

(f) the term "enterprise" applies to the carrying on of any business;

(g) the terms "enterprise of a Contracting State" and "enterprise of the other Contracting State" mean respectively an enterprise carried on by a resident of a Contracting State and an enterprise carried on by a resident of the other Contracting State;

(h) the term "international traffic" means any transport by a ship, aircraft or road vehicle operated by an enterprise that has its place of effective management in a Contracting State, except when the ship, aircraft or road vehicle is operated solely between places in the other Contracting State;

(i) the term "competent authority" means:

   (i) in the case of Hungary, the minister responsible for tax policy or his authorised representative;

   (ii) in the case of Luxembourg, the Minister of Finance or his authorised representative;

(j) the term "national", in relation to a Contracting State, means:

   (i) any individual possessing the nationality of that Contracting State; and

   (ii) any legal person, partnership, association or other entity deriving its status as such from the laws in force in that Contracting State;

(k) the term "business" includes the performance of professional services and of other activities of an independent character;

(l) the "place of effective management" is the place where the key management and commercial decisions that are necessary for the conduct of the entity's business are in substance made. The place of effective management will ordinarily be the place where the most senior person or group of persons makes its decisions, and the day-to-day management is conducted, the place where the actions to be taken by the entity as a whole are determined.

2. As regards the application of the Convention at any time by a Contracting State, any term not defined therein shall, unless the context otherwise requires, have the meaning that it has at that time under the law of that State for the purposes of the taxes to which the Convention applies, any meaning under the applicable tax laws of that State prevailing over a meaning given to the term under other laws of that State.

Article 4
RESIDENT

1. For the purposes of this Convention, the term "resident of a Contracting State" means any person who, under the laws of that State, is liable to tax therein by reason of his domicile, residence, place of management, place of incorporation or any other criterion of a similar nature, and also includes that State and any local authority thereof, as well as a collective investment vehicle established in that State. This term, however, does not include any person who is liable to tax in that State in respect only of income from sources in that State or capital situated therein.

2. Where by reason of the provisions of paragraph 1 an individual is a resident of both Contracting States, then his status shall be determined as follows:

(a) he shall be deemed to be a resident only of the State in which he has a permanent home available to him; if he has a permanent home available to him in both States, he shall be deemed to be a resident only of the State with which his personal and economic relations are closer (centre of vital interests);

(b) if the State in which he has his centre of vital interests cannot be determined, or if he has not a permanent home available to him in either State, he shall be deemed to be a resident only of the State in which he has an habitual abode;

(c) if he has an habitual abode in both States or in neither of them, he shall be deemed to be a resident only of the State of which he is a national;

(d) if he is a national of both States or of neither of them, the competent authorities of the Contracting States shall settle the question by mutual agreement.

3. Where by reason of the provisions of paragraph 1 a person other than an individual is a resident of both Contracting States, then it shall be deemed to be a resident only of the State in which its place of effective management is situated.

Article 5

PERMANENT ESTABLISHMENT

1. For the purposes of this Convention, the term "permanent establishment" means a fixed place of business through which the business of an enterprise is wholly or partly carried on.

2. The term "permanent establishment" includes especially:

(a) a place of management;

(b) a branch;

(c) an office;

(d) a factory;

(e) a workshop; and

(f) a mine, an oil or gas well, a quarry or any other place of extraction of natural resources.

3. A building site, a construction, assembly, installation or dredging project constitutes a permanent establishment only if it lasts more than twelve months.

4. Notwithstanding the preceding provisions of this Article, the term "permanent establishment" shall be deemed not to include:

(a) the use of facilities solely for the purpose of storage, display or delivery of goods or merchandise belonging to the enterprise;

(b) the maintenance of a stock of goods or merchandise belonging to the enterprise solely for the purpose of storage, display or delivery;

(c) the maintenance of a stock of goods or merchandise belonging to the enterprise solely for the purpose of processing by another enterprise;

(d) the maintenance of a fixed place of business solely for the purpose of purchasing goods or merchandise or of collecting information, for the enterprise;

(e) the maintenance of a fixed place of business solely for the purpose of carrying on, for the enterprise, any other activity of a preparatory or auxiliary character;

(f) the maintenance of a fixed place of business solely for any combination of activities mentioned in subparagraphs (a) to (e), provided that the overall activity of the fixed place of business resulting from this combination is of a preparatory or auxiliary character.

5. Notwithstanding the provisions of paragraphs 1 and 2, where a person – other than an agent of an independent status to whom paragraph 6 applies – is acting on behalf of an enterprise and has, and habitually exercises, in a Contracting State an authority to conclude contracts in the name of the enterprise, that enterprise shall be deemed to have a permanent establishment in that State in respect of any activities which that person undertakes for the enterprise, unless the activities of such person are limited to those mentioned in paragraph 4 which, if exercised through a fixed place of business, would not make this fixed place of business a permanent establishment under the provisions of that paragraph.

6. An enterprise shall not be deemed to have a permanent establishment in a Contracting State merely because it carries on business in that State through a broker, general commission agent or any other agent of an independent status, provided that such persons are acting in the ordinary course of their business.

7. The fact that a company which is a resident of a Contracting State controls or is controlled by a company which is a resident of the other Contracting State, or which carries on business in that other State (whether through a permanent establishment or otherwise), shall not of itself constitute either company a permanent establishment of the other.

Article 6
INCOME FROM IMMOVABLE PROPERTY

1. Income derived by a resident of a Contracting State from immovable property (including income from agriculture or forestry) situated in the other Contracting State may be taxed in that other State.

2. The term "immovable property" shall have the meaning which it has under the law of the Contracting State in which the property in question is situated. The term shall in any case include property accessory to immovable property, livestock and equipment used in agriculture and forestry, rights to which the provisions of general law respecting landed property apply, usufruct of immovable property and rights to variable or fixed payments as consideration for the working of, or the right to work, mineral deposits, sources and other natural resources; ships, boats and aircraft shall not be regarded as immovable property.

3. The provisions of paragraph 1 shall apply to income derived from the direct use, letting or use in any other form of immovable property.

4. The provisions of paragraphs 1 and 3 shall also apply to the income from immovable property of an enterprise.

Article 7
BUSINESS PROFITS

1. Profits of an enterprise of a Contracting State shall be taxable only in that State unless the enterprise carries on business in the other Contracting State through a permanent establishment situated therein. If the enterprise carries on business as aforesaid, the profits that are attributable to the permanent establishment in accordance with the provisions of paragraph 2 may be taxed in that other State.

2. For the purposes of this Article and Article 23, the profits that are attributable in each Contracting State to the permanent establishment referred to in paragraph 1 are the profits it might be expected to make, in particular in its dealings with other parts of the enterprise, if it were a seperate and independent enterprise engaged in the same or similar activities under the same or similar conditions, taking into account the functions performed, assets used and risks assumed by the enterprise through the permanent establishment and through the other parts of the enterprise.

3. Where in accordance with paragraph 2, a Contracting State adjusts the profits that are attributable to a permanent establishment of an enterprise of one of the Contracting States and taxes accordingly profits of the enterprise that have been charged to tax in the other State, the other State shall, to the extent necessary to eliminate double taxation on these profits, make an appropriate adjustment to the amount of the tax charged on those profits. In determining such adjustment, the competent authorities of the Contracting States shall if necessary consult each other.

4. Where profits include items of income which are dealt with separately in other Articles of this Convention, then the provisions of those Articles shall not be affected by the provisions of this Article.

Article 8
SHIPPING, INLAND WATERWAYS TRANSPORT AND AIR TRANSPORT

1. Profits from the operation of ships or aircraft in international traffic shall be taxable only in the Contracting State in which the place of effective management of the enterprise is situated.

2. Profits from the operation of boats engaged in inland waterways transport shall be taxable only in the Contracting State in which the place of effective management of the enterprise is situated.

3. If the place of effective management of a shipping enterprise or of an inland waterways transport enterprise is aboard a ship or boat, then it shall be deemed to be situated in the Contracting State in which the home harbour of the ship or boat is situated, or, if there is no such home harbour, in the Contracting State of which the operator of the ship or boat is a resident.

4. The provisions of paragraph 1 shall also apply to profits from the participation in a pool, a joint business or an international operating agency.

Article 9
ASSOCIATED ENTERPRISES

1. Where

(a) an enterprise of a Contracting State participates directly or indirectly in the management, control or capital of an enterprise of the other Contracting State, or

(b) the same persons participate directly or indirectly in the management, control or capital of an enterprise of a Contracting State and an enterprise of the other Contracting State,

and in either case conditions are made or imposed between the two enterprises in their commercial or financial relations which differ from those which would be made between independent enterprises, then any profits which would, but for those conditions, have accrued to one of the enterprises, but, by reason of those conditions, have not so accrued, may be included in the profits of that enterprise and taxed accordingly.

2. Where a Contracting State includes in the profits of an enterprise of that State – and taxes accordingly – profits on which an enterprise of the other Contracting State has been charged to tax in that other State and the profits so included are profits which would have accrued to the enterprise of the first-mentioned State if the conditions made between the two enterprises had been those which would have been made between independent enterprises, then that other State shall make an appropriate adjustment to the amount of the tax charged therein on those profits. In determining such adjustment, due regard shall be had to the other provisions of this Convention and the competent authorities of the Contracting States shall if necessary consult each other.

Article 10
DIVIDENDS

1. Dividends paid by a company which is a resident of a Contracting State to a resident of the other Contracting State may be taxed in that other State.

2. However, such dividends may also be taxed in the Contracting State of which the company paying the dividends is a resident and according to the laws of that State, but if the beneficial owner of the dividends is a resident of the other Contracting State, the tax so charged shall not exceed:

(a) 0 per cent of the gross amount of the dividends if the beneficial owner is a company (other than a partnership that is not liable to tax), which holds directly at least 10 per cent of the capital of the company paying the dividends;

(b) 10 per cent of the gross amount of the dividends in all other cases.

This paragraph shall not affect the taxation of the company in respect of the profits out of which the dividends are paid.

3. The term "dividends" as used in this Article means income from shares, "jouissance" shares or "jouissance" rights, minig shares, founders' shares or other rights, not being debt-claims, participating in profits, as well as income from other corporate rights which is subjected to the same taxation treatment as income from shares by the laws of the State of which the company making the distribution is a resident.

4. The provisions of paragraphs 1 and 2 shall not apply if the beneficial owner of the dividends, being a resident of a Contracting State, carries on business in the other Contracting State of which the company paying the dividends is a resident through a permanent establishment situated therein and the holding in respect of which the dividends are paid is effectively connected with such permanent establishment. In such case the provisions of Article 7 shall apply.

5. Where a company which is a resident of a Contracting State derives profits or income from the other Contracting State, that other State may not impose any tax on the dividends paid by the company, except insofar as such dividends are paid to a resident of that other State or insofar as the holding in respect of which the dividends are paid is effectively connected with a permanent establishment situated in that other State, nor subject the company's undistributed profits to a tax on the company's undistributed profits, even if the dividends paid or the undistributed profits consist wholly or partly of profits or income arising in such other State.

Article 11
INTEREST

1. Interest arising in a Contracting State and beneficially owned by a resident of the other Contracting State shall be taxable only in that other State.

2. The term "interest" as used in this Article means income from debt-claims of every kind, whether or not secured by mortgage and whether or not carrying a right to participate in the debtor's profits, and in particular, income from government securities and income from bonds or debentures, including premiums and prizes attaching to such securities, bonds or debentures, but does not include income dealt with in Article 10. Penalty charges for late payment shall not be regarded as interest for the purpose of this Article.

3. The provisions of paragraph 1 shall not apply if the beneficial owner of the interest, being a resident of a Contracting State, carries on business in the other Contracting State in which the interest arises, through a permanent establishment situated therein, and the debt-claim in respect of which the interest is paid is effectively connected with such permanent establishment. In such case the provisions of Article 7 shall apply.

4. Where, by reason of a special relationship between the payer and the beneficial owner or between both of them and some other person, the amount of the interest, having regard to the debt-claim for which it is paid, exceeds the amount which would have been agreed upon by the payer and the beneficial owner in the absence of such relationship, the provisions of this Article shall apply only to the last-mentioned amount. In such case, the excess part of the payments shall remain taxable according to the laws of each Contracting State, due regard being had to the other provisions of this Convention.

Article 12
ROYALTIES

1. Royalties arising in a Contracting State and beneficially owned by a resident of the other Contracting State shall be taxable only in that other State.

2. The term "royalties" as used in this Article means payments of any kind received as a consideration for the use of, or the right to use, any copyright of literary, artistic or scientific work (including cinematograph films), any patent, trade mark, design or model, plan, secret formula or process, or for information concerning industrial, commercial or scientific experience.

3. The provisions of paragraph 1 shall not apply if the beneficial owner of the royalties, being a resident of a Contracting State, carries on business in the other Contracting State in which the royalties arise, through a permanent establishment situated therein, and the right or property in respect of which the royalties are paid is effectively connected with such permanent establishment. In such case the provisions of Article 7 shall apply.

4. Where, by reason of a special relationship between the payer and the beneficial owner or between both of them and some other person, the amount of the royalties, having regard to the use, right or information for which they are paid, exceeds the amount which would have been agreed upon by the payer and the beneficial owner in the absence of such relationship, the provisions of this Article shall apply only to the last-mentioned amount. In such case, the excess part of the payments shall remain taxable according to the laws of each Contracting State, due regard being had to the other provisions of this Convention.

Article 13
CAPITAL GAINS

1. Gains derived by a resident of a Contracting State from the alienation of immovable property referred to in Article 6 and situated in the other Contracting State may be taxed in that other State.

2. Gains derived by a resident of a Contracting State from the alienation of shares or comparable interests deriving more than 50 per cent of their value directly or indirectly from immovable property situated in the other Contracting State may be taxed in that other State.

3. Gains, other than those dealt with in paragraph 2 of this Article, from the alienation of movable property forming part of the business property of a permanent establishment which an enterprise of a Contracting State has in the other Contracting State, including such gains from the alienation of such a permanent establishment (alone or with the whole enterprise), may be taxed in that other State.

4. Gains from the alienation of ships or aircraft operated in international traffic, boats engaged in inland waterways transport or movable property pertaining to the operation of such ships, aircraft or boats, shall be taxable only in the Contracting State in which the place of effective management of the enterprise is situated.

5. Gains from the alienation of any property other than that referred to in paragraphs 1, 2, 3 and 4, shall be taxable only in the Contracting State of which the alienator is a resident.

Article 14
INCOME FROM EMPLOYMENT

1. Subject to the provisions of Articles 15, 17, 18 and 20, salaries, wages and other similar remuneration derived by a resident of a Contracting State in respect of an employment shall be taxable only in that State unless the employment is exercised in the other Contracting State. If the employment is so exercised, such remuneration as is derived therefrom may be taxed in that other State.

2. Notwithstanding the provisions of paragraph 1, remuneration derived by a resident of a Contracting State in respect of an employment exercised in the other Contracting State shall be taxable only in the first-mentioned State if:

(a) the recipient is present in the other State for a period or periods not exceeding in the aggregate 183 days in any twelve-month period commencing or ending in the calendar year concerned, and

(b) the remuneration is paid by, or on behalf of, an employer who is not a resident of the other State, and

(c) the remuneration is not borne by a permanent establishment which the employer has in the other State.

3. Notwithstanding the preceding provisions of this Article, remuneration derived in respect of an employment exercised aboard a ship, aircraft or road vehicle operated in international traffic, or aboard a boat engaged in inland waterways transport, may be taxed in the Contracting State in which the place of effective management of the enterprise is situated.

Article 15
DIRECTORS' FEES

Directors' fees and other similar payments derived by a resident of a Contracting State in his capacity as a member of the board of directors or the supervisory board of a company which is a resident of the other Contracting State may be taxed in that other State.

Article 16
ARTISTES AND SPORTSPERSONS

1. Notwithstanding the provisions of Articles 7 and 14, income derived by a resident of a Contracting State as an entertainer, such as a theatre, motion picture, radio or television artiste, or a musician, or as a sportsperson, from his personal activities as such exercised in the other Contracting State, may be taxed in that other State.

2. Where income in respect of personal activities exercised by an entertainer or a sportsperson in his capacity as such accrues not to the entertainer or sportsperson himself but to another person, that income may, notwithstanding the provisions of Articles 7 and 14, be taxed in the Contracting State in which the activities of the entertainer or sportsperson are exercised.

3. The provisions of paragraphs 1 and 2 shall not apply to income derived from activities performed in a Contracting State by artistes or sportspersons if the visit to that State is wholly or mainly supported by public funds of one or both of the Contracting States or local authorities thereof. In such a case, the income is taxable only in the Contracting State in which the artiste or sportsperson is a resident.

Article 17
PENSIONS

Pensions and other similar remuneration arising in a Contracting State and paid to a resident of the other Contracting State shall be taxable only in the first-mentioned State.

Article 18
GOVERNMENT SERVICE

1. (a) Salaries, wages and other similar remuneration paid by a Contracting State or a local authority thereof to an individual in respect of services rendered to that State or authority shall be taxable only in that State.

(b) However, such salaries, wages and other similar remuneration shall be taxable only in the other Contracting State if the services are rendered in that State and the individual is a resident of that State who

(i) is a national of that State; or

(ii) did not become a resident of that State solely for the purpose of rendering the services.

2. The provisions of Articles 14, 15 and 16 shall apply to salaries, wages and other similar remuneration in respect of services rendered in connection with a business carried on by a Contracting State or a local authority thereof.

Article 19
STUDENTS

Payments which a student, apprentice or business trainee who is or was immediately before visiting a Contracting State a resident of the other Contracting State and who is present in the first-mentioned State solely for the purpose of his education or training receives for the purpose of his maintenance, education or training shall not be taxed in that State, provided that such payments arise from sources outside that State.

Article 20
PROFESSORS, TEACHERS AND RESEARCHERS

1. An individual who visits a Contracting State for the purpose of teaching or carrying out research at a university, college, school or other recognised educational institution in that State and who is or was immediately before that visit a resident of the other Contracting State, shall be exempt from taxation in the first-mentioned Contracting State on remuneration for such teaching or research for a period not exceeding two years from the date of his first visit for that purpose.

2. The provisions of paragraph 1 of this Article shall not apply to remuneration from research if such research is undertaken not in the public interest but primarily for the private benefit of a specific person or persons.

Article 21
OTHER INCOME

1. Items of income of a resident of a Contracting State, wherever arising, not dealt with in the foregoing Articles of this Convention shall be taxable only in that State.

2. The provisions of paragraph 1 shall not apply to income, other than income from immovable property as defined in paragraph 2 of Article 6, if the recipient of such income, being a resident of a Contracting State, carries on business in the other Contracting State through a permanent establishment situated therein and the right or property in respect of which the income is paid is effectively connected with such permanent establishment. In such case the provisions of Article 7 shall apply.

Article 22
CAPITAL

1. Capital represented by immovable property referred to in Article 6, owned by a resident of a Contracting State and situated in the other Contracting State, may be taxed in that other State.

2. Capital represented by movable property forming part of the business property of a permanent establishment which an enterprise of a Contracting State has in the other Contracting State may be taxed in that other State.

3. Capital represented by ships and aircraft operated in international traffic and by boats engaged in inland waterways transport, and by movable property pertaining to the operation of such ships, aircraft and boats, shall be taxable only in the Contracting State in which the place of effective management of the enterprise is situated.

4 All other elements of capital of a resident of a Contracting State shall be taxable only in that State

Article 23
ELIMINATION OF DOUBLE TAXATION

1. In Hungary double taxation shall be eliminated as follows:

(a) Where a resident of Hungary derives income or owns capital which, in accordance with the provisions of this Convention may be taxed in Luxembourg, Hungary shall, subject to the provisions of subparagraphs (b) and (c), exempt such income or capital from tax.

(b) Where a resident of Hungary derives items of income which, in accordance with the provisions of Article 10 and paragraph 2 of Article 13, may be taxed in Luxembourg, Hungary shall allow as a deduction from the tax on the income of that resident an amount equal to the tax paid in Luxembourg. Such deduction shall not, however, exceed that part of the tax, as computed before the deduction is given, which is attributable to such items of income derived from Luxembourg.

(c) Where in accordance with any provision of the Convention income derived or capital owned by a resident of Hungary is exempt from tax in Hungary, Hungary may nevertheless, in calculating the amount of tax on the remaining income or capital of such resident, take into account the exempted income or capital.

(d) The provisions of subparagraph (a) shall not apply to income derived or capital owned by a resident of Hungary where Luxembourg applies the provisions of this Convention to exempt such income or capital from tax or applies the provisions of paragraph 2 of Article 10 to such income.

2. Subject to the provisions of the law of Luxembourg regarding the elimination of double taxation which shall not affect the general principle hereof, double taxation shall be eliminated as follows:

(a) Where a resident of Luxembourg derives income or owns capital which, in accordance with the provisions of this Convention, may be taxed in Hungary, Luxembourg shall, subject to the provisions of subparagraphs (b) and (c), exempt such income or capital from tax, but may, in order to calculate the amount of tax on the remaining income or capital of the resident, apply the same rates of tax as if the income or capital had not been exempted.

(b) Where a resident of Luxembourg derives income which, in accordance with the provisions of Article 10, paragraph 2 of Article 13 and Article 16 may be taxed in Hungary, Luxembourg shall allow as a deduction from the income tax on individuals or from the corporation tax of that resident an amount equal to the tax paid in Hungary. Such deduction shall not, however, exceed that part of the tax, as computed before the deduction is given, which is attributable to such items of income derived from Hungary.

(c) The provisions of subparagraph (a) shall not apply to income derived or capital owned by a resident of Luxembourg where Hungary applies the provisions of this Convention to exempt such income or capital from tax or applies the provisions of paragraph 2 of Article 10 to such income.

Article 24
NON-DISCRIMINATION

1. Nationals of a Contracting State shall not be subjected in the other Contracting State to any taxation or any requirement connected therewith, which is other or more burdensome than the taxation and connected requirements to which nationals of that other State in the same circumstances, in particular with respect to residence, are or may be subjected. This provision shall, notwithstanding the provisions of Article 1, also apply to persons who are not residents of one or both of the Contracting States.

2 Stateless persons who are residents of a Contracting State shall not be subjected in either Contracting State to any taxation or any requirement connected therewith, which is other or more burdensome than the taxation and connected requirements to which nationals of the State concerned in the same circumstances, in particular with respect to residence, are or may be subjected.

3 The taxation on a permanent establishment which an enterprise of a Contracting State has in the other Contracting State shall not be less favourably levied in that other State than the taxation levied on enterprises of that other State carrying on the same activities. This provision shall not be construed as obliging a Contracting State to grant to residents of the other Contracting State any personal allowances, reliefs and reductions for taxation purposes on account of civil status or family responsibilities which it grants to its own residents

4 Except where the provisions of paragraph 1 of Article 9, paragraph 4 of Article 11, or paragraph 4 of Article 12, apply, interest, royalties and other disbursements paid by an enterprise of a Contracting State to a resident of the other Contracting State shall, for the purpose of determining the taxable profits of such enterprise, be deductible under the same conditions as if they had been paid to a resident of the first-mentioned State Similarly, any debts of an enterprise of a Contracting State to a resident of the other Contracting State shall, for the purpose of determining the taxable capital of such enterprise, be deductible under the same conditions as if they had been contracted to a resident of the first-mentioned Contracting State

5 Enterprises of a Contracting State, the capital of which is wholly or partly owned or controlled, directly or indirectly, by one or more residents of the other Contracting State, shall not be subjected in the first-mentioned Contracting State to any taxation or any requirement connected therewith which is other or more burdensome than the taxation and connected requirements to which other similar enterprises of the first-mentioned State are or may be subjected

6 The provisions of this Article shall, notwithstanding the provisions of Article 2, apply to taxes of every kind and description.

Article 25
MUTUAL AGREEMENT PROCEDURE

1. Where a person considers that the actions of one or both of the Contracting States result or will result for him in taxation not in accordance with the provisions of this Convention, he may, irrespective of the remedies provided by the domestic law of those States, present his case to the competent authority of the Contracting State of which he is a resident or, if his case comes under paragraph 1 of Article 24, to that of the Contracting State of which he is a national. The case must be presented within three years from the first notification of the action resulting in taxation not in accordance with the provisions of the Convention.

2 The competent authority shall endeavour, if the objection appears to it to be justified and if it is not itself able to arrive at a satisfactory solution, to resolve the case by mutual agreement with the competent authority of the other Contracting State, with a view to the avoidance of taxation which is not in accordance with the Convention Any agreement reached shall be implemented notwithstanding any time limits in the domestic law of the Contracting States.

3 The competent authorities of the Contracting States shall endeavour to resolve by mutual agreement any difficulties or doubts arising as to the interpretation or application of the Convention. They may also consult together for the elimination of double taxation in cases not provided for in the Convention.

4 The competent authorities of the Contracting States may communicate with each other directly including through a joint commission consisting of themselves or their representatives, for the purpose of reaching an agreement in the sense of the preceding paragraphs.

Article 26
EXCHANGE OF INFORMATION

1 The competent authorities of the Contracting States shall exchange such information as is foreseeably relevant for carrying out the provisions of this Convention or to the administration or enforcement of the domestic laws concerning taxes of every kind and description imposed on behalf of the Contracting States or of their local authorities insofar as the taxation thereunder is not contrary to the Convention. The exchange of information is not restricted by Articles 1 and 2.

2 Any information received under paragraph 1 by a Contracting State shall be treated as secret in the same manner as information obtained under the domestic laws of that State and shall be disclosed only to persons or authorities (including courts and administrative bodies) concerned with the assessment or collection of, the enforcement or prosecution in respect of, the determination of appeals in relation to the taxes referred to in paragraph 1, or the oversight of the above. Such persons or authorities shall use the information only for such purposes They may disclose the information in public court proceedings or in judicial decisions

3 In no case shall the provisions of paragraphs 1 and 2 be construed so as to impose on a Contracting State the obligation

(a) to carry out administrative measures at variance with the laws and administrative practice of that or of the other Contracting State

(b) to supply information which is not obtainable under the laws or in the normal course of the administration of that or of the other Contracting State

(c) to supply information which would disclose any trade, business, industrial, commercial or professional secret or trade process, or information the disclosure of which would be contrary to public policy (ordre public)

4 If information is requested by a Contracting State in accordance with this Article, the other Contracting State shall use its information gathering measures to obtain the requested information, even though that other State may not need such information for its own tax purposes. The obligation contained in the preceding sentence is subject to the limitations of paragraph 3 but in no case shall such limitations be construed to permit a Contracting State to decline to supply information solely because it has no domestic interest in such information

5 In no case shall the provisions of paragraph 3 be construed to permit a Contracting State to decline to supply information solely because the information is held by a bank, other financial institution, nominee or person acting in an agency or a fiduciary capacity or because it relates to ownership interests in a person

Article 27
MEMBERS OF DIPLOMATIC MISSIONS AND CONSULAR POSTS

Nothing in this Convention shall affect the fiscal privileges of members of diplomatic missions or consular posts under the general rules of international law or under the provisions of special agreements.

Article 28
ENTRY INTO FORCE

1 Each of the Contracting States shall notify each other in writing, through diplomatic channels of the completion of the procedures required by its law for the bringing into force of this Convention.

2 This Convention shall enter into force on the 30th day following the date of receipt of the latter of the notifications referred to in paragraph 1 and its provisions shall have effect in both Contracting States:

(a) in respect of taxes withheld at source, to income derived on or after 1 January of the calendar year next following the year in which the Convention enters into force;
(b) in respect of other taxes on income and taxes on capital, to taxes chargeable for any tax year beginning on or after 1 January of the calendar year next following the year in which the Convention enters into force

3 Upon the entry into force of this Convention, the Convention between the Republic of Hungary and the Grand Duchy of Luxembourg for the avoidance of double taxation with respect to taxes on income and on capital and the Protocol signed at Budapest on 15th January 1990, shall be terminated and cease to have effect

(a) in respect of taxes withheld at source to income derived on or after 1 January of the calendar year next following the year in which this Convention enters into force;
(b) in respect of other taxes on income and on capital, to taxes chargeable for any tax year beginning on or after 1 January of the calendar year next following the year in which this Convention enters into force.

Article 29
TERMINATION

1 This Convention shall remain in force until terminated by a Contracting State. Either Contracting State may terminate the Convention through diplomatic channels, by giving notice of termination at least six months before the end of any calendar year beginning after the expiration of a period of five years from the date of its entry into force

2 In such event this Convention shall cease to have effect in both Contracting States:

(a) in respect of taxes withheld at source, to income derived on or after 1 January of the calendar year next following the year in which the notice is given,
(b) in respect of other taxes on income and taxes on capital, to taxes chargeable for any tax year beginning on or after 1 January of the calendar year next following the year in which the notice is given.

IN WITNESS WHEREOF the undersigned, duly authorised thereto, have signed this Convention.

Done in duplicate at Brussels this 10th day of march 2015., in the French, Hungarian and English languages, each text being equally authentic. In case of divergence of interpretation the English text shall prevail.

For the Grand Duchy of Luxembourg

For Hungary

PROTOCOL

At the moment of the signing of the Convention between Hungary and the Grand Duchy of Luxembourg for the avoidance of double taxation and the prevention of fiscal evasion with respect to taxes on income and on capital, both sides have agreed upon the following provisions, which shall form an integral part of the Convention:

I. With reference to paragraph 1 of Article 4:

It is understood that the term "collective investment vehicle" means:

(a) in the case of Hungary, any investment fund established on the basis of the Act on collective investment schemes and their management;

(b) in the case of Luxembourg,

- (i) an investment company with variable capital (société d'investissement à capital variable);
- (ii) an investment company with fixed capital (société d'investissement à capital fixe);
- (iii) an investment company in risk capital (société d'investissement en capital à risque);
- (iv) a collective investment fund (fonds commun de placement),

as well as any other collective investment vehicle established in either Contracting State which the competent authorities of the Contracting States agree to regard as a collective investment vehicle for purposes of this paragraph.

This provision shall not be construed as restricting in any way a Contracting State's right to tax the residents of that State.

II. With reference to paragraphs 1 and 4 of Article 8, paragraph 4 of Article 13 and paragraph 3 of Article 22:

Both Contracting States have agreed that the term "international traffic" does not cover international traffic by road vehicles.

III. With reference to Article 26:

The competent authority of the requesting State shall provide the following information to the competent authority of the requested State when making a request for information under the Convention to demonstrate the foreseeable relevance of the information to the request:

(a) the identity of the person under examination or investigation;

(b) a statement of the information sought including its nature and the form in which the requesting State wishes to receive the information from the requested State;

(c) the tax purpose for which the information is sought;

(d) the taxable period for which the information is requested;

(e) grounds for believing that the information requested is held in the requested State or is in the possession or control of a person within the jurisdiction of the requested State;

(f) to the extent known the name and address of any person believed to be in possession of the requested information;

(g) a statement that the requesting State has pursued all means available in its own territory to obtain the information, except those that would give rise to disproportionate difficulties.

IV. Legal acts of the European Union:

It is understood that the Convention shall not affect legal acts of the European Union and corresponding provisions of the Contracting States.

IN WITNESS WHEREOF the undersigned, duly authorised thereto, have signed this Protocol.

Done in duplicate at Brussels this 10th day of March 2015, in the French, Hungarian and English languages, each text being equally authentic. In case of divergence of interpretation the English text shall prevail.

For the Grand Duchy of Luxembourg

For Hungary

[TEXT IN FRENCH – TEXTE EN FRANÇAIS]

CONVENTION

ENTRE

LE GRAND-DUCHE DE LUXEMBOURG

ET

LA HONGRIE

TENDANT A EVITER LES DOUBLES IMPOSITIONS

ET A PREVENIR LA FRAUDE FISCALE EN MATIERE

D'IMPOTS SUR LE REVENU ET SUR LA FORTUNE

Le Grand-Duché de Luxembourg et la Hongrie, désireux de conclure une Convention tendant à éviter les doubles impositions et à prévenir la fraude fiscale en matière d'impôts sur le revenu et sur la fortune, et en vue de développer et de faciliter d'avantage leurs relations, sont convenus de ce qui suit:

Article 1
PERSONNES VISÉES

La présente Convention s'applique aux personnes qui sont des résidents d'un État contractant ou des deux États contractants.

Article 2
IMPÔTS VISÉS

1. La présente Convention s'applique aux impôts sur le revenu et sur la fortune perçus pour le compte d'un État contractant ou de ses collectivités locales, quel que soit le système de perception.

2. Sont considérés comme impôts sur le revenu et sur la fortune les impôts perçus sur le revenu total, sur la fortune totale, ou sur des éléments du revenu ou de la fortune, y compris les impôts sur les gains provenant de l'aliénation de biens mobiliers ou immobiliers, les impôts sur le montant global des salaires payés par les entreprises, ainsi que les impôts sur les plus-values.

3. Les impôts actuels auxquels s'applique la Convention sont notamment:

(a) en Hongrie:
(i) l'impôt sur le revenu des personnes physiques;
(ii) l'impôt sur le revenu des collectivités;
(iii) l'impôt sur les propriétés non bâties; et
(iv) l'impôt sur les propriétés bâties;
(ci-après dénommés «impôt hongrois»);

(b) au Luxembourg:
(i) l'impôt sur le revenu des personnes physiques;
(ii) l'impôt sur le revenu des collectivités;
(iii) l'impôt sur la fortune; et
(iv) l'impôt commercial communal;
(ci-après dénommés «impôt luxembourgeois»).

4. La Convention s'applique aussi aux impôts de nature identique ou analogue qui seraient établis après la date de signature de la Convention et qui s'ajouteraient aux impôts actuels ou qui les remplaceraient. Les autorités compétentes des États contractants se communiquent les modifications significatives apportées à leurs législations fiscales.

Article 3
DÉFINITIONS GÉNÉRALES

1. Au sens de la présente Convention, à moins que le contexte n'exige une interprétation différente:

(a) le terme «Hongrie» désigne le territoire de la Hongrie tel qu'il est défini dans sa législation conformément au droit international;

(b) le terme «Luxembourg» désigne le Grand-Duché de Luxembourg et, lorsqu'il est employé dans un sens géographique, il désigne le territoire du Grand-Duché de Luxembourg;
(c) les expressions «un État contractant» et «l'autre État contractant» désignent, suivant le contexte, la Hongrie ou le Luxembourg;
(d) le terme «personne» comprend les personnes physiques, les sociétés et tous autres groupements de personnes;
(e) le terme «société» désigne toute personne morale ou toute entité qui est considérée comme une personne morale aux fins d'imposition;
(f) le terme «entreprise» s'applique à l'exercice de toute activité ou affaire;
(g) les expressions «entreprise d'un État contractant» et «entreprise de l'autre État contractant» désignent respectivement une entreprise exploitée par un résident d'un État contractant et une entreprise exploitée par un résident de l'autre État contractant;
(h) l'expression «trafic international» désigne tout transport effectué par un navire, un aéronef ou un véhicule routier exploité par une entreprise dont le siège de direction effective est situé dans un État contractant, sauf lorsque le navire, l'aéronef ou le véhicule routier n'est exploité qu'entre des points situés dans l'autre État contractant;
(i) l'expression «autorité compétente» désigne:
   (i) en ce qui concerne la Hongrie, le ministre responsable pour la politique fiscale ou son représentant autorisé;
   (ii) en ce qui concerne le Luxembourg, le Ministre des Finances ou son représentant autorisé;
(j) le terme «national», en ce qui concerne un État contractant, désigne:
   (i) toute personne physique qui possède la nationalité de cet État contractant; et
   (ii) toute personne morale, société de personnes, association ou autre entité constituée conformément à la législation en vigueur dans cet État contractant;
(k) les termes «activité», par rapport à une entreprise, et «affaires» comprennent l'exercice de professions libérales ou d'autres activités de caractère indépendant;
(l) le «siège de direction effective» est le lieu où sont prises, quant au fond, les décisions clés sur le plan de la gestion et sur le plan commercial qui sont nécessaires pour la conduite des activités de l'entité. Le siège de direction effective est généralement le lieu où le dirigeant ou un groupe de dirigeants prend ses décisions, et où s'exerce la gestion des affaires courantes, le lieu où les activités à exercer par l'entreprise dans son ensemble sont déterminées.

2. Pour l'application de la Convention à un moment donné par un État contractant, tout terme ou expression qui n'y est pas défini a, sauf si le contexte exige une interprétation différente, le sens que lui attribue, à ce moment, le droit de cet État concernant les impôts auxquels s'applique la Convention, le sens attribué à ce terme ou expression par le droit fiscal de cet État prévalant sur le sens que lui attribuent les autres branches du droit de cet État.

Article 4
RÉSIDENT

1. Au sens de la présente Convention, l'expression «résident d'un État contractant» désigne toute personne qui, en vertu de la législation de cet État, est assujettie à l'impôt dans cet État, en raison de son domicile, de sa résidence, de son siège de direction, de son lieu d'enregistrement ou de tout autre critère de nature analogue et s'applique aussi à cet État et à toutes ses collectivités locales, ainsi qu'à un organisme de placement collectif établi dans cet État. Toutefois, cette expression ne comprend pas les personnes qui ne sont assujetties à l'impôt dans cet État que pour les revenus de sources situées dans cet État ou pour la fortune qui y est située.

2. Lorsque, selon les dispositions du paragraphe 1, une personne physique est un résident des deux États contractants, sa situation est réglée de la manière suivante:

(a) cette personne est considérée comme un résident seulement de l'État où elle dispose d'un foyer d'habitation permanent; si elle dispose d'un foyer d'habitation permanent dans les deux États, elle est considérée comme un résident seulement de l'État avec lequel ses liens personnels et économiques sont les plus étroits (centre des intérêts vitaux);
(b) si l'État où cette personne a le centre de ses intérêts vitaux ne peut pas être déterminé, ou si elle ne dispose d'un foyer d'habitation permanent dans aucun des États, elle est considérée comme un résident seulement de l'État où elle séjourne de façon habituelle;
(c) si cette personne séjourne de façon habituelle dans les deux États ou si elle ne séjourne de façon habituelle dans aucun d'eux, elle est considérée comme un résident seulement de l'État dont elle possède la nationalité;
(d) si cette personne possède la nationalité des deux États ou si elle ne possède la nationalité d'aucun d'eux, les autorités compétentes des États contractants tranchent la question d'un commun accord.

3. Lorsque, selon les dispositions du paragraphe 1, une personne autre qu'une personne physique est un résident des deux États contractants, elle est considérée comme un résident seulement de l'État où son siège de direction effective est situé.

Article 5
ÉTABLISSEMENT STABLE

1. Au sens de la présente Convention, l'expression «établissement stable» désigne une installation fixe d'affaires par l'intermédiaire de laquelle une entreprise exerce tout ou partie de son activité.

2. L'expression «établissement stable» comprend notamment:

(a) un siège de direction,
(b) une succursale,
(c) un bureau,
(d) une usine,
(e) un atelier et
(f) une mine, un puits de pétrole ou de gaz, une carrière ou tout autre lieu d'extraction de ressources naturelles.

3. Un chantier de construction, de montage ou de dragage ne constitue un établissement stable que si sa durée dépasse douze mois.

4. Nonobstant les dispositions précédentes du présent article, on considère qu'il n'y a pas «établissement stable» si:

(a) il est fait usage d'installations aux seules fins de stockage, d'exposition ou de livraison de marchandises appartenant à l'entreprise;
(b) des marchandises appartenant à l'entreprise sont entreposées aux seules fins de stockage, d'exposition ou de livraison;
(c) des marchandises appartenant à l'entreprise sont entreposées aux seules fins de transformation par une autre entreprise;
(d) une installation fixe d'affaires est utilisée aux seules fins d'acheter des marchandises ou de réunir des informations, pour l'entreprise;
(e) une installation fixe d'affaires est utilisée aux seules fins d'exercer, pour l'entreprise, toute autre activité de caractère préparatoire ou auxiliaire;

(f) une installation fixe d'affaires est utilisée aux seules fins de l'exercice cumulé d'activités mentionnées aux alinéas (a) à (e), à condition que l'activité d'ensemble de l'installation fixe d'affaires résultant de ce cumul garde un caractère préparatoire ou auxiliaire.

5. Nonobstant les dispositions des paragraphes 1 et 2, lorsqu'une personne - autre qu'un agent jouissant d'un statut indépendant auquel s'applique le paragraphe 6 - agit pour le compte d'une entreprise et dispose dans un État contractant de pouvoirs qu'elle y exerce habituellement lui permettant de conclure des contrats au nom de l'entreprise, cette entreprise est considérée comme ayant un établissement stable dans cet État pour toutes les activités que cette personne exerce pour l'entreprise, à moins que les activités de cette personne ne soient limitées à celles qui sont mentionnées au paragraphe 4 et qui, si elles étaient exercées par l'intermédiaire d'une installation fixe d'affaires, ne permettraient pas de considérer cette installation comme un établissement stable selon les dispositions de ce paragraphe.

6. Une entreprise n'est pas considérée comme ayant un établissement stable dans un État contractant du seul fait qu'elle y exerce son activité par l'entremise d'un courtier, d'un commissionnaire général ou de tout autre agent jouissant d'un statut indépendant, à condition que ces personnes agissent dans le cadre ordinaire de leur activité.

7. Le fait qu'une société qui est un résident d'un État contractant contrôle ou est contrôlée par une société qui est un résident de l'autre État contractant ou qui y exerce son activité (que ce soit par l'intermédiaire d'un établissement stable ou non) ne suffit pas, en lui-même, à faire de l'une quelconque de ces sociétés un établissement stable de l'autre.

Article 6
REVENUS IMMOBILIERS

1. Les revenus qu'un résident d'un État contractant tire de biens immobiliers (y compris les revenus des exploitations agricoles ou forestières) situés dans l'autre État contractant, sont imposables dans cet autre État.

2. L'expression «biens immobiliers» a le sens que lui attribue le droit de l'État contractant où les biens considérés sont situés. L'expression comprend en tous cas les accessoires, le cheptel mort ou vif des exploitations agricoles et forestières, les droits auxquels s'appliquent les dispositions du droit privé concernant la propriété foncière, l'usufruit des biens immobiliers et les droits à des paiements variables ou fixes pour l'exploitation ou la concession de l'exploitation de gisements minéraux, sources et autres ressources naturelles; les navires, bateaux et aéronefs ne sont pas considérés comme des biens immobiliers.

3. Les dispositions du paragraphe 1 s'appliquent aux revenus provenant de l'exploitation directe, de la location ou de l'affermage, ainsi que de toute autre forme d'exploitation des biens immobiliers.

4. Les dispositions des paragraphes 1 et 3 s'appliquent également aux revenus provenant des biens immobiliers d'une entreprise.

Article 7
BÉNÉFICES DES ENTREPRISES

1. Les bénéfices d'une entreprise d'un État contractant ne sont imposables que dans cet État, à moins que l'entreprise n'exerce son activité dans l'autre État contractant par l'intermédiaire d'un établissement stable qui y est situé. Si l'entreprise exerce son activité d'une telle façon, les bénéfices qui sont attribuables à l'établissement stable conformément aux dispositions du paragraphe 2 sont imposables dans l'autre État.

2. Aux fins de cet article et de l'article 23, les bénéfices qui sont attribuables dans chaque État contractant à l'établissement stable mentionné au paragraphe 1 sont ceux qu'il aurait pu réaliser, en particulier dans ses opérations internes avec d'autres parties de l'entreprise, s'il avait constitué une entreprise distincte et indépendante exerçant des activités identiques ou analogues dans des conditions identiques ou analogues, compte tenu des fonctions exercées, des actifs utilisés et des risques assumés par l'entreprise par l'intermédiaire de l'établissement stable et des autres parties de l'entreprise.

3. Lorsque, conformément au paragraphe 2, un État contractant ajuste les bénéfices qui sont attribuables à un établissement stable d'une entreprise d'un des États contractants et impose en conséquence des bénéfices de l'entreprise qui ont été imposés dans l'autre État, cet autre État procède à un ajustement approprié du montant de l'impôt qui a été perçu sur ces bénéfices dans la mesure nécessaire pour éliminer la double imposition de ces bénéfices. Pour déterminer cet ajustement, les autorités compétentes des États contractants se consultent si nécessaire.

4. Lorsque les bénéfices comprennent des éléments de revenu traités séparément dans d'autres articles de la présente Convention, les dispositions de ces articles ne sont pas affectées par les dispositions du présent article.

Article 8

NAVIGATION MARITIME, INTERIEURE ET AÉRIENNE

1. Les bénéfices provenant de l'exploitation, en trafic international, de navires ou d'aéronefs ne sont imposables que dans l'État contractant où le siège de direction effective de l'entreprise est situé.

2. Les bénéfices provenant de l'exploitation de bateaux servant à la navigation intérieure ne sont imposables que dans l'État contractant où le siège de direction effective de l'entreprise est situé.

3. Si le siège de direction effective d'une entreprise de navigation maritime ou intérieure est à bord d'un navire ou d'un bateau, ce siège est considéré comme situé dans l'État contractant où se trouve le port d'attache de ce navire ou de ce bateau, ou à défaut de port d'attache, dans l'État contractant dont l'exploitant du navire ou du bateau est un résident.

4. Les dispositions du paragraphe 1 s'appliquent aussi aux bénéfices provenant de la participation à un pool, une exploitation en commun ou un organisme international d'exploitation.

Article 9

ENTREPRISES ASSOCIÉES

1. Lorsque

(a) une entreprise d'un État contractant participe directement ou indirectement à la direction, au contrôle ou au capital d'une entreprise de l'autre État contractant, ou que

(b) les mêmes personnes participent directement ou indirectement à la direction, au contrôle ou au capital d'une entreprise d'un État contractant et d'une entreprise de l'autre État contractant,

et que, dans l'un et l'autre cas, les deux entreprises sont, dans leurs relations commerciales ou financières, liées par des conditions convenues ou imposées, qui diffèrent de celles qui seraient convenues entre des entreprises indépendantes, les bénéfices qui, sans ces conditions, auraient été réalisés par l'une des entreprises, mais n'ont pu l'être en fait à cause de ces conditions, peuvent être inclus dans les bénéfices de cette entreprise et imposés en conséquence.

2. Lorsqu'un État contractant inclut dans les bénéfices d'une entreprise de cet État - et impose en conséquence - des bénéfices sur lesquels une entreprise de l'autre État contractant a été imposée dans cet autre État, et que les bénéfices ainsi inclus sont des bénéfices qui auraient été réalisés par l'entreprise du premier État si les conditions convenues entre les deux entreprises avaient été celles qui auraient été convenues entre des entreprises indépendantes, l'autre État procède à un ajustement approprié du montant de l'impôt qui y a été perçu sur ces bénéfices. Pour déterminer cet ajustement, il est tenu compte des autres dispositions de la présente Convention et, si c'est nécessaire, les autorités compétentes des États contractants se consultent.

Article 10
DIVIDENDES

1. Les dividendes payés par une société qui est un résident d'un État contractant à un résident de l'autre État contractant, sont imposables dans cet autre État.

2. Toutefois, ces dividendes sont aussi imposables dans l'État contractant dont la société qui paie les dividendes est un résident, et selon la législation de cet État, mais si le bénéficiaire effectif des dividendes est un résident de l'autre État contractant, l'impôt ainsi établi ne peut excéder:
(a) 0 pour cent du montant brut des dividendes, si le bénéficiaire effectif est une société (autre qu'une société de personnes qui n'est pas assujettie à l'impôt) qui détient directement au moins 10 pour cent du capital de la société qui paie les dividendes;
(b) 10 pour cent du montant brut des dividendes, dans tous les autres cas.

Le présent paragraphe n'affecte pas l'imposition de la société au titre des bénéfices qui servent au paiement des dividendes.

3. Le terme «dividendes» employé dans le présent article désigne les revenus provenant d'actions, actions ou bons de jouissance, parts de mine, parts de fondateur ou autres parts bénéficiaires à l'exception des créances, ainsi que les revenus d'autres parts sociales soumis au même régime fiscal que les revenus d'actions par la législation de l'État dont la société distributrice est un résident.

4. Les dispositions des paragraphes 1 et 2 ne s'appliquent pas lorsque le bénéficiaire effectif des dividendes, résident d'un État contractant, exerce dans l'autre État contractant dont la société qui paie les dividendes est un résident, une activité d'entreprise par l'intermédiaire d'un établissement stable qui y est situé, et que la participation génératrice des dividendes s'y rattache effectivement. Dans ce cas, les dispositions de l'article 7 sont applicables.

5. Lorsqu'une société qui est un résident d'un État contractant tire des bénéfices ou des revenus de l'autre État contractant, cet autre État ne peut percevoir aucun impôt sur les dividendes payés par la société, sauf dans la mesure où ces dividendes sont payés à un résident de cet autre État ou dans la mesure où la participation génératrice des dividendes se rattache effectivement à un établissement stable situé dans cet autre État, ni prélever aucun impôt, au titre de l'imposition des bénéfices non distribués, sur les bénéfices non distribués de la société, même si les dividendes payés ou les bénéfices non distribués consistent en tout ou en partie en bénéfices ou revenus provenant de cet autre État.

Article 11
INTÉRÊTS

1. Les intérêts provenant d'un État contractant et dont le bénéficiaire effectif est un résident de l'autre État contractant ne sont imposables que dans cet autre État.

2. Le terme «intérêts» employé dans le présent article désigne les revenus des créances de toute nature, assorties ou non de garanties hypothécaires ou d'une clause de participation aux bénéfices du débiteur, et notamment les revenus des fonds publics et des obligations d'emprunts, y compris les primes et lots attachés à ces titres, mais ne comprend pas les revenus visés à l'article 10. Les pénalisations pour paiement tardif ne sont pas considérées comme des intérêts au sens du présent article.

3. Les dispositions du paragraphe 1 ne s'appliquent pas lorsque le bénéficiaire effectif des intérêts, résident d'un État contractant, exerce dans l'autre État contractant d'où proviennent les intérêts, une activité d'entreprise par l'intermédiaire d'un établissement stable qui y est situé, et que la créance génératrice des intérêts s'y rattache effectivement. Dans ce cas, les dispositions de l'article 7 sont applicables.

4. Lorsque, en raison de relations spéciales existant entre le débiteur et le bénéficiaire effectif ou que l'un et l'autre entretiennent avec de tierces personnes, le montant des intérêts, compte tenu de la créance pour laquelle ils sont payés, excède celui dont seraient convenus le débiteur et le bénéficiaire effectif en l'absence de pareilles relations, les dispositions du présent article ne s'appliquent qu'à ce dernier montant. Dans ce cas, la partie excédentaire des paiements reste imposable selon la législation de chaque État contractant et compte tenu des autres dispositions de la présente Convention.

Article 12
REDEVANCES

1. Les redevances provenant d'un État contractant et dont le bénéficiaire effectif est un résident de l'autre État contractant ne sont imposables que dans cet autre État.

2. Le terme «redevances» employé dans le présent article, désigne les rémunérations de toute nature payées pour l'usage ou la concession de l'usage d'un droit d'auteur sur une oeuvre littéraire, artistique ou scientifique (y compris les films cinématographiques), d'un brevet, d'une marque de fabrique ou de commerce, d'un dessin ou d'un modèle, d'un plan, d'une formule ou d'un procédé secrets et pour des informations ayant trait à une expérience acquise dans le domaine industriel, commercial ou scientifique.

3. Les dispositions du paragraphe 1 ne s'appliquent pas, lorsque le bénéficiaire effectif des redevances, résident d'un État contractant, exerce dans l'autre État contractant d'où proviennent les redevances, une activité d'entreprise par l'intermédiaire d'un établissement stable qui y est situé, et que le droit ou le bien générateur des redevances s'y rattache effectivement. Dans ce cas, les dispositions de l'article 7 sont applicables.

4. Lorsque, en raison de relations spéciales existant entre le débiteur et le bénéficiaire effectif ou que l'un et l'autre entretiennent avec de tierces personnes, le montant des redevances, compte tenu de la prestation pour laquelle elles sont payées, excède celui dont seraient convenus le débiteur et le bénéficiaire effectif en l'absence de pareilles relations, les dispositions du présent article ne s'appliquent qu'à ce dernier montant. Dans ce cas, la partie excédentaire des paiements reste imposable selon la législation de chaque État contractant et compte tenu des autres dispositions de la présente Convention.

Article 13
GAINS EN CAPITAL

1. Les gains qu'un résident d'un État contractant tire de l'aliénation de biens immobiliers visés à l'article 6, et situés dans l'autre État contractant, sont imposables dans cet autre État.

2. Les gains qu'un résident d'un État contractant tire de l'aliénation d'actions ou d'intérêts similaires qui tirent directement ou indirectement plus de 50 pour cent de leur valeur de biens immobiliers situés dans l'autre État contractant sont imposables dans cet autre État.

3. Les gains, autres que ceux visés au paragraphe 2 du présent article, provenant de l'aliénation de biens mobiliers qui font partie de l'actif d'un établissement stable qu'une entreprise d'un État contractant a dans l'autre État contractant, y compris de tels gains provenant de l'aliénation de cet établissement stable (seul ou avec l'ensemble de l'entreprise) sont imposables dans cet autre État.

4. Les gains provenant de l'aliénation de navires ou aéronefs exploités en trafic international, de bateaux servant à la navigation intérieure ou de biens mobiliers affectés à l'exploitation de ces navires, aéronefs ou bateaux, ne sont imposables que dans l'État contractant où le siège de direction effective de l'entreprise est situé.

5. Les gains provenant de l'aliénation de tous biens autres que ceux visés aux paragraphes 1, 2, 3 et 4, ne sont imposables que dans l'État contractant dont le cédant est un résident.

Article 14
REVENUS D'EMPLOI

1. Sous réserve des dispositions des articles 15, 17, 18 et 20, les salaires, traitements et autres rémunérations similaires qu'un résident d'un État contractant reçoit au titre d'un emploi salarié, ne sont imposables que dans cet État, à moins que l'emploi ne soit exercé dans l'autre État contractant. Si l'emploi y est exercé, les rémunérations reçues à ce titre sont imposables dans cet autre État.

2. Nonobstant les dispositions du paragraphe 1, les rémunérations qu'un résident d'un État contractant reçoit au titre d'un emploi salarié exercé dans l'autre État contractant, ne sont imposables que dans le premier État si:

(a) le bénéficiaire séjourne dans l'autre État pendant une période ou des périodes n'excédant pas au total 183 jours durant toute période de douze mois commençant ou se terminant durant l'année civile considérée, et

(b) les rémunérations sont payées par un employeur, ou pour le compte d'un employeur, qui n'est pas un résident de l'autre État, et

(c) la charge des rémunérations n'est pas supportée par un établissement stable que l'employeur a dans l'autre État.

3. Nonobstant les dispositions précédentes du présent article, les rémunérations reçues au titre d'un emploi salarié exercé à bord d'un navire, d'un aéronef ou d'un véhicule routier exploité en trafic international, ou à bord d'un bateau servant à la navigation intérieure, sont imposables dans l'État contractant où le siège de direction effective de l'entreprise est situé.

Article 15
TANTIÈMES

Les tantièmes, jetons de présence et autres rétributions similaires qu'un résident d'un État contractant reçoit en sa qualité de membre du conseil d'administration ou de surveillance d'une société qui est un résident de l'autre État contractant, sont imposables dans cet autre État.

Article 16
ARTISTES ET SPORTIFS

1. Nonobstant les dispositions des articles 7 et 14, les revenus qu'un résident d'un État contractant tire de ses activités personnelles exercées dans l'autre État contractant en tant qu'artiste du spectacle, tel qu'un artiste de théâtre, de cinéma, de la radio ou de la télévision, ou qu'un musicien, ou en tant que sportif, sont imposables dans cet autre État.

2. Lorsque les revenus d'activités qu'un artiste du spectacle ou un sportif exerce personnellement et en cette qualité sont attribués non pas à l'artiste ou au sportif lui-même mais à une autre personne, ces revenus sont imposables, nonobstant les dispositions des articles 7 et 14, dans l'État contractant où les activités de l'artiste ou du sportif sont exercées.

3. Les dispositions des paragraphes 1 et 2 ne s'appliquent pas aux revenus tirés d'activités exercées par des artistes ou des sportifs dans un État contractant si la visite dans cet État est entièrement ou principalement financée par des fonds publics d'un ou des deux États contractants ou de leurs collectivités locales. Dans ce cas, le revenu n'est imposable que dans l'État contractant dont l'artiste ou le sportif est un résident.

Article 17
PENSIONS

Les pensions et autres rémunérations similaires provenant d'un État contractant et payées à un résident de l'autre État contractant ne sont imposables que dans le premier État.

Article 18
FONCTIONS PUBLIQUES

1. (a) Les salaires, traitements et autres rémunérations similaires payés par un État contractant ou l'une de ses collectivités locales à une personne physique au titre de services rendus à cet État ou à cette collectivité ne sont imposables que dans cet État.
   (b) Toutefois, ces salaires, traitements et autres rémunérations similaires ne sont imposables que dans l'autre État contractant si les services sont rendus dans cet État et si la personne physique est un résident de cet État qui:
      (i) possède la nationalité de cet État, ou
      (ii) n'est pas devenu un résident de cet État à seule fin de rendre les services.

2. Les dispositions des articles 14, 15 et 16 s'appliquent aux salaires, traitements et autres rémunérations similaires payés au titre de services rendus dans le cadre d'une activité d'entreprise exercée par un État contractant ou l'une de ses collectivités locales.

Article 19
ÉTUDIANTS

Les sommes qu'un étudiant, un apprenti ou un stagiaire qui est, ou qui était immédiatement avant de se rendre dans un État contractant, un résident de l'autre État contractant et qui séjourne dans le premier État à seule fin d'y poursuivre ses études ou sa formation, reçoit pour couvrir ses frais d'entretien, d'études ou de formation ne sont pas imposables dans cet État, à condition qu'elles proviennent de sources situées en dehors de cet État.

Article 20
PROFESSEURS, ENSEIGNANTS ET CHERCHEURS

1. Une personne physique qui se rend dans un État contractant afin d'y enseigner ou de s'y livrer à des recherches à une université, un collège, une école ou une autre institution d'enseignement reconnue dans cet État et qui immédiatement avant ce départ est ou était un résident de l'autre État contractant, est exemptée d'impôts dans le premier État contractant sur les rémunérations reçues au titre de cet enseignement ou ces recherches pour une période n'excédant pas deux ans à partir de la date de sa première arrivée à cette fin.

2. Les dispositions du paragraphe 1 du présent article ne s'appliquent pas aux rémunérations touchées pour des recherches, si ces recherches sont entreprises non pas dans l'intérêt public mais principalement au profit privé d'une ou de personnes déterminées.

Article 21
AUTRES REVENUS

1. Les éléments du revenu d'un résident d'un État contractant, d'où qu'ils proviennent, qui ne sont pas traités dans les articles précédents de la présente Convention, ne sont imposables que dans cet État.

2. Les dispositions du paragraphe 1 ne s'appliquent pas aux revenus autres que les revenus provenant de biens immobiliers tels qu'ils sont définis au paragraphe 2 de l'article 6, lorsque le bénéficiaire de tels revenus, résident d'un État contractant, exerce dans l'autre État contractant une activité d'entreprise par l'intermédiaire d'un établissement stable qui y est situé et que le droit ou le bien générateur des revenus s'y rattache effectivement. Dans ce cas, les dispositions de l'article 7 sont applicables.

Article 22
FORTUNE

1. La fortune constituée par des biens immobiliers visés à l'article 6, que possède un résident d'un État contractant et qui sont situés dans l'autre État contractant, est imposable dans cet autre État.

2. La fortune constituée par des biens mobiliers qui font partie de l'actif d'un établissement stable qu'une entreprise d'un État contractant a dans l'autre État contractant, est imposable dans cet autre État.

3. La fortune constituée par des navires et des aéronefs exploités en trafic international, par des bateaux servant à la navigation intérieure ainsi que par des biens mobiliers affectés à l'exploitation de ces navires, aéronefs ou bateaux, n'est imposable que dans l'État contractant où le siège de direction effective de l'entreprise est situé.

4. Tous les autres éléments de la fortune d'un résident d'un État contractant ne sont imposables que dans cet État.

Article 23
ÉLIMINATION DES DOUBLES IMPOSITIONS

1. En Hongrie, la double imposition est éliminée de la manière suivante:

(a) Lorsqu'un résident de la Hongrie reçoit des revenus ou possède de la fortune qui, conformément aux dispositions de la présente Convention, sont imposables au Luxembourg, la Hongrie exempte de l'impôt ces revenus ou cette fortune, sous réserve des dispositions des sous-paragraphes (b) et (c).

(b) Lorsqu'un résident de la Hongrie reçoit des éléments de revenu qui, conformément aux dispositions de l'article 10 et du paragraphe 2 de l'article 13, sont imposables au Luxembourg, la Hongrie accorde, sur l'impôt qu'il perçoit sur les revenus de ce résident, une déduction d'un montant égal à l'impôt payé au Luxembourg. Cette déduction ne peut toutefois excéder la fraction de l'impôt, calculé avant déduction, correspondant à ces éléments de revenus reçus du Luxembourg.

(c) Lorsque, conformément à une disposition quelconque de la Convention, les revenus qu'un résident de la Hongrie reçoit ou la fortune qu'il possède sont exempts d'impôt en Hongrie, la Hongrie peut néanmoins, pour calculer le montant de l'impôt sur le reste des revenus ou de la fortune de ce résident, tenir compte des revenus ou de la fortune exemptés.

(d) Les dispositions du sous-paragraphe (a) ne s'appliquent pas au revenu reçu ou à la fortune possédée par un résident de la Hongrie lorsque le Luxembourg applique les dispositions de la présente Convention pour exempter d'impôt ce revenu ou cette fortune ou applique les dispositions du paragraphe 2 de l'article 10 à ce revenu.

2. Sous réserve des dispositions de la législation luxembourgeoise concernant l'élimination de la double imposition qui n'en affectent pas le principe général, la double imposition est éliminée de la manière suivante:

(a) Lorsqu'un résident du Luxembourg reçoit des revenus ou possède de la fortune qui, conformément aux dispositions de la présente Convention, sont imposables en Hongrie, le Luxembourg exempte de l'impôt ces revenus ou cette fortune, sous réserve des dispositions des sous-paragraphes (b) et (c), mais peut, pour calculer le montant de l'impôt sur le reste du revenu ou de la fortune du résident, appliquer les mêmes taux d'impôt que si les revenus ou la fortune n'avaient pas été exemptés.

(b) Lorsqu'un résident du Luxembourg reçoit des éléments de revenu qui, conformément aux dispositions de l'article 10, du paragraphe 2 de l'article 13 et de l'article 16, sont imposables en Hongrie, le Luxembourg accorde sur l'impôt sur le revenu des personnes physiques ou sur l'impôt sur le revenu des collectivités de ce résident, une déduction d'un montant égal à l'impôt payé en Hongrie. Cette déduction ne peut toutefois excéder la fraction de l'impôt, calculé avant déduction, correspondant à ces éléments de revenus reçus de Hongrie.

(c) Les dispositions du sous-paragraphe (a) ne s'appliquent pas au revenu reçu ou à la fortune possédée par un résident du Luxembourg, lorsque la Hongrie applique les dispositions de la présente Convention pour exempter d'impôt ce revenu ou cette fortune ou applique les dispositions du paragraphe 2 de l'article 10 à ce revenu.

Article 24
NON-DISCRIMINATION

1. Les nationaux d'un État contractant ne sont soumis dans l'autre État contractant à aucune imposition ou obligation y relative, qui est autre ou plus lourde que celles auxquelles sont ou pourront être assujettis les nationaux de cet autre État qui se trouvent dans la même situation, notamment au regard de la résidence. La présente disposition s'applique aussi, nonobstant les dispositions de l'article 1, aux personnes qui ne sont pas des résidents d'un État contractant ou des deux États contractants.

2. Les apatrides qui sont des résidents d'un État contractant ne sont soumis dans l'un ou l'autre État contractant à aucune imposition ou obligation y relative, qui est autre ou plus lourde que celles auxquelles sont ou pourront être assujettis les nationaux de l'État concerné qui se trouvent dans la même situation, notamment au regard de la résidence.

3. L'imposition d'un établissement stable qu'une entreprise d'un État contractant a dans l'autre État contractant n'est pas établie dans cet autre État d'une façon moins favorable que l'imposition des entreprises de cet autre État qui exercent la même activité. La présente disposition ne peut être interprétée comme obligeant un État contractant à accorder aux résidents de l'autre État contractant les déductions personnelles, abattements et réductions d'impôt en fonction de la situation ou des charges de famille qu'il accorde à ses propres résidents.

4. A moins que les dispositions du paragraphe 1 de l'article 9, du paragraphe 4 de l'article 11 ou du paragraphe 4 de l'article 12 ne soient applicables, les intérêts, redevances et autres dépenses payés par une entreprise d'un État contractant à un résident de l'autre État contractant sont déductibles, pour la détermination des bénéfices imposables de cette entreprise, dans les mêmes conditions que s'ils avaient été payés à un résident du premier État. De même, les dettes d'une entreprise d'un État contractant envers un résident de l'autre État contractant sont déductibles, pour la détermination de la fortune imposable de cette entreprise, dans les mêmes conditions que si elles avaient été contractées envers un résident du premier État contractant.

5. Les entreprises d'un État contractant, dont le capital est en totalité ou en partie, directement ou indirectement, détenu ou contrôlé par un ou plusieurs résidents de l'autre État contractant, ne sont soumises dans le premier État contractant à aucune imposition ou obligation y relative, qui est autre ou plus lourde que celles auxquelles sont ou pourront être assujetties les autres entreprises similaires du premier État.

6. Les dispositions du présent article s'appliquent, nonobstant les dispositions de l'article 2, aux impôts de toute nature ou dénomination.

Article 25
PROCÉDURE AMIABLE

1. Lorsqu'une personne estime que les mesures prises par un État contractant ou par les deux États contractants entraînent ou entraîneront pour elle une imposition non conforme aux dispositions de la présente Convention, elle peut, indépendamment des recours prévus par le droit interne de ces États, soumettre son cas à l'autorité compétente de l'État contractant dont elle est un résident ou, si son cas relève du paragraphe 1 de l'article 24, à celle de l'État contractant dont elle possède la nationalité. Le cas doit être soumis dans les trois ans qui suivent la première notification de la mesure qui entraîne une imposition non conforme aux dispositions de la Convention.

2. L'autorité compétente s'efforce, si la réclamation lui paraît fondée et si elle n'est pas elle-même en mesure d'y apporter une solution satisfaisante, de résoudre le cas par voie d'accord amiable avec l'autorité compétente de l'autre État contractant, en vue d'éviter une imposition non conforme à la Convention. L'accord est appliqué quels que soient les délais prévus par le droit interne des États contractants.

3. Les autorités compétentes des États contractants s'efforcent, par voie d'accord amiable, de résoudre les difficultés ou de dissiper les doutes auxquels peuvent donner lieu l'interprétation ou l'application de la Convention. Elles peuvent aussi se concerter en vue d'éliminer la double imposition dans les cas non prévus par la Convention.

4. Les autorités compétentes des États contractants peuvent communiquer directement entre elles, y compris au sein d'une commission mixte composée de ces autorités ou de leurs représentants, en vue de parvenir à un accord comme il est indiqué aux paragraphes précédents.

Article 26

ÉCHANGE DE RENSEIGNEMENTS

1. Les autorités compétentes des États contractants échangent les renseignements vraisemblablement pertinents pour appliquer les dispositions de la présente Convention ou pour l'administration ou l'application de la législation interne relative aux impôts de toute nature ou dénomination perçus pour le compte des États contractants ou de leurs collectivités locales dans la mesure où l'imposition qu'elle prévoit n'est pas contraire à la Convention. L'échange de renseignements n'est pas restreint par les articles 1 et 2.

2. Les renseignements reçus en vertu du paragraphe 1 par un État contractant sont tenus secrets de la même manière que les renseignements obtenus en application de la législation interne de cet État et ne sont communiqués qu'aux personnes ou autorités (y compris les tribunaux et organes administratifs) concernées par l'établissement ou le recouvrement des impôts mentionnés au paragraphe 1, par les procédures ou poursuites concernant ces impôts, par les décisions sur les recours relatifs à ces impôts, ou par le contrôle de ce qui précède. Ces personnes ou autorités n'utilisent ces renseignements qu'à ces fins. Elles peuvent révéler ces renseignements au cours d'audiences publiques de tribunaux ou dans des jugements.

3. Les dispositions des paragraphes 1 et 2 ne peuvent en aucun cas être interprétées comme imposant à un État contractant l'obligation:

(a) de prendre des mesures administratives dérogeant à sa législation et à sa pratique administrative ou à celles de l'autre État contractant;

(b) de fournir des renseignements qui ne pourraient être obtenus sur la base de sa législation ou dans le cadre de sa pratique administrative normale ou de celles de l'autre État contractant;

(c) de fournir des renseignements qui révéleraient un secret commercial, industriel, professionnel ou un procédé commercial ou des renseignements dont la communication serait contraire à l'ordre public.

4. Si des renseignements sont demandés par un État contractant conformément à cet article, l'autre État contractant utilise les pouvoirs dont il dispose pour obtenir les renseignements demandés, même s'il n'en a pas besoin à ses propres fins fiscales. L'obligation qui figure dans la phrase précédente est soumise aux limitations prévues au paragraphe 3 sauf si ces limitations sont susceptibles d'empêcher un État contractant de communiquer des renseignements uniquement parce que ceux-ci ne présentent pas d'intérêt pour lui dans le cadre national.

5. En aucun cas les dispositions du paragraphe 3 ne peuvent être interprétées comme permettant à un État contractant de refuser de communiquer des renseignements uniquement parce que ceux-ci sont détenus par une banque, un autre établissement financier, un mandataire ou une personne agissant en tant qu'agent ou fiduciaire ou parce que ces renseignements se rattachent aux droits de propriété d'une personne.

Article 27
MEMBRES DES MISSIONS DIPLOMATIQUES ET POSTES CONSULAIRES

Les dispositions de la présente Convention ne portent pas atteinte aux privilèges fiscaux dont bénéficient les membres des missions diplomatiques ou postes consulaires en vertu soit des règles générales du droit international, soit des dispositions d'accords particuliers.

Article 28
ENTRÉE EN VIGUEUR

1. Chacun des États contractants notifiera à l'autre par écrit, par la voie diplomatique, l'accomplissement des procédures requises par sa législation pour la mise en vigueur de la présente Convention.

2. La présente Convention entrera en vigueur le 30ième jour suivant la date de réception de la dernière des notifications visées au paragraphe 1 et ses dispositions seront applicables dans les deux États contractants:

(a) en ce qui concerne les impôts retenus à la source, aux revenus attribués le ou après le 1er janvier de l'année civile suivant immédiatement l'année au cours de laquelle la Convention entrera en vigueur;

(b) en ce qui concerne les autres impôts sur le revenu et les impôts sur la fortune, aux impôts dus pour toute année d'imposition commençant le ou après le 1er janvier de l'année civile suivant immédiatement l'année au cours de laquelle la Convention entrera en vigueur.

3. Au moment de l'entrée en vigueur de la présente Convention, la Convention entre la République de Hongrie et le Grand-Duché de Luxembourg tendant à éviter les doubles impositions en matière d'impôts sur le revenu et sur la fortune, et le Protocole y relatif, signés à Budapest le 15 janvier 1990, sont dénoncés et cessent de s'appliquer:

(a) en ce qui concerne les impôts retenus à la source, aux revenus attribués le ou après le 1er janvier de l'année civile suivant immédiatement l'année au cours de laquelle la présente Convention entrera en vigueur;

(b) en ce qui concerne les autres impôts sur le revenu et les impôts sur la fortune, aux impôts dus pour toute année d'imposition commençant le ou après le 1er janvier de l'année civile suivant immédiatement l'année au cours de laquelle la présente Convention entrera en vigueur.

Article 29
DÉNONCIATION

1. La présente Convention demeurera en vigueur tant qu'elle n'aura pas été dénoncée par un État contractant. Chaque État contractant peut dénoncer la Convention par voie diplomatique avec un préavis minimum de six mois avant la fin de chaque année civile commençant après l'expiration d'une période de cinq années à partir de la date de son entrée en vigueur.

2. Dans ce cas, la Convention cessera d'être applicable dans les deux États contractants:

(a) en ce qui concerne les impôts retenus à la source, aux revenus attribués le ou après le 1er janvier de l'année civile suivant immédiatement l'année au cours de laquelle le préavis est donné;

(b) en ce qui concerne les autres impôts sur le revenu et les impôts sur la fortune, aux impôts dus pour toute année d'imposition commençant le ou après le 1er janvier de l'année civile suivant immédiatement l'année au cours de laquelle le préavis est donné.

EN FOI DE QUOI, les soussignés, dûment autorisés à cet effet, ont signé la présente Convention.

Fait en deux exemplaires à Bruxelles, le 10 mars 2015

en langues française, hongroise et anglaise, tous les textes faisant également foi. En cas de divergence dans l'interprétation, le texte anglais prévaut.

Pour le Grand-Duché de Luxembourg

Pour la Hongrie

PROTOCOLE

Au moment de procéder à la signature de la Convention entre le Grand-Duché de Luxembourg et la Hongrie tendant à éviter les doubles impositions et à prévenir la fraude fiscale en matière d'impôts sur le revenu et sur la fortune, les deux parties sont convenues que les dispositions suivantes forment partie intégrante de la Convention:

I. En référence au paragraphe 1 de l'article 4:

Il est convenu que l'expression «organisme de placement collectif» désigne:

(a) en ce qui concerne la Hongrie, tout fonds d'investissement établi conformément à la loi sur les organismes de placement collectif et leur gestion (Act on collective investment schemes and their management);

(b) en ce qui concerne le Luxembourg,
   (i) une société d'investissement à capital variable;
   (ii) une société d'investissement à capital fixe;
   (iii) une société d'investissement en capital à risque;
   (iv) un fonds commun de placement,

ainsi que tout autre organisme de placement collectif établi dans chacun des États contractants que les autorités compétentes des États contractants conviennent de considérer comme un organisme de placement collectif aux fins du présent paragraphe.

La présente disposition ne peut être interprétée comme limitant d'une quelconque manière le droit d'un État contractant d'imposer les résidents de cet État.

II. En référence aux paragraphes 1 et 4 de l'article 8, au paragraphe 4 de l'article 13 et au paragraphe 3 de l'article 22:

Les deux États contractants sont convenus que l'expression «trafic international» ne couvre pas le trafic international des véhicules routiers.

III. En référence à l'article 26:

L'autorité compétente de l'État requérant fournit les informations suivantes à l'autorité compétente de l'État requis lorsqu'elle soumet une demande de renseignements en vertu de la Convention, afin de démontrer la pertinence vraisemblable des renseignements demandés:

(a) l'identité de la personne faisant l'objet d'un contrôle ou d'une enquête;
(b) les indications concernant les renseignements recherchés, notamment leur nature et la forme sous laquelle l'État requérant souhaite recevoir les renseignements de l'État requis;
(c) le but fiscal dans lequel les renseignements sont demandés;
(d) la période sur laquelle portent les renseignements;
(e) les raisons qui donnent à penser que les renseignements demandés sont détenus dans l'État requis ou sont en la possession ou sous le contrôle d'une personne relevant de la compétence de l'État requis;
(f) dans la mesure où ils sont connus, les nom et adresse de toute personne dont il y a lieu de penser qu'elle est en possession des renseignements demandés;
(g) une déclaration précisant que l'État requérant a utilisé pour obtenir les renseignements tous les moyens disponibles sur son propre territoire, hormis ceux qui susciteraient des difficultés disproportionnées

IV. Actes légaux de l'Union Européenne:
Il est convenu que la Convention n'affecte pas les actes légaux de l'Union Européenne et les dispositions correspondantes des États contractants.

EN FOI DE QUOI, les soussignés, dûment autorisés à cet effet, ont signé le présent Protocole.

Fait en deux exemplaires à Bruxelles, le 10 mars 2015

en langues française, hongroise et anglaise, tous les textes faisant également foi. En cas de divergence dans l'interprétation, le texte anglais prévaut.

Pour le Grand-Duché de Luxembourg

Pour la Hongrie

[TEXT IN HUNGARIAN – TEXTE EN HONGROIS]

EGYEZMÉNY

A LUXEMBURGI NAGYHERCESÉG

ÉS

MAGYARORSZÁG

KÖZÖTT

A KETTŐS ADÓZTATÁS ELKERÜLÉSÉRŐL

ÉS AZ ADÓZTATÁS KIJÁTSZÁSÁNAK

MEGAKADÁLYOZÁSÁRÓL

A JÖVEDELEM- ÉS A VAGYONADÓK TERÜLETÉN

A Luxemburgi Nagyhercegség és Magyarország, attól az óhajtól vezérelve, hogy Egyezményt kössenek a kettős adóztatás elkerüléséről és az adóztatás kijátszásának megakadályozásáról a jövedelem- és vagyonadók területén, és hogy kapcsolatukat továbbfejlesszék és előmozdítsák,

az alábbiak szerint állapodtak meg:

1. Cikk
SZEMÉLYI HATÁLY

Ez az Egyezmény azokra a személyekre terjed ki, akik az egyik vagy mindkét Szerződő Államban belföldi illetőségűek.

2. Cikk
AZ EGYEZMÉNY HATÁLYA ALÁ TARTOZÓ ADÓK

1. Ez az Egyezmény azokra a jövedelem- és vagyonadókra terjed ki, amelyeket az egyik Szerződő Állam vagy annak helyi hatóságai vetnek ki, a beszedés módjára való tekintet nélkül.

2. Jövedelem- és vagyonadóknak tekintendők mindazok az adók, amelyeket a teljes jövedelem vagy teljes vagyon, illetve a jövedelem vagy vagyon részei után vetnek ki, beleértve az ingó vagy ingatlan vagyon elidegenítéséből származó nyereség utáni adókat, a vállalkozások által fizetett bérek és fizetések teljes összege utáni adókat, valamint a tőke értéknövekedésének adóját.

3. Azok a jelenleg létező adók, amelyekre az Egyezmény különösen kiterjed:

(a) Magyarország esetében:
- (i) a személyi jövedelemadó;
- (ii) a társasági adó;
- (iii) a telekadó; és
- (iv) az építményadó;
- (a továbbiakban: „magyar adó");

(b) Luxemburg esetében:
- (i) a magánszemélyek jövedelemadója;
- (ii) a társasági adó;
- (iii) a vagyonadó; és
- (iv) a kommunális kereskedelmi adó;
- (a továbbiakban: „luxemburgi adó").

4. Az Egyezmény kiterjed minden olyan azonos vagy lényegét tekintve hasonló adóra is, amelyet az Egyezmény aláírása után a jelenleg létező adók mellett vagy azok helyett vezetnek be. A Szerződő Államok illetékes hatóságai értesíteni fogják egymást az adójogszabályaikban végrehajtott bármely lényeges változásról.

3. Cikk
ÁLTALÁNOS MEGHATÁROZÁSOK

1. Az Egyezmény alkalmazásában, ha a szövegösszefüggés mást nem kíván:

(a) a „Magyarország" kifejezés a nemzetközi joggal összhangban lévő magyar jogszabályok által meghatározott földrajzi területet jelenti;

(b) a „Luxemburg" kifejezés a Luxemburgi Nagyhercegséget, és földrajzi értelemben használva a Luxemburgi Nagyhercegség területét jelenti;

(c) az „egyik Szerződő Állam" és a „másik Szerződő Állam" kifejezés Luxemburgot vagy Magyarországot jelenti a szövegösszefüggésnek megfelelően;

(d) a „személy" kifejezés magában foglalja a természetes személyt, a társaságot és bármely más személyi egyesülést;

(e) a „társaság" kifejezés bármely jogi személyt vagy egyéb olyan jogalanyt jelent, amely az adóztatás szempontjából a jogi személyekkel azonos módon kezelendő;

(f) a „vállalkozás" kifejezés bármely üzleti tevékenység végzésére vonatkozik;

(g) az „egyik Szerződő Állam vállalkozása" és „a másik Szerződő Állam vállalkozása" kifejezések az egyik Szerződő Államban belföldi illetőségű személy, illetve a másik Szerződő Államban belföldi illetőségű személy által folytatott vállalkozást jelentik;

(h) a „nemzetközi forgalom" kifejezés az egyik Szerződő Államban tényleges üzletvezetési hellyel rendelkező vállalkozás által üzemeltetett hajó, légi vagy közúti jármű igénybevételével végzett bármilyen szállítást jelent, kivéve, ha a hajót, légi vagy közúti járművet kizárólag a másik Szerződő Államban lévő helyek között üzemeltetik;

(i) az „illetékes hatóság" kifejezés a következőt jelenti:

(i) Magyarország esetében az adópolitikáért felelős minisztert vagy meghatalmazott képviselőjét;

(ii) Luxemburg esetében a pénzügyminisztert vagy meghatalmazott képviselőjét;

(j) az „állampolgár" kifejezés, egy Szerződő Állam vonatkozásában, a következőt jelenti:

(i) bármely természetes személyt, aki annak a Szerződő Államnak az állampolgárságával rendelkezik; és

(ii) bármely jogi személyt, személyegyesítő társaságot, egyesülést vagy egyéb olyan jogalanyt, amely ezt a jogállását abban a Szerződő Államban hatályos jogszabályokból nyeri;

(k) az „üzleti tevékenység" kifejezés magában foglalja a szabad foglalkozás vagy más önálló jellegű tevékenység végzését;

(l) a „tényleges üzletvezetés helye" az a hely, ahol a jogalany üzletvezetéséhez szükséges kulcsfontosságú vezetési és kereskedelmi döntéseket lényegében meghozzák. A tényleges üzletvezetés helye rendszerint az a hely lesz, ahol a legmagasabb rangú személy vagy személyek csoportja döntéseit meghozza, és a mindennapi vezetési tevékenységet végzik, a hely, ahol a jogalany egésze által végrehajtandó intézkedéseket meghatározzák.

2. Az Egyezménynek az egyik Szerződő Állam által bármely időpontban történő alkalmazásánál az Egyezményben meghatározás nélkül szereplő kifejezéseknek – ha a szövegösszefüggés mást nem kíván – olyan jelentésük van, mint amit ennek az államnak a jogszabályaiban abban az időpontban jelentenek azokra az adókra vonatkozóan, amelyekre az Egyezmény alkalmazást nyer; ennek az államnak az adójogszabályaiban foglalt meghatározások az irányadók ennek az államnak az egyéb jogszabályaiban foglalt meghatározásokkal szemben.

4. Cikk

BELFÖLDI ILLETŐSÉGŰ SZEMÉLY

1. Az Egyezmény alkalmazásában az „egyik Szerződő Államban belföldi illetőségű személy" kifejezés olyan személyt jelent, aki ennek a Szerződő Államnak a jogszabályai szerint lakóhelye, székhelye, üzletvezetési helye, bejegyzési helye vagy bármely más hasonló ismérv alapján adóköteles, beleértve az államot és annak bármely helyi hatóságát, valamint az abban az Államban létrehozott kollektív befektetési eszközt. Ez a kifejezés azonban nem foglalja magában azokat a személyeket, akik ebben az államban kizárólag az ebben az államban lévő forrásokból származó jövedelem vagy az ott lévő vagyon alapján adókötelesek.

2. Amennyiben egy természetes személy az 1. bekezdés rendelkezései értelmében mindkét Szerződő Államban belföldi illetőségű, helyzetét az alábbiak szerint kell meghatározni:

(a) csak abban az államban tekintendő belföldi illetőségűnek, amelyben állandó lakóhellyel rendelkezik; amennyiben mindkét államban rendelkezik állandó lakóhellyel, csak abban az államban tekintendő belföldi illetőségűnek, amellyel személyi és gazdasági kapcsolatai szorosabbak (a létérdekek központja);

(b) amennyiben nem határozható meg, hogy melyik államban van létérdekeinek a központja, vagy ha egyik államban sem rendelkezik állandó lakóhellyel, csak abban az államban tekintendő belföldi illetőségűnek, amelyben szokásos tartózkodási helye van;

(c) amennyiben mindkét államban van szokásos tartózkodási helye, vagy egyikben sincs, csak abban az államban tekintendő belföldi illetőségűnek, amelynek állampolgára;

(d) amennyiben mindkét Szerződő Állam állampolgára, vagy egyiké sem, a Szerződő Államok illetékes hatóságai kölcsönös egyetértéssel rendezik a kérdést.

3. Amennyiben az 1. bekezdés rendelkezései értelmében valamely nem természetes személy mindkét Szerződő Államban belföldi illetőségű, csak abban az államban tekintendő belföldi illetőségűnek, amelyben a tényleges üzletvezetésének helye található.

5. Cikk
TELEPHELY

1. Az Egyezmény alkalmazásában a „telephely" kifejezés olyan állandó üzleti helyet jelent, amelyen keresztül a vállalkozás üzleti tevékenységét egészben vagy részben kifejti.

2. A „telephely" kifejezés magában foglalja különösen:

(a) az üzletvezetés helyét;

(b) a fióktelepet;

(c) az irodát;

(d) a gyártelepet;

(e) a műhelyt; és

(f) a bányát, az olaj- és a földgázkutat, a kőfejtőt és a természeti kincsek kiaknázására szolgáló bármely más telepet.

3. Az építési terület, az építkezési, szerelési, beszerelési vagy kotrási munkálatok telephelyet keletkeztetnek, de csak ha 12 hónapnál tovább tartanak.

4. E cikk előző rendelkezéseire tekintet nélkül nem minősül „telephelynek":

(a) létesítmények használata kizárólag a vállalkozás javainak vagy áruinak raktározása, kiállítása vagy kiszolgáltatása céljára;

(b) készletek tartása a vállalkozás javaiból vagy áruiból kizárólag raktározás, kiállítás vagy kiszolgáltatás céljára;

(c) készletek tartása a vállalkozás javaiból vagy áruiból kizárólag abból a célból, hogy azokat egy másik vállalkozás feldolgozza;

(d) állandó üzleti hely fenntartása kizárólag arra a célra, hogy a vállalkozás részére javakat vagy árukat vásároljanak vagy információkat szerezzenek;

(e) állandó üzleti hely fenntartása kizárólag arra a célra, hogy a vállalkozás részére bármilyen más előkészítő vagy kisegítő jellegű tevékenységet folytassanak;

(f) állandó üzleti hely fenntartása kizárólag arra a célra, hogy az a)–e) pontokban említett tevékenységek bármely kombinációját végezze, feltéve, hogy az állandó üzleti helynek az ilyen kombinációból származó teljes tevékenysége előkészítő vagy kisegítő jellegű.

5. Tekintet nélkül az 1. és 2. bekezdések rendelkezéseire, ha egy személy – kivéve a független képviselőt, akire a 6. bekezdés rendelkezése alkalmazandó – egy vállalkozás számára tevékenykedik és az egyik Szerződő Államban meghatalmazása van, amellyel ott rendszeresen él, arra, hogy a vállalkozás nevében szerződéseket kössön, úgy ez a vállalkozás telephellyel bírónak tekintendő ebben az államban minden olyan tevékenység tekintetében, amelyet ez a személy a vállalkozás részére kifejt, kivéve, ha az ilyen személy tevékenysége a 4. bekezdésben említett tevékenységekre korlátozódik, amelyek, ha azokat egy állandó üzleti helyen keresztül fejtenék ki, az említett bekezdés rendelkezései értelmében nem tennék ezt az állandó üzleti helyet telephellyé.

6. Egy vállalkozást nem lehet úgy tekinteni, mintha annak az egyik Szerződő Államban telephelye lenne csupán azért, mert tevékenységét ebben az államban alkusz, bizományos vagy más független képviselő útján fejti ki, feltéve, hogy ezek a személyek rendes üzleti tevékenységük keretében járnak el.

7. Az a tény, hogy az egyik Szerződő Államban belföldi illetőségű társaság olyan társaságot ellenőriz, vagy olyan társaság ellenőrzése alatt áll, amely a másik Szerződő Államban belföldi illetőségű, vagy üzleti tevékenységet fejt ki ebben a másik államban (akár telephely útján, akár más módon), önmagában még nem teszi egyik társaságot sem a másik telephelyévé.

6. Cikk
INGATLAN VAGYONBÓL SZÁRMAZÓ JÖVEDELEM

1. Az a jövedelem, amelyet az egyik Szerződő Államban belföldi illetőségű személy a másik Szerződő Államban fekvő ingatlan vagyonból szerez (beleértve a mezőgazdaságból és az erdőgazdálkodásból származó jövedelmet), megadóztatható ebben a másik államban.

2. Az „ingatlan vagyon" kifejezésnek olyan jelentése van, amit annak a Szerződő Államnak jogszabályai szerint jelent, amelyikben a szóban forgó vagyon fekszik. Ez a kifejezés minden esetben magában foglalja az ingatlan vagyon tartozékának minősülő vagyont, az állatállományt és a mezőgazdaságban és az erdőgazdálkodásban használatos berendezéseket, azokat a jogokat, amelyekre a földtulajdonra vonatkozó magánjogi rendelkezések nyernek alkalmazást, az ingatlan vagyon haszonélvezeti jogát, valamint az ásványlelőhelyek, források és más természeti erőforrások kitermelésének vagy kitermelési jogának ellenértékeként járó változó vagy állandó kifizetésekhez való jogot; hajók, belvízi hajók és légi járművek nem tekintendők ingatlan vagyonnak.

3. Az 1. bekezdés rendelkezései ingatlan vagyon közvetlen használatából, bérbeadásából, vagy hasznosításának bármely más formájából származó jövedelemre is alkalmazandók.

4. Az 1. és 3. bekezdés rendelkezései a vállalkozás ingatlan vagyonából származó jövedelemre is alkalmazandók.

7. Cikk
VÁLLALKOZÁSI NYERESÉG

1. Az egyik Szerződő Állam vállalkozásának nyeresége csak ebben az államban adóztatható, kivéve, ha a vállalkozás a másik Szerződő Államban egy ott lévő telephelyen keresztül fejt ki üzleti tevékenységet. Amennyiben a vállalkozás ily módon fejt ki üzleti tevékenységet, a telephelynek a 2. bekezdés rendelkezéseinek megfelelően betudható nyereség megadóztatható ebben a másik államban.

2. Az e cikk és a 23. cikk alkalmazásában, az egyik Szerződő Államban lévő, 1. bekezdésben meghatározott telephelynek betudható nyereségnek azt a nyereséget kell tekinteni, amelyet akkor érhetne el, különösen a vállalkozás más részeivel folytatott ügyleteiben, ha önálló és elkülönült vállalkozásként azonos vagy hasonló tevékenységet végezne azonos vagy hasonló feltételek mellett, figyelembe véve a vállalkozás által a telephelyen vagy a vállalkozás más részein keresztül elvégzett feladatokat, felhasznált eszközöket és vállalt kockázatokat.

3. Amennyiben az egyik Szerződő Állam a 2. bekezdéssel összhangban megállapítja az egyik Szerződő Állam vállalkozása telephelyének betudható nyereséget, és ennek megfelelően megadóztatja a vállalkozás olyan nyereségét, amely a másik államban adókötelezettség alá esett, a másik állam, az e nyereséget terhelő kettős adóztatás elkerülése érdekében a szükséges mértékben megfelelő kiigazítást tesz az erre a nyereségre számított adó összegére vonatkozóan. Ennek a kiigazításnak a megállapításánál a Szerződő Államok illetékes hatóságai szükség esetén konzultálnak egymással.

4. Amennyiben a nyereség olyan jövedelemtételeket tartalmaz, amelyekkel a jelen Egyezmény más cikkei külön foglalkoznak, úgy azoknak a cikkeknek a rendelkezéseit e cikk rendelkezései nem érintik.

8. Cikk
HAJÓZÁS, BELVÍZI SZÁLLÍTÁS ÉS LÉGI SZÁLLÍTÁS

1. A nyereség, amely a vízi vagy légi járművek nemzetközi forgalomban történő üzemeltetéséből származik csak abban a Szerződő Államban adóztatható, amelyben a vállalkozás tényleges üzletvezetésének helye található.

2. A nyereség, amely a belvízi szállítást végző hajók üzemeltetéséből származik csak abban a Szerződő Államban adóztatható, amelyben a vállalkozás tényleges üzletvezetésének helye található.

3. Ha egy hajózási vállalkozás vagy egy belvízi szállítást végző vállalkozás tényleges üzletvezetésének helye egy vízi jármű vagy hajó fedélzetén van, akkor azt abban a Szerződő Államban találhatónak kell tekinteni, ahol a vízi jármű vagy hajó lajstromozási kikötője található, vagy ha nincs ilyen kikötő, akkor abban a Szerződő Államban, ahol a vízi jármű vagy hajó üzemeltetője belföldi illetőségű.

4. Az 1. bekezdés rendelkezései alkalmazandók azokra a nyereségekre is, amelyek valamely poolban, közös üzemeltetésben vagy nemzetközi üzemeltetésű szervezetben való részvételből származnak.

9. Cikk
KAPCSOLT VÁLLALKOZÁSOK

1. Amennyiben
(a) az egyik Szerződő Állam vállalkozása közvetlenül vagy közvetve a másik Szerződő Állam vállalkozásának vezetésében, ellenőrzésében vagy tőkéjében részesedik, vagy
(b) ugyanazok a személyek közvetlenül vagy közvetve az egyik Szerződő Állam vállalkozásának és a másik Szerződő Állam vállalkozásának vezetésében, ellenőrzésében vagy tőkéjében részesednek,
és bármelyik esetben a két vállalkozás egymás közötti kereskedelmi vagy pénzügyi kapcsolataiban olyan feltételekben állapodik meg vagy olyan feltételeket szab, amelyek eltérnek azoktól, amelyekben független vállalkozások egymással megállapodnának, úgy az a nyereség, amelyet a vállalkozások egyike e feltételek nélkül elért volna, de e feltételek miatt nem ért el, beszámítható ennek a vállalkozásnak a nyereségébe, és megfelelően megadóztatható.

2. Ha az egyik Szerződő Állam ezen állam valamely vállalkozásának a nyereségéhez olyan nyereséget számít hozzá – és adóztat meg ennek megfelelően –, amelyet a másik Szerződő Állam vállalkozásánál megadóztattak ebben a másik államban, és az így hozzászámított nyereség olyan nyereség, amelyet az elsőként említett állam vállalkozása ért volna el, ha a két vállalkozás olyan feltételekben állapodott volna meg, mint amelyekben független vállalkozások egymással megállapodnának, úgy ez a másik állam megfelelően kiigazítja az ilyen nyereségre ott kivetett adó összegét. Az ilyen kiigazítás megállapításánál kellően figyelembe kell venni jelen Egyezmény egyéb rendelkezéseit, és a Szerződő Államok illetékes hatóságai szükség esetén egyeztetnek egymással.

10. Cikk
OSZTALÉK

1. Az osztalék, amelyet az egyik Szerződő Államban belföldi illetőségű társaság a másik Szerződő Államban belföldi illetőségű személynek fizet, megadóztatható ebben a másik államban.

2. Mindazonáltal ez az osztalék abban a Szerződő Államban is megadóztatható, és annak az államnak a jogszabályai szerint, amelyben az osztalékot fizető társaság belföldi illetőségű, ha azonban az osztalék haszonhúzója a másik Szerződő Államban belföldi illetőségű személy, az így megállapított adó nem haladhatja meg:

(a) az osztalék bruttó összegének 0 százalékát, ha a haszonhúzó egy olyan társaság (a nem adóköteles személyegyesítő társaság kivételével), amely az osztalékot fizető társaság tőkéjében legalább 10 százalékos közvetlen részesedéssel bír;

(b) az osztalék bruttó összegének 10 százalékát minden más esetben.

E bekezdés rendelkezései nem érintik a társaság adóztatását azon nyereség után, amelyből az osztalékot fizetik.

3. E cikk alkalmazásában az „osztalék" kifejezés részvényekből, élvezeti jegyekből vagy élvezeti jogokból, bányarészjegyekből, alapítói részvényekből vagy más nyereségből való részesedést biztosító jogokból – kivéve a hitelköveteléseket – származó jövedelmet, valamint olyan más társasági jogokból származó jövedelmet jelent, amelyet annak az Államnak az adózási jogszabályai, amelyben a nyereséget felosztó társaság belföldi illetőségű, a részvényekből származó jövedelemmel azonos adóztatási elbánás alá vetnek.

4. Az 1. és 2. bekezdés rendelkezései nem alkalmazandók, ha az osztaléknak egyik Szerződő Államban belföldi illetőségű haszonhúzója a másik Szerződő Államban, amelyben az osztalékot fizető társaság belföldi illetőségű, egy ott lévő telephely útján üzleti tevékenységet fejt ki, és az érdekeltség, amelyre tekintettel az osztalékot fizetik, ténylegesen ehhez a telephelyhez kapcsolódik. Ebben az esetben a 7. cikk rendelkezéseit kell alkalmazni.

5. Ha az egyik Szerződő Államban belföldi illetőségű társaság nyereséget vagy jövedelmet élvez a másik Szerződő Államból, úgy ez a másik állam nem adóztathatja meg a társaság által kifizetett osztalékot, kivéve, ha az osztalékot ebben a másik államban belföldi illetőségű személynek fizetik, vagy ha az érdekeltség, amelyre tekintettel az osztalékot fizetik, ténylegesen a másik államban lévő telephelyhez kapcsolódik, sem pedig a társaság fel nem osztott nyereségét nem terhelheti a társaság fel nem osztott nyeresége után kivetett adóval, még akkor sem, ha a kifizetett osztalék vagy a fel nem osztott nyereség egészben vagy részben ebben a másik államban keletkező nyereségből vagy jövedelemből áll.

11. Cikk
KAMAT

1. A kamat, amely az egyik Szerződő Államban keletkezik, és amelynek haszonhúzója a másik Szerződő Államban belföldi illetőségű személy, csak ebben a másik államban adóztatható.

2. E cikk alkalmazásában a „kamat" kifejezés mindenfajta követelésből származó jövedelmet jelent, akár van jelzáloggal biztosítva, akár nem, és akár ad jogot az adós nyereségéből való részesedésre, akár nem, és magában foglalja különösen az állami értékpapírokból származó jövedelmet, a kötvényekből és az adósságlevelekből származó jövedelmet, beleértve az ilyen értékpapírokhoz, kötvényekhez vagy adósságlevelekhez kapcsolódó prémiumokat és díjakat, de nem foglalja magában a 10. cikkben említett jövedelmet. E cikk alkalmazásában a késedelmes fizetés utáni büntető terhek nem tekintendők kamatnak.

3. Az 1. bekezdés rendelkezései nem alkalmazandók, ha a kamat egyik Szerződő Államban belföldi illetőségű haszonhúzója a másik Szerződő Államban, amelyben a kamat keletkezik, egy ott lévő telephely útján üzleti tevékenységet folytat, és a követelés, amely után a kamatot fizetik, ténylegesen ehhez a telephelyhez kapcsolódik. Ebben az esetben a 7. cikk rendelkezéseit kell alkalmazni.

4. Ha a kamatot fizető személy és a haszonhúzó közötti, vagy kettejük és egy harmadik személy közötti különleges kapcsolat miatt a kamat összege ahhoz a követeléshez viszonyítva, amely után fizetik, meghaladja azt az összeget, amelyben a kamatot fizető személy és a haszonhúzó ilyen kapcsolat hiányában megállapodtak volna, úgy e cikk rendelkezéseit csak az utóbb említett összegre kell alkalmazni. Ebben az esetben a kifizetett többletösszeg mindkét Szerződő Állam jogszabályai szerint megadóztatható marad, az Egyezmény egyéb rendelkezéseinek kellő figyelembevételével.

12. Cikk
JOGDÍJ

1. A jogdíj, amely az egyik Szerződő Államban keletkezik, és amelynek haszonhúzója a másik Szerződő Államban belföldi illetőségű személy, csak ebben a másik államban adóztatható.

2. E cikk alkalmazásában a „jogdíj" kifejezés bármely olyan jellegű kifizetést jelent, amelyet irodalmi, művészeti vagy tudományos művek (ideértve a filmalkotást) szerzői jogának, bármilyen szabadalomnak, védjegynek, formatervezési vagy más mintának, tervnek, titkos formulának vagy eljárásnak a hasznosításáért vagy hasznosítási jogáért, valamint ipari, kereskedelmi vagy tudományos tapasztalatokra vonatkozó információért ellenértékként kapnak.

3. Az 1. bekezdés rendelkezései nem alkalmazandók, ha a jogdíj egyik Szerződő Államban belföldi illetőségű haszonhúzója a másik Szerződő Államban, amelyben a jogdíj keletkezik, egy ott lévő telephely útján üzleti tevékenységet folytat, és a jog vagy vagyoni érték, amely után a jogdíjat fizetik, ténylegesen ehhez a telephelyhez kapcsolódik. Ebben az esetben a 7. cikk rendelkezéseit kell alkalmazni.

4. Ha a jogdíjat fizető személy és a haszonhúzó, vagy kettejük és egy harmadik személy közötti különleges kapcsolat miatt a jogdíj összege azon hasznosításhoz, joghoz vagy információhoz mérten, amiért fizetik, meghaladja azt az összeget, amelyben a jogdíjat fizető személy és a haszonhúzó ilyen kapcsolat hiányában megállapodott volna, úgy e cikk rendelkezéseit csak az utóbb említett összegre kell alkalmazni. Ebben az esetben a kifizetett többletösszeg mindkét Szerződő Állam jogszabályai szerint megadóztatható marad, az Egyezmény egyéb rendelkezéseinek kellő figyelembevételével.

13. Cikk
ELIDEGENÍTÉSBŐL SZÁRMAZÓ NYERESÉG

1. Az egyik Szerződő Államban belföldi illetőségű személynek a 6. cikkben meghatározott és a másik Szerződő Államban fekvő ingatlan vagyona elidegenítéséből származó nyeresége megadóztatható ebben a másik államban.

2. Az egyik Szerződő Államban belföldi illetőségű személynek olyan részvények vagy hasonló érdekeltségek elidegenítéséből származó nyeresége, amelyek értékének több mint 50 százaléka közvetlenül vagy közvetve a másik Szerződő Államban fekvő ingatlan vagyonból származik, megadóztatható ebben a másik államban.

3. Az e cikk 2. bekezdésében nem említett egyéb nyereség, amely olyan ingó vagyon elidegenítéséből származik, amely az egyik Szerződő Állam vállalkozása másik Szerződő Államban lévő telephelye üzleti vagyonának része, beleértve az ilyen telephelynek (önmagában vagy az egész vállalkozással együtt történő) elidegenítéséből elért nyereséget, megadóztatható ebben a másik államban.

4. A nemzetközi forgalomban üzemeltetett vízi vagy légi járművek, illetve belvízi szállítást végző hajók elidegenítéséből, vagy az ilyen vízi járművek, légi járművek vagy hajók üzemeltetését szolgáló ingó vagyon elidegenítéséből származó nyereség csak abban a Szerződő Államban adóztatható, ahol a vállalkozás tényleges üzletvezetésének helye található.

5. Az 1., 2., 3. és 4. bekezdésekben nem említett bármely vagyon elidegenítéséből származó nyereség csak abban a Szerződő Államban adóztatható, amelyben az elidegenítő belföldi illetőségű.

14. Cikk
MUNKAVISZONYBÓL SZÁRMAZÓ JÖVEDELEM

1. A 15., 17., 18. és 20. cikkek rendelkezéseinek fenntartásával a fizetés, a bér és más hasonló díjazás, amelyet az egyik Szerződő Államban belföldi illetőségű személy munkaviszonyra tekintettel kap, csak ebben az államban adóztatható, kivéve, ha a munkát a másik Szerződő Államban végzik. Amennyiben a munkát ott végzik, úgy az ezért kapott díjazás megadóztatható ebben a másik államban.

2. Tekintet nélkül az 1. bekezdés rendelkezéseire, az a díjazás, amelyet az egyik Szerződő Államban belföldi illetőségű személy a másik Szerződő Államban végzett munkára tekintettel kap, csak az elsőként említett államban adóztatható, ha:

(a) a kedvezményezett a másik államban nem tartózkodik egyfolytában vagy megszakításokkal összesen 183 napnál hosszabb időszakot az adott naptári évben kezdődő vagy végződő bármely tizenkét hónapos időtartamon belül, és
(b) a díjazást olyan munkaadó fizeti, vagy azt olyan munkaadó nevében fizetik, aki nem belföldi illetőségű a másik államban, és
(c) a díjazást nem a munkaadónak a másik államban lévő telephelye viseli.

3. Tekintet nélkül e cikk előző rendelkezéseire, a nemzetközi forgalomban üzemeltetett vízi, légi vagy közúti járművön vagy belvízi szállítást végző hajó fedélzetén végzett munkáért kapott díjazás megadóztatható abban a Szerződő Államban, amelyben a vállalkozás tényleges üzletvezetésének helye található.

15. Cikk
IGAZGATÓK TISZTELETDÍJA

Az igazgatói tiszteletdíj és más hasonló kifizetés, amelyet az egyik Szerződő Államban belföldi illetőségű személy a másik Szerződő Államban belföldi illetőségű társaság igazgatótanácsának vagy felügyelőbizottságának tagjaként kap, megadóztatható ebben a másik államban.

16. Cikk
MŰVÉSZEK ÉS SPORTOLÓK

1. Tekintet nélkül a 7. és a 14. cikkek rendelkezéseire, az a jövedelem, amelyet az egyik Szerződő Államban belföldi illetőségű személy előadóművészként, mint színpadi, film-, rádió- vagy televíziós művész vagy zeneművész, vagy sportolóként élvez a másik Szerződő Államban ilyen minőségében kifejtett személyes tevékenységéből, megadóztatható ebben a másik államban.

2. Amennyiben egy előadóművész vagy egy sportoló által ilyen minőségében kifejtett személyes tevékenységéből származó jövedelem nem az előadóművésznél vagy sportolónál magánál, hanem egy másik személynél jelentkezik, úgy ez a jövedelem, tekintet nélkül a 7. és a 14. cikkek rendelkezéseire, megadóztatható abban a Szerződő Államban, amelyben az előadóművész vagy a sportoló a tevékenységét kifejti.

3. Az 1. és 2. bekezdés rendelkezései nem alkalmazandók a művészek és sportolók egyik Szerződő Államban kifejtett tevékenységéből származó jövedelemére, ha az abba az Államba tett látogatást az egyik vagy mindkét Szerződő Állam vagy helyi hatóságaik teljes egészében vagy nagyrészben közalapjaiból támogatják. Ilyen esetben a jövedelem csak abban a Szerződő Államban adóztatható, amelyben a művész vagy sportoló belföldi illetőségű.

17. Cikk
NYUGDÍJAK

A nyugdíj és más hasonló térítés, amely az egyik Szerződő Államban keletkezik, és amelyet a másik Szerződő Államban belföldi illetőségű személynek fizetnek, csak az elsőként említett államban adóztatható.

18. Cikk
KÖZSZOLGÁLAT

1. (a) A fizetések, bérek és más hasonló díjazások, amelyeket az egyik Szerződő Állam vagy annak helyi hatósága fizet természetes személynek az ezen államnak vagy hatóságnak teljesített szolgálatért, csak ebben az államban adóztathatók.
(b) Ezen fizetések, bérek és más hasonló díjazások azonban csak a másik Szerződő Államban adóztathatók, ha a szolgálatot ebben a másik államban teljesítették, és a természetes személy ebben az államban olyan belföldi illetőségű személy, aki:
(i) ennek az államnak az állampolgára; vagy
(ii) nem kizárólag a szolgálat teljesítése céljából vált ebben az államban belföldi illetőségű személlyé.

2. Az egyik Szerződő Állam vagy annak helyi hatósága által folytatott üzleti tevékenységgel kapcsolatosan teljesített szolgálatért fizetett fizetésekre, bérekre és más hasonló díjazásokra a 14., 15. és 16. cikkek rendelkezései alkalmazandók.

19. Cikk
TANULÓK

Azok a kifizetések, amelyeket olyan tanuló, ipari és kereskedelmi tanuló vagy gyakornok kap ellátására, tanulmányi vagy képzési célokra, aki közvetlenül az egyik Szerződő Államba való utazás előtt a másik Szerződő Államban belföldi illetőségű volt, vagy jelenleg is az, és aki az elsőként említett államban kizárólag tanulmányi vagy képzési célból tartózkodik, nem adóztatható meg ebben az államban, amennyiben az ilyen kifizetések ezen az államon kívüli forrásból származnak.

20. Cikk
OKTATÓK, TANÁROK ÉS KUTATÓK

1. Egy természetes személy, aki az egyik Szerződő Államot az abban az Államban lévő egyetemen, főiskolán, iskolában vagy más elismert oktatási intézetben való tanítás vagy kutatás folytatása céljából látogatja meg, és aki közvetlenül ezen látogatás előtt a másik Szerződő Államban belföldi illetőségű volt, vagy jelenleg is az, az elsőként említett Szerződő Államban mentes az adó alól az ilyen tanításért vagy kutatásért kapott díjazás után az e célból tett első látogatásának időpontjától számított két évet meg nem haladó időtartamra.

2. Ezen cikk 1. bekezdésének rendelkezései nem alkalmazandók a kutatásból származó díjazásra, ha az ilyen kutatást nem a köz érdekében, hanem elsősorban egy meghatározott személy vagy személyek egyéni haszna érdekében végzik.

21. Cikk
EGYÉB JÖVEDELEM

1. Az egyik Szerződő Államban belföldi illetőségű személy jövedelmének az Egyezmény előző cikkeiben nem tárgyalt részei, bárhol is keletkeznek, csak ebben az államban adóztathatók.

2. Az 1. bekezdés rendelkezései nem alkalmazandók a 6. cikk 2. bekezdésében meghatározott ingatlan vagyonból származó jövedelmen kívüli jövedelemre, ha az ilyen jövedelemnek az egyik Szerződő Államban belföldi illetőségű kedvezményezettje a másik Szerződő Államban egy ott lévő telephely útján üzleti tevékenységet fejt ki, és a jog vagy vagyoni érték, amelyre tekintettel a jövedelmet fizetik, ténylegesen ehhez a telephelyhez kapcsolódik. Ebben az esetben a 7. cikk rendelkezéseit kell alkalmazni.

22. Cikk
VAGYON

1. A 6. cikkben említett olyan ingatlan vagyon, amely az egyik Szerződő Államban belföldi illetőségű személy tulajdonát képezi és a másik Szerződő Államban fekszik, megadóztatható ebben a másik államban.

2. Az ingó vagyon, amely az egyik Szerződő Állam vállalkozásának a másik Szerződő Államban lévő telephelye üzleti vagyonának részét képezi, megadóztatható ebben a másik államban.

3. A nemzetközi forgalomban üzemeltetett vízi és légi járművekből és a belvízi szállítást végző hajókból álló vagyon, és az ilyen vízi járművek, légi járművek és hajók üzemeltetésére szolgáló ingó vagyon csak abban a Szerződő Államban adóztatható, amelyben a vállalkozás tényleges üzletvezetésének helye található.

4. Az egyik Szerződő Államban belföldi illetőségű személy minden más vagyonrésze csak ebben az államban adóztatható.

23. Cikk
A KETTŐS ADÓZTATÁS ELKERÜLÉSE

1. Magyarországon a kettős adóztatást a következő módon kell elkerülni:

(a) Amennyiben egy Magyarországon belföldi illetőségű személy olyan jövedelmet élvez, vagy olyan vagyona van, amely ezen Egyezmény rendelkezései szerint megadóztatható Luxemburgban, Magyarország a (b) és (c) albekezdésben foglalt rendelkezések fenntartásával mentesíti az ilyen jövedelmet vagy vagyont az adó alól.
(b) Amennyiben egy Magyarországon belföldi illetőségű személy olyan jövedelemtételeket élvez, amelyek a 10. cikk és a 13. cikk 2. bekezdésének rendelkezései szerint megadóztathatók Luxemburgban, Magyarország megengedi az ilyen belföldi illetőségű személy jövedelmét terhelő adóból azon összeg levonását, amely megegyezik a Luxemburgban megfizetett adóval. Az így levont összeg azonban nem haladhatja meg a levonás előtt számított adónak azt a részét, amely a Luxemburgból származó ilyen jövedelemtételekre esik.
(c) Amennyiben ezen Egyezmény bármely rendelkezése szerint valamely, Magyarországon belföldi illetőségű személy által élvezett jövedelem, vagy a tulajdonát képező vagyon mentesül az adó alól Magyarországon, Magyarország mindazonáltal ennek a belföldi illetőségű személynek a többi jövedelme vagy vagyona utáni adó kiszámításánál figyelembe veheti a mentesített jövedelmet vagy vagyont.
(d) Az (a) albekezdés rendelkezései nem alkalmazandók egy Magyarországon belföldi illetőségű személy jövedelmére vagy vagyonára, ha Luxemburg ezen Egyezmény rendelkezéseit alkalmazva mentesíti az ilyen jövedelmet vagy vagyont az adó alól, vagy az ilyen jövedelemre a 10. cikk 2. bekezdése rendelkezéseit alkalmazza.

2. A kettős adóztatás elkerülésére vonatkozó luxemburgi jog rendelkezéseinek fenntartásával, amelyek nem érintik a bemutatott általános alapelvet, a kettős adóztatást a következő módon kell elkerülni:
(a) Amennyiben egy Luxemburgban belföldi illetőségű személy olyan jövedelem élvez, vagy olyan vagyona van, amely ezen Egyezmény rendelkezései szerint megadóztatható Magyarországon, Luxemburg a (b) és (c) albekezdésben foglalt rendelkezések fenntartásával mentesíti az ilyen jövedelmet vagy vagyont az adó alól, mindazonáltal a belföldi illetőségű személynek a többi jövedelme vagy vagyona utáni adó kiszámításánál ugyanazokat az adókulcsokat alkalmazhatja, mintha a jövedelem vagy vagyon nem lett volna mentesítve.
(b) Amennyiben egy Luxemburgban belföldi illetőségű személy olyan jövedelmet élvez, amely a 10. cikk, a 13. cikk 2. bekezdésének és a 16. cikk rendelkezései szerint megadóztatható Magyarországon, Luxemburg megengedi az ilyen belföldi illetőségű személy jövedelmét terhelő személyi jövedelemadóból vagy társasági adóból azon összeg levonását, amely megegyezik a Magyarországon megfizetett adóval. Az így levont összeg azonban nem haladhatja meg a levonás előtt számított adónak azt a részét, amely a Magyarországból származó ilyen jövedelemtételekre esik.
(c) Az (a) albekezdés rendelkezései nem alkalmazandók egy Luxemburgban belföldi illetőségű személy jövedelmére vagy vagyonára, ha Magyarország ezen Egyezmény rendelkezéseit alkalmazva mentesíti az ilyen jövedelmet vagy vagyont az adó alól, vagy az ilyen jövedelemre a 10. cikk 2. bekezdése rendelkezéseit alkalmazza.

24. Cikk
EGYENLŐ ELBÁNÁS

1. Az egyik Szerződő Állam állampolgárai nem vethetők a másik Szerződő Államban olyan adóztatás, vagy azzal összefüggő kötelezettség alá, amely más vagy terhesebb, mint az az adóztatás vagy azzal összefüggő kötelezettség, amelynek e másik állam állampolgárai azonos körülmények között – különös tekintettel a belföldi illetőségre – alá vannak vagy alá lehetnek vetve. Ez a rendelkezés, tekintet nélkül az 1. cikk rendelkezéseire, azokra a személyekre is alkalmazandó, akik nem belföldi illetőségűek az egyik vagy mindkét Szerződő Államban.

2. Az egyik Szerződő Államban belföldi illetőségű hontalan személyek egyik Szerződő Államban sem vethetők olyan adóztatás vagy azzal összefüggő kötelezettség alá, amely más vagy terhesebb, mint az az adóztatás vagy azzal összefüggő kötelezettség, amelynek az adott állam állampolgárai azonos körülmények között – különös tekintettel a belföldi illetőségre – alá vannak vagy alá lehetnek vetve.

3. Az egyik Szerződő Állam vállalkozásának a másik Szerződő Államban lévő telephelyét ebben a másik államban nem lehet kedvezőtlenebb adóztatás alá vetni, mint ennek a másik államnak azonos tevékenységet folytató vállalkozásait. Ez a rendelkezés nem értelmezendő akként, mintha az egyik Szerződő Államot arra kötelezné, hogy a másik Szerződő Államban belföldi illetőségű személyeknek a polgári jogállás vagy családi kötelezettségek alapján adózási célból olyan személyi kedvezményeket, mentességeket és levonásokat nyújtson, amelyeket a saját belföldi illetőségű személyeinek nyújt.

4. Az egyik Szerződő Állam vállalkozása által a másik Szerződő Államban belföldi illetőségű személynek fizetett kamat, jogdíj és más kifizetések az ilyen vállalkozás adóköteles nyereségének megállapításánál ugyanolyan feltételek mellett vonhatók le, mintha azokat az elsőként említett államban belföldi illetőségű személy részére fizették volna, kivéve, ha a 9. cikk 1. bekezdésének, a 11. cikk 4. bekezdésének vagy a 12. cikk 4. bekezdésének rendelkezései alkalmazandók. Hasonlóképpen az egyik Szerződő Állam vállalkozásának a másik Szerződő Államban belföldi illetőségű személlyel szemben fennálló tartozásai az ilyen vállalkozás adóköteles vagyonának megállapításánál ugyanolyan feltételek mellett vonhatók le, mintha azok az elsőként említett Szerződő Államban belföldi illetőségű személlyel szemben álltak volna fenn.

5. Az egyik Szerződő Állam olyan vállalkozásai, amelyeknek tőkéje teljesen vagy részben, közvetlenül vagy közvetve, a másik Szerződő Államban belföldi illetőségű egy vagy több személy tulajdonában vagy ellenőrzése alatt van, nem vethetők az elsőként említett Szerződő Államban olyan adóztatás vagy azzal összefüggő kötelezettség alá, amely más vagy terhesebb, mint az az adóztatás és azzal összefüggő kötelezettség, amelynek az elsőként említett állam más hasonló vállalkozásai alá vannak vagy alá lehetnek vetve.

6. E cikk rendelkezései, tekintet nélkül a 2. cikk rendelkezéseire, bármilyen fajtájú és megnevezésű adóra alkalmazandók.

25. Cikk
KÖLCSÖNÖS EGYEZTETŐ ELJÁRÁS

1. Ha egy személy véleménye szerint az egyik vagy mindkét Szerződő Állam intézkedései rá nézve olyan adóztatáshoz vezetnek vagy fognak vezetni, amely nem felel meg ezen Egyezmény rendelkezéseinek, úgy ezeknek az államoknak a belső jogszabályai által biztosított jogorvoslati lehetőségektől függetlenül, ügyét előterjesztheti annak a Szerződő Államnak az illetékes hatóságához, amelyben belföldi illetőségű, vagy ha ügye a 24. cikk 1. bekezdése alá tartozik, annak a Szerződő Államnak az illetékes hatóságához, amelynek állampolgára. Az ügyet az Egyezmény rendelkezéseinek meg nem felelő adóztatáshoz vezető intézkedésre vonatkozó első értesítést követő három éven belül kell előterjeszteni.

2. Az illetékes hatóság, amennyiben a kifogást megalapozottnak találja, és önmaga nem képes kielégítő megoldást találni, törekedni fog arra, hogy az ügyet a másik Szerződő Állam illetékes hatóságával együtt kölcsönös egyetértéssel rendezze azzal a céllal, hogy elkerüljék az olyan adóztatást, amely nem áll összhangban az Egyezménnyel. Az így létrejött megállapodást a Szerződő Államok belső jogszabályaiban előírt határidőktől függetlenül végre kell hajtani.

3. A Szerződő Államok illetékes hatóságai törekedni fognak arra, hogy az Egyezmény értelmezésével vagy alkalmazásával kapcsolatos nehézségeket vagy kétségeket kölcsönös egyetértéssel oldják fel. Közös tanácskozásokat tarthatnak annak érdekében, hogy olyan esetekben is elkerüljék a kettős adóztatást, amelyekről az Egyezmény nem rendelkezik.

4. A Szerződő Államok illetékes hatóságai közvetlenül érintkezhetnek egymással, beleértve egy saját magukból vagy képviselőikből álló közös bizottságot, abból a célból, hogy az előző bekezdések értelmében egyetértésre jussanak.

26. Cikk
INFORMÁCIÓCSERE

1. A Szerződő Államok illetékes hatóságai tájékoztatni fogják egymást a jelen Egyezmény rendelkezéseinek végrehajtásához, vagy a Szerződő Államok vagy azok helyi hatóságai által kivetett, bármilyen fajtájú vagy megnevezésű adóra vonatkozó belső jogszabályi rendelkezések végrehajtásához és érvényesítéséhez előreláthatóan fontos információról, amennyiben az ezek alapján való adóztatás nem ellentétes az Egyezménnyel. Az információcserét az 1. és a 2. cikk nem korlátozza.

2. A Szerződő Államnak az 1. bekezdés alapján kapott bármely információt ugyanúgy titokként kell kezelnie, mint az ennek az államnak a saját belső jogszabályai alapján megszerzett információkat és csak olyan személyek vagy hatóságok (beleértve a bíróságokat és a közigazgatási szerveket) részére szabad felfednie, amelyek az 1. bekezdésben említett adók megállapításával vagy beszedésével, ezek érvényesítésével és a vonatkozó peres eljárással, vagy az ezekkel az adókkal kapcsolatos jogorvoslat elbírálásával vagy a fentiek felügyeletével foglalkoznak. Ezek a személyek vagy hatóságok az információt csak ilyen célokra használhatják fel. Nyilvános bírósági tárgyalásokon vagy bírósági határozatokban az információt nyilvánosságra hozhatják.

3. Az 1. és 2. bekezdés rendelkezései semmilyen esetben sem értelmezhetők úgy, mintha valamelyik Szerződő Államot arra köteleznék, hogy:

(a) az egyik vagy a másik Szerződő Állam jogszabályaitól vagy államigazgatási gyakorlatától eltérő államigazgatási intézkedést hozzon;

(b) olyan információt nyújtson, amely az egyik vagy másik Szerződő Állam jogszabályai szerint, vagy az államigazgatás szokásos rendjében nem szerezhető be;

(c) olyan információt nyújtson, amely bármely szakmai, üzleti, ipari, kereskedelmi vagy foglalkozási titkot vagy szakmai eljárást fedne fel, vagy amelynek felfedése sértené a közrendet.

4. Ha az egyik Szerződő Állam a jelen cikknek megfelelően információt kér, a másik Szerződő Állam saját információszerzési intézkedéseit alkalmazza a kért információ megszerzése érdekében, még akkor is, ha a másik Államnak az információra saját adóügyi céljaira nincs szüksége. A megelőző mondatban foglalt kötelezettségre a 3. bekezdés korlátozásai vonatkoznak, de ezek a korlátozások semmilyen esetben sem értelmezhetők úgy, hogy a Szerződő Állam számára megengedik az információszolgáltatás megtagadását kizárólag azért, mert az információhoz nem kapcsolódik hazai érdeke.

5. A 3. bekezdés rendelkezései semmilyen esetben nem értelmezhetők úgy, hogy a Szerződő Állam számára megengedik az információszolgáltatás megtagadását kizárólag azért, mert az információ banknak, más pénzintézetnek, kijelölt személynek vagy képviselői vagy bizalmi minőségben eljáró személynek áll rendelkezésére, vagy mert az egy személyben lévő tulajdonosi érdekeltségre vonatkozik.

27. Cikk
DIPLOMÁCIAI ÉS KONZULI KÉPVISELETEK TAGJAI

Az Egyezmény semmilyen módon nem érinti a diplomáciai vagy konzuli képviseletek tagjait a nemzetközi jog általános szabályai szerint vagy külön egyezmények rendelkezései alapján megillető adózási kiváltságokat.

28. Cikk
HATÁLYBALÉPÉS

1. Az egyes Szerződő Államok írásban, diplomáciai úton értesítik egymást arról, hogy az ezen Egyezmény hatálybalépéséhez szükséges belső követelményeknek eleget tettek.

2. Az Egyezmény az 1. bekezdésben említett értesítések közül a későbbi kézhezvételének időpontját követő 30. napon lép hatályba, és rendelkezései mindkét Szerződő Államban alkalmazandók:
(a) a forrásnál levont adók tekintetében az Egyezmény hatálybalépésének évét követő első naptári év január 1-jén vagy azt követően keletkezett jövedelmekre;
(b) az egyéb jövedelemadók és a vagyonadók tekintetében az Egyezmény hatálybalépésének évét követő első naptári év január 1-jén vagy azután kezdődő bármely adóévre kivethető adókra.

3. Ezen Egyezmény hatályba lépésekor a Magyar Köztársaság és a Luxemburgi Nagyhercegség között a kettős adózás elkerüléséről a jövedelem- és vagyonadók tekintetében, Budapesten, 1990. január hó 15. napján aláírt Egyezmény és Jegyzőkönyv hatályát veszíti és nem kell alkalmazni:
(a) a forrásnál levont adók tekintetében ezen Egyezmény hatálybalépésének évét követő első naptári év január 1-jén vagy azt követően keletkezett jövedelmekre;
(b) az egyéb jövedelem- és a vagyonadók tekintetében ezen Egyezmény hatálybalépésének évét követő első naptári év január 1-jén vagy azután kezdődő bármely adóévre kivethető adókra.

29. Cikk
FELMONDÁS

1. Ez az Egyezmény mindaddig hatályban marad, ameddig az egyik Szerződő Állam fel nem mondja. Az Egyezményt annak hatályba lépésétől számított öt éves időszak lejártától kezdődően bármelyik Szerződő Állam felmondhatja úgy, hogy legalább hat hónappal bármely naptári év vége előtt a felmondásról diplomáciai úton értesítést küld.

2. Ebben az esetben ez az Egyezmény mindkét Szerződő Államban hatályát veszti:
(a) a forrásnál levont adók tekintetében az értesítés átadásának évét követő első naptári év január 1-jén vagy azt követően keletkezett jövedelmekre;
(b) az egyéb jövedelem- és a vagyonadók tekintetében az értesítés átadásának évét követő első naptári év január 1-jén vagy azután kezdődő bármely adóévre kivethető adókra.

ENNEK HITELÉÜL az arra kellő meghatalmazással rendelkező alulírottak ezt az Egyezményt aláírták.

Készült két példányban Brüsszel 2015, Március 10 napján francia, magyar és angol nyelven, mindegyik szöveg egyaránt hiteles. Eltérő értelmezés esetén az angol nyelvű szöveg irányadó.

a Luxemburgi Nagyhercegség nevében

Magyarország nevében

JEGYZŐKÖNY

A Luxemburgi Nagyhercegség és Magyarország között a jövedelem- és a vagyonadók területén a kettős adóztatás elkerüléséről és az adóztatás kijátszásának megakadályozásáról szóló Egyezmény aláírásának pillanatában a felek a következő rendelkezésekben állapodtak meg, amelyek az Egyezmény szerves részét alkotják:

I. A 4. cikk 1. bekezdésének tekintetében:

Megállapításra került, hogy a „kollektív befektetési eszköz" kifejezés a következőt jelenti:

(a) Magyarország esetében bármely befektetési alapot, amit a kollektív befektetési formákról és kezelőikről szóló törvény alapján hoztak létre;

(b) Luxemburg esetében,
   (i) egy nyiltvégi befektetési társaságot;
   (ii) egy zártvégű befektetési társaságot;
   (iii) egy kockázati tőke befektetési társaságot;
   (iv) egy kollektív befektetési alapot,

valamint bármely olyan valamelyik Szerződő Államban létrehozott kollektív befektetési eszközt, amit a Szerződő Államok illetékes hatóságai megegyezésük alapján ezen bekezdés céljából kollektív befektetési eszköznek tekintenek.

E bekezdés nem értelmezendő úgy, hogy az bármely formában korlátozná egy Szerződő Állam jogát arra, hogy az abban az államban belföldi illetőséggel bírókat adóztassa.

II. A 8. cikk 1. és 4. bekezdéseinek, a 13. cikk 4. bekezdésének és a 22. cikk 3. bekezdésének tekintetében:

A Szerződő Államok megállapodtak, hogy a "nemzetközi forgalom" kifejezés nem terjed ki a nemzetközi forgalomban szereplő közúti járművekre.

III. A 26. cikk tekintetében:

A megkereső Állam illetékes hatóságának biztosítania kell a következő információkat a megkeresett Állam illetékes hatóságának, amikor az Egyezmény alapján információt kér annak érdekében, hogy alátámassza, hogy a kéréshez az információ előreláthatólag releváns:

(a) annak a személynek az azonosító adatait, akivel szemben a vizsgálatot vagy a nyomozást folytatják;
(b) egy nyilatkozatot a kért információ természetére és formájára vonatkozóan, amelyben a megkereső Állam azt meg kívánja kapni a megkeresett Államtól;
(c) azt az adózási célt, amelyre az információt keresik;
(d) azt az időszakot, amelyre vonatkozóan az információt kérik;
(e) az indokokat, amelyek alapján feltételezhető, hogy a kért információ a megkeresett Államnál van, vagy a megkeresett Állam joghatósága alatt levő személy birtokában vagy ellenőrzése alatt;
(f) az ismert mértékig bármely személy nevét és címét, akiről úgy hiszik, hogy a kért információ birtokában van;
(g) nyilatkozatot arról, hogy a megkereső Állam minden elérhető eszközt foganatosított a saját hatáskörén belül az információ megszerzésére, kivéve, ahol ez aránytalan nehézségeket okozna.

IV. Az Európai Unió jogi aktusai:

Megállapításra került, hogy az Egyezmény nem befolyásolja az Európai Unió jogi aktusait és a Szerződő Államok ezekhez kapcsolódó rendelkezéseit.

ENNEK HITELÉÜL az arra kellő meghatalmazással rendelkező alulírottak ezt a Jegyzőkönyvet aláírták.

Készült két példányban Brüsszel 2015, Március 10 napján francia, magyar és angol nyelven, mindegyik szöveg egyaránt hiteles. Eltérő értelmezés esetén az angol nyelvű szöveg irányadó.

a Luxemburgi Nagyhercegség nevében

Magyarország nevében

No. 54782

Luxembourg
and
Ukraine

Convention between the Government of the Grand Duchy of Luxembourg and the Government of Ukraine for the avoidance of double taxation and the prevention of fiscal evasion with respect to taxes on income and on capital. Kiev, 6 September 1997

Entry into force: *18 April 2017 by notification, in accordance with article 29*

Authentic texts: *English, French and Ukrainian*

Registration with the Secretariat of the United Nations: *Luxembourg, 7 November 2017*

Luxembourg
et
Ukraine

Convention entre le Gouvernement du Grand-Duché de Luxembourg et le Gouvernement de l'Ukraine tendant à éviter les doubles impositions et à prévenir la fraude fiscale en matière d'impôts sur le revenu et sur la fortune. Kiev, 6 septembre 1997

Entrée en vigueur : *18 avril 2017 par notification, conformément à l'article 29*

Textes authentiques : *anglais, français et ukrainien*

Enregistrement au Secrétariat de l'Organisation des Nations Unies : *Luxembourg, 7 novembre 2017*

[TEXT IN ENGLISH – TEXTE EN ANGLAIS]

CONVENTION

BETWEEN

THE GOVERNMENT OF THE GRAND DUCHY OF LUXEMBOURG

AND

THE GOVERNMENT OF UKRAINE

FOR THE AVOIDANCE OF DOUBLE TAXATION AND THE PREVENTION OF FISCAL EVASION WITH RESPECT TO TAXES ON INCOME AND ON CAPITAL

The Government of the Grand Duchy of Luxembourg and the Government of Ukraine desiring to conclude a Convention for the avoidance of double taxation and the prevention of fiscal evasion with respect to taxes on income and on capital and confirming their endeavour to develop and deepen mutual economic relations, have agreed as follows:

Article 1

PERSONAL SCOPE

This Convention shall apply to persons who are residents of one or both of the Contracting States.

Article 2

TAXES COVERED

1. This Convention shall apply to taxes on income and on capital imposed on behalf of a Contracting State or of its political subdivisions or local authorities, irrespective of the manner in which they are levied.

2. There shall be regarded as taxes on income and on capital all taxes imposed on total income, on total capital or on elements of income or of capital including taxes on gains from the alienation of movable or immovable property and taxes on the total amounts of wages or salaries paid by enterprises.

3. The existing taxes which are the subject of this Convention are:

a) in the case of the Grand Duchy of Luxembourg:

(i) the income tax on individuals;

(ii) the corporation tax;

(iii) the tax on fees of directors of companies;

(iv) the capital tax; and

(v) the communal trade tax;

(hereinafter referred to as "Luxembourg tax");

b) in the case of Ukraine:
   (i) the tax on profits of enterprises; and
   (ii) the individual income tax;
   (hereinafter referred to as "Ukrainian tax").

4. The Convention shall apply also to any identical or substantially similar taxes which are imposed by either Contracting State after the date of signature of this Convention in addition to, or in place of, the existing taxes. The competent authorities of the Contracting States shall notify each other of any substantial changes which have been made in their respective taxation laws.

Article 3

GENERAL DEFINITIONS

1. For the purposes of this Convention, unless the context otherwise requires:

a) the term "Luxembourg" when used in geographical sense, means the territory of the Grand of Luxembourg;
b) the term "Ukraine" when used in geographical sense, means the territory of Ukraine, its Continental Shelf and its exclusive (maritime) economic zone, including any area outside the territorial sea of Ukraine which in accordance with international law has been or may hereafter be designated, as an area within which the rights of Ukraine with respect to the sea bed and sub-soil and their natural resources may be exercised;
c) the term "national" means:
   (i) any individual possessing the nationality of a Contracting State;
   (ii) any legal person, partnership or association deriving its status as such from the laws in force in a Contracting State;
d) the terms "a Contracting State" and "the other Contracting State" mean Ukraine or Luxembourg, as the context requires;

e) the term "person" includes an individual, a company and any other body of persons;
f) the term "company" means any body corporate or any entity which is treated as a body corporate for tax purposes;
g) the terms "enterprise of a Contracting State" and "enterprise of the other Contracting State" mean respectively an enterprise carried on by a resident of a Contracting State and an enterprise carried on by a resident of the other Contracting State;
h) the term "international traffic" means any transport by a ship, boat or aircraft operated by an enterprise of a Contracting State, except when the ship, boat or aircraft is operated solely between places in the other Contracting State;
i) the term "competent authority" means, in the case of Ukraine, the Ministry of Finance of Ukraine or its authorized representative, and, in case of Luxembourg, the Minister of Finance or his authorized representative.

2. As regards the application of the Convention at any time by a Contracting State any term not defined therein shall, unless the context otherwise requires, have the meaning that it has at that time under the law of that State for the purpose of the taxes to which the Convention applies. Any meaning under the applicable tax laws of that State prevails over a meaning given to the term under other laws of that State.

Article 4

RESIDENT

1. For the purposes of this Convention, the term "resident of a Contracting State" means any person who, under the laws of that State, is liable to tax therein by reason of his domicile, residence, place of management, place of registration or any other criterion of a similar nature, and also includes that State and any political subdivision or local authority thereof. But this term does not include any person who is liable to tax in that State in respect only of income from sources in that State or capital situated therein.

2. Where by reason of the provisions of paragraph 1 of this Article an individual is a resident of both Contracting States, then his status shall be determined as follows:

a) he shall be deemed to be a resident of the Contracting State in which he has a permanent home available to him; if he has a permanent home available to him in both Contracting States, he shall be deemed to be a resident of the Contracting State with which his personal and economic relations are closer (centre of vital interests);

b) if the Contracting State in which he has his centre of vital interests cannot be determined, or if he has no permanent home available to him in either Contracting State, he shall be deemed to be a resident only of the Contracting State in which he has an habitual abode;

c) if he has an habitual abode in both Contracting States or in neither of them, he shall be deemed to be a resident only of the Contracting State of which he is a national;

d) if he is a national of both Contracting States or of neither of them, the competent authorities of the Contracting States shall settle the question by mutual agreement.

3. Where by reason of the provisions of paragraph 1 of this Article a person other than an individual is a resident of both Contracting States, then it shall be deemed to be a resident only of the Contracting State in which its place of effective management is situated.

Article 5

PERMANENT ESTABLISHMENT

1. For the purposes of this Convention, the term "permanent establishment" means a fixed place of business through which the business of an enterprise is wholly or partly carried on.

2. The term "permanent establishment" includes especially:

a) a place of management;

b) a branch;

c) an office;
d) a factory;
e) a workshop;
f) an installation or structure for the exploration of natural resources;
g) a mine, an oil or gas well, a quarry or any other place of extraction of natural resources; and
h) a warehouse or other structure used as a sales outlet.

3. A building site or construction or installation project constitutes a permanent establishment only if it lasts more than twelve months.

4. Notwithstanding the preceding provisions of this Article, the term "permanent establishment" shall be deemed not to include:
a) the use of facilities solely for the purpose of storage, display or delivery of goods or merchandise belonging to the enterprise;
b) the maintenance of a stock of goods or merchandise belonging to the enterprise solely for the purpose of storage, display or delivery;
c) the maintenance of a stock of goods or merchandise belonging to the enterprise solely for the purpose of processing by another enterprise;
d) the maintenance of a fixed place of business solely for the purpose of purchasing goods or merchandise or of collecting information, for the enterprise;
e) the maintenance of a fixed place of business solely for the purpose of carrying on, for the enterprise, any other activity of a preparatory or auxiliary character;
f) the maintenance of a fixed place of business solely for any combination of activities mentioned in sub-paragraphs a) to e), provided that the overall activity of the fixed place of business resulting from this combination is of a preparatory or auxiliary character.

5. Notwithstanding the provisions of paragraphs 1 and 2 of this Article, where a person other than an agent of an independent status to whom paragraph 6 of this Article applies is

acting on behalf of an enterprise and has, and habitually exercises, in a Contracting State an authority to conclude contracts on behalf of the enterprise, or maintains a stock of goods or merchandise belonging to the enterprise, from which regular sales of such goods and merchandise are carried on in the name of the enterprise, that enterprise shall be deemed to have a permanent establishment in that State in respect of any activities which that person undertakes for the enterprise, unless the activities of such person are limited to those mentioned in paragraph 4 of this Article which, if exercised through a fixed place of business, would not make this fixed place of business a permanent establishment under the provisions of that paragraph.

6. An enterprise shall not be deemed to have a permanent establishment in a Contracting State merely because it carries on business in that State through a broker, general commission agent or any other agent of an independent status, provided that such persons are acting in the ordinary course of their business.

7. The fact that a company which is a resident of a Contracting State controls or is controlled by a company which is a resident of the other Contracting State, or which carries on business in that other State (whether through a permanent establishment or otherwise), shall not of itself constitute either company a permanent establishment of the other.

Article 6

INCOME FROM IMMOVABLE PROPERTY

1. Income derived by a resident of a Contracting State from immovable property (including income from agriculture or forestry) situated in the other Contracting State may be taxed in that other State.

2. The term "immovable property" shall have the meaning which it has under the law of the Contracting State in which the property in question is situated. The term shall in any case

include property accessory to immovable property, livestock and equipment used in agriculture and forestry, rights to which the provisions of general law respecting landed property apply, usufruct of immovable property and rights to variable or fixed payments as consideration for the working of, or the right to work, mineral deposits, sources and other natural resources. Ships, boats and aircraft shall not be regarded as immovable property.

3. The provisions of paragraph 1 of this Article shall apply to income derived from the direct use, letting, or use in any other form of immovable property.

4. The provisions of paragraphs 1 and 3 of this Article shall also apply to the income from immovable property of an enterprise and to income from immovable property used for the performance of independent personal services.

Article 7

BUSINESS PROFITS

1. The profits of an enterprise of a Contracting State shall be taxable only in that State unless the enterprise carries on business in the other Contracting State through a permanent establishment situated therein. If the enterprise carries on business as aforesaid, the profits of the enterprise may be taxed in the other State but only so much of them as is attributable to that permanent establishment.

2. Subject to the provisions of paragraph 3 of this Article, where an enterprise of a Contracting State carries on business in the other Contracting State through a permanent establishment situated therein, there shall in each Contracting State be attributed to that permanent establishment the profits which it might be expected to make if it were a distinct and separate enterprise engaged in the same or similar activities under the same or similar conditions and dealing wholly independently with the enterprise of which it is a permanent establishment.

3. In determining the profits of a permanent establishment, there shall be allowed as deductions expenses which are incurred for the purposes of the permanent establishment, including executive and general administrative expenses so incurred, whether in the State in which the permanent establishment is situated or elsewhere. However, no such deduction shall be allowed in respect of amounts, if any, paid (otherwise than towards reimbursement of actual expenses) by the permanent establishment to the enterprise or any of its other offices, by way of royalties, fees or other similar payments in return for the use of patents or other rights, or by way of commission, for specific services performed or for management, or, except in case of a banking enterprise, by way of interest on money lent to the permanent establishment by the enterprise.

4. Insofar as it has been customary in a Contracting State to determine, according to its laws, the profits to be attributed to a permanent establishment on the basis of an apportionment of the total profits of the enterprise to its various parts, nothing in paragraph 2 of this Article shall preclude that Contracting State from determining the profits to be taxed by such an apportionment as may be customary; the method of apportionment adopted shall, however, be such that the result shall be in accordance with the principles contained in this Article.

5. No profits shall be attributed to a permanent establishment by reason of the mere purchase by that permanent establishment of goods or merchandise for the enterprise.

6. For the purposes of the preceding paragraphs, the profits to be attributed to the permanent establishment shall be determined by the same method year by year unless there is good and sufficient reason to the contrary.

7. Where profits include items of income which are dealt with separately in other Articles of this Convention, then the provisions of those Articles shall not be affected by the provisions of this Article.

Article 8

INTERNATIONAL TRANSPORT

1. Profits derived by a resident of a Contracting State from the operation of ships, boats or aircraft in international traffic shall be taxable only in that State.

2. For the purposes of this Article, profits from the operation of ships or aircraft in international traffic include:

a) income from the rental on a bareboat basis of ships or aircraft; and

b) profits from the use, maintenance or rental of containers (including trailers and related equipment for the transport of containers) used for the transport of goods or merchandise;

where such rental or such use, maintenance or rental, as the case may be, is incidental to the operation of ships or aircraft in international traffic.

3. Where profits within paragraph 1 of this Article are derived by a resident of a Contracting State from participation in a pool, a joint business or an international operating agency, the profits attributable to that resident shall be taxable only in the Contracting State of which he is a resident.

Article 9

ASSOCIATED ENTERPRISES

1. Where:

a) an enterprise of a Contracting State participates directly or indirectly in the management, control or capital of an enterprise of the other Contracting State; or

b) the same persons participate directly or indirectly in the management, control or capital of an enterprise of a Contracting State and an enterprise of the other Contracting State,

and in either case conditions are made or imposed between the two enterprises in their commercial or financial relations which differ from those which would be made between independent enterprises, then any profits which would, but for those conditions, have accrued to one of the enterprises, but by reason of those conditions, have not so accrued, may be included by a Contracting State in the profits of that enterprise and taxed accordingly.

2. Where a Contracting State includes in the profits of an enterprise of that State - and taxes accordingly - profits on which an enterprise of the other Contracting State has been charged to tax in that other State and the profits so included are profits which would have accrued to the enterprise of the first-mentioned State if the conditions made between the two enterprises had been those which would have been made between independent enterprises, then that other State shall make an appropriate adjustment to the amount of the tax charged therein on those profits. In determining such adjustment, due regard shall be had to the other provisions of this Convention and the competent authorities of the Contracting States shall if necessary consult each other.

Article 10

DIVIDENDS

1. Dividends paid by a company which is a resident of a Contracting State to a resident of the other Contracting State may be taxed in that other State.

2. However, such dividends may also be taxed in the Contracting State of which the company paying the dividends is a resident and according to the laws of that State, but if the recipient is the beneficial owner of the dividends the tax so charged shall not exceed:

a) 5 per cent of the gross amount of the dividends if the beneficial owner is a company (other than a partnership) which holds directly at least 20 per cent of the capital of the company paying the dividends;
b) 15 per cent of the gross amount of the dividends in all other cases.

3. Notwithstanding the provisions of paragraph 2 of this Article, dividends paid by a company that is a resident of a Contracting State shall not be taxable in that State if the beneficial owner of the dividends is a company that is a resident of the other Contracting State and that has had, during an uninterrupted period of three years preceding the date of payment of the dividends, a direct shareholding of at least 50 per cent of the company paying the dividends and provided that an investment of at least 1.000.000 US dollars or its equivalent in the national currencies of the Contracting States has been made in the capital of the company paying the dividends. This provision only applies to dividends attributable to the part of the shareholding that has been owned without interruption by the beneficial owner during such three-year period. Furthermore, the provision of this paragraph shall only apply if the distributed dividend is derived from the active conduct of trade or business in the first-mentioned State (other than the business of making or managing investments, unless such business is carried on by a banking or insurance company).

4. The term "dividends" as used in this Article means income from shares, or other rights, not being debt-claims, participating in profits, as well as income from other corporate rights which is subjected to the same taxation treatment as income from shares by the laws of the State of which the company making the distribution is a resident.

5. The provisions of paragraphs 1, 2 and 3 of this Article shall not apply if the beneficial owner of the dividends, being a resident of a Contracting State, carries on business in the other Contracting State of which the company paying the dividends is a resident, through a permanent establishment situated therein, or performs in that other State independent personal services from a fixed base situated therein, and the holding in respect of which the dividends are paid is effectively connected with such permanent establishment or fixed base. In such case the provisions of Article 7 or Article 14 of this Convention, as the case may be, shall apply.

6. Where a company which is a resident of a Contracting State derives profits or income from the other Contracting State, that other State may not impose any tax on the dividends paid by the company, except insofar as such dividends are paid to a resident of that other State or insofar as the holding in respect of which the dividends are paid is effectively connected with a permanent establishment or a fixed base situated in that other State, nor subject the company's undistributed profits to a tax on the company's undistributed profits, even if the dividends paid or the undistributed profits consist wholly or partly of profits or income arising in such other State.

Article 11

INTEREST

1. Interest arising in a Contracting State and paid to a resident of the other Contracting State may be taxed in that other State.

2. However, such interest may also be taxed in the Contracting State in which it arises and according to the laws of that State, but if the recipient is the beneficial owner of the interest the tax so charged shall not exceed:

a) 2 per cent of the gross amount of the interest, in the case of interest arising in a Contracting State and paid on any loans of whatever kind granted by a bank or any other financial institution of the other State, including investment banks and saving banks, and insurance companies;

b) 10 per cent of the gross amount of the interest in all other cases.

3. Notwithstanding the provisions of paragraph 2 of this Article, interest arising in a Contracting State paid to a resident of the other Contracting State who is the beneficial owner, shall be exempt from tax in the first-mentioned State if it was paid in respect of a loan made, guaranteed or insured, or in respect of any other debt-claim or credit guaranteed or insured on behalf of the other Contracting State by its authorized organ.

4. The term "interest" as used in this Article means income from debt-claims of every kind, whether or not secured by mortgage and whether or not carrying a right to participate in the debtor's profits, and in particular, income from government securities and income from bonds or debentures, including premiums and prizes attaching to such securities, bonds or debentures.

5. The provisions of paragraphs 1, 2 and 3 of this Article shall not apply if the beneficial owner of the interest, being a resident of a Contracting State, carries on business in the other Contracting State in which the interest arises, through a permanent establishment situated therein, or performs in that other State independent personal services from a fixed base situated therein, and the debt-claim in respect of which the interest is paid is effectively connected with such permanent establishment or fixed base. In such case the provisions of Article 7 or Article 14 of this Convention, as the case may be, shall apply.

6. Interest shall be deemed to arise in a Contracting State when the payer is a resident of that State. Where, however, the person paying the interest, whether he is a resident of a Contracting State or not, has in a Contracting State a permanent establishment or a fixed base in connection with which the indebtedness on which the interest is paid was incurred, and such interest is borne by such permanent establishment or fixed base, then such interest shall be deemed to arise in the State in which the permanent establishment or fixed base is situated.

7. Where, by reason of a special relationship between the payer and the beneficial owner or between both of them and some other person, the amount of the interest, having regard to the debt-claim for which it is paid, exceeds the amount which would have been agreed upon by the payer and the beneficial owner in the absence of such relationship, the provisions of this Article shall apply only to the last-mentioned amount. In such case, the excess part of the payments shall remain taxable according to the laws of each Contracting State, due regard being had to the other provisions of this Convention.

Article 12

ROYALTIES

1. Royalties arising in a Contracting State and paid to a resident of the other Contracting State may be taxed in that other State.

2. However, such royalties may also be taxed in the Contracting State in which they arise and according to the laws of that State, but if the recipient is the beneficial owner of the royalties the tax so charged shall not exceed:

a) 5 per cent of the gross amount of the payments referred to in sub-paragraph a) of paragraph 3 of this Article;

b) 10 per cent of the gross amount of the payments referred to in sub-paragraph b) of paragraph 3 of this Article.

3. The term "royalties" as used in this Article means payments of any kind received as a consideration for:

a) the use of, or the right to use any patent, trade mark, design or model, plan, secret formula or process, or for information (know-how) concerning industrial, commercial or scientific experience;

b) the use of, or the right to use, any copyright of literary, artistic or scientific work (including cinematograph films, and films or tapes for radio or television broadcasting).

4. The provisions of paragraphs 1 and 2 of this Article shall not apply if the beneficial owner of the royalties, being a resident of a Contracting State, carries on business in the other Contracting State in which the royalties arise, through a permanent establishment situated therein, or performs in that other State independent personal services from a fixed base situated therein, and the right or property in respect of which the royalties are paid is effectively connected with such permanent establishment or fixed base. In such case the provisions of Article 7 or Article 14 of this Convention, as the case may be, shall apply.

5. Royalties shall be deemed to arise in a Contracting State when the payer is a resident of that State. Where, however, the person paying the royalties, whether he is a resident of a Contracting State or not, has in a Contracting State a permanent establishment or a fixed base in connection with which the indebtedness on which the royalties are paid was incurred, and such royalties are borne by such permanent establishment or fixed base, then such royalties shall be deemed to arise in the State in which the permanent establishment or fixed base is situated.

6. Where, by reason of a special relationship between the payer and the beneficial owner or between both of them and some other person, the amount of the royalties, having regard to the use, right or information for which they are paid, exceeds, for whatever reason, the amount which would have been agreed upon by the payer and the beneficial owner in the absence of such relationship, the provisions of this Article shall apply only to the last-mentioned amount. In such case, the excess part of the payments shall remain taxable according to the laws of each Contracting State, due regard being had to the other provisions of this Convention.

Article 13

CAPITAL GAINS

1. Gains derived by a resident of a Contracting State from the alienation of immovable property referred to in Article 6 of this Convention and situated in the other Contracting State may be taxed in that other State.

2. Gains derived by a resident of a Contracting State from the alienation of:

a) shares, other than shares quoted on an approved Stock Exchange, deriving their value or the greater part of their value directly or indirectly from immovable property situated in the other Contracting State, or

b) an interest in a partnership the assets of which consist principally of immovable property situated in the other Contracting State, or of shares referred to in sub-paragraph a) above,

may be taxed in that other State.

3. Gains from the alienation of movable property forming part of the business property of a permanent establishment which an enterprise of a Contracting State has in the other Contracting State or of movable property pertaining to a fixed base available to a resident of a Contracting State in the other Contracting State for the purpose of performing independent personal services, including such gains from the alienation of such a permanent establishment (alone or with the whole enterprise) or of such fixed base, may be taxed in that other State.

4. Gains from the alienation of ships, boats or aircraft operated in international traffic by an enterprise of a Contracting State or movable property pertaining to the operation of such ships, boats or aircraft, shall be taxable only in that Contracting State.

5. Gains from the alienation of any property other than that referred to in paragraphs 1, 2, 3 and 4 of this Article shall be taxable only in the Contracting State of which the alienator is a resident.

Article 14

INDEPENDENT PERSONAL SERVICES

1. Income derived by a resident of a Contracting State in respect of professional services or other activities of an independent character shall be taxable only in that State unless he has a fixed base regularly available to him in the other Contracting State for the purpose of performing his activities. If he has such a fixed base, the income may be taxed in the other State but only so much of it as is attributable to that fixed base.

2. The term "professional services" includes especially independent scientific, literary, artistic, educational or teaching activities as well as the independent activities of physicians, lawyers, engineers, architects, dentists and accountants.

Article 15

DEPENDENT PERSONAL SERVICES

1. Subject to the provisions of Articles 16, 18, 19 and 20 of this Convention, salaries, wages and other similar remuneration derived by a resident of a Contracting State in respect of an employment shall be taxable only in that State unless the employment is exercised in the other Contracting State. If the employment is so exercised, such remuneration as is derived therefrom may be taxed in that other State.

2. Notwithstanding the provisions of paragraph 1 of this Article, remuneration derived by a resident of a Contracting State in respect of an employment exercised in the other Contracting State shall be taxable only in the first-mentioned State if:

a) the recipient is present in the other State for a period or periods not exceeding in the aggregate 183 days in any twelve month period commencing or ending in the calendar year concerned; and
b) the remuneration is paid by, or on behalf of, an employer who is not a resident of the other State; and
c) the remuneration is not borne by a permanent establishment or a fixed base which the employer has in the other State.

3. Notwithstanding the preceding provisions of this Article, remuneration derived in respect of an employment exercised aboard a ship, a boat or aircraft operated in international traffic, may be taxed in the Contracting State of which the enterprise operating the ship, boat or aircraft is a resident.

Article 16

DIRECTORS' FEES

Directors' fees and other similar payments derived by a resident of a Contracting State in his capacity as a member of the board of directors or any other similar organ of a company which is a resident of the other Contracting State may be taxed in that other State.

Article 17

ARTISTES AND SPORTSMEN

1. Notwithstanding the provisions of Articles 14 and 15 of this Convention, income derived by a resident of a Contracting State as an entertainer, such as a theatre, motion picture, radio or television artiste, or a musician, or as a sportsman, from his personal activities as such exercised in the other Contracting State, may be taxed in that other State.

2. Where income in respect of personal activities exercised by an entertainer or a sportsman in his capacity as such accrues not to the entertainer or sportsman himself but to another person, that income may, notwithstanding the provisions of Articles 7, 14 and 15 of this Convention, be taxed in the Contracting State in which the activities of the entertainer or sportsman are exercised.

3. Notwithstanding the provisions of paragraphs 1 and 2 of this Article, income referred to in this Article shall be exempt from tax in the Contracting State in which the activities of the entertainer or sportsman are exercised, if such activities are substantially financed from the public funds of one or both of the Contracting States, or are carried on under culture co-operation agreement between the Contracting States.

Article 18

PENSIONS

1. Subject to the provisions of paragraph 2 of Article 19 of this Convention, pensions and other similar remuneration paid to a resident of a Contracting State in consideration of past employment shall be taxable only in that State.

2. Notwithstanding the provisions of paragraph 1 of this Article, pensions and payments made under the social security legislation or under State Pension Plan of a Contracting State, shall be taxable only in that State.

Article 19

GOVERNMENT SERVICE

1. a) Remuneration, other than a pension, paid by a Contracting State or a political subdivision or a local authority thereof to an individual in respect of services rendered to that State or subdivision or authority shall be taxable only in that State.
   b) Notwithstanding the provisions of sub-paragraph a) of this paragraph, such remuneration shall be taxable only in the other Contracting State if the services are rendered in that State and the individual is a resident of that State who:
   (i) is a national of that State; or
   (ii) did not become a resident of that State solely for the purpose of rendering the services.

2. a) Any pension paid by, or out of funds created by, a Contracting State or a political subdivision or a local authority thereof to an individual in respect of services rendered to that State or subdivision or authority shall be taxable only in that State.
   b) Notwithstanding the provisions of sub-paragraph a) of this paragraph, such pension shall be taxable only in the other Contracting State if the individual is a resident of, and a national of, that State.

3. The provisions of Articles 15, 16, 17 and 18 of this Convention shall apply to remuneration and pensions in respect of services rendered in connection with a business carried on by a Contracting State or a political subdivision or a local authority thereof.

Article 20

STUDENTS

1. Payments which a student or business apprentice who is or was immediately before visiting a Contracting State a resident of the other Contracting State and who is present in the first-mentioned State solely for the purpose of his education or training receives for the purpose of his maintenance, education or training shall not be taxed in the first-mentioned State, provided that such payments arise from sources outside that State.

2. Income which a student or apprentice receives for his activities performed in the Contracting State in which he is present solely for the purpose of his education or training shall not be taxed in that State. This exemption shall apply only for a period of time not exceeding two years from the date he first arrives in this State for the purpose of his education or training.

Article 21

OTHER INCOME

1. Items of income of a resident of a Contracting State, wherever arising, not dealt with in the foregoing Articles of this Convention, shall be taxable only in the first-mentioned State.

2. The provisions of paragraph 1 of this Article shall not apply to income, other than income from immovable property as defined in paragraph 2 of Article 6 of this Convention, if the

recipient of such income, being a resident of a Contracting State, carries on business in the other Contracting State through a permanent establishment situated therein, or performs in that other State independent personal services from a fixed base situated therein, and the right or property in respect of which the income is paid is effectively connected with such permanent establishment or fixed base. In such case the provisions of Article 7 or Article 14 of this Convention, as the case may be, shall apply.

Article 22

CAPITAL

1. Capital represented by immovable property referred to in Article 6 of this Convention, owned by a resident of a Contracting State and situated in the other Contracting State, may be taxed in that other State.

2. Capital represented by movable property forming part of the business property of a permanent establishment which an enterprise of a Contracting State has in the other Contracting State or by movable property pertaining to a fixed base available to a resident of a Contracting State in the other Contracting State for the purpose of performing independent personal services, may be taxed in that other State.

3. Capital represented by ships, boats and aircraft operated by an enterprise of a Contracting State in international traffic, and by movable property pertaining to the operation of such ships, boats and aircraft, shall be taxable only in that Contracting State.

4. All other elements of capital of a resident of a Contracting State shall be taxable only in that State.

Article 23

ELIMINATION OF DOUBLE TAXATION

1. Subject to the provisions of the law of Ukraine regarding the elimination of double taxation (which shall not affect the general principle hereof), Luxembourg tax paid under the laws of Luxembourg and in accordance with this Convention on profits, income from sources within or chargeable capital situated in Luxembourg shall be allowed as a credit against any Ukrainian tax computed by reference to the same profits, income or capital on which the Luxembourg tax is paid.

2. Subject to the provisions of the law of Luxembourg regarding the elimination of double taxation (which shall not affect the general principle hereof), double taxation shall be eliminated in Luxembourg as follows:

a) Where a resident of Luxembourg derives income or owns capital which, in accordance with the provisions of this Convention may be taxed in Ukraine, Luxembourg shall, subject to the provisions of sub-paragraphs b) and c), exempt such income or capital from tax.

b) Where a resident of Luxembourg derives income which, in accordance with the provisions of Articles 10, 11 and 12 of this Convention may be taxed in Ukraine, Luxembourg shall allow as a deduction from the tax on the income of that resident an amount equal to the tax paid in Ukraine.

c) Where a company which is a resident of Luxembourg derives dividends from Ukrainian sources, Luxembourg shall exempt such dividends from tax, provided that the company which is a resident of Luxembourg holds since the beginning of its accounting year directly at least 10 per cent of the capital of the company paying the dividends and if this company is subject in Ukraine to an income tax corresponding to the Luxembourg corporation tax. The above-mentioned shares in the Ukrainian company are, under the same conditions, exempt from the Luxembourg capital tax.

3. The deductions provided for in a Contracting State under paragraph 1 or sub-paragraph b) of paragraph 2 of this Article in either case shall not exceed that part of income tax or capital tax, as computed before the deduction is given, which is attributable, as the case may be, to the income or the capital which may be taxed in the other State.

4. Where in accordance with any provision of the Convention income derived or capital owned by a resident of a Contracting State is exempt from tax in that State, such State may nevertheless, in calculating the amount of tax on the remaining income or capital of such resident, take into account the exempted income or capital.

5. For the purposes of paragraphs 1 and 2 of this Article, profits, income and capital gains derived by a resident of a Contracting State which may be taxed in the other Contracting State in accordance with this Convention shall be deemed to arise from sources in that other Contracting State.

Article 24

NON-DISCRIMINATION

1. Nationals of a Contracting State shall not be subjected in the other Contracting State to any taxation or any requirement connected therewith, which is other or more burdensome than the taxation and connected requirements to which nationals of that other State in the same circumstances, in particular with respect to residence, are or may be subjected. This provision shall, notwithstanding the provisions of Article 1 of this Convention, also apply to persons who are not residents of one or both of the Contracting States.

2. Stateless persons who are residents of a Contracting State shall not be subjected in either Contracting State to any taxation or any requirement connected therewith, which is other or more burdensome than the taxation and connected requirements to

which nationals of the State concerned in the same circumstances are or may be subjected.

3. The taxation on a permanent establishment which an enterprise of a Contracting State has in the other Contracting State shall not be less favourably levied in that other State than the taxation levied on enterprises of that other State carrying on the same activities.

4. Except where the provisions of paragraph 1 of Article 9, paragraph 7 of Article 11, or paragraph 6 of Article 12 of this Convention apply, interest, royalties and other disbursements paid by an enterprise of a Contracting State to a resident of the other Contracting State shall, for the purpose of determining the taxable profits of such enterprise, be deductible under the same conditions as if they had been paid to a resident of the first-mentioned State. Similarly, any debts of an enterprise of a Contracting State to a resident of the other Contracting State shall, for the purpose of determining the taxable capital of such enterprise, be deductible under the same conditions as if they had been contracted to a resident of the first-mentioned State.

5. Enterprises of a Contracting State, the capital of which is wholly or partly owned or controlled, directly or indirectly, by one or more residents of the other Contracting State, shall not be subjected in the first-mentioned State to any taxation or any requirement connected therewith which is other or more burdensome than the taxation and connected requirements to which other similar enterprises of the first-mentioned State are or may be subjected.

6. Nothing contained in this Article shall be construed as obliging either Contracting State to grant to individuals not resident in that State any personal allowances, reliefs and reductions for taxation purposes on account of civil status or family responsibilities which it grants to its own residents or any of the personal allowances, reliefs and reductions for tax purposes which are granted to individuals so resident under the criteria not contained in general tax laws.

7. The provisions of this Article shall apply to taxes covered by this Convention.

Article 25

MUTUAL AGREEMENT PROCEDURE

1. Where a resident of a Contracting State considers that the actions of one or both of the Contracting States result or will result for him in taxation not in accordance with the provisions of this Convention, he may, irrespective of the remedies provided by the domestic law of those States, present his case to the competent authority of the Contracting State of which he is a resident or, if his case comes under paragraph 1 of Article 24 of this Convention, to that of the Contracting State of which he is a national. The case must be presented within three years from the first notification of the action resulting in taxation not in accordance with the provisions of this Convention.

2. The competent authority shall endeavour, if the objection appears to it to be justified and if it is not itself able to arrive at a satisfactory solution, to resolve the case by mutual agreement with the competent authority of the other Contracting State, with a view to the avoidance of taxation which is not in accordance with the Convention. Any agreement reached shall be implemented notwithstanding any time limits in the domestic law of the Contracting States.

3. The competent authorities of the Contracting States shall endeavour to resolve by mutual agreement any difficulties or doubts arising as to the interpretation or the application of the Convention.

4. The competent authorities of the Contracting States may communicate with each other directly for the purpose of reaching an agreement in the sense of the preceding paragraphs.

Article 26

EXCHANGE OF INFORMATION

1. The competent authorities of the Contracting States shall exchange such information as is necessary for carrying out the provisions of this Convention or of the domestic laws of the Contracting States concerning taxes covered by the Convention insofar as the taxation there under is not contrary to the Convention, in particular, to prevent evasion and to facilitate the administration of statutory provisions against legal avoidance. The exchange of information is not restricted by Article 1 of this Convention. Any information received by a Contracting State shall be treated as secret in the same manner as information obtained under the domestic laws of that State and shall be disclosed only to persons or authorities (including courts and administrative bodies) involved in the assessment or collection of, the enforcement or prosecution in respect of, or the determination of appeals in relation to, the taxes covered by the Convention. Such persons or authorities shall use the information only for such purposes. They may disclose the information in public court proceedings or in judicial decisions.

The competent authorities shall develop the appropriate conditions, methods and technics regarding cases, in respect of which such exchange of information may be done, including where it is necessary exchange of information regarding tax evasions, by way of consultations.

2. In no case shall the provisions of paragraph 1 of this Article be construed so as to impose on the competent authority of either Contracting State the obligation:

a) to carry out administrative measures at variance with the laws and administrative practice prevailing in either Contracting State;
b) to supply information which is not obtainable under the laws or in the normal course of the administration of either Contracting State;
c) to supply information which would disclose any trade, business, industrial, commercial or professional secret or trade process, or information, the disclosure of which would be contrary to public policy.

Article 27

MEMBERS OF DIPLOMATIC OR PERMANENT MISSIONS AND CONSULAR POSTS

Nothing in this Convention shall affect the fiscal privileges accorded to members of diplomatic or permanent missions or consular posts under the general rules of international law or under the provisions of special agreements.

Article 28

EXCLUSION OF CERTAIN COMPANIES

This Convention shall not apply to holding companies within the meaning of special Luxembourg laws, currently the Act of 31 July 1929 and the Decree of 17 December 1938. Neither shall it apply to income derived from such companies by a resident of Ukraine, nor to shares or other rights in such companies owned by such a person.

Article 29

ENTRY INTO FORCE

Each of the Contracting States shall notify to the other, through the diplomatic channel the completion of the procedures required by its domestic law for the bringing into force of this Convention. This Convention shall enter into force on the date of the later of these notifications and shall thereupon have effect:

a) in respect of taxes withheld at source, to income derived on or after 1 of January of the calendar year next following the year in which the Convention enters into force;
b) in respect of other taxes on income, and taxes on capital, to taxes chargeable for any taxable year beginning on or after 1 January of the calendar year next following the year in which the Convention enters into force.

Article 30

TERMINATION

This Convention shall remain in force until terminated by one of the Contracting States. Either Contracting State may terminate the Convention, through diplomatic channel, by giving notice of termination at least six months before the end of any calendar year beginning after the expiry of five years from the date of entry into force of the Convention.

In such event, the Convention shall cease to have effect:

a) in respect of taxes withheld at source, to income derived on or after 1 of January of the calendar year next following the year in which the notice is given;

b) in respect of other taxes on income, and taxes on capital, to taxes chargeable for any taxable year beginning on or after 1 January of the calendar year next following the year in which the notice is given.

In witness whereof the undersigned, duly authorized thereto have signed this Convention.

Done in duplicate at Kyiv this 6 day of September 1997, in French, Ukrainian and English languages, all texts being equally authentic.

For the Government of the Grand Duchy of Luxembourg

For the Government of Ukraine

[TEXT IN FRENCH – TEXTE EN FRANÇAIS]

CONVENTION

ENTRE

LE GOUVERNEMENT DU GRAND-DUCHE DE LUXEMBOURG

ET

LE GOUVERNEMENT DE L'UKRAINE

TENDANT A EVITER LES DOUBLES IMPOSITIONS ET

A PREVENIR LA FRAUDE FISCALE EN MATIERE

D'IMPOTS SUR LE REVENU ET SUR LA FORTUNE

Le Gouvernement du Grand-Duché de Luxembourg et le Gouvernement de l'Ukraine désireux de conclure une Convention tendant à éviter les doubles impositions et à prévenir la fraude fiscale en matière d'impôts sur le revenu et sur la fortune et confirmant leurs efforts de développer et d'approfondir leurs relations économiques mutuelles, sont convenus de ce qui suit:

Article 1

PERSONNES VISEES

La présente Convention s'applique aux personnes qui sont des résidents d'un Etat contractant ou des deux Etats contractants.

Article 2

IMPOTS VISES

1. La présente Convention s'applique aux impôts sur le revenu et sur la fortune perçus pour le compte d'un Etat contractant, de ses subdivisions politiques ou de ses collectivités locales, quel que soit le système de perception.

2. Sont considérés comme impôts sur le revenu et sur la fortune les impôts perçus sur le revenu total, sur la fortune totale, ou sur des éléments du revenu ou de la fortune, y compris les impôts sur les gains provenant de l'aliénation de biens mobiliers ou immobiliers et les impôts sur le montant global des salaires payés par les entreprises.

3. Les impôts actuels qui font l'objet de la présente Convention sont:

a) en ce qui concerne le Grand-Duché de Luxembourg:
   (i) l'impôt sur le revenu des personnes physiques;
   (ii) l'impôt sur le revenu des collectivités;
   (iii) l'impôt spécial sur les tantièmes;

(iv) l'impôt sur la fortune; et
(v) l'impôt commercial communal;
(ci-après dénommés "impôt luxembourgeois");

b) en ce qui concerne l'Ukraine:
(i) l'impôt sur les bénéfices des entreprises; et
(ii) l'impôt sur le revenu des personnes physiques;
(ci-après dénommés "impôt ukrainien").

4. La Convention s'applique aussi aux impôts de nature identique ou analogue qui seraient établis par l'un ou l'autre Etat contractant après la date de signature de la présente Convention et qui s'ajouteraient aux impôts actuels ou qui les remplaceraient. Les autorités compétentes des Etats contractants se communiqueront les modifications importantes apportées à leurs législations fiscales respectives.

Article 3

DEFINITIONS GENERALES

1. Au sens de la présente Convention, à moins que le contexte n'exige une interprétation différente:

a) le terme "Luxembourg" utilisé dans un sens géographique, désigne le territoire du Grand-Duché de Luxembourg;

b) le terme "Ukraine" utilisé dans un sens géographique, désigne le territoire de l'Ukraine, son plateau continental et sa zone (maritime) économique exclusive, comprenant toute zone au-delà des eaux territoriales de l'Ukraine qui, conformément au droit international, a été ou sera ultérieurement désignée comme une zone sur laquelle l'Ukraine peut exercer ses droits en ce qui concerne le lit de mer, son sous-sol et leurs ressources naturelles;

c) le terme "national" désigne:
(i) toute personne physique qui possède la nationalité d'un Etat contractant;
(ii) toute personne morale, société de personnes ou association constituée conformément à la législation en vigueur dans un Etat contractant;

d) les expressions "un Etat contractant" et "l'autre Etat contractant" désignent, suivant le cas, le Luxembourg ou l'Ukraine;
e) le terme "personne" comprend les personnes physiques, les sociétés et tous autres groupements de personnes;
f) le terme "société" désigne toute personne morale ou toute entité qui est considérée comme une personne morale aux fins d'imposition;
g) les expressions "entreprise d'un Etat contractant" et "entreprise de l'autre Etat contractant" désignent respectivement une entreprise exploitée par un résident d'un Etat contractant et une entreprise exploitée par un résident de l'autre Etat contractant;
h) l'expression "trafic international" désigne tout transport effectué par un navire, un bateau ou un aéronef exploité par une entreprise d'un Etat contractant, sauf lorsque le navire, le bateau ou l'aéronef n'est exploité qu'entre des points situés dans l'autre Etat contractant;
i) l'expression "autorité compétente" désigne, en ce qui concerne l'Ukraine, le Ministère des Finances de l'Ukraine ou son représentant autorisé, et, en ce qui concerne le Luxembourg, le Ministre des Finances ou son représentant autorisé.

2. Pour l'application de la Convention à un moment donné par un Etat contractant, tout terme ou expression qui n'y est pas défini a, sauf si le contexte exige une interprétation différente, le sens que lui attribue à ce moment le droit de cet Etat concernant les impôts auxquels s'applique la Convention. Le sens attribué à ce terme ou expression par le droit fiscal de cet Etat prévaut sur le sens que lui attribuent les autres branches du droit de cet Etat.

Article 4

RESIDENT

1. Au sens de la présente Convention, l'expression "résident d'un Etat contractant" désigne toute personne qui, en vertu de la législation de cet Etat, est assujettie à l'impôt dans

cet Etat, en raison de son domicile, de sa résidence, de son siège de direction, de son lieu d'enregistrement ou de tout autre critère de nature analogue et s'applique aussi à cet Etat ainsi qu'à toutes ses subdivisions politiques ou à ses collectivités locales. Mais cette expression ne comprend pas les personnes qui ne sont assujetties à l'impôt dans cet Etat que pour les revenus de sources situées dans cet Etat ou pour la fortune qui y est située.

2. Lorsque, selon les dispositions du paragraphe 1 du présent article, une personne physique est un résident des deux Etats contractants, sa situation est réglée de la manière suivante:

a) cette personne est considérée comme un résident de l'Etat contractant où elle dispose d'un foyer d'habitation permanent; si elle dispose d'un foyer d'habitation permanent dans les deux Etats contractants, elle est considérée comme un résident de l'Etat contractant avec lequel ses liens personnels et économiques sont les plus étroits (centre des intérêts vitaux);
b) si l'Etat contractant où cette personne a le centre de ses intérêts vitaux ne peut pas être déterminé, ou si elle ne dispose d'un foyer d'habitation permanent dans aucun des Etats, elle est considérée comme un résident seulement de l'Etat contractant où elle séjourne de façon habituelle;
c) si cette personne séjourne de façon habituelle dans les deux Etats contractants ou si elle ne séjourne de façon habituelle dans aucun d'eux, elle est considérée comme un résident seulement de l'Etat contractant dont elle possède la nationalité;
d) si cette personne possède la nationalité des deux Etats contractants ou si elle ne possède la nationalité d'aucun d'eux, les autorités compétentes des Etats contractants tranchent la question d'un commun accord.

3. Lorsque, selon les dispositions du paragraphe 1 du présent article, une personne autre qu'une personne physique est un résident des deux Etats contractants, elle est considérée comme un résident seulement de l'Etat contractant où son siège de direction effective est situé.

Article 5

ETABLISSEMENT STABLE

1. Au sens de la présente Convention, l'expression "établissement stable" désigne une installation fixe d'affaires par l'intermédiaire de laquelle une entreprise exerce tout ou partie de son activité.

2. L'expression "établissement stable" comprend notamment:

a) un siège de direction;
b) une succursale;
c) un bureau;
d) une usine;
e) un atelier;
f) une installation ou un dispositif pour l'exploration des ressources naturelles;
g) une mine, un puits de pétrole ou de gaz, une carrière ou tout autre lieu d'extraction de ressources naturelles; et
h) un magasin ou un autre dispositif utilisé comme point de vente.

3. Un chantier de construction ou de montage ne constitue un établissement stable que si sa durée dépasse douze mois.

4. Nonobstant les dispositions précédentes du présent article, on considère qu'il n'y a pas "établissement stable" si:

a) il est fait usage d'installations aux seules fins de stockage, d'exposition ou de livraison de marchandises appartenant à l'entreprise;
b) des marchandises appartenant à l'entreprise sont entreposées aux seules fins de stockage, d'exposition ou de livraison;
c) des marchandises appartenant à l'entreprise sont entreposées aux seules fins de transformation par une autre entreprise;
d) une installation fixe d'affaires est utilisée aux seules fins d'acheter des marchandises ou de réunir des informations, pour l'entreprise;

e) une installation fixe d'affaires est utilisée aux seules fins d'exercer, pour l'entreprise, toute autre activité de caractère préparatoire ou auxiliaire;

f) une installation fixe d'affaires est utilisée aux seules fins de l'exercice cumulé d'activités mentionnées aux alinéas a) à e), à condition que l'activité d'ensemble de l'installation fixe d'affaires résultant de ce cumul garde un caractère préparatoire ou auxiliaire.

5. Nonobstant les dispositions des paragraphes 1 et 2 du présent article, lorsqu'une personne autre qu'un agent jouissant d'un statut indépendant auquel s'applique le paragraphe 6 du présent article agit pour le compte d'une entreprise et dispose dans un Etat contractant de pouvoirs qu'elle y exerce habituellement lui permettant de conclure des contrats au nom de l'entreprise, ou entrepose un stock de marchandises appartenant à l'entreprise et servant à effectuer des ventes régulières au nom de l'entreprise, cette entreprise est considérée comme ayant un établissement stable dans cet Etat pour toutes les activités que cette personne exerce pour l'entreprise, à moins que les activités de cette personne ne soient limitées à celles qui sont mentionnées au paragraphe 4 et qui, si elles étaient exercées par l'intermédiaire d'une installation fixe d'affaires, ne permettraient pas de considérer cette installation comme un établissement stable selon les dispositions de ce paragraphe.

6. Une entreprise n'est pas considérée comme ayant un établissement stable dans un Etat contractant du seul fait qu'elle y exerce son activité par l'entremise d'un courtier, d'un commissionnaire général ou de tout autre agent jouissant d'un statut indépendant, à condition que ces personnes agissent dans le cadre ordinaire de leur activité.

7. Le fait qu'une société qui est un résident d'un Etat contractant contrôle ou est contrôlée par une société qui est un résident de l'autre Etat contractant ou qui y exerce son activité (que ce soit par l'intermédiaire d'un établissement stable ou non) ne suffit pas, en lui-même, à faire de l'une quelconque de ces sociétés un établissement stable de l'autre.

Article 6

REVENUS IMMOBILIERS

1. Les revenus qu'un résident d'un Etat contractant tire de biens immobiliers (y compris les revenus des exploitations agricoles ou forestières) situés dans l'autre Etat contractant, sont imposables dans cet autre Etat.

2. L'expression "biens immobiliers" a le sens que lui attribue le droit de l'Etat contractant où les biens considérés sont situés. L'expression comprend en tous cas les accessoires, le cheptel mort ou vif des exploitations agricoles et forestières, les droits auxquels s'appliquent les dispositions du droit privé concernant la propriété foncière, l'usufruit des biens immobiliers et les droits à des paiements variables ou fixes pour l'exploitation ou la concession de l'exploitation de gisements minéraux, sources et autres ressources naturelles. Les navires, bateaux et aéronefs ne sont pas considérés comme des biens immobiliers.

3. Les dispositions du paragraphe 1 du présent article s'appliquent aux revenus provenant de l'exploitation directe, de la location ou de l'affermage, ainsi que de toute autre forme d'exploitation des biens immobiliers.

4. Les dispositions des paragraphes 1 et 3 du présent article s'appliquent également aux revenus provenant des biens immobiliers d'une entreprise ainsi qu'aux revenus des biens immobiliers servant à l'exercice d'une profession indépendante.

Article 7

BENEFICES DES ENTREPRISES

1. Les bénéfices d'une entreprise d'un Etat contractant ne sont imposables que dans cet Etat, à moins que l'entreprise n'exerce son activité dans l'autre Etat contractant par

l'intermédiaire d'un établissement stable qui y est situé. Si l'entreprise exerce son activité d'une telle façon, les bénéfices de l'entreprise sont imposables dans l'autre Etat mais uniquement dans la mesure où ils sont imputables à cet établissement stable.

2. Sous réserve des dispositions du paragraphe 3 du présent article, lorsqu'une entreprise d'un Etat contractant exerce son activité dans l'autre Etat contractant par l'intermédiaire d'un établissement stable qui y est situé, il est imputé, dans chaque Etat contractant, à cet établissement stable les bénéfices qu'il aurait pu réaliser s'il avait constitué une entreprise distincte exerçant des activités identiques ou analogues dans des conditions identiques ou analogues et traitant en toute indépendance avec l'entreprise dont il constitue un établissement stable.

3. Pour déterminer les bénéfices d'un établissement stable, sont admises en déduction les dépenses exposées aux fins poursuivies par cet établissement stable, y compris les dépenses de direction et les frais généraux d'administration ainsi exposés, soit dans l'Etat où est situé cet établissement stable, soit ailleurs. Toutefois, aucune déduction n'est admise pour les sommes qui seraient, le cas échéant, versées (à d'autres titres que le remboursement de frais encourus) par l'établissement stable à l'entreprise ou à l'un quelconque de ses bureaux, comme redevances, honoraires ou autres paiements similaires, pour l'usage de brevets ou d'autres droits, ou comme commission, pour des services spécifiques rendus ou pour une activité de direction ou, sauf dans le cas d'une entreprise bancaire, comme intérêts sur des sommes prêtées par l'entreprise à l'établissement stable.

4. S'il est d'usage, dans un Etat contractant, de déterminer les bénéfices imputables à un établissement stable sur la base d'une répartition des bénéfices totaux de l'entreprise entre ses diverses parties, aucune disposition du paragraphe 2 du présent article n'empêche cet Etat contractant de déterminer les bénéfices imposables selon la répartition en usage; la méthode de répartition adoptée doit cependant être telle que le résultat obtenu soit conforme aux principes contenus dans le présent article.

5. Aucun bénéfice n'est imputé à un établissement stable du fait qu'il a simplement acheté des marchandises pour l'entreprise.

6. Aux fins des paragraphes précédents, les bénéfices à imputer à l'établissement stable sont déterminés chaque année selon la même méthode, à moins qu'il n'existe des motifs valables et suffisants de procéder autrement.

7. Lorsque les bénéfices comprennent des éléments de revenu traités séparément dans d'autres articles de la présente Convention, les dispositions de ces articles ne sont pas affectées par les dispositions du présent article.

Article 8

TRANSPORT INTERNATIONAL

1. Les bénéfices qu'un résident d'un Etat contractant tire de l'exploitation, en trafic international, de navires, bateaux ou aéronefs ne sont imposables que dans cet Etat.

2. Au sens du présent article, les bénéfices provenant de l'exploitation, en trafic international, de navires ou aéronefs comprennent:

a) les revenus provenant de la location coque nue de navires ou d'aéronefs; et

b) les bénéfices provenant de l'utilisation, de la maintenance ou de la location de conteneurs (y compris les remorques et l'équipement relatif au transport des conteneurs) utilisés pour le transport de marchandises;

lorsque cette location ou cette utilisation, maintenance ou location, suivant les cas, est accessoire à l'exploitation, en trafic international, de navires ou d'aéronefs.

3. Lorsque les bénéfices visés au paragraphe 1 du présent article sont tirés par un résident d'un Etat contractant de la participation à un pool, une exploitation en commun ou un organisme international d'exploitation, les bénéfices imputables à ce résident ne sont imposables que dans l'Etat contractant dont il est un résident.

Article 9

ENTREPRISES ASSOCIEES

1. Lorsque

a) une entreprise d'un Etat contractant participe directement ou indirectement à la direction, au contrôle ou au capital d'une entreprise de l'autre Etat contractant, ou que

b) les mêmes personnes participent directement ou indirectement à la direction, au contrôle ou au capital d'une entreprise d'un Etat contractant et d'une entreprise de l'autre Etat contractant,

et que, dans l'un et l'autre cas, les deux entreprises sont, dans leurs relations commerciales ou financières, liées par des conditions convenues ou imposées, qui diffèrent de celles qui seraient convenues entre des entreprises indépendantes, les bénéfices qui, sans ces conditions, auraient été réalisés par l'une des entreprises mais n'ont pu l'être en fait à cause de ces conditions, peuvent être inclus dans les bénéfices de cette entreprise et imposés en conséquence.

2. Lorsqu'un Etat contractant inclut dans les bénéfices d'une entreprise de cet Etat - et impose en conséquence - des bénéfices sur lesquels une entreprise de l'autre Etat contractant a été imposée dans cet autre Etat, et que les bénéfices ainsi inclus sont des bénéfices qui auraient été réalisés par l'entreprise du premier Etat si les conditions convenues entre les deux entreprises avaient été celles qui auraient été convenues entre des entreprises indépendantes, l'autre Etat procède à un ajustement approprié du montant de l'impôt qui y a été perçu sur ces bénéfices. Pour

déterminer cet ajustement, il est tenu compte des autres dispositions de la présente Convention et, si c'est nécessaire, les autorités compétentes des Etats contractants se consultent.

Article 10

DIVIDENDES

1. Les dividendes payés par une société qui est un résident d'un Etat contractant à un résident de l'autre Etat contractant sont imposables dans cet autre Etat.

2. Toutefois, ces dividendes sont aussi imposables dans l'Etat contractant dont la société qui paie les dividendes est un résident, et selon la législation de cet Etat, mais si la personne qui reçoit les dividendes en est le bénéficiaire effectif, l'impôt ainsi établi ne peut excéder:

a) 5 pour cent du montant brut des dividendes si le bénéficiaire effectif est une société (autre qu'une société de personnes) qui détient directement au moins 20 pour cent du capital de la société qui paie les dividendes;

b) 15 pour cent du montant brut des dividendes, dans tous les autres cas.

3. Nonobstant les dispositions du paragraphe 2 du présent article, les dividendes payés par une société qui est un résident d'un Etat contractant ne sont pas imposables dans cet Etat si le bénéficiaire effectif des dividendes est une société qui est un résident de l'autre Etat contractant et qui a détenu durant une période ininterrompue de trois ans précédant la date du paiement des dividendes, une participation directe d'au moins 50 pour cent dans la société qui paie les dividendes et à condition qu'un investissement d'au moins 1.000.000 US dollars ou de son équivalent dans les monnaies nationales des Etats contractants ait été effectué dans le capital de la société qui paie les dividendes. Cette disposition ne s'applique qu'aux dividendes provenant de la fraction de la participation qui a été détenue par le bénéficiaire

effectif sans interruption durant cette période de trois ans. Par ailleurs, la disposition du présent paragraphe ne s'applique que si le dividende distribué provient d'une activité industrielle ou commerciale effective exercée dans le premier Etat (autre qu'une activité consistant à effectuer ou à gérer des investissements, à moins qu'il ne s'agisse d'une activité exercée par une société bancaire ou d'assurance).

4. Le terme "dividendes" employé dans le présent article désigne les revenus provenant d'actions ou autres parts bénéficiaires à l'exception des créances, ainsi que les revenus d'autres parts sociales soumis au même régime fiscal que les revenus d'actions par la législation de l'Etat dont la société distributrice est un résident.

5. Les dispositions des paragraphes 1, 2 et 3 du présent article ne s'appliquent pas lorsque le bénéficiaire effectif des dividendes, résident d'un Etat contractant, exerce dans l'autre Etat contractant dont la société qui paie les dividendes est un résident, soit une activité industrielle ou commerciale par l'intermédiaire d'un établissement stable qui y est situé, soit une profession indépendante au moyen d'une base fixe qui y est située, et que la participation génératrice des dividendes s'y rattache effectivement. Dans ce cas, les dispositions de l'article 7 ou de l'article 14 de la présente Convention, suivant les cas, sont applicables.

6. Lorsqu'une société qui est un résident d'un Etat contractant tire des bénéfices ou des revenus de l'autre Etat contractant, cet autre Etat ne peut percevoir aucun impôt sur les dividendes payés par la société, sauf dans la mesure où ces dividendes sont payés à un résident de cet autre Etat ou dans la mesure où la participation génératrice des dividendes se rattache effectivement à un établissement stable ou à une base fixe situés dans cet autre Etat, ni prélever aucun impôt, au titre de l'imposition des bénéfices non distribués, sur les bénéfices non distribués de la société, même si les dividendes payés ou les bénéfices non distribués consistent en tout ou en partie en bénéfices ou revenus provenant de cet autre Etat.

Article 11

INTERETS

1. Les intérêts provenant d'un Etat contractant et payés à un résident de l'autre Etat contractant sont imposables dans cet autre Etat.

2. Toutefois, ces intérêts sont aussi imposables dans l'Etat contractant d'où ils proviennent et selon la législation de cet Etat, mais si la personne qui reçoit les intérêts en est le bénéficiaire effectif, l'impôt ainsi établi ne peut excéder:

a) 2 pour cent du montant brut des intérêts, dans le cas des intérêts provenant d'un Etat contractant et payés en raison de prêts de toutes sortes accordés par une banque ou un autre établissement financier de l'autre Etat, y compris les banques d'investissement et les caisses d'épargne, et les sociétés d'assurance;

b) 10 pour cent du montant brut des intérêts, dans tous les autres cas.

3. Nonobstant les dispositions du paragraphe 2 du présent article, les intérêts provenant d'un Etat contractant et payés à un résident de l'autre Etat contractant qui en est le bénéficiaire effectif, sont exempts d'impôt dans le premier Etat s'ils sont payés en raison de prêts faits, garantis ou assurés, ou en vertu de toute autre créance ou crédit garantis ou assurés pour le compte de l'autre Etat contractant par son organe autorisé.

4. Le terme "intérêts" employé dans le présent article désigne les revenus des créances de toute nature, assorties ou non de garanties hypothécaires ou d'une clause de participation aux bénéfices du débiteur, et notamment les revenus des fonds publics et des obligations d'emprunts, y compris les primes et lots attachés à ces titres.

5. Les dispositions des paragraphes 1, 2 et 3 du présent article ne s'appliquent pas lorsque le bénéficiaire effectif des intérêts, résident d'un Etat contractant, exerce dans l'autre Etat contractant d'où proviennent les intérêts, soit une activité industrielle ou commerciale par l'intermédiaire d'un établissement stable qui y est situé, soit une profession indépendante au moyen d'une base fixe qui y est située, et que la créance génératrice des intérêts s'y rattache effectivement. Dans ce cas, les dispositions de l'article 7 ou de l'article 14 de la présente Convention, suivant les cas, sont applicables.

6. Les intérêts sont considérés comme provenant d'un Etat contractant lorsque le débiteur est un résident de cet Etat. Toutefois, lorsque le débiteur des intérêts, qu'il soit ou non un résident d'un Etat contractant, a dans un Etat contractant un établissement stable, ou une base fixe, pour lequel la dette donnant lieu au paiement des intérêts a été contractée et qui supporte la charge de ces intérêts, ceux-ci sont considérés comme provenant de l'Etat où l'établissement stable, ou la base fixe, est situé.

7. Lorsque, en raison de relations spéciales existant entre le débiteur et le bénéficiaire effectif ou que l'un et l'autre entretiennent avec de tierces personnes, le montant des intérêts, compte tenu de la créance pour laquelle ils sont payés, excède celui dont seraient convenus le débiteur et le bénéficiaire effectif en l'absence de pareilles relations, les dispositions du présent article ne s'appliquent qu'à ce dernier montant. Dans ce cas, la partie excédentaire des paiements reste imposable selon la législation de chaque Etat contractant et compte tenu des autres dispositions de la présente Convention.

Article 12

REDEVANCES

1. Les redevances provenant d'un Etat contractant et payées à un résident de l'autre Etat contractant sont imposables dans cet autre Etat.

2. Toutefois, ces redevances sont aussi imposables dans l'Etat contractant d'où elles proviennent et selon la législation de cet Etat, mais si la personne qui reçoit les redevances en est le bénéficiaire effectif, l'impôt ainsi établi ne peut excéder:

a) 5 pour cent du montant brut des rémunérations visées au sous-paragraphe a) du paragraphe 3 du présent article;

b) 10 pour cent du montant brut des rémunérations visées au sous-paragraphe b) du paragraphe 3 du présent article.

3. Le terme "redevances" employé dans le présent article désigne les rémunérations de toute nature payées pour:

a) l'usage ou la concession de l'usage d'un brevet, d'une marque de fabrique ou de commerce, d'un dessin ou d'un modèle, d'un plan, d'une formule ou d'un procédé secrets, et pour des informations (know-how) ayant trait à une expérience acquise dans le domaine industriel, commercial ou scientifique;

b) l'usage ou la concession de l'usage d'un droit d'auteur sur une oeuvre littéraire, artistique ou scientifique (y compris les films cinématographiques, et les films ou bandes utilisés pour les émissions radiophoniques ou télévisées).

4. Les dispositions des paragraphes 1 et 2 du présent article ne s'appliquent pas lorsque le bénéficiaire effectif des redevances, résident d'un Etat contractant, exerce dans l'autre Etat contractant d'où proviennent les redevances, soit une activité industrielle ou commerciale par l'intermédiaire d'un établissement stable qui y est situé, soit une profession indépendante au moyen d'une base fixe qui y est située, et que le droit ou le bien générateur des redevances s'y rattache effectivement. Dans ce cas, les dispositions de l'article 7 ou de l'article 14 de la présente Convention, suivant les cas, sont applicables.

5. Les redevances sont considérées comme provenant d'un Etat contractant lorsque le débiteur est un résident de cet Etat. Toutefois, lorsque le débiteur des redevances, qu'il soit ou non un résident d'un Etat contractant, a dans un Etat contractant un établissement stable, ou une base fixe, pour lequel l'engagement donnant lieu au paiement des redevances a été contracté et qui

supporte la charge de ces redevances, celles-ci sont considérées comme provenant de l'Etat où l'établissement stable, ou la base fixe, est situé.

6. Lorsque, en raison de relations spéciales existant entre le débiteur et le bénéficiaire effectif ou que l'un et l'autre entretiennent avec de tierces personnes, le montant des redevances, compte tenu de la prestation pour laquelle elles sont payées, excède pour une raison quelconque celui dont seraient convenus le débiteur et le bénéficiaire effectif en l'absence de pareilles relations, les dispositions du présent article ne s'appliquent qu'à ce dernier montant. Dans ce cas, la partie excédentaire des paiements reste imposable selon la législation de chaque Etat contractant et compte tenu des autres dispositions de la présente Convention.

Article 13

GAINS EN CAPITAL

1. Les gains qu'un résident d'un Etat contractant tire de l'aliénation de biens immobiliers visés à l'article 6 de la présente Convention, et situés dans l'autre Etat contractant, sont imposables dans cet autre Etat.

2. Les gains qu'un résident d'un Etat contractant tire de l'aliénation:

a) d'actions, autres que des actions cotées en bourse reconnue, dont la valeur ou la plus grande partie de la valeur provient directement ou indirectement de biens immobiliers situés dans l'autre Etat contractant, ou

b) d'une participation dans une société de personnes dont l'actif est constitué en majeure partie de biens immobiliers situés dans l'autre Etat contractant ou d'actions visées ci-dessus au sous-paragraphe a),

sont imposables dans cet autre Etat.

3. Les gains provenant de l'aliénation de biens mobiliers qui font partie de l'actif d'un établissement stable qu'une entreprise d'un Etat contractant a dans l'autre Etat contractant, ou de biens mobiliers qui appartiennent à une base fixe dont un résident d'un Etat contractant dispose dans l'autre Etat contractant pour l'exercice d'une profession indépendante, y compris de tels gains provenant de l'aliénation de cet établissement stable (seul ou avec l'ensemble de l'entreprise) ou de cette base fixe, sont imposables dans cet autre Etat.

4. Les gains qu'une entreprise d'un Etat contractant tire de l'aliénation de navires, de bateaux ou d'aéronefs exploités en trafic international, ou de biens mobiliers affectés à l'exploitation de ces navires, bateaux ou aéronefs, ne sont imposables que dans cet Etat contractant.

5. Les gains provenant de l'aliénation de tous biens autres que ceux visés aux paragraphes 1, 2, 3 et 4 du présent article ne sont imposables que dans l'Etat contractant dont le cédant est un résident.

Article 14

PROFESSIONS INDEPENDANTES

1. Les revenus qu'un résident d'un Etat contractant tire d'une profession libérale ou d'autres activités de caractère indépendant ne sont imposables que dans cet Etat, à moins que ce résident ne dispose de façon habituelle dans l'autre Etat contractant d'une base fixe pour l'exercice de ses activités. S'il dispose d'une telle base fixe, les revenus sont imposables dans l'autre Etat mais uniquement dans la mesure où ils sont imputables à cette base fixe.

2. L'expression "profession libérale" comprend notamment les activités indépendantes d'ordre scientifique, littéraire, artistique, éducatif ou pédagogique, ainsi que les activités indépendantes des médecins, avocats, ingénieurs, architectes, dentistes et comptables.

Article 15

PROFESSIONS DEPENDANTES

1. Sous réserve des dispositions des articles 16, 18, 19 et 20 de la présente Convention, les salaires, traitements et autres rémunérations similaires qu'un résident d'un Etat contractant reçoit au titre d'un emploi salarié ne sont imposables que dans cet Etat, à moins que l'emploi ne soit exercé dans l'autre Etat contractant. Si l'emploi y est exercé, les rémunérations reçues à ce titre sont imposables dans cet autre Etat.

2. Nonobstant les dispositions du paragraphe 1 du présent article, les rémunérations qu'un résident d'un Etat contractant reçoit au titre d'un emploi salarié exercé dans l'autre Etat contractant ne sont imposables que dans le premier Etat si:

a) le bénéficiaire séjourne dans l'autre Etat pendant une période ou des périodes n'excédant pas au total 183 jours durant toute période de douze mois commençant ou se terminant durant l'année civile considérée, et

b) les rémunérations sont payées par un employeur ou pour le compte d'un employeur qui n'est pas un résident de l'autre Etat, et

c) la charge des rémunérations n'est pas supportée par un établissement stable ou une base fixe que l'employeur a dans l'autre Etat.

3. Nonobstant les dispositions précédentes du présent article, les rémunérations reçues au titre d'un emploi salarié exercé à bord d'un navire, d'un bateau ou d'un aéronef exploité en trafic international, sont imposables dans l'Etat contractant dont l'entreprise exploitant le navire, bateau ou aéronef est un résident.

Article 16

TANTIEMES

Les tantièmes, jetons de présence et autres rétributions similaires qu'un résident d'un Etat contractant reçoit en sa qualité de membre du conseil d'administration ou de surveillance ou de tout autre organe similaire d'une société qui est un résident de l'autre Etat contractant sont imposables dans cet autre Etat.

Article 17

ARTISTES ET SPORTIFS

1. Nonobstant les dispositions des articles 14 et 15 de la présente Convention, les revenus qu'un résident d'un Etat contractant tire de ses activités personnelles exercées dans l'autre Etat contractant en tant qu'artiste du spectacle, tel qu'un artiste de théâtre, de cinéma, de la radio ou de la télévision, ou qu'un musicien, ou en tant que sportif, sont imposables dans cet autre Etat.

2. Lorsque les revenus d'activités qu'un artiste du spectacle ou un sportif exerce personnellement et en cette qualité sont attribués non pas à l'artiste ou au sportif lui-même mais à une autre personne, ces revenus sont imposables, nonobstant les dispositions des articles 7, 14 et 15 de la présente Convention, dans l'Etat contractant où les activités de l'artiste ou du sportif sont exercées.

3. Nonobstant les dispositions des paragraphes 1 et 2 du présent article, les revenus visés au présent article sont exempts d'impôt dans l'Etat contractant où les activités de l'artiste ou du sportif sont exercées, si ces activités sont financées pour une grande part par des fonds publics d'un ou des deux Etats contractants, ou sont exercées dans le cadre d'un accord de coopération culturelle entre les Etats contractants.

Article 18

PENSIONS

1. Sous réserve des dispositions du paragraphe 2 de l'article 19 de la présente Convention, les pensions et autres

rémunérations similaires, payées à un résident d'un Etat contractant au titre d'un emploi antérieur, ne sont imposables que dans cet Etat.

2. Nonobstant les dispositions du paragraphe 1 du présent article, les pensions et autres sommes payées en application de la législation sur la sécurité sociale ou en application d'un Plan d'Etat de Pension d'un Etat contractant ne sont imposables que dans cet Etat.

Article 19

FONCTIONS PUBLIQUES

1. a) Les rémunérations, autres que les pensions, payées par un Etat contractant ou l'une de ses subdivisions politiques ou collectivités locales à une personne physique, au titre de services rendus à cet Etat ou à cette subdivision ou collectivité, ne sont imposables que dans cet Etat.
   b) Nonobstant les dispositions du sous-paragraphe a) du présent paragraphe, ces rémunérations ne sont imposables que dans l'autre Etat contractant si les services sont rendus dans cet Etat et si la personne physique est un résident de cet Etat qui:
      (i) possède la nationalité de cet Etat, ou
      (ii) n'est pas devenu un résident de cet Etat à seule fin de rendre les services.

2. a) Les pensions payées par un Etat contractant ou l'une de ses subdivisions politiques ou collectivités locales, soit directement soit par prélèvement sur des fonds qu'ils ont constitués, à une personne physique, au titre de services rendus à cet Etat ou à cette subdivision ou collectivité, ne sont imposables que dans cet Etat.
   b) Nonobstant les dispositions du sous-paragraphe a) du présent paragraphe, ces pensions ne sont imposables que dans l'autre Etat contractant si la personne physique est un résident de cet Etat et en possède la nationalité.

3. Les dispositions des articles 15, 16, 17 et 18 de la présente Convention s'appliquent aux rémunérations ainsi qu'aux pensions payées au titre de services rendus dans le cadre d'une activité industrielle ou commerciale exercée par un Etat contractant ou l'une de ses subdivisions politiques ou collectivités locales.

Article 20

ETUDIANTS

1. Les sommes qu'un étudiant ou un stagiaire qui est, ou qui était immédiatement avant de se rendre dans un Etat contractant, un résident de l'autre Etat contractant et qui séjourne dans le premier Etat à seule fin d'y poursuivre ses études ou sa formation, reçoit pour couvrir ses frais d'entretien, d'études ou de formation ne sont pas imposables dans le premier Etat, à condition qu'elles proviennent de sources situées en dehors de cet Etat.

2. Les revenus qu'un étudiant ou stagiaire reçoit pour les activités exercées dans l'Etat contractant où il ne séjourne que pour poursuivre ses études ou sa formation, ne sont pas imposables dans cet Etat. Cette exemption ne s'applique que pour une période n'excédant pas 2 ans à partir de la date où il est arrivé pour la première fois dans cet Etat pour poursuivre ses études ou sa formation.

Article 21

AUTRES REVENUS

1. Les éléments du revenu d'un résident d'un Etat contractant, d'où qu'ils proviennent, qui ne sont pas traités dans les articles précédents de la présente Convention ne sont imposables que dans le premier Etat.

2. Les dispositions du paragraphe 1 du présent article ne s'appliquent pas aux revenus autres que les revenus provenant de biens immobiliers tels qu'ils sont définis au paragraphe 2 de l'article 6 de la présente Convention, lorsque le bénéficiaire de tels revenus, résident d'un Etat contractant, exerce dans l'autre Etat contractant, soit une activité industrielle ou commerciale par l'intermédiaire d'un établissement stable qui y est situé, soit une profession indépendante au moyen d'une base fixe qui y est située, et que le droit ou le bien générateur des revenus s'y rattache effectivement. Dans ce cas, les dispositions de l'article 7 ou de l'article 14 de la présente Convention, suivant les cas, sont applicables.

Article 22

FORTUNE

1. La fortune constituée par des biens immobiliers visés à l'article 6 de la présente Convention, que possède un résident d'un Etat contractant et qui sont situés dans l'autre Etat contractant, est imposable dans cet autre Etat.

2. La fortune constituée par des biens mobiliers qui font partie de l'actif d'un établissement stable qu'une entreprise d'un Etat contractant a dans l'autre Etat contractant, ou par des biens mobiliers qui appartiennent à une base fixe dont un résident d'un Etat contractant dispose dans l'autre Etat contractant pour l'exercice d'une profession indépendante, est imposable dans cet autre Etat.

3. La fortune constituée par des navires, des bateaux et des aéronefs exploités en trafic international par une entreprise d'un Etat contractant, ainsi que par des biens mobiliers affectés à l'exploitation de ces navires, bateaux et aéronefs, n'est imposable que dans cet Etat contractant.

4. Tous les autres éléments de la fortune d'un résident d'un Etat contractant ne sont imposables que dans cet Etat.

Article 23

ELIMINATION DE LA DOUBLE IMPOSITION

1. Sous réserve des dispositions de la législation de l'Ukraine concernant l'élimination de la double imposition (qui n'en affectent pas le principe général), l'impôt luxembourgeois payé en vertu de la législation luxembourgeoise et conformément à la présente Convention, sur les bénéfices et les revenus de sources luxembourgeoises ou sur la fortune située au Luxembourg, est déduit de tout impôt ukrainien calculé sur les mêmes bénéfices et revenus ou sur la même fortune sur lesquels l'impôt luxembourgeois est payé.

2. Sous réserve des dispositions de la législation du Luxembourg concernant l'élimination de la double imposition (qui n'en affectent pas le principe général), la double imposition est évitée au Luxembourg de la manière suivante:

a) Lorsqu'un résident du Luxembourg reçoit des revenus ou possède de la fortune qui, conformément aux dispositions de la présente Convention, sont imposables en Ukraine, le Luxembourg exempte de l'impôt ces revenus ou cette fortune, sous réserve des dispositions des sous-paragraphes b) et c).

b) Lorsqu'un résident du Luxembourg reçoit des revenus qui, conformément aux dispositions des articles 10, 11 et 12 de la présente Convention sont imposables en Ukraine, le Luxembourg accorde sur l'impôt qu'il perçoit sur les revenus de ce résident, une déduction d'un montant égal à l'impôt payé en Ukraine.

c) Lorsqu'une société qui est un résident du Luxembourg reçoit des dividendes de sources ukrainiennes, le Luxembourg exempte de l'impôt ces dividendes, pourvu que cette société qui est un résident du Luxembourg détienne directement depuis le début de son exercice social au moins 10 pour cent du capital de la société qui paie les dividendes et que cette société soit soumise en Ukraine à un impôt correspondant à l'impôt luxembourgeois sur le revenu des collectivités. Les actions ou parts susvisées de la société ukrainienne sont, aux mêmes conditions, exonérées de l'impôt luxembourgeois sur la fortune.

3. Les déductions accordées par un Etat contractant en vertu du paragraphe 1 ou du sous-paragraphe b) du paragraphe 2 du présent article ne peuvent dans l'un ou l'autre cas excéder la fraction de l'impôt sur le revenu ou de l'impôt sur la fortune, calculé avant déduction, correspondant selon le cas aux revenus ou à la fortune qui sont imposables dans l'autre Etat.

4. Lorsque, conformément à une disposition quelconque de la Convention, les revenus qu'un résident d'un Etat contractant reçoit ou la fortune qu'il possède sont exempts d'impôt dans cet Etat, cet Etat peut néanmoins, pour calculer le montant de l'impôt sur le reste des revenus ou de la fortune de ce résident, tenir compte des revenus ou de la fortune exemptés.

5. Pour les besoins des paragraphes 1 et 2 du présent article, les bénéfices, les revenus et les gains en capital reçus par un résident d'un Etat contractant et qui, conformément à la présente Convention, sont imposables dans l'autre Etat contractant, sont considérés comme provenant de sources de cet autre Etat contractant.

Article 24

NON-DISCRIMINATION

1. Les nationaux d'un Etat contractant ne sont soumis dans l'autre Etat contractant à aucune imposition ou obligation y relative, qui est autre ou plus lourde que celles auxquelles sont ou pourront être assujettis les nationaux de cet autre Etat qui se trouvent dans la même situation, notamment au regard de la résidence. La présente disposition s'applique aussi, nonobstant les dispositions de l'article 1 de la présente Convention, aux

personnes qui ne sont pas des résidents d'un Etat contractant ou des deux Etats contractants.

2. Les apatrides qui sont des résidents d'un Etat contractant ne sont soumis dans l'un ou l'autre Etat contractant à aucune imposition ou obligation y relative, qui est autre ou plus lourde que celles auxquelles sont ou pourront être assujettis les nationaux de l'Etat concerné qui se trouvent dans la même situation.

3. L'imposition d'un établissement stable qu'une entreprise d'un Etat contractant a dans l'autre Etat contractant n'est pas établie dans cet autre Etat d'une façon moins favorable que l'imposition des entreprises de cet autre Etat qui exercent la même activité.

4. A moins que les dispositions du paragraphe 1 de l'article 9, du paragraphe 7 de l'article 11 ou du paragraphe 6 de l'article 12 de la présente Convention ne soient applicables, les intérêts, redevances et autres dépenses payés par une entreprise d'un Etat contractant à un résident de l'autre Etat contractant sont déductibles, pour la détermination des bénéfices imposables de cette entreprise, dans les mêmes conditions que s'ils avaient été payés à un résident du premier Etat. De même, les dettes d'une entreprise d'un Etat contractant envers un résident de l'autre Etat contractant sont déductibles, pour la détermination de la fortune imposable de cette entreprise, dans les mêmes conditions que si elles avaient été contractées envers un résident du premier Etat.

5. Les entreprises d'un Etat contractant, dont le capital est en totalité ou en partie, directement ou indirectement, détenu ou contrôlé par un ou plusieurs résidents de l'autre Etat contractant, ne sont soumises dans le premier Etat à aucune imposition ou obligation y relative, qui est autre ou plus lourde que celles auxquelles sont ou pourront être assujetties les autres entreprises similaires du premier Etat.

6. Aucune disposition du présent article ne peut être interprétée comme obligeant l'un ou l'autre Etat contractant à accorder aux personnes physiques qui ne sont pas des résidents de cet Etat les déductions personnelles, abattements et réductions d'impôt en fonction de la situation ou des charges de famille qu'il accorde à ses propres résidents ou une des déductions personnelles, un des abattements ou une des réductions d'impôt qui sont accordés à des personnes physiques qui sont des résidents selon des critères non prévus par la législation générale des impôts.

7. Les dispositions du présent article s'appliquent aux impôts visés par la présente Convention.

Article 25

PROCEDURE AMIABLE

1. Lorsqu'un résident d'un Etat contractant estime que les mesures prises par un Etat contractant ou par les deux Etats contractants entraînent ou entraîneront pour lui une imposition non conforme aux dispositions de la présente Convention, elle peut, indépendamment des recours prévus par le droit interne de ces Etats, soumettre son cas à l'autorité compétente de l'Etat contractant dont elle est un résident ou, si son cas relève du paragraphe 1 de l'article 24 de la présente Convention, à celle de l'Etat contractant dont elle possède la nationalité. Le cas doit être soumis dans les trois ans qui suivent la première notification de la mesure qui entraîne une imposition non conforme aux dispositions de la Convention.

2. L'autorité compétente s'efforce, si la réclamation lui paraît fondée et si elle n'est pas elle-même en mesure d'y apporter une solution satisfaisante, de résoudre le cas par voie d'accord amiable avec l'autorité compétente de l'autre Etat contractant, en vue d'éviter une imposition non conforme à la Convention. L'accord est appliqué quels que soient les délais prévus par le droit interne des Etats contractants.

3. Les autorités compétentes des Etats contractants s'efforcent, par voie d'accord amiable, de résoudre les difficultés ou de dissiper les doutes auxquels peuvent donner lieu l'interprétation ou l'application de la Convention.

4. Les autorités compétentes des Etats contractants peuvent communiquer directement entre elles en vue de parvenir à un accord comme il est indiqué aux paragraphes précédents.

Article 26

ECHANGE DE RENSEIGNEMENTS

1. Les autorités compétentes des Etats contractants échangent les renseignements nécessaires pour appliquer les dispositions de la présente Convention ou celles de la législation interne des Etats contractants relative aux impôts visés par la Convention dans la mesure où l'imposition qu'elle prévoit n'est pas contraire à la Convention, en particulier, pour prévenir la fraude et pour faciliter l'application des dispositions légales contre l'évasion légale. L'échange de renseignements n'est pas restreint par l'article 1 de la présente Convention. Les renseignements reçus par un Etat contractant sont tenus secrets de la même manière que les renseignements obtenus en application de la législation interne de cet Etat et ne sont communiqués qu'aux personnes ou autorités (y compris les tribunaux et organes administratifs) impliquées dans l'établissement ou le recouvrement des impôts visés par la Convention, dans les procédures ou poursuites concernant ces impôts, ou dans les décisions sur les recours relatifs à ces impôts. Ces personnes ou autorités n'utilisent ces renseignements qu'à ces fins. Elles peuvent révéler ces renseignements au cours d'audiences publiques de tribunaux ou dans des jugements.
Les autorités compétentes développent les conditions, méthodes et techniques appropriées concernant les cas pour lesquels l'échange de renseignements est pratiqué, y compris si nécessaire l'échange de renseignements par voie de consultations dans des cas de fraude fiscale.

2. Les dispositions du paragraphe 1 du présent article ne peuvent en aucun cas être interprétées comme imposant à l'autorité compétente de l'un ou l'autre Etat contractant l'obligation:

a) de prendre des mesures administratives dérogeant à la législation et à la pratique administrative prévalant dans l'un ou l'autre Etat contractant;
b) de fournir des renseignements qui ne pourraient être obtenus sur la base de la législation ou dans le cadre de la pratique administrative normale de l'un ou l'autre Etat contractant;
c) de fournir des renseignements qui révéleraient un secret commercial, industriel, professionnel ou un procédé commercial ou des renseignements dont la communication serait contraire à l'ordre public.

Article 27

MEMBRES DES MISSIONS DIPLOMATIQUES OU REPRESENTATIONS PERMANENTES ET POSTES CONSULAIRES

Les dispositions de la présente Convention ne portent pas atteinte aux privilèges fiscaux dont bénéficient les membres des missions diplomatiques ou représentations permanentes ou postes consulaires en vertu soit des règles générales du droit international, soit des dispositions d'accords particuliers.

Article 28

EXCLUSION DE CERTAINES SOCIETES

La présente Convention ne s'applique pas aux sociétés holding au sens de la législation particulière luxembourgeoise régie actuellement par la loi du 31 juillet 1929 et l'arrêté grand-ducal du 17 décembre 1938. Elle ne s'applique pas non plus aux revenus qu'un résident de l'Ukraine tire de pareilles sociétés ni aux actions ou autres titres de capital de telles sociétés que cette personne possède.

Article 29

ENTRER EN VIGUEUR

Chaque Etat contractant notifiera à l'autre Etat contractant par la voie diplomatique l'accomplissement des procédures requises par sa législation interne pour l'entrée en vigueur de la présente Convention. La Convention entrera en vigueur à la date de la dernière de ces notifications et s'appliquera:

a) en ce qui concerne les impôts retenus à la source, aux revenus attribués le ou après le 1er janvier de l'année civile suivant immédiatement l'année au cours de laquelle la Convention entrera en vigueur;

b) en ce qui concerne les autres impôts sur le revenu et sur la fortune, aux impôts dus pour toute année d'imposition commençant le ou après le 1er janvier de l'année civile suivant immédiatement l'année au cours de laquelle la Convention entrera en vigueur.

Article 30

DENONCIATION

La présente Convention demeurera en vigueur tant qu'elle n'aura pas été dénoncée par un des Etats contractants. Chacun des Etats contractants peut, par la voie diplomatique, dénoncer la Convention avec un préavis écrit de dénonciation fait au moins six mois avant la fin de toute année civile commençant après l'expiration d'un délai de cinq ans à partir de la date de l'entrée en vigueur de la Convention.

Dans ce cas, la Convention cessera de s'appliquer:

a) en ce qui concerne les impôts retenus à la source, aux revenus attribués le ou après le 1er janvier de l'année civile suivant immédiatement l'année au cours de laquelle l'avis est donné;

b) en ce qui concerne les autres impôts sur le revenu et sur la fortune, aux impôts dus pour toute année d'imposition commençant le ou après le 1er janvier de l'année civile suivant immédiatement l'année au cours de laquelle l'avis est donné.

EN FOI DE QUOI les soussignés, dûment autorisés à cet effet, ont signé la présente Convention.

Fait en double exemplaire à Kyiv le 6 septembre 1997, en langues française, ukrainienne et anglaise, les trois textes faisant également foi.

Pour le Gouvernement du Grand-Duché de Luxembourg

Pour le Gouvernement de l'Ukraine

[TEXT IN UKRAINIAN – TEXTE EN UKRAINIEN]

КОНВЕНЦІЯ

МІЖ УРЯДОМ ВЕЛИКОГО ГЕРЦОГСТВА ЛЮКСЕМБУРГ І УРЯДОМ УКРАЇНИ

про уникнення подвійного оподаткування та попередження податкових ухилень стосовно податків на доходи і на капітал

Уряд Великого Герцогства Люксембург і Уряд України, бажаючи укласти Конвенцію про уникнення подвійного оподаткування та попередження податкових ухилень стосовно податків на доходи і на капітал,

і, підтверджуючи своє прагнення до розвитку та поглиблення взаємних економічних стосунків,

домовились про таке:

СТАТТЯ 1
Особи, до яких застосовується Конвенція

Ця Конвенція буде застосовуватись до осіб, які є резидентами однієї або обох Договірних Держав.

СТАТТЯ 2
Податки, на які поширюється Конвенція

1. Ця Конвенція застосовується до податків на доходи і на капітал, що стягуються від імені Договірної Держави або її політико-адміністративних підрозділів, або місцевих органів влади, незалежно від способу їх стягнення.

2. Податками на доходи і на капітал вважаються всі податки, що справляються від загальної суми доходів, від всього капіталу або з окремих їх елементів, включаючи податки на доходи від відчужування рухомого або нерухомого майна і податки на загальну суму заробітної плати або платні, сплачуваних підприємствами.

3. Існуючими податками, на які поширюється ця Конвенція, зокрема, є:

a) в Україні:

(i) податок на прибуток підприємств; і
(ii)податок на доходи фізичних осіб;
(далі "український податок");

b) у Великому Герцогстві Люксембург:

(i) прибутковий податок з фізичних осіб;
(ii) корпоративний податок;
(iii)податок на гонорари директорів компаній;
(iv) податок на капітал; і
(v)податок на комунальну торгівлю;
(далі "люксембурзький податок").

4. Конвенція застосовується також до всіх ідентичних або по суті подібних податків, які будуть стягуватись кожною з Договірних Держав після дати підписання цієї Конвенції, в доповнення до або замість існуючих податків. Компетентні органи Договірних Держав повідомлять один одного про будь-які істотні зміни, що відбудуться в їх законодавствах щодо оподаткування.

СТАТТЯ 3
Загальні визначення

1. У розумінні цієї Конвенції, якщо із контексту не випливає інше:

a) термін "Україна" при використанні в географічному значенні означає територію України, її континентальний шельф і її виключну (морську) економічну зону, а також будь-яку іншу територію за межами територіальних вод України, яка відповідно до міжнародного права визначається або може бути в подальшому визначена як територія, в межах якої можуть здійснюватись права України стосовно морського дна, надр та їх природних ресурсів;

b) термін «Люксембург» при використанні в географічному значенні, означає територію Великого Герцогства Люксембург;

c) термін "національна особа" означає:

(i) будь-яку фізичну особу, яка має громадянство Договірної Держави;

(ii) будь-яку юридичну особу, товариство або асоціацію, що одержують свій статус як такий за чинним законодавством Договірної Держави;

d) терміни «Договірна Держава» і «друга Договірна Держава» означають Люксембург або Україну, залежно від контексту;

e) термін "особа" включає фізичну особу, компанію і будь-яке інше об'єднання осіб;

f) термін "компанія" означає будь-яке корпоративне об'єднання або будь-яку іншу організацію, що розглядається з метою оподаткування як корпоративне об'єднання;

g) терміни "підприємство Договірної Держави" та "підприємство другої Договірної Держави" означають відповідно підприємство, що керується резидентом Договірної Держави, та підприємство, що керується резидентом другої Договірної Держави;

h) термін "міжнародне перевезення" означає будь-яке перевезення морським, річковим або повітряним судном, що експлуатується підприємством Договірної Держави, крім випадків, коли морське, річкове або повітряне судно експлуатується виключно між пунктами в другій Договірній Державі;

і) термін "компетентний орган" означає в Люксембурзі Міністра фінансів або його повноважного представника, і в Україні -Міністерство фінансів України або його повноважного представника.

2. При застосуванні Договірною Державою цієї Конвенції в будь-який час будь-який термін, не визначений у ній, якщо з контексту не випливає інше, має те значення, яке в цей час надається законодавством цієї Держави щодо податків, на які поширюється ця Конвенція. Будь-яке значення згідно із податковим законодавством, що застосовується, цієї Держави переважає над значенням цього терміну згідно з іншими законами цієї Держави.

СТАТТЯ 4
Резидент

1. Для цілей цієї Конвенції вираз "резидент однієї Договірної Держави" означає будь-яку особу, яка за законодавством цієї Держави підлягає оподаткуванню в ній на підставі місця її проживання, постійного місця перебування, місцезнаходження керівного органу або будь-якого іншого аналогічного критерію, а також включає цю Державу та її будь-який політико-адміністративній підрозділ або місцевий орган влади. Цей термін разом з тим не включає будь-яку особу, яка підлягає оподаткуванню в цій Державі, тільки якщо ця особа одержує доходи з джерел в цій Державі або стосовно капіталу, що в ній знаходиться.

2. У разі, коли відповідно до положень пункту 1 цієї статті фізична особа є резидентом обох Договірних Держав, її положення визначається відповідно до таких правил:

a) вона вважається резидентом тієї Договірної Держави, де вона має постійне житло; якщо вона має постійне житло в обох Договірних Державах, вона вважається резидентом тієї Договірної Держави, де вона має більш тісні особисті і економічні зв'язки (центр життєвих інтересів);

b) якщо Договірна Держава, в якій вона має центр життєвих інтересів, не може бути визначена або коли вона не має постійного житла в жодній з Договірних Держав, вона вважається резидентом тільки тієї Договірної Держави, де вона звичайно проживає;

c) якщо вона звичайно проживає в обох Договірних Державах або коли вона звичайно не проживає в жодній з них, вона вважається резидентом тільки тієї Договірної Держави, національною особою якої вона є;

d) якщо вона є національною особою обох Договірних Держав або якщо вона не є національною особою жодної з них, компетентні органи Договірних Держав будуть прагнути вирішити питання оподаткування такого резидента за взаємною згодою.

3. У випадку, коли відповідно до положень пункту 1 цієї статті особа, що не є фізичною особою, є резидентом обох Договірних Держав, вона вважається резидентом тільки тієї Договірної Держави, де розміщений її фактичний керівний орган.

СТАТТЯ 5
Постійне представництво

1. Для цілей цієї Конвенції термін "постійне представництво" означає постійне місце діяльності, через яке повністю або частково здійснюється підприємницька діяльність підприємства.

2. Термін "постійне представництво", зокрема, включає:

a) місце управління;
b) відділення;
c) контору;
d) фабрику;
e) майстерню;
f) установку або споруду для розвідки природних ресурсів;
g) шахту, нафтову або газову свердловину, кар'єр або будь-яке інше місце видобутку природних ресурсів; і
h) склад або іншу споруду, що використовується як торговельна точка.

3. Будівельний майданчик або монтажний чи складальний об'єкт є постійними представництвами лише в тому разі, якщо вони існують більше дванадцяти місяців.

4. Незважаючи на попередні положення цієї статті, термін "постійне представництво" не розглядається як такий, що включає:

a) використання споруд виключно з метою зберігання, показу або поставки товарів чи виробів, що належать підприємству;

b) утримання запасів товарів або виробів, що належать підприємству, виключно з метою зберігання, показу або поставки;

c) утримання запасів товарів або виробів, що належать підприємству, виключно з метою переробки іншим підприємством;

d) утримання постійного місця діяльності виключно з метою закупівлі товарів чи виробів або для збирання інформації для підприємства;

e) утримання постійного місця діяльності виключно з метою здійснення для підприємства будь-якої іншої діяльності, яка має підготовчий або допоміжний характер;

f) утримання постійного місця діяльності виключно для здійснення будь-якої комбінації видів діяльності, перелічених у підпунктах від a) до e), за умови, що сукупна діяльність постійного місця діяльності, яка виникає внаслідок такої комбінації, має підготовчий або допоміжний характер.

5. Якщо, крім агента з незалежним статусом, про якого йдеться в 6-му пункті цієї статті, інша особа, незалежно від положень пунктів 1 і 2 цієї статті, діє від імені підприємства і має, і звичайно використовує в Договірній Державі повноваження укладати контракти від імені підприємства, або утримує запаси товарів та виробів, що належать підприємству, з яких здійснюється регулярний продаж цих товарів та виробів від імені підприємства, то це підприємство розглядається як таке, що має постійне представництво в цій Державі щодо будь-якої діяльності, яку ця особа здійснює для підприємства, за винятком, якщо діяльність цієї особи обмежується тією, що зазначена в пункті 4 цієї статті, яка, якщо і здійснюється через постійне місце діяльності, не робить з цього постійного місця діяльності постійного представництва відповідно до положень цього пункту.

6. Підприємство не розглядається як таке, що має постійне представництво в Договірній Державі, лише якщо воно здійснює підприємницьку діяльність у цій Державі через брокера, комісіонера чи будь-якого іншого агента з незалежним статусом за умови, що ці особи діють у межах своєї звичайної діяльності.

7. Той факт, що компанія, яка є резидентом Договірної Держави, контролює чи контролюється компанією, що є резидентом другої Договірної Держави або яка здійснює підприємницьку діяльність у цій другій Державі (або через постійне представництво або будь-яким іншим чином), сам по собі не перетворює одну з цих компаній у постійне представництво другої компанії.

СТАТТЯ 6
Доходи від нерухомого майна

1. Доходи, що одержуються резидентом Договірної Держави від нерухомого майна (включаючи доход від сільського або лісового господарства), яке міститься в другій Договірній Державі, можуть оподатковуватись у цій другій Державі.

2. Термін "нерухоме майно" повинен мати те значення, яке він має у законодавстві Договірної Держави, в якій міститься це майно. Цей термін повинен у будь-якому випадку включати майно, допоміжне щодо нерухомого майна, худобу і обладнання, використовувані в сільському і лісовому господарстві, права, до яких застосовуються положення загального права щодо земельної власності, узуфрукт нерухомого майна і права на перемінні або фіксовані платежі як компенсації за розробку або право на розробку мінеральних запасів, джерел та інших природних ресурсів. Морські, річкові і повітряні судна не розглядаються як нерухоме майно.

3. Положення пункту 1 цієї статті застосовуються до доходів, одержуваних від прямого використання, здавання в оренду або використання в будь-якій іншій формі нерухомого майна.

4. Положення пунктів 1 і 3 цієї статті застосовуються також до доходів від нерухомого майна підприємства і до доходів від нерухомого майна, використовуваного для здійснення незалежних особистих послуг.

СТАТТЯ 7
Прибуток від підприємницької діяльності

1. Прибуток підприємства Договірної Держави оподатковується тільки у цій Державі, якщо це підприємство не здійснює підприємницької діяльності в другій Договірній Державі через розташоване в ній постійне представництво. Якщо підприємство здійснює підприємницьку діяльність як вказано вище, прибуток підприємства може оподатковуватись у другій Державі, але тільки в тій частині, яка стосується цього постійного представництва.

2. З урахуванням положень пункту 3 цієї статті, якщо підприємство однієї Договірної Держави здійснює підприємницьку діяльність у другій Договірній Державі через розташоване там постійне представництво, то в кожній Договірній Державі до такого постійного представництва відноситься прибуток, який воно могло б одержати, якби було окремим та самостійним підприємством, зайнятим такою ж або аналогічною діяльністю в таких же або аналогічних умовах і діяло в повній незалежності від підприємства, постійним представництвом якого воно є.

3. У визначенні прибутку постійного представництва допускається віднімання витрат, понесених для цілей постійного представництва, включаючи раціональний розподіл управлінських та загальноадміністративних витрат, понесених для цілей підприемства в цілому як у Державі, де розташоване постійне представництво, так і в будь-якому іншому місці. У будь-якому випадку такі витрати не повинні включати будь-які суми, що сплачуються (інакше, ніж покриття витрат, що дійсно мали місце) постійним представництвом підприємству або його іншому підрозділу як роялті, гонорар або інші подібні платежі за користування патентами або іншими правами, або як комісійні за надані особливі послуги чи управління, чи, виключаючи банки, як проценти за позику, надану підприемством постійному представництву.

4. В міру того, як визначення в Договірній Державі відповідно до її законодавства прибутку, що стосується постійного представництва, на базі пропорційного розподілу загальної суми прибутку підприємства його різним підрозділам, є звичайною практикою, ніщо в пункті 2 цієї статті не буде перешкоджати цій Договірній Державі визначати оподатковуваний прибуток шляхом такого розподілу, як це диктується практикою; обраний спосіб розподілу, однак, повинен бути таким, що його результати будуть відповідати принципам, які містяться в цій статті.

5. Жодний прибуток не відноситься до постійного представництва на основі простої закупівлі постійним представництвом товарів або виробів для підприємства.

6. Для цілей попередніх пунктів прибуток, що відноситься до постійного представництва, визначається щорічно одним і тим же методом, якщо тільки немає достатньої і вагомої причини для зміни.

7. Якщо прибуток включає види доходів, які розглядаються окремо в інших статтях цієї Конвенції, положення цих статей не будуть зачіпатися положеннями цієї статті.

СТАТТЯ 8
Міжнародний транспорт

1. Прибуток, що отримується резидентом Договірної Держави від експлуатації морських, річкових або повітряних суден у міжнародних перевезеннях будуть оподатковуватись лише в цій Державі.

2. Для цілей цієї статті прибутки від експлуатації морських або повітряних суден у міжнародних перевезеннях включають:

a) доход від здавання в оренду порожніх морських або повітряних суден; і

b) прибутки від використання, утримання або здавання в оренду контейнерів (включаючи трейлери і супутнє устаткування для транспортування контейнерів), використовуваних для транспортування товарів чи виробів,

де така оренда або таке використання або утримання, залежно від випадку, є побічними стосовно експлуатації морського або повітряного судна у міжнародних перевезеннях.

3. Якщо прибутки, відповідно до пункту 1 цієї статті, отримуються резидентом Договірної Держави від участі у пулі, спільному підприємстві чи міжнародному транспортному агентстві, прибутки, що відносяться до такого резидента, будуть оподатковуватись тільки в Договорній Державі, резидентом якої він є.

СТАТТЯ 9
Асоційовані підприємства

1. У випадку, коли:

a) підприємство Договірної Держави прямо або посередньо бере участь у керівництві, контролі або капіталі підприємства другої Договірної Держави, або

b) одні й ті ж особи прямо або посередньо беруть участь у керівництві, контролі або капіталі підприємства однієї Договірної Держави і підприємства другої Договірної Держави і в кожному випадку між двома підприємствами в їх комерційних та фінансових взаємовідносинах створюються або встановлюються умови, відмінні від тих, які мали б місце між двома незалежними підприємствами, тоді будь-який прибуток, який міг би бути нарахований одному з них, але з причин наявності цих умов не був йому нарахований, може бути включений до прибутку цього підприємства і відповідно оподаткований.

2. У випадку, коли одна Договірна Держава включає в прибуток підприємства цієї Держави - і відповідно оподатковує - прибутки, по яких підприємство другої Договірної Держави було оподатковано в цій другій Державі, і прибутки, таким чином включені, є прибутками, які були б нараховані підприємству першої згаданої Держави, якби умови взаємовідносин між двома підприємствами були б умовами, які існують між незалежними підприємствами, тоді ця друга Держава повинна зробити відповідні поправки в сумі податку, що стягується з цих прибутків. При визначенні такої поправки повинні бути розглянуті інші положення цієї Конвенції, а компетентні органи Договірних Держав можуть проконсультуватися один з одним при необхідності.

СТАТТЯ 10
Дивіденди

1. Дивіденди, що сплачуються компанією, яка є резидентом Договірної Держави, резиденту другої Договірної Держави, можуть оподатковуватись у цій другій Державі.

2. Однак такі дивіденди можуть також оподатковуватись у тій Договірній Державі, резидентом якої є компанія, що сплачує дивіденди, і відповідно до законодавства цієї Держави, але якщо одержувач є фактичним власником дивідендів, то податок, що стягується таким чином, не повинен перевищувати :

a) 5 відсотків загальної суми дивідендів, якщо фактичним власником дивідендів є компанія (інша, ніж товариство), яка безпосередньо володіє принаймні 20 відсотками капіталу компанії, яка сплачує дивіденди;

b) 15 відсотків загальної суми дивідендів в усіх інших випадках.

3. Незважаючи на положення пункту 2 цієї статті, дівіденди, що сплачуються компанією, яка є резидентом однієї Договірної Держави, не будуть оподатковуватись в цій Державі, якщо фактичним власником дивідендів є компанія, що є резидентом другої Договірної Держави, і яка протягом безперервного періоду 3 років до дати виплати дивідендів прямо володіла 50% акцій компанії, що сплачує дивіденди, та при умові, що до капіталу компанії , яка сплачує дивіденди, було вкладено інвестицію у розмірі принаймні 1000000 доларів США або їх еквіваленту в національних валютах Договірних Держав. Це положення застосовується тільки до дивідендів, що стосуються тієї частини акцій, яка належала фактичному власнику безперервно протягом такого трьохрічного періоду. Більше того, положення цього підпункту будуть застосовуватись тільки якщо дивіденди, що розподіляються, будуть отримані від активного проведення торгової, підприємницької діяльності в першій згаданій Державі (іншої, ніж діяльність по здійсненню або управлінню інвестиціями, якщо тільки така діяльність не здійснюється банківською або страховою компанією).

4. Термін "дивіденди" при використанні в цій статті означає доход від акцій чи інших прав, які не є борговими вимогами, що дають право на участь у прибутку, також як доход від інших корпоративних прав, який підлягає такому ж оподаткуванню, як доходи від акцій відповідно до податкового законодавства Держави, резидентом якої є компанія, що розподіляє прибуток.

5. Положення пунктів 1, 2 і 3 цієї статті не застосовуються, якщо особа, що фактично має право на дивіденди, яка є резидентом Договірної Держави, здійснює підприємницьку діяльність у другій Договірній Державі, резидентом якої є компанія, що сплачує дивіденди, через розташоване в ній постійне представництво, або надає в цій другій Державі незалежні особисті послуги з розташованої в ній постійної бази, і холдінг, стосовно якого сплачуються дивіденди, дійсно відноситься до таких постійного представництва або постійної бази. В такому випадку, залежно від обставин, застосовуються положення статті 7 або статті 14 цієї Конвенції.

6. У випадку, коли компанія, яка є резидентом однієї Договірної Держави, одержує прибуток або доходи з другої Договірної Держави, ця друга Держава може не стягувати будь-яких податків на дивіденди, що сплачуються компанією, за винятком, коли ці дивіденди сплачуються резиденту цієї другої Держави, або якщо холдінг, стосовно якого сплачуються дивіденди, дійсно відноситься до постійного представництва або постійної бази, розташованих у цій другій Державі, і з нерозподіленого прибутку не стягуються податки на

нерозподілений прибуток, навіть якщо дивіденди сплачуються або нерозподілений прибуток складається повністю або частково з прибутку або доходу, що утворюються у цій Державі.

СТАТТЯ 11
Проценти

1. Проценти, що виникають в одній Договірній Державі і сплачуються резиденту другої Договірної Держави, можуть оподатковуватись у цій другій Державі.

2. Однак такі проценти можуть також оподатковуватись у тій Договірній Державі, в якій вони виникають, і відповідно до законодавства цієї Держави, але якщо одержувач фактично має право на проценти, податок, що стягується таким чином, не повинен перевищувати:

a) 2 відсотки від загальної суми процентів у випадку процентів, які виникають в Договірній Державі і сплачуються за будь-якими позиками будь-якого виду, що надаються банком або будь-якою іншою фінансовою установою другої Держави, включаючи інвестиційні банки та ощадні банки і страхові компанії; або

b) 10 відсотків загальної суми процентів в усіх інших випадках.

3. Незважаючи на положення пункту 2 цієї статті, проценти, що виникають в одній Договірній Державі, які сплачуються резиденту другої Договірної Держави, яка є фактичним власником процентів, повинні звільнятися від податку в першій згаданій Державі, якщо вони сплачені стосовно позики, наданої, гарантованої або застрахованої, або будь-якої іншої боргової вимоги чи кредиту, гарантованого або застрахованого від імені другої Договірної Держави уповноваженим на те органом.

4. Термін "проценти" при використанні в цій статті означає доход від боргових вимог будь-якого виду, незалежно від іпотечного забезпечення і незалежно від володіння правом на участь у прибутках боржника, і, зокрема, доход від урядових цінних паперів і доход від облігацій чи боргових вимог, включаючи премії та винагороди, що сплачуються стосовно таких цінних паперів, облігацій та боргових зобов'язань.

5. Положення пунктів 1, 2 і 3 цієї статті не застосовуються, якщо особа, що фактично має право на проценти, яка є резидентом однієї Договірної

Держави, здійснює підприємницьку діяльність у другій Договірній Державі, в якій виникають проценти, через розташоване там постійне представництво або надає в цій другій Державі незалежні особисті послуги з розташованої там постійної бази, і боргова вимога, на підставі якої сплачуються проценти, дійсно відноситься до такого постійного представництва або постійної бази. У такому випадку, залежно від обставин, застосовуються положення статті 7 або статті 14 цієї Конвенції.

6. Вважається, що проценти виникають у Договірній Державі, якщо платником є резидент цієї Держави. Якщо, проте, особа, що сплачує проценти, незалежно від того, є вона резидентом Договірної Держави чи ні, має в Договірній Державі постійне представництво або постійну базу, у зв'язку з якими виникла заборгованість, по якій сплачуються проценти, і витрати по сплаті цих процентів несе постійне представництво або постійна база, то вважається, що такі проценти виникають у Державі, в якій знаходиться постійне представництво або постійна база.

7. Якщо з причин особливих відносин між платником і особою, яка фактично має право на проценти, або між ними обома і будь-якою третьою особою, сума сплачуваних процентів, що стосується боргової вимоги, на підставі якої вона сплачується, перевищує з будь-яких причин суму, яка була б погоджена між платником і особою, яка фактично має право на одержання процентів, при відсутності таких відносин, положення цієї статті будуть застосовуватись тільки до останньої згаданої суми процентів. У такому випадку надмірна частина платежу, як і раніше, підлягає оподаткуванню відповідно до законодавства кожної Договірної Держави з належним урахуванням інших положень цієї Конвенції.

СТАТТЯ 12
Роялті

1. Роялті, які виникають в одній Договірній Державі і сплачуються резиденту другої Договірної Держави, можуть оподатковуватись у цій другій Державі.

2. Однак такі роялті можуть також оподатковуватись у Договірній Державі, в якій вони виникають, і відповідно до законодавства цієї Держави, але якщо отримувач є фактичним власником роялті, податок, що визначається таким чином, не повинен перевищувати:

а) 5 відсотків загальної суми платежів, про які йдеться в підпункті а) пункту 3;

b) 10 відсотків загальної суми платежів, про які йдеться в підпункті b) пункту 3.

3. Термін "роялті" при використанні в цій статті означає платежі будь-якого виду, що одержуються як відшкодування за:

a) користування або за надання права користування будь-яким патентом, торговою маркою, дизайном або моделлю, планом, таємною формулою або процесом, або за інформацію (ноу-хау), що стосується промислового, комерційного або наукового досвіду;

b) користування або за надання права користування будь-яким авторським правом на літературні твори, твори мистецтва або науки (включаючи кінематографічні фільми і будь-які фільми або плівки для радіомовлення чи телебачення).

4. Положення пунктів 1 і 2 цієї статті не застосовуються, якщо фактичний власник роялті, який є резидентом однієї Договірної Держави, проводить підприємницьку діяльність у другій Договірній Державі, в якій виникають роялті, через розташоване там постійне представництво, або надає в цій другій Державі незалежні особисті послуги з розташованої там постійної бази, і право або майно, стосовно яких сплачуються роялті, дійсно пов'язані з цим постійним представництвом чи постійною базою. У такому випадку застосовуються положення статті 7 або 14 цієї Конвенції, залежно від обставин.

5. Вважається, що роялті виникають у Договірній Державі, якщо платником є резидент цієї Держави. Якщо, проте, особа, що сплачує роялті, незалежно від того, є вона резидентом Договірної Держави чи ні, має у Договірній Державі постійне представництво або постійну базу, у зв'язку з якими виникло зобов'язання сплатити роялті, і витрати по сплаті цих роялті несе постійне представництво або постійна база, то вважається, що такі роялті виникають у Державі, в якій розташоване постійне представництво або постійна база.

6. Якщо з причин особливих відносин між платником і фактичним власником, або між ними обома і будь-якою третьою особою, сума роялті, яка відноситься до використання, права або інформації, на підставі яких вони сплачуються, перевищує, з будь-яких причин, суму, яка була б узгоджена між платником і фактичним власником за відсутністю таких відносин, положення цієї статті будуть застосовуватись тільки до останньої згаданої

суми. У цьому випадку надмірна частина платежу, як і раніше, підлягає оподаткуванню відповідно до законодавства кожної Договірної Держави, з належним урахуванням інших положень цієї Конвенції.

СТАТТЯ 13
Доходи від відчужування майна

1. Доходи, що одержуються резидентом Договірної Держави від відчужування нерухомого майна, як воно визначено у статті 6 цієї Конвенції і яке знаходиться у другій Договірній Державі, можуть оподатковуватись у цій другій Державі.

2. Доходи, одержувані резидентом Договірної Держави від відчужування:

a) акцій, інших ніж ті акції, що котируються на визнаній фондовій біржі, які одержують їх вартість або більшу частину вартості прямо або посередньо від нерухомого майна, розташованого в другій Договірній Державі; або

b) паїв у товаристві, активи якого складаються переважно з нерухомого майна, розташованого в другій Договірній Державі, або з акцій, як вони визначені в підпункті a) вище, можуть оподатковуватись у цій другій Державі.

3. Доходи від відчужування рухомого майна, що формує частину комерційного майна постійного представництва, яке підприємство Договірної Держави має в другій Договірній Державі, або рухомого майна, яке відноситься до постійної бази, регулярно доступної резиденту Договірної Держави в другій Договірній Державі для цілей надання незалежних особистих послуг, які включають такі доходи від відчужування такого постійного представництва (окремо чи в сукупності з цілим підприємством) або такої постійної бази, можуть оподатковуватись у цій другій Державі.

4. Доходи від відчужування морських, річкових або повітряних суден, що експлуатуються в міжнародних перевезеннях підприємством Договірної Держави, або рухомого майна, що відноситься до експлуатації таких морських, річкових або повітряних суден, оподатковуються тільки в цій Договірній Державі.

5. Доходи від відчужування будь-якого майна, іншого ніж те, про яке йдеться у пунктах 1, 2, 3 і 4 цієї статті, оподатковуються тільки в Договірній Державі, резидентом якої є особа, що відчужує майно.

СТАТТЯ 14
Незалежні особисті послуги

1. Доход, що одержується резидентом однієї Договірної Держави щодо професійних послуг чи іншої діяльності незалежного характеру, оподатковується тільки в цій Державі, за винятком випадку, коли він володіє регулярно доступною постійною базою в другій Договірній Державі з метою проведення цієї діяльності. Якщо у нього є така постійна база, доход може оподатковуватись у другій Договірній Державі, але тільки стосовно доходу, що приписується до цієї постійної бази.

2. Термін "професійні послуги" включає, зокрема, незалежну наукову, літературну, артистичну, художню, освітню або викладацьку діяльність, так само, як і незалежну діяльність лікарів, адвокатів, інженерів, архітекторів, стоматологів і бухгалтерів.

СТАТТЯ 15
Залежні особисті послуги

1. З урахуванням положень статей 16, 18, 19 і 20 цієї Конвенції платня, заробітна плата та інші подібні винагороди, одержувані резидентом Договірної Держави у зв'язку з роботою за наймом, оподатковуються тільки в цій Державі, якщо тільки робота за наймом не здійснюється в другій Договірній Державі. Якщо робота за наймом здійснюється таким чином, така винагорода, одержана у зв'язку з цим, може оподатковуватись у цій другій Державі.

2. Незалежно від положень пункту 1 цієї статті, винагорода, що одержується резидентом Договірної Держави у зв'язку з роботою за наймом, здійснюваною в другій Договірній Державі, оподатковується тільки в першій згаданій Державі, якщо:

a) одержувач перебуває в другій Державі протягом періоду або періодів, що не перевищують у сукупності 183 днів у будь-якому дванадцятимісячному періоді, що починається або закінчується в поточному календарному році; і

b) винагорода сплачується наймачем або від імені наймача, який не є резидентом другої Держави; і

c) витрати по сплаті винагород не несуть постійне представництво або постійна база, які наймач має в другій Державі.

3. Незалежно від попередніх положень цієї статті, винагорода, одержувана у зв'язку з роботою за наймом, що здійснюється на борту морського, річкового або повітряного судна, яке експлуатується в міжнародних перевезеннях, може оподатковуватись в Договірній Державі, резидентом якої є підприємство, що експлуатує морське, річкове або повітряне судно.

СТАТТЯ 16
Директорські гонорари

Директорські гонорари та інші аналогічні виплати, які одержуються резидентом однієї Договірної Держави як членом ради директорів або іншого подібного органу компанії, яка є резидентом другої Договірної Держави, можуть оподатковуватись у цій другій Державі.

СТАТТЯ 17
Артисти і спортсмени

1. Незалежно від положень статей 14 і 15 цієї Конвенції, доход, що одержується резидентом Договірної Держави як працівником мистецтв, таким як артист театру, кіно, радіо чи телебачення, або музикантом, або як спортсменом від його особистої діяльності, здійснюваної в другій Договірній Державі, може оподатковуватись у цій другій Державі.

2. Якщо доход від особистої діяльності, здійснюваної працівником мистецтв або спортсменом у цій своїй якості, нараховується не самому працівнику мистецтв чи спортсмену, а іншій особі, цей доход може, незалежно від положень статей 7, 14 і 15 цієї Конвенції, оподатковуватись у Договірній Державі, в якій здійснюється діяльність працівника мистецтв чи спортсмена.

3. Незважаючи на положення пунктів 1 і 2 цієї статті, доход, вказаний у цій статті, буде звільнений від оподаткування в тій Договірній Державі, в якій діяльність артиста або спортсмена здійснюється, якщо ця діяльність суттєвою мірою фінансується за рахунок суспільних фондів однієї або обох Договірних Держав, або якщо ця діяльність виконується на підставі угоди про культурне співробітництво, укладеної між Договірними Державами.

СТАТТЯ 18
Пенсії

1. З урахуванням положень пункту 2 статті 19 цієї Конвенції пенсії та інші подібні винагороди, що сплачуються у зв'язку з минулою роботою резиденту

Договірної Держави, будуть оподатковуватись тільки в цій Державі.

2. Незважаючи на положення пункту 1 цієї статті, пенсії та інші платежі, які здійснюються на підставі законодавства стосовно соціального забезпечення або на підставі Державної пенсійної програми Договірної Держави, підлягають оподаткуванню тільки в цій Державі.

СТАТТЯ 19
Державна служба

1. а) Винагорода інша, ніж пенсія, що сплачується Договірною Державою або її політико-адміністративним підрозділом, або місцевим органом влади будь-якій фізичній особі за службу, здійснювану для цієї Держави або її політико-адміністративного підрозділу, або місцевого органу влади, оподатковується тільки в цій Державі;

b) Незважаючи на положення підпункту а) цього пункту, така винагорода оподатковується тільки в другій Договірній Державі, якщо служба здійснюється в цій Державі, і фізична особа є резидентом цієї Держави, яка:

(і) є національною особою цієї Держави; або

(іі) не стала резидентом цієї Держави тільки з метою здійснення служби.

2. а) Будь-яка пенсія, яка сплачується Договірною Державою або її політико-адміністративним підрозділом, або місцевим органом влади, або із створених ними фондів фізичній особі за службу, здійснювану для цієї Держави або її політико-адміністративного підрозділу, або місцевого органу влади, оподатковується тільки в цій Державі.

b) Незважаючи на положення підпункту а) цього пункту, така пенсія оподатковується тільки в другій Договірній Державі, якщо фізична особа є її резидентом або національною особою.

3. Положення статей 15, 16, 17 і 18 цієї Конвенції застосовуються до винагород та пенсій стосовно служби, що здійснюється у зв'язку з проведенням підприємницької діяльності Договірною Державою або її політико-адміністративним підрозділом, або місцевим органом влади.

СТАТТЯ 20
Студенти

1. Платежі, одержувані студентом або стажувальником, які є або були безпосередньо до приїзду в одну Договірну Державу резидентами другої Договірної Держави і перебувають у першій згаданій Державі виключно з метою навчання або одержання освіти, і призначені для проживання, навчання і одержання освіти, не оподатковуються в першій згаданій Державі, якщо джерела цих платежів знаходяться за межами цієї Держави.

2. Доход, який одержується студентом або стажувальником у зв'язку з діяльністю, що виконується в Договірній Державі, в якій він перебуває виключно з метою одержання освіти чи навчання, не буде оподатковуватись у цій Державі. Це звільнення застосовується тільки протягом періоду, що не перевищує 2 років з дня їх першого прибуття до цієї Держави з метою навчання або одержання освіти.

СТАТТЯ 21
Інші доходи

1. Види доходів резидента Договірної Держави, незалежно від джерела їх виникнення, про які не йдеться мова у попередніх статтях цієї Конвенції, оподатковуються тількі в першій Державі.

2. Положення пункту 1 цієї статті не застосовуються до доходів інших, ніж доходи від нерухомого майна, визначеного в пункті 2 статті 6 цієї Конвенції, якщо одержувач таких доходів є резидентом однієї Договірної Держави, здійснює підприємницьку діяльність у другій Договірній Державі через розташоване в ній постійне представництво і надає в цій Державі незалежні особисті послуги через розташовану там постійну базу, і право або майно, у зв'язку з яким одержано доход, дійсно пов'язані з таким постійним представництвом або постійною базою. В такому випадку застосовуються положення статті 7 або статті 14 цієї Конвенції залежно від обставин.

СТАТТЯ 22
Капітал

1. Капітал, представлений нерухомим майном, про яке йдеться у статті 6 цієї Конвенції, що є власністю резидента однієї Договірної Держави та знаходиться в другій Договірній Державі, може оподатковуватись у цій другій Державі.

2. Капітал, представлений рухомим майном, що є частиною комерційного майна постійного представництва, яке підприємство однієї Договірної Держави має в другій Договірній Державі, або представлене рухомим майном, пов'язаним з постійною базою, доступною резиденту однієї Договірної Держави в другій Договірній Державі з метою надання незалежних особистих послуг, може оподатковуватись у цій другій Державі.

3. Капітал, представлений морськими, річковими та повітряними судами, що експлуатуються підприємством Договірної Держави у міжнародних перевезеннях, а також рухомим майном, пов'язаним з експлуатацією цих морських, річкових та повітряних суден, оподатковується тільки в цій Договірній Державі.

4. Усі інші елементи капітала резидента Договірної Держави оподатковуються тільки у цій Державі.

СТАТТЯ 23
Усунення подвійного оподаткування

1. З урахуванням положень законодавства України, що стосується усунення подвійного оподаткування (які не будуть суперечити головним принципам цього пункту), на люксембурзький податок, сплачуваний за законодавством Люгсембурга, та відповідно до цієї Конвенції з прибутку, доходів із джерел в Люксембурзі або капітала, що підлягає оподаткуванню, який знаходиться в Люксембурзі, буде робитись знижка у вигляді кредиту проти будь-якого українського податку, обчислюваного стосовно того ж прибутку, доходу або капіталу, стосовно яких сплачується люксембурзький податок.

2. З урахуванням положень законодавства Люксембурга, що стосується усунення подвійного оподаткування (які не будуть суперечити головним принципам цього пункту), в Люксембурзі подвійне оподаткування усувається таким чином:

a) якщо резидент Люксембургу одержує доход або володіє капіталом, які згідно з положеннями цієї Конвенції можуть оподатковуватись в Україні, то Люксембург з урахуванням положень підпунктів b) і c) звільняє цей доход або капітал від оподаткування.

b) якщо резидент Люксембургу одержує доход, який згідно з положеннями статей 10, 11 і 12 цієї Конвенції можуть оподатковуватись в Україні, то Люксембург дозволяє вирахування з податку на доход цього резидента суми, що дорівнює податку, сплаченому в Україні.

c) якщо компанія, що є резидентом Люксембурга, отримує дивиденди із джерел в Україні, то Люксембург звільняє такі дивиденди від податку за умови, що ця компанія, що є резидентом Люксембурга, з початку її звітного року є безпосереднім власником хоча б 10 відсотків капиталу компанії, що сплачує дивіденди, і якщо ця компанія підлягає в Україні оподаткуванню на доход, що є відповідним до люксембургського корпоративного податку. Вищезгадані акції української компанії належать на тих же умовах звільненню від люксембурзького податку на капітал.

3. Вирахування, що надаються в Договірній Державі на підставі пункту 1 або підпункту b) пункту 2 цієї статті в будь-якому випадку не повинні перевищувати тієї частини податку з доходу або капіталу, як було підраховано до надання вирахування, яка стосується доходу або капіталу, залежно від обставин, які можуть оподатковуватись у цій другій Державі.

4. Якщо відповідно до будь-якого положення Конвенції одержуваний доход або капітал резидента Договірної Держави звільнено від податку в цій Державі, ця Держава може, незважаючи на це, при підрахунку суми оподаткування на частину доходу або капіталу цього резидента, що залишилась, взяти до уваги звільнений доход або капітал.

5. Для цілей пунктів 1 і 2 цієї статті прибуток, доход і приріст вартості нерухомого майна, що належать резиденту Договірної Держави, які можуть оподатковуватись у другій Договірній Державі відповідно до цієї Конвенції, будуть вважатись такими, що виникають із джерел у цій другій Договірній Державі.

СТАТТЯ 24
Недискримінація

1. Національні особи однієї Договірної Держави не будуть підлягати у другій Договірній Державі будь-якому оподаткуванню або пов'язаному з ним зобов'язанню, яке є іншим або більш обтяжливим ніж оподаткування і пов'язане з ним зобов'язання, яким піддаються або можуть піддаватися національні особи цієї другої Держави за тих же обставин, зокрема, з точки зору резиденції. Це положення також застосовується, незважаючи на положення статті 1 цієї Конвенції, до фізичних осіб, які не є резидентами однієї або обох Договірних Держав.

2. Особи без громадянства, які є резидентами Договірної Держави, не будуть піддаватися в жодній з Договірних Держав будь-якому оподаткуванню або пов'язаному з ним зобов'язанню, іншому або більш обтяжливому, ніж оподаткування і пов'язані з ним зобов'язання, яким національні особи Держави, що відносяться до них, піддаються або можуть піддаватися за тих же умов.

3. Оподаткування постійного представництва, яке підприємство Договірної Держави має в другій Договірній Державі, не буде менш сприятливим у цій другій Державі, ніж оподаткування підприємств цієї другої Держави, які здійснюють подібну діяльність у цій другій Державі.

4. За винятком випадків, коли застосовуються положення пункту 1 статті 9, пункту 7 статті 11 або пункту 6 статті 12 цієї Конвенції, проценти, роялті та інші виплати, що сплачуються підприємством Договірної Держави резиденту другої Договірної Держави, з метою визначення оподатковуваного прибутку такого підприємства будуть обчислюватись за таких же умов, за яких вони сплачувались резиденту першої згаданої Держави. Таким же чином будь-які борги підприємства однієї Договірної Держави резиденту другої Договірної Держави повинні, з метою визначення оподатковуваного майна цього підприємства, підлягати вирахуванням за таких же умов, що й борги резидента першої згаданої Держави.

5. Підприємства Договірної Держави, капітал яких повністю або частково належить або контролюється прямо чи посередньо одним або кількома резидентами другої Договірної Держави, не будуть піддаватися в першій згаданій Державі будь-якому оподаткуванню або пов'язаному з ним зобов'язанню, яке є іншим або більш обтяжливим ніж оподаткування і пов'язані з ним зобов'язання, яким піддаються або можуть піддаватися інші подібні підприємства першої згаданої Держави.

6. Ніякі положення цієї статті не будуть мати тлумачення як зобов'язання будь-якої з Договірних Держав надавати фізичній особі, що не є резидентом цієї Держави, будь-яких персональних звільнень, пільг і вирахувань для податкових цілей на підставі громадянського статусу або сімейних зобов'язань, які надаються її власним резидентам, або будь-яких персональних звільнень, пільг і вирахувань для податкових цілей, які надаються фізичним особам, які є такими резидентами на підставі критеріїв, не передбачених загальним податковим законодавством.

7. Положення цієї статті будуть застосовуватись до податків, які розглядаються цією Конвенцією.

СТАТТЯ 25
Процедура взаємного узгодження

1. Якщо резидент Договірної Держави вважає, що дії однієї або обох Договірних Держав призводять або призведуть до його оподаткування не відповідно до положень цієї Конвенції, він може, незалежно від засобів захисту, передбачених національним законодавством цих Держав, подати свій випадок до компетентних органів Договірної Держави, резидентом якої він є, або, якщо його випадок підпадає під дію пункту 1 статті 24 цієї Конвенції, тієї Договірної Держави, національною особою якої він є. Заява повинна бути подана протягом трьох років з моменту першого повідомлення про дії, що призводять до оподаткування не у відповідності до положень Конвенції.

2. Компетентний орган прагнутиме, якщо він буде вважати заперечення обгрунтованим і якщо він сам не в змозі дійти до задовільного рішення, вирішити випадок за взаємною згодою з компетентним органом другої Договірної Держави з метою уникнення оподаткування, невідповідного Конвенції. Будь-яка досягнута домовленість повинна виконуватись незалежно від будь-яких обмежень часу, передбачених внутрішнім законодавством Договірних Держав.

3. Компетентні органи Договірних Держав будуть прагнути вирішити за взаємною згодою будь-які труднощі або сумніви, що виникають при тлумаченні або застосуванні Конвенції.

4. Компетентні органи Договірних Держав можуть вступати в прямі контакти один з одним з метою досягнення згоди в розумінні попередніх пунктів.

СТАТТЯ 26
Обмін інформацією

1. Компетентні органи Договірних Держав обмінюються інформацією, необхідною для виконання положень цієї Конвенції або національних законодавств Договірних Держав, що стосуються податків, на які поширюється Конвенція, тією мірою, в якій оподаткування не суперечить цій

Конвенції, зокрема, щоб попереджувати ухилення від сплати податків і полегшувати застосування встановлених законом положень проти легальних ухилень. Обмін інформацією не обмежується статею 1 цієї Конвенції. Будь-яка інформація, одержана Договірною Державою, буде розглядатися як конфіденційна таким же чином як і інформація, одержана в рамках внутрішнього законодавства цієї Держави, і буде розкрита тільки особам або органам влади (включаючи суди і адміністративні органи), зайнятим оцінкою або збором, примусовим стягненням або судовим переслідуванням, або розглядом апеляцій стосовно податків, на які поширюється ця Конвенція. Такі особи або органи будуть використовувати інформацію тільки з цією метою. Вони можуть розкривати цю інформацію на публічних судових засіданнях і при прийнятті судових рішень.
Компетентні органи шляхом консультацій будуть розвивати відповідні умови, методи та техніку, що стосуються справ, щодо яких такий обмін інформацією може бути зроблений, включаючи, якщо необхідно, обмін інформацією, яка стосується податкових ухилень.

2. В жодному випадку положення пункту 1 цієї статті не будуть тлумачитись як такі, що покладають на компетентні органи однієї з Договірних Держав зобов'язання:

a) здійснювати адміністративні заходи, такі, що відрізняються від законів адміністративної практики, яка має перевагу в одній з Договірних Держав;

b) надавати інформацію, яку неможливо одержати за законодавством або в ході звичайного управління в одній з Договірних Держав;

c) надавати інформацію, яка буде розкривати будь-яку торговельну, підприємницьку, промислову, комерційну або професійну таємницю або торговельний процес, або інформацію, розкриття якої суперечило б установленій практиці.

СТАТТЯ 27
Члени дипломатичних або постійних місій і консульських установ

Ніщо в цій Конвенції не буде зачіпати податкових привілеїв, наданих членам дипломатичних або постійних місій або консульських установ за загальними нормами міжнародного права або на підставі спеціальних угод.

СТАТТЯ 28
Виключення деяких компаній

Ця Конвенція не застосовується до холдингових компаній в рамках значення спеціальних законів Люксембургу, існуючого Закону від 31 липня 1929 року та Декрету від 17 грудня 1938 року. Таким же чином вона не буде застосовуватись до доходу, отриманого від таких компаній резидентом України і до акцій або інших прав такої особи в таких компаніях.

СТАТТЯ 29
Набуття чинності

Кожна із Договірних Держав повідомлять одна одну по дипломатичних каналах про завершення необхідної відповідно до внутрішнього законодавства процедури набуття чинності цією Конвенцією. Ця Конвенція набуває чинності в день останнього такого повідомлення, і її положення будуть застосовуватись:

a) стосовно податків, утриманих у джерела щодо доходів, які отримані на або після першого січня календарного року, наступного за роком набуття Конвенцією чинності; та

b) стосовно інших податків на доходи та податків на капітал, щодо податків які стягуються за будь-який податковий рік, що починається на або після першого січня календарного року, наступного за роком набуття Конвенцією чинності.

СТАТТЯ 30
Завершення чинності

Ця Конвенція буде залишатися чинною до припинення її дії однією з Договірних Держав. Кожна Договірна Держава може припинити дію Конвенції шляхом передачі через дипломатичні канали повідомлення про припинення дії принаймні за шість місяців до закінчення будь-якого календарного року, що починається після закінчення п'яти років після дня набуття чинності Конвенцією.

У такому випадку чинність Конвенції буде припинено:

a) стосовно податків, утриманих у джерела щодо доходів, які отримані на або після першого січня календарного року, наступного за роком подачі

b) стосовно інших податків щодо податків на доходи та податків на капітал, які стягуються за будь-який податковий рік, що починається на або після першого січня календарного року, наступного за роком подачі повідомлення.

У засвідчення чого ті, що нижче підписалися, відповідним чином на те уповноважені, підписали цю Конвенцію.

Вчинено в м.Києві, 6 вересня 1997 року в двох примірниках кожний французькою, українською та англійською мовами, при цьому всі тексти є автентичні.

За Уряд
Великого Герцогства Люксембург

За Уряд
України

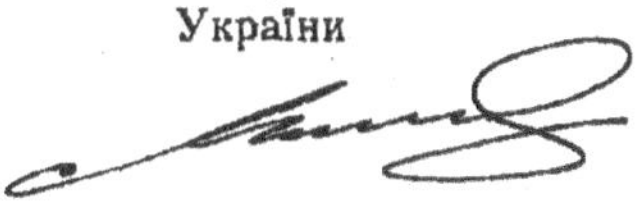

No. 54783

Mexico
and
Argentina

Agreement between the United Mexican States and the Argentine Republic for the avoidance of double taxation and the prevention of fiscal evasion with respect to taxes on income and on capital (with protocol). Mexico City, 4 November 2015

Entry into force: *23 August 2017, in accordance with article 30*

Authentic text: *Spanish*

Registration with the Secretariat of the United Nations: *Mexico, 22 November 2017*

Mexique
et
Argentine

Accord entre les États-Unis du Mexique et la République argentine tendant à éviter les doubles impositions et à prévenir la fraude fiscale en matière d'impôts sur le revenu et sur la fortune (avec protocole). Mexico, 4 novembre 2015

Entrée en vigueur : *23 août 2017, conformément à l'article 30*

Texte authentique : *espagnol*

Enregistrement au Secrétariat de l'Organisation des Nations Unies : *Mexique, 22 novembre 2017*

[TEXT IN SPANISH – TEXTE EN ESPAGNOL]

ACUERDO ENTRE LOS ESTADOS UNIDOS MEXICANOS Y LA REPÚBLICA ARGENTINA PARA EVITAR LA DOBLE IMPOSICIÓN Y PREVENIR LA EVASIÓN FISCAL CON RESPECTO A LOS IMPUESTOS SOBRE LA RENTA Y SOBRE EL PATRIMONIO

Los Estados Unidos Mexicanos y la República Argentina, con el objeto de promover el desarrollo de sus relaciones económicas y la cooperación en materia fiscal, y deseosos de concluir un Acuerdo para evitar la doble imposición y prevenir la evasión fiscal con respecto a los impuestos sobre la renta y el patrimonio, sin crear oportunidades para la no imposición o imposición reducida a través de la evasión o elusión fiscal (incluyendo a través de acuerdos para el uso abusivo de tratados cuyo objetivo es extender indirectamente los beneficios previstos en este Acuerdo a residentes de terceros Estados), han acordado lo siguiente:

ÁMBITO DE APLICACIÓN DEL ACUERDO

ARTÍCULO 1
PERSONAS COMPRENDIDAS

El presente Acuerdo se aplica a las personas residentes de uno o de ambos Estados Contratantes.

ARTÍCULO 2
IMPUESTOS COMPRENDIDOS

1. El presente Acuerdo se aplica a los impuestos sobre la renta y sobre el patrimonio, exigibles por cada Estado Contratante, cualquiera que fuera el sistema de recaudación.

2. Se consideran impuestos sobre la renta y sobre el patrimonio los impuestos que gravan la renta total, o el patrimonio total, o cualquier parte de los mismos, incluidos los impuestos sobre las ganancias provenientes de la enajenación de bienes muebles e inmuebles, así como los impuestos sobre las plusvalías.

3. Los impuestos actuales a los cuales se aplica el presente Acuerdo son, en particular:

a) en el caso de Argentina:

4. No obstante las disposiciones precedentes en este Artículo se considera que el término "establecimiento permanente" no incluye:

a) la utilización de instalaciones con el único fin de almacenar o exponer bienes o mercancías pertenecientes a la empresa;

b) el mantenimiento de un depósito de bienes o mercancías pertenecientes a la empresa con el único fin de almacenarlas o exponerlas;

c) el mantenimiento de un depósito de bienes o mercancías pertenecientes a la empresa con el único fin de que sean transformadas por otra empresa;

d) el mantenimiento de un lugar fijo de negocios con el único fin de comprar bienes o mercancías o de recoger información para la empresa;

e) el mantenimiento de un lugar fijo de negocios con el único fin de realizar para la empresa cualquier otra actividad de carácter preparatorio o auxiliar;

f) el mantenimiento de un lugar fijo de negocios con el único fin de realizar cualquier combinación de las actividades mencionadas en los subapartados a) a e), a condición de que el conjunto de la actividad del lugar fijo de negocios que resulte de esa combinación conserve su carácter auxiliar o preparatorio.

5. No obstante lo dispuesto en los apartados 1 y 2, cuando una persona distinta de un agente independiente, al que será aplicable el apartado 7, actúe en un Estado Contratante por cuenta de una empresa del otro Estado Contratante, se considerará que dicha empresa tiene un establecimiento permanente en el Estado Contratante mencionado en primer lugar, con relación a cualquier actividad que esa persona realice para la empresa, si dicha persona:

a) posee y habitualmente ejerce en dicho Estado poderes que la faculten para concluir contratos en nombre de la empresa, a menos que las actividades de esta persona se limiten a las mencionadas en el apartado 4 que, de haber sido realizadas por medio de un lugar fijo de negocios, no se hubiera considerado ese lugar fijo de negocios como un establecimiento permanente de acuerdo con las disposiciones de ese apartado; o

b) no posee tales poderes, pero mantiene habitualmente en el Estado Contratante mencionado en primer lugar un depósito de bienes o mercancías desde el cual regularmente entrega bienes o mercancías por cuenta de la empresa.

6. No obstante las disposiciones anteriores del presente Artículo, se considera que una empresa aseguradora de un Estado Contratante tiene un establecimiento permanente en el otro Estado Contratante si recauda primas en el territorio de ese otro Estado o si asegura contra riesgos situados en él por medio de una persona distinta de un agente independiente al cual se le aplica el apartado 7 del presente Artículo.

7. No se considera que una empresa tiene un establecimiento permanente en un Estado Contratante por el mero hecho de que realice sus actividades en ese Estado por medio de un corredor, un comisionista general, o cualquier otro agente independiente, siempre que dichas personas actúen dentro del marco ordinario de su actividad y en sus relaciones comerciales o financieras con la empresa, las condiciones no difieren de aquellas generalmente acordadas por agentes independientes. No obstante, cuando las actividades de dicho agente sean ejercidas total o principalmente para dicha empresa, la persona no será considerada un agente independiente de acuerdo con las disposiciones de este apartado.

8. El hecho de que una sociedad residente de un Estado Contratante controle o sea controlada por una sociedad que es residente del otro Estado Contratante, o que realiza actividades empresariales en ese otro Estado (ya sea por medio de un establecimiento permanente o de otra forma) no convierte por sí solo a cualquiera de estas sociedades en un establecimiento permanente de la otra.

IMPOSICIÓN DE LA RENTA

ARTÍCULO 6
RENTAS DE LA PROPIEDAD INMUEBLE

1. Las rentas que un residente de un Estado Contratante obtenga de bienes inmuebles (incluidas las rentas de explotaciones agrícolas, pecuarias o forestales) situados en el otro Estado Contratante pueden someterse a imposición en ese otro Estado.

2. La expresión "bienes inmuebles" tendrá el significado que le atribuya la legislación del Estado Contratante en que los bienes en cuestion estén situados. Dicha expresión comprende, asimismo, los bienes accesorios a los bienes

inmuebles, el ganado y el equipo utilizado en las explotaciones agrícolas, pecuarias y forestales, los derechos a los que se apliquen las disposiciones del derecho privado relativas a los bienes raíces, el usufructo de bienes inmuebles y el derecho a percibir pagos variables o fijos por la explotación, o la concesión de la explotación, de yacimientos minerales, fuentes y otros recursos naturales; los buques, embarcaciones y aeronaves no se considerarán bienes inmuebles.

3. Las disposiciones del apartado 1 se aplicarán a las rentas derivadas de la utilización directa, del arrendamiento o aparcería, así como de cualquier otra forma de explotación de los bienes inmuebles.

4. Las disposiciones de los apartados 1 y 3 se aplicarán igualmente a las rentas derivadas de los bienes inmuebles de una empresa y de los bienes inmuebles utilizados para la prestación de servicios personales independientes.

ARTÍCULO 7
BENEFICIOS EMPRESARIALES

1. Los beneficios de una empresa de un Estado Contratante solamente pueden someterse a imposición en ese Estado, a no ser que la empresa realice su actividad en el otro Estado Contratante por medio de un establecimiento permanente situado en él. Si la empresa realiza o ha realizado su actividad de dicha manera, los beneficios de la empresa pueden someterse a imposición en el otro Estado, pero sólo en la medida en que sean atribuibles a ese establecimiento permanente. A tales efectos, serán atribuibles al establecimiento permanente los beneficios de la empresa provenientes de:

a) las ventas o actividades realizadas por el propio establecimiento permanente;

b) las ventas en ese otro Estado de bienes o mercancías de tipo idéntico o similar al de las vendidas por medio de ese establecimiento permanente; o

c) otras actividades empresariales llevadas a cabo en ese otro Estado de naturaleza idéntica o similar a las efectuadas por medio del citado establecimiento permanente.

Sin embargo, los beneficios obtenidos de las actividades descritas en los incisos b) y c) no serán sometidos a imposición en el otro Estado Contratante si la empresa demuestra que dichas actividades han sido realizadas por razones distintas a las de obtener un beneficio del presente Acuerdo.

2. Sin perjuicio de las disposiciones del apartado 3, cuando una empresa de un Estado Contratante realice su actividad en el otro Estado Contratante por medio de un establecimiento permanente situado en él, en cada Estado Contratante se atribuirán al establecimiento permanente los beneficios que el mismo hubiera podido obtener de ser una empresa distinta y separada que realizase las mismas o similares actividades, en las mismas o similares condiciones, y tratase con total independencia con la empresa de la que es establecimiento permanente.

3. Para la determinación de los beneficios del establecimiento permanente se permitirá la deducción de los gastos realizados para los fines del establecimiento permanente, comprendidos los gastos de dirección y generales de administración para los mismos fines, tanto si se efectúan en el Estado en que se encuentra el establecimiento permanente como en otra parte. A tal fin, sólo se tendrán en cuenta los gastos que resultan deducibles por el establecimiento permanente de conformidad con las disposiciones de la legislación impositiva del Estado Contratante en el cual el establecimiento permanente está situado.

4. En el caso en que un establecimiento permanente participe de manera importante y activa en la negociación y conclusión de contratos celebrados por la empresa, no obstante que otras partes de la empresa también hayan participado en esas operaciones, se atribuirá al establecimiento permanente aquella proporción de los beneficios de la empresa originados por dichos contratos que representen la contribución efectuada por el establecimiento permanente a las transacciones de la empresa en su conjunto.

5. No obstante lo establecido en el apartado 2, no se atribuirá ningún beneficio a un establecimiento permanente por el mero hecho de que este establecimiento permanente compre bienes o mercancías para la empresa.

6. A los efectos de los apartados anteriores, los beneficios atribuibles a un establecimiento permanente se calcularán cada año por el mismo método, a no ser que existan motivos válidos y suficientes para proceder de otra forma.

7. Cuando los beneficios comprendan rentas reguladas separadamente en otros Artículos del presente Acuerdo, las disposiciones de aquéllos no quedarán afectadas por las del presente Artículo.

ARTÍCULO 8
TRANSPORTE INTERNACIONAL

1. Los beneficios obtenidos por una empresa de un Estado Contratante procedentes de la explotación de buques o aeronaves en el transporte internacional sólo podrán someterse a imposición en ese Estado.

2. A los efectos del presente Artículo, los beneficios provenientes de la operación de buques o aeronaves en el transporte internacional comprenden:

a) la renta proveniente del alquiler o arrendamiento de buques o aeronaves a casco desnudo; y

b) los beneficios provenientes del uso o alquiler de contenedores (incluidos los remolques y equipos vinculados para el transporte de contenedores) usados para el transporte de bienes o mercancías;

cuando dicho alquiler o dicho uso, según se trate del inciso a) o del inciso b), es incidental a la operación de buques o aeronaves en el transporte internacional.

3. Cuando los beneficios incluidos dentro de los apartados 1 y 2 del presente Artículo son obtenidos por un residente de un Estado Contratante proveniente de su participación en un consorcio ("*pool*"), en una explotación en común o en una agencia internacional de explotación, los beneficios atribuibles a ese residente serán solamente sometidos a imposición en el Estado Contratante en el cual el mismo reside.

ARTÍCULO 9
EMPRESAS ASOCIADAS

1. Cuando:

a) una empresa de un Estado Contratante participe, directa o indirectamente, en la dirección, el control o el capital de una empresa del otro Estado Contratante; o

b) unas mismas personas participen, directa o indirectamente, en la dirección, el control o el capital de una empresa de un Estado Contratante y de una empresa del otro Estado Contratante,

y en uno y otro caso las dos empresas estén, en sus relaciones comerciales o financieras unidas por condiciones aceptadas o impuestas que difieran de las que serían acordadas por empresas independientes, los beneficios que habrían sido obtenidos por una de las empresas de no existir dichas condiciones, pero que de hecho no se han realizado a causa de las mismas, podrán incluirse en los beneficios de esa empresa y someterse a imposición en consecuencia.

2. Cuando un Estado Contratante incluya en los beneficios de una empresa de ese Estado —y someta, en consecuencia, a imposición— los beneficios sobre los cuales una empresa del otro Estado Contratante ha sido sometida a imposición en ese otro Estado, y los beneficios así incluidos son beneficios que habrían sido realizados por la empresa del Estado mencionado en primer lugar si las condiciones convenidas entre las dos empresas hubieran sido las que se hubiesen convenido entre empresas independientes, ese otro Estado practicará el ajuste correspondiente de la cuantía del impuesto que ha percibido sobre esos beneficios. Para determinar dicho ajuste se tendrán debidamente en cuenta las demás disposiciones del presente Acuerdo y las Autoridades Competentes de los Estados Contratantes se consultarán mutuamente, si fuese necesario.

3. Las disposiciones del apartado 2 no se aplicarán en el caso que un procedimiento judicial o administrativo, u otro procedimiento legal, haya resultado en una sentencia firme en virtud de la cual, por acciones que hayan originado un ajuste de beneficios de conformidad con el apartado 1, una de las empresas involucradas sea sujeto de sanciones por fraude, negligencia u omisión culposa.

ARTÍCULO 10
DIVIDENDOS

1. Los dividendos pagados por una sociedad residente de un Estado Contratante a un residente del otro Estado Contratante pueden someterse a imposición en ese otro Estado.

2. Sin embargo, dichos dividendos podrán ser gravados en el Estado Contratante en el que resida la sociedad que paga los dividendos y de conformidad con las leyes de dicho Estado, pero si el beneficiario efectivo de los dividendos es un residente del otro Estado Contratante, el impuesto así exigido no podrá exceder del:

a) 10 por ciento del importe bruto de los dividendos si el beneficiario efectivo es una sociedad que tenga la propiedad de por lo menos el 25 por ciento del capital de la sociedad que paga los dividendos; o

b) 15 por ciento del importe bruto de los dividendos en todos los demás casos.

Las disposiciones del presente apartado no afectan la imposición de la sociedad respecto de los beneficios con cargo a los cuales se paguen los dividendos.

3. El término "dividendos" empleado en el presente Artículo significa los rendimientos de las acciones, acciones de goce o derechos de goce, de las partes de minas, de las partes de fundador u otros derechos, excepto los de crédito, que permitan participar en los beneficios, así como los ingresos de otras participaciones sociales y otros ingresos asimilables sujetos al mismo tratamiento fiscal que los rendimientos de las acciones por la legislación del Estado en que resida la sociedad que los distribuya.

4. Las disposiciones de los apartados 1 y 2 no se aplicarán si el beneficiario efectivo de los dividendos, residente de un Estado Contratante, realiza una actividad empresarial en el otro Estado Contratante, del que es residente la sociedad que paga los dividendos, por medio de un establecimiento permanente allí situado, o presta en ese otro Estado servicios personales independientes por medio de una base fija allí situada, y la participación que genera los dividendos está efectivamente vinculada con dicho establecimiento permanente o base fija. En tal caso, serán aplicables las disposiciones del Artículo 7 ó del Artículo 14, según corresponda.

5. Cuando una sociedad residente de un Estado Contratante obtenga beneficios o rentas procedentes del otro Estado Contratante, ese otro Estado no podrá exigir ningún impuesto sobre los dividendos pagados por la sociedad, salvo en la medida en que esos dividendos sean pagados a un residente de ese otro Estado o la participación que genera los dividendos esté vinculada efectivamente a un establecimiento permanente o a una base fija situados en ese otro Estado, ni someter los beneficios no distribuidos de la sociedad a un impuesto sobre los mismos, aunque los dividendos pagados o los beneficios no distribuidos consistan, total o parcialmente, en beneficios o rentas procedentes de ese otro Estado.

6. No obstante lo señalado en otra disposición del presente Acuerdo, cuando una sociedad que sea residente de un Estado Contratante tenga un establecimiento permanente en el otro Estado Contratante, los beneficios que se sometan a imposición conforme al apartado 1 del Artículo 7, podrán estar sujetos a una retención de impuestos adicional en el otro Estado, de conformidad con su legislación fiscal, cuando los beneficios se remitan a la oficina central, pero la retención no excederá del 10 por ciento del monto de dichos beneficios, después de deducir de los mismos el impuesto corporativo gravado en ese otro Estado.

ARTÍCULO 11
INTERESES

1. Los intereses procedentes de un Estado Contratante y pagados a un residente del otro Estado Contratante podrán someterse a imposición en ese otro Estado.

2. Sin embargo, dichos intereses pueden someterse a imposición también en el Estado Contratante del que procedan y de conformidad con las leyes de ese Estado, pero si el beneficiario efectivo de los intereses es residente del otro Estado Contratante, el impuesto así exigido no puede exceder del 12 por ciento.

3. No obstante las disposiciones del apartado 2, los intereses mencionados en el apartado 1 solo pueden someterse a imposición en el Estado Contratante del que es residente el beneficiario efectivo de los intereses, si:

a) el beneficiario efectivo es uno de los Estados Contratantes, una subdivisión política o una entidad local del mismo, o el Banco Central de un Estado Contratante;

b) los intereses son pagados por cualquiera de las entidades mencionadas en el inciso a);

c) los intereses proceden de Argentina y son pagados respecto de un préstamo por un periodo no menor a tres (3) años otorgado por el Banco Nacional de Comercio Exterior, S. N. C., Nacional Financiera, S. N. C., o el Banco Nacional de Obras y Servicios Públicos, S. N. C., o por cualquier otra institución acordada por las Autoridades Competentes de los Estados Contratantes; o

d) los intereses proceden de México y son pagados respecto de un préstamo por un periodo no menor a tres (3) años, otorgado por el Banco de la Nación Argentina y el Banco de Inversión y Comercio Exterior, o por cualquier otra institución acordada por las Autoridades Competentes de los Estados Contratantes.

4. El término "intereses" empleado en el presente Artículo significa los rendimientos de créditos de cualquier naturaleza, con o sin garantías hipotecarias o cláusula de participación en los beneficios del deudor y, especialmente, las rentas de fondos públicos y bonos u obligaciones, incluidas las primas y premios unidos a estos títulos, así como cualquier otra renta que se asimile a los rendimientos de las cantidades dadas en préstamo bajo la legislación del Estado Contratante de donde procedan las rentas. El término "intereses" no incluye a los ingresos considerados como dividendos de conformidad con el apartado 3 del Artículo 10.

5. Las disposiciones de los apartados 1, 2 y 3 no serán aplicables si el beneficiario efectivo de los intereses, residente de un Estado Contratante, realiza en el otro Estado Contratante, del que proceden los intereses, una actividad empresarial por medio de un establecimiento permanente situado allí o presta servicios personales independientes en ese otro Estado por medio de una base fija

situada allí, y el crédito que genera los intereses está vinculado efectivamente con: (a) dicho establecimiento permanente o base fija, o con (b) actividades empresariales a que se refiere el inciso (c) del apartado 1 del Artículo 7. En tal caso, se aplicarán las disposiciones del Artículo 7 ó del Artículo 14, según corresponda.

6. Los intereses se considerarán procedentes de un Estado Contratante cuando el deudor sea un residente de ese Estado. Sin embargo, cuando el deudor de los intereses, sea o no residente de un Estado Contratante, tenga en un Estado Contratante un establecimiento permanente o una base fija en relación con los cuales se haya contraído la deuda por la que se pagan los intereses, y dicho establecimiento o base fija soporta la carga de los mismos, dichos intereses se considerarán procedentes del Estado Contratante donde estén situados el establecimiento permanente o la base fija.

ARTÍCULO 12
REGALÍAS

1. Las regalías procedentes de un Estado Contratante y pagadas a un residente del otro Estado Contratante pueden someterse a imposición en este otro Estado.

2. Sin embargo, dichas regalías también pueden someterse a imposición en el Estado Contratante del que procedan y de conformidad con la legislación de ese Estado, pero si el beneficiario efectivo de las regalías es residente del otro Estado Contratante, el impuesto así exigido no podrá exceder del:

a) 10 por ciento del importe bruto pagado por el uso o la concesión del uso de derechos de autor sobre obras literarias, teatrales, musicales, artísticas o científicas; del importe bruto pagado por el uso o la concesión del uso de patentes, diseños y modelos, planos, fórmulas o procedimientos secretos, de programas de computadora, de equipos comerciales, industriales o científicos, o por informaciones relativas a experiencias industriales, comerciales o científicas, así como por la prestación de servicios de asistencia técnica; o

b) 15 por ciento del importe bruto de las regalías en los demás casos.

No obstante lo dispuesto en el Artículo 13, el término "regalías" también incluye las ganancias obtenidas por la enajenación de cualquiera de dichos derechos o bienes que estén condicionados a la productividad, uso o posterior disposicion de los mismos.

3. El término "regalías" empleado en el presente Artículo significa las cantidades de cualquier clase pagadas por el uso o la concesión de uso de un derecho de autor sobre una obra literaria, musical, teatral, artística o científica, programas de computación, patentes, marcas de fábrica o de comercio, diseño o modelo, plano, fórmula o procedimientos secretos o por cualquier otra propiedad intangible o por el uso o el derecho al uso de equipos industriales, comerciales o científicos, o por la información relacionada con experiencias industriales, comerciales o científicas e incluye los pagos por la prestación de asistencia técnica y pagos de cualquier clase con respecto a películas cinematográficas y obras de cine, o bandas magnetofónicas, u otros medios de reproducción en relación con emisiones de televisión.

4. Las disposiciones de los apartados 1 y 2 no se aplicarán si el beneficiario efectivo de las regalías, residente de un Estado Contratante, realiza en el otro Estado Contratante del que procedan las regalías una actividad empresarial por medio de un establecimiento permanente allí situado, o presta en ese otro Estado servicios personales independientes a través de una base fija situada allí, y el derecho o bien por el que se pagan las regalías están vinculados efectivamente con: (a) dicho establecimiento permanente o base fija, o con (b) actividades empresariales a que se refiere el inciso (c) del apartado 1 del Artículo 7. En tal caso, se aplicarán las disposiciones del Artículo 7 ó del Artículo 14, según corresponda.

5. Las regalías se considerarán procedentes de un Estado Contratante cuando el deudor sea un residente de ese Estado. Sin embargo, cuando el deudor de las regalías sea o no residente de un Estado Contratante, tenga en uno de los Estados Contratantes un establecimiento permanente o una base fija en relación con los cuales se haya contraído la obligación del pago de las regalías, y dicho establecimiento permanente o base fija soporte la carga de las mismas, tales regalías se considerarán procedentes del Estado donde estén situados el establecimiento permanente o la base fija.

ARTÍCULO 13
GANANCIAS DE CAPITAL

1. Las ganancias que un residente de un Estado Contratante obtenga de la enajenación de bienes inmuebles, a los que se refiere el Artículo 6, y situados en el otro Estado Contratante, pueden someterse a imposición en este Estado.

2. Las ganancias derivadas de la enajenación de bienes muebles que forman parte del activo de un establecimiento permanente que una empresa de un Estado Contratante tenga en el otro Estado Contratante, o de bienes muebles que pertenezcan a una base fija que un residente de un Estado Contratante tenga en el

otro Estado Contratante para la prestación de servicios personales independientes, comprendidas las ganancias derivadas de la enajenación de este establecimiento permanente (solo o con el conjunto de la empresa) o de esta base fija, pueden someterse a imposición en este otro Estado.

3. Las ganancias derivadas de la enajenación de buques o aeronaves explotados en el transporte internacional, o de bienes muebles afectados al giro específico de la explotación de tales buques o aeronaves, sólo podrán someterse a imposición en el Estado Contratante donde esté situada la sede de dirección efectiva de la empresa.

4. Las ganancias que un residente de un Estado Contratante obtenga de la enajenación de acciones o de otros derechos de participación cuyo valor se derive directa o indirectamente en más de un 50 por ciento de bienes inmuebles situados en el otro Estado Contratante, pueden someterse a imposición en ese otro Estado.

5. Las ganancias derivadas de la enajenación de acciones o participaciones en el capital o el patrimonio de una sociedad residente de un Estado Contratante, distintas de las mencionadas en el apartado 4 del presente Artículo, pueden someterse a imposición en este Estado. Sin embargo, el impuesto así exigido no podrá exceder del:

a) 10 por ciento de la ganancia cuando se trate de una participación directa en el capital de al menos el 25 por ciento;

b) 15 por ciento de la ganancia en los demás casos.

6. Las ganancias derivadas de la enajenación de cualquier otro bien distinto de los mencionados en los apartados precedentes pueden someterse a imposición solo en el Estado Contratante en que resida quien enajena.

ARTÍCULO 14
SERVICIOS PERSONALES INDEPENDIENTES

1. Las rentas obtenidas por un residente de un Estado Contratante por la prestación de servicios profesionales o el ejercicio de otras actividades de carácter independiente solo podrán someterse a imposición en ese Estado excepto en las siguientes circunstancias, en que esas rentas podrán ser gravadas también en el otro Estado Contratante:

a) si dicho residente tiene en el otro Estado Contratante una base fija de la que disponga regularmente para el desempeño de sus actividades; en tal caso, solo podrá gravarse en ese otro Estado Contratante la parte de las rentas que sea atribuible a dicha base fija; o

b) si su estancia en el otro Estado Contratante es por un periodo o periodos que sumen o excedan en total ciento ochenta y tres (183) días en todo periodo de doce (12) meses que empiece o termine durante el año fiscal considerado; en tal caso, solo podrá gravarse en ese otro Estado la parte de la renta obtenida de las actividades desempeñadas por él en ese otro Estado.

2. La expresión "servicios profesionales" comprende especialmente las actividades, científicas, literarias, artísticas, de educación o enseñanza independientes, así como las actividades independientes de los médicos, abogados, ingenieros, arquitectos, odontólogos y contadores.

ARTÍCULO 15
SERVICIOS PERSONALES DEPENDIENTES

1. Sujeto a las disposiciones de los Artículos 16, 18 y 19, los sueldos, salarios y otras remuneraciones similares obtenidos por un residente de un Estado Contratante por razón de un empleo, sólo pueden someterse a imposición en ese Estado a no ser que el empleo se realice en el otro Estado Contratante. Si el empleo se realiza de esa forma, las remuneraciones derivadas del mismo pueden someterse a imposición en ese otro Estado.

2. No obstante lo dispuesto en el apartado 1, las remuneraciones obtenidas por un residente de un Estado Contratante por razón de un empleo realizado en el otro Estado Contratante, sólo pueden someterse a imposición en el Estado mencionado en primer término si:

a) el perceptor permanece en el otro Estado durante un periodo o periodos cuya duración no exceda en conjunto de ciento ochenta y tres (183) días en cualquier periodo de doce (12) meses que comience o termine en el año fiscal respectivo; y

b) las remuneraciones se pagan por, o en nombre de, un empleador que no es residente del otro Estado; y

c) las remuneraciones no son soportadas por un establecimiento permanente o una base fija que el empleador tenga en el otro Estado.

3. No obstante las disposiciones precedentes de este Artículo, las remuneraciones obtenidas por razón de un empleo realizado a bordo de un buque o aeronave explotados en el transporte internacional, sólo pueden someterse a imposición en el Estado Contratante en el cual la empresa que opera los buques y aeronaves es residente.

ARTÍCULO 16
HONORARIOS DE DIRECTORES

Los honorarios y otras retribuciones similares que un residente de un Estado Contratante obtenga como miembro del directorio, consejo de administración o de vigilancia, de una sociedad residente del otro Estado Contratante, pueden someterse a imposición en este otro Estado.

ARTÍCULO 17
ARTISTAS Y DEPORTISTAS

1. No obstante las disposiciones de los Artículos 14 y 15, las rentas que un residente de un Estado Contratante obtenga del ejercicio de sus actividades personales en el otro Estado Contratante en calidad de artista del espectáculo, tal como actor de teatro, cine, radio o televisión, músico, o como deportista, pueden someterse a imposición en ese otro Estado.

2. Cuando las rentas derivadas de las actividades ejercidas por un artista o un deportista personalmente y en calidad de tal se atribuyan, no al propio artista o deportista, sino a otra persona, dichas rentas pueden, no obstante las disposiciones de los Artículos 7, 14 y 15, someterse a imposición en el Estado Contratante en el que se realicen las actividades del artista o del deportista.

3. Sin perjuicio de lo dispuesto en los apartados 1 y 2, los ingresos obtenidos por un residente de un Estado Contratante en su calidad de artista o deportista estarán exentos en el otro Estado Contratante siempre que la visita a ese otro Estado esté sustancialmente financiada por fondos públicos del Estado mencionado en primer lugar o una subdivisión política o entidad local del mismo.

ARTÍCULO 18
PENSIONES

Sin perjuicio de las disposiciones del apartado 2 del Artículo 19.

a) las pensiones originadas en un Estado Contratante y pagadas a un residente del otro Estado Contratante;

b) cualquier tipo de pagos, sean estos periódicos o no, establecidos en la legislación de seguridad social de un Estado Contratante o programado bajo cualquier tipo de sistema público que tenga como propósito disponer el bienestar social en un Estado Contratante;

pueden someterse a imposición en ambos Estados Contratantes. Sin embargo, los pagos referidos en el subapartado b) no serán sometidos a imposición en el Estado Contratante en el cual el perceptor es residente, si dichos pagos, dada su naturaleza, están exentos de impuesto en el otro Estado Contratante en el cual se originan.

ARTÍCULO 19
FUNCIONES PÚBLICAS

1. Los sueldos, salarios y otras remuneraciones similares, distintas de las pensiones, pagadas por un Estado Contratante o una de sus subdivisiones políticas o autoridades locales del mismo, a una persona física por razón de servicios prestados a ese Estado o a esa subdivisión o autoridad, sólo pueden someterse a imposición en ese Estado.

2. Sin embargo, dichos sueldos, salarios y remuneraciones similares pueden someterse a imposición en el otro Estado Contratante si los servicios son prestados en ese otro Estado y la persona física es un residente de ese Estado que:

a) es nacional de ese Estado; o

b) no ha adquirido la condición de residente de ese Estado solamente para prestar los servicios.

3. No obstante las disposiciones del apartado 1, cualquier pensión u otra remuneración similar pagada, o con cargo a fondos constituidos, por un Estado Contratante o subdivisión política o entidad local del mismo, a una persona física por razón de servicios prestados a ese Estado o subdivisión o entidad solo pueden someterse a imposición en ese Estado.

ARTÍCULO 20
ESTUDIANTES

Las cantidades que un estudiante o una persona en prácticas, que sea o que haya sido inmediatamente antes de visitar un Estado Contratante, residente del otro Estado y que se encuentre en el Estado mencionado en primer lugar con el único fin de proseguir sus estudios o su formación práctica, reciba para cubrir sus gastos de mantenimiento, estudios o de formación práctica, no pueden someterse a imposición en ese Estado, siempre que dichos pagos procedan de fuentes situadas fuera de ese Estado.

ARTÍCULO 21
HIDROCARBUROS

1. Lo dispuesto en este Artículo se aplicará no obstante cualquier otra disposición del presente Acuerdo.

2. Cuando una persona residente de un Estado Contratante realice actividades empresariales que consistan o estén relacionadas con la exploración, producción, refinación, procesamiento, transportación, distribución, almacenamiento o comercialización de hidrocarburos, situados en el otro Estado Contratante y dichas actividades se realicen por un periodo o periodos que en conjunto excedan treinta (30) días en cualquier periodo de doce (12) meses, se considera a tales actividades como realizadas a través de un establecimiento permanente situado en ese otro Estado.

3. Para los efectos del cómputo del plazo al que se refiere el apartado anterior, las actividades realizadas por una empresa asociada con otra empresa serán consideradas como realizadas por la empresa con la que está asociada si las actividades en cuestión son idénticas o sustancialmente similares que aquéllas realizadas por la empresa mencionada en último lugar o son parte del mismo proyecto. Para los efectos de este apartado, la expresión "empresa asociada" tendrá el significado que le otorgue la legislación del Estado donde las actividades son realizadas.

4. Los sueldos, salarios y remuneraciones similares obtenidas por un residente de un Estado Contratante respecto de un empleo relacionado con la exploración, producción, refinación, procesamiento, transportación, distribución, almacenamiento o comercialización de hidrocarburos situados en el otro Estado Contratante pueden someterse a imposición en ese otro Estado. Sin embargo, dichas remuneraciones se someterán a imposición solo en el Estado mencionado en primer lugar si el

empleo es realizado para un empleador que no sea residente del otro Estado y siempre que el empleo sea realizado por un periodo o periodos que en conjunto no excedan treinta (30) días en cualquier periodo de doce (12) meses que inicie o termine en el ejercicio fiscal respectivo.

ARTÍCULO 22
OTRAS RENTAS

1. Las rentas de un residente de un Estado Contratante, cualquiera que fuese su procedencia, no mencionadas en los Artículos precedentes del presente Acuerdo, sólo pueden someterse a imposición en ese Estado.

2. Lo dispuesto en el apartado 1 no es aplicable a las rentas, distintas de las derivadas de bienes inmuebles en el sentido del apartado 2 del Artículo 6, cuando el beneficiario de dichas rentas, residente de un Estado Contratante, realice en el otro Estado Contratante una actividad empresarial por medio de un establecimiento permanente situado en ese otro Estado o preste servicios personales independientes por medio de una base fija situada en ese otro Estado, y el derecho o bien por el que se pagan las rentas estén vinculados efectivamente con dicho establecimiento permanente o base fija. En tal caso, son aplicables las disposiciones del Artículo 7 ó del Artículo 14, según proceda.

3. No obstante lo dispuesto en los apartados 1 y 2, las rentas de un residente de un Estado Contratante no mencionadas en los Artículos precedentes del presente Acuerdo y procedentes del otro Estado Contratante pueden también someterse a imposición en ese otro Estado.

IMPOSICIÓN DEL PATRIMONIO

ARTÍCULO 23
PATRIMONIO

1. El patrimonio que posea un residente de un Estado Contratante y que esté situado en el otro Estado Contratante, puede someterse a imposición en ambos Estados.

2. No obstante las disposiciones del apartado 1, el patrimonio constituido por buques, embarcaciones o aeronaves explotados por un residente de un Estado Contratante en el transporte internacional, y por bienes muebles afectados a esa explotación de tales buques, embarcaciones o aeronaves, sólo puede someterse a imposición en ese Estado.

MÉTODOS PARA ELIMINAR LA DOBLE IMPOSICIÓN

ARTÍCULO 24
ELIMINACIÓN DE LA DOBLE IMPOSICIÓN

1. En Argentina, la doble imposición se evitará de la siguiente manera:

Cuando un residente de Argentina obtenga rentas o posea un patrimonio que, de conformidad con las disposiciones del presente Acuerdo, pueden someterse a imposición en México, Argentina permitirá:

a) deducir del impuesto a la renta de ese residente un importe equivalente al impuesto sobre la renta pagado en México conforme a las previsiones del presente Acuerdo;

b) deducir del impuesto sobre el patrimonio de ese residente correspondiente a los bienes situados en México, un importe equivalente al impuesto sobre el patrimonio pagado en México.

Sin embargo, esta deducción en ambos casos no podrá exceder de la parte del impuesto sobre la renta o sobre el patrimonio, calculado antes de la deducción, correspondiente, según el caso, a las rentas o al patrimonio que pueden someterse a imposición en México.

Cuando de conformidad con cualquier disposición del presente Acuerdo, las rentas obtenidas por un residente de Argentina o el patrimonio que éste posea estén exentos de imposición en Argentina, Argentina podrá, sin embargo, tener en cuenta las rentas o el patrimonio exentos a efectos de calcular el importe del impuesto sobre las demás rentas o el patrimonio de dicho residente.

2. En México, con arreglo a las disposiciones y sin perjuicio de las limitaciones establecidas en la legislación de México, conforme a las modificaciones ocasionales de esta legislación que no afecten sus principios generales, México permitirá a sus residentes acreditar contra el impuesto mexicano:

a) el impuesto argentino pagado por ingresos que conforme el presente Acuerdo pueden someterse a imposición en Argentina en una cantidad que no exceda del impuesto exigible en México sobre dichos ingresos; y

b) en el caso de una sociedad que detente al menos el 10 por ciento del capital de una sociedad residente de Argentina y de la cual la sociedad mencionada en primer lugar recibe dividendos, el impuesto argentino pagado por la sociedad que distribuye dichos dividendos, respecto de los beneficios con cargo a los cuales se pagan los dividendos.

DISPOSICIONES ESPECIALES

ARTÍCULO 25
NO DISCRIMINACIÓN

1. Los nacionales de un Estado Contratante no serán sometidos en el otro Estado Contratante a ningún impuesto u obligación relativa al mismo que no se exijan o que sean más gravosos que aquéllos a los que estén o puedan estar sometidos los nacionales de este otro Estado que se encuentren en las mismas condiciones, en particular con respecto a la residencia. No obstante las disposiciones del Artículo 1, la presente disposición también es aplicable a las personas que no sean residentes de uno o de ambos Estados Contratantes.

2. Los establecimientos permanentes que una empresa de un Estado Contratante tenga en el otro Estado Contratante, no serán sometidos a imposición en ese Estado de manera menos favorable que las empresas de ese otro Estado que realicen las mismas actividades. Esta disposición no podrá interpretarse en el sentido de obligar a un Estado Contratante a conceder a los residentes del otro Estado Contratante las deducciones personales, desgravaciones y reducciones impositivas que otorgue a sus propios residentes en consideración a su estado civil o cargas familiares.

3. A menos que se apliquen las disposiciones del Artículo 9, apartado 1, los intereses, las regalías y demás gastos pagados por una empresa de un Estado Contratante a un residente del otro Estado Contratante, serán deducibles, para efectos de determinar los beneficios sujetos a imposición de esta empresa, en las mismas condiciones que si hubieran sido pagados a un residente del Estado mencionado en primer lugar.

4. Las empresas de un Estado Contratante cuyo capital esté, total o parcialmente, detentado o controlado, directa o indirectamente, por uno o varios residentes del otro Estado Contratante, no se someterán en el Estado mencionado en primer lugar a ningún impuesto u obligación relativa al mismo que no se exijan o que sean más gravosos que aquéllos a los que estén o pueden estar sometidas otras empresas similares del Estado mencionado en primer lugar.

5. No obstante lo dispuesto por el Artículo 2, las disposiciones del presente Artículo se aplicarán a los impuestos de cualquier naturaleza y denominación.

ARTÍCULO 26
PROCEDIMIENTO DE ACUERDO MUTUO

1. Cuando una persona considere que las medidas adoptadas por uno o ambos Estados Contratantes implican o pueden implicar para ella una imposición que no esté conforme con las disposiciones del presente Acuerdo, con independencia de los recursos previstos por el derecho interno de esos Estados, podrá someter su caso a las Autoridades Competentes del Estado Contratante del que sea residente o, si fuera aplicable el apartado 1 del Artículo 25, a la del Estado Contratante del que sea nacional. El caso deberá ser planteado dentro de los tres (3) años siguientes a la primera notificación de la medida que implique una imposición no conforme con las disposiciones del presente Acuerdo.

2. La Autoridad Competente, si el reclamo le parece fundado y si no puede por sí misma encontrar una solución satisfactoria, hará lo posible por resolver la cuestión mediante un acuerdo mutuo con la Autoridad Competente del otro Estado Contratante a fin de evitar una imposición que no se ajuste al presente Acuerdo siempre que la Autoridad Competente del otro Estado Contratante sea notificada del caso dentro de los cuatro (4) años siguientes a la fecha en la que se presentó o debió haberse presentado la declaración en este otro Estado, lo que ocurra posteriormente.

3. Las Autoridades Competentes de los Estados Contratantes harán lo posible por resolver mediante acuerdo mutuo, las dificultades o las dudas que plantee la interpretación o aplicación del presente Acuerdo.

4. Las Autoridades Competentes de los Estados Contratantes podrán comunicarse directamente, incluso en el seno de una Comisión Mixta integrada por ellas mismas o sus representantes, a fin de llegar a un acuerdo en el sentido de los apartados anteriores. Las Autoridades Competentes desarrollarán, a través de consultas, los procedimientos, condiciones, métodos y técnicas bilaterales apropiados para la implementación del procedimiento de acuerdo mutuo previsto en el presente apartado. Además, una Autoridad Competente puede desarrollar procedimientos, condiciones, métodos y técnicas unilaterales apropiados para facilitar las acciones bilaterales mencionadas precedentemente, así como la implementación del procedimiento de acuerdo mutuo.

5. No obstante lo dispuesto en cualquier otro tratado del que los Estados Contratantes sean o puedan ser partes, cualquier controversia sobre una medida adoptada por un Estado Contratante, que se relacione con alguno de los impuestos comprendidos en el Artículo 2, o sobre la eventual discriminación vinculada a una medida impositiva adoptada por un Estado Contratante, incluyendo una controversia sobre la aplicabilidad del presente Acuerdo, deberá ser sometida únicamente a la consideración de las Autoridades Competentes de los Estados Contratantes, quienes harán lo posible por resolverla mediante un procedimiento de acuerdo mutuo.

ARTÍCULO 27
INTERCAMBIO DE INFORMACIÓN

1. Las Autoridades Competentes de los Estados Contratantes intercambiarán la información que previsiblemente sea relevante para aplicar lo dispuesto en el presente Acuerdo o para la administración o ejecución del derecho interno, relativa a los impuestos de cualquier naturaleza y denominación establecidos por los Estados Contratantes. El intercambio de información no está limitado por los Artículos 1 y 2.

2. Cualquier información recibida de conformidad con el apartado 1 por un Estado Contratante será mantenida secreta al igual que la información obtenida con base en el derecho interno de este Estado y sólo se revelará a las personas o autoridades (incluidos los tribunales y órganos administrativos) encargadas de la determinación o recaudación de los impuestos a que se refiere el apartado 1, de los procedimientos declarativos o ejecutivos relativos a dichos impuestos, de la resolución de los recursos relativos a los mismos, o de la vigilancia de todo lo anterior. Dichas personas o autoridades sólo utilizarán esta información para tales propósitos. Podrán revelar la información en las audiencias públicas de los tribunales o en las sentencias judiciales. No obstante lo antes dispuesto, la información recibida por un Estado Contratante podrá utilizarse para otros fines cuando dicha información pueda ser utilizada de esa forma de conformidad con la legislación de ambos Estados y la Autoridad Competente del Estado que proporciona la información autorice dicho uso.

3. En ningún caso las disposiciones de los apartados 1 y 2 podrán interpretarse en el sentido de obligar a un Estado Contratante a:

a) adoptar medidas administrativas contrarias a la legislación y práctica administrativa de éste o del otro Estado Contratante;

b) suministrar información que no se pueda obtener según la legislación o en el ejercicio de la práctica administrativa normal de éste o del otro Estado Contratante;

c) suministrar información que revele cualquier secreto comercial, empresarial, industrial, mercantil o profesional o procedimientos comerciales, o información cuya revelación sería contraria al orden público (*ordre public*).

4. Cuando la información sea solicitada por un Estado Contratante de conformidad con el presente Artículo, el otro Estado Contratante utilizará todas las medidas de recopilación de información para obtener la información solicitada, incluso si el otro Estado no necesita dicha información para sus propios efectos impositivos. La obligación a que se refiere la oración anterior está sujeta a las limitaciones del apartado 3 pero en ningún caso, dichas limitaciones deberán interpretarse en el sentido de permitir que un Estado Contratante se niegue a proporcionar información únicamente porque no tiene un interés interno sobre la misma.

5. En ningún caso las disposiciones del apartado 3 deberán interpretarse en el sentido de permitir que un Estado Contratante se niegue a proporcionar información únicamente debido a que la misma está en poder de un banco, otra institución financiera, beneficiario u otra persona que actúe en calidad de agente o fiduciario, o porque dicha información se relaciona con la tenencia de una participación en una persona.

ARTÍCULO 28
LIMITACIÓN DE BENEFICIOS

1. Salvo que en el presente Artículo se disponga lo contrario, una persona (distinta de una persona física), que sea residente de un Estado Contratante y que obtenga ingresos del otro Estado Contratante tendrá derecho a todos los beneficios del presente Acuerdo previstos para los residentes de un Estado Contratante, únicamente si dicha persona satisface los requisitos señalados en el apartado 2 y cumple con las demás condiciones del presente Acuerdo para la obtención de cualquiera de dichos beneficios.

2. Una persona de un Estado Contratante es una persona que cumple con los requisitos para un ejercicio fiscal únicamente si dicha persona es:

a) una entidad Gubernamental; o

b) una compañía constituida en cualquiera de los Estados Contratantes, si:

(i) la principal clase de sus acciones se encuentra listada en un mercado de valores reconocido, definido en el apartado 4 de este Artículo y son negociadas regularmente en uno o más mercados de valores reconocidos; o

(ii) al menos el 50 por ciento de los derechos de voto o del valor de las acciones de la compañía sea propiedad directa o indirectamente de una o más personas físicas residentes en cualquiera de los Estados Contratantes y/o de otras personas constituidas en cualquiera de los Estados Contratantes, en las que al menos el 50 por ciento de los derechos de voto o del valor de las acciones o de la participación en los beneficios sean propiedad directa o indirectamente de una o más personas físicas residentes en cualquiera de los Estados Contratantes; o

c) una sociedad de personas o una asociación de personas, en la que al menos el 50 por ciento o más de la participación en los beneficios sea propiedad de una o más personas físicas residentes en cualquiera de los Estados Contratantes y/o de otras personas constituidas en cualquiera de los Estados Contratantes, en las que al menos el 50 por ciento de los derechos de voto o del valor de las acciones o la participación en los beneficios sean propiedad directa o indirectamente de una o más personas físicas residentes en cualquiera de los Estados Contratantes; o

d) una institución de beneficencia u otra entidad que se encuentre exenta para efectos fiscales, cuyas principales actividades sean realizadas en cualquiera de los Estados Contratantes.

Las personas mencionadas anteriormente no tendrán derecho a los beneficios del presente Acuerdo, si más del 50 por ciento de su ingreso bruto, en el ejercicio fiscal de que se trate, es pagado directa o indirectamente a personas que no sean residentes de ninguno de los Estados Contratantes mediante pagos que sean deducibles para efectos de determinar el impuesto comprendido en el presente Acuerdo en el Estado de residencia de la persona.

3. Sin embargo, un residente de un Estado Contratante tendrá derecho a los beneficios del presente Acuerdo si la Autoridad Competente del otro Estado Contratante determina que dicho residente lleva a cabo activamente actividades empresariales en el otro Estado y que el establecimiento o adquisición o mantenimiento de dicha persona y la realización de dichas operaciones no ha tenido como uno de sus principales fines la obtención de los beneficios del Acuerdo.

4. Para efectos de este Artículo, el término "mercado de valores reconocido" significa:

a) en Argentina, los mercados de valores que operan bajo el control de la Comisión Nacional de Valores;

b) en México, la Bolsa Mexicana de Valores; y

c) cualquier otro mercado de valores que se determine de común acuerdo por las Autoridades Competentes de los Estados Contratantes.

5. Antes de que a un residente de un Estado Contratante se le niegue la desgravación fiscal en el otro Estado Contratante debido a lo dispuesto en los apartados anteriores, las Autoridades Competentes de los Estados Contratantes se consultarán mutuamente. Asimismo, las Autoridades Competentes de los Estados Contratantes podrán consultarse mutuamente con respecto a la aplicación de este Artículo.

6. Las disposiciones del presente Acuerdo no impedirán a un Estado Contratante aplicar sus disposiciones relacionadas con capitalización delgada y empresas extranjeras controladas (en el caso de México, regímenes fiscales preferentes) o cualquier normativa anti-abuso que se encuentre vigente en la legislación interna de los Estados Contratantes.

7. No obstante las demás disposiciones del presente Acuerdo y teniendo en consideración todos los hechos y circunstancias pertinentes, no se otorgará un beneficio tributario conforme al presente Acuerdo, respecto a un elemento de un ingreso, si se concluye que uno de los principales propósitos de cualquier arreglo o transacción fue obtener un beneficio, a menos que éste se otorgue de conformidad con el objeto y propósito de las disposiciones pertinentes del presente Acuerdo.

ARTÍCULO 29
MIEMBROS DE MISIONES DIPLOMÁTICAS Y DE OFICINAS CONSULARES

Las disposiciones del presente Acuerdo no afectarán los privilegios fiscales que disfruten los miembros de las misiones diplomáticas o de las oficinas consulares, de conformidad con los principios generales del Derecho Internacional o en virtud de acuerdos especiales.

DISPOSICIONES FINALES

ARTÍCULO 30
ENTRADA EN VIGOR

1. Cada uno de los Estados Contratantes notificará al otro, a través de la vía diplomática, el cumplimiento de los procedimientos exigidos por su legislación para la entrada en vigor del presente Acuerdo.

2. El presente Acuerdo entrará en vigor treinta (30) días después de la fecha de recepción de la última de dichas notificaciones y sus disposiciones surtirán efectos:

a) con respecto a impuestos retenidos en la fuente, sobre los montos pagados a partir del primero de enero, inclusive, del año calendario siguiente a aquel en que el presente Acuerdo entre en vigor; y

b) con respecto a otros impuestos sobre la renta y el patrimonio, para los ejercicios fiscales que comiencen a partir del primero de enero, inclusive, del año calendario siguiente a aquel en que el presente Acuerdo entre en vigor.

3. El Convenio entre el Gobierno de los Estados Unidos Mexicanos y el Gobierno de la República Argentina para Evitar la Doble Imposición e Impedir la Evasión Fiscal en materia de Impuestos sobre la Renta Provenientes de la Operación de Buques y Aeronaves en el Transporte Internacional, firmado en la Ciudad de México, el 26 de noviembre de 1997, quedará terminado de forma definitiva a partir del momento en que el presente Acuerdo resulte aplicable.

ARTÍCULO 31
DENUNCIA

El presente Acuerdo permanecerá en vigor mientras no se denuncie por uno de los Estados Contratantes. Cualquiera de los Estados Contratantes puede denunciar el presente Acuerdo por la vía diplomática, comunicándolo al menos seis (6) meses antes de la terminación de cualquier año calendario siguiente a la expiración de un periodo de tres (3) años contados a partir de la fecha de su entrada en vigor. En tal caso, el Acuerdo dejará de aplicarse:

a) con respecto a impuestos retenidos en la fuente, sobre los montos pagados a partir del primero de enero, inclusive, del año calendario siguiente a la fecha de notificación de la denuncia; y

b) con respecto a otros impuestos sobre la renta y el patrimonio, para los ejercicios fiscales que comiencen a partir del primero de enero, inclusive, del año calendario siguiente a la fecha de notificación de la denuncia.

En fe de lo cual los signatarios, debidamente autorizados al efecto, han firmado el presente Acuerdo.

Hecho en la Ciudad de México, el cuatro de noviembre de dos mil quince, en dos originales en idioma español, siendo ambos textos igualmente auténticos.

POR LOS ESTADOS UNIDOS MEXICANOS

Luis Videgaray Caso
Secretario de Hacienda y Crédito Público

POR LA REPÚBLICA ARGENTINA

Ricardo Daniel Echegaray
Administrador Federal de Ingresos Públicos

PROTOCOLO AL ACUERDO ENTRE LOS ESTADOS UNIDOS MEXICANOS Y LA REPÚBLICA ARGENTINA PARA EVITAR LA DOBLE IMPOSICIÓN Y PREVENIR LA EVASIÓN FISCAL CON RESPECTO A LOS IMPUESTOS SOBRE LA RENTA Y SOBRE EL PATRIMONIO

En el momento de la firma del "Acuerdo entre los Estados Unidos Mexicanos y la República Argentina para Evitar la Doble Imposición y Prevenir la Evasión Fiscal con respecto a los Impuestos sobre la Renta y sobre el Patrimonio", los Estados Contratantes han acordado las siguientes disposiciones que forman parte integrante del Acuerdo:

1. Con referencia a los Artículos 5 y 7:

Para los efectos de la aplicación de lo establecido en el Artículo 5, apartado 4, inciso d) y en el Artículo 7, apartado 5, la exportación de bienes o mercancías comprados para la empresa deberá cumplir con lo previsto en materia de precios de transferencia conforme al presente Acuerdo y a la legislación interna de cada Estado Contratante.

2. Con referencia al Artículo 5, apartado 2, literal f):

Se entiende que la actividad pesquera constituye un establecimiento permanente aun sin un lugar fijo de negocios.

3. Con referencia al Artículo 5, apartado 6:

Queda establecido que, no obstante lo dispuesto en el Acuerdo, en el caso de actividades de reaseguro se aplicará la legislación interna de cada uno de los Estados Contratantes.

4. Con referencia al Artículo 8:

Se entiende que los beneficios a que se refiere el apartado 1 no comprenden aquellos provenientes del transporte terrestre.

5. Con referencia al Artículo 10:

Cuando una empresa residente en Argentina pague dividendos o distribuya utilidades que excedan los resultados acumulados sujetos a imposición al final del año fiscal inmediatamente anterior al día del pago o de la distribución, determinado de conformidad con las disposiciones de la Ley de Impuesto a las Ganancias argentina, la limitación del apartado 2 del Artículo 10 no se aplicará respecto del importe de la retención correspondiente por aplicación de las disposiciones de la mencionada Ley de Impuesto a las Ganancias.

6. Con referencia al Artículo 12:

   a) En el caso de Argentina, se entiende que la limitación de la retención en la fuente procederá siempre que se cumplimenten los requisitos de registro, verificación y autorización previstos en su legislación interna.

   b) El límite a la imposición exigible en el Estado de procedencia de las regalías que establece el apartado 2, inciso a) solo será aplicable, en casos de derechos de autor, cuando dichas regalías se perciban por el propio autor o sus legítimos herederos.

7. Con referencia al Artículo 12, apartado 3:

   a) Se entiende que los pagos relativos a las aplicaciones informáticas –software– se encuentran dentro del ámbito de aplicación del Artículo cuando se transfiere solamente una parte de los derechos sobre el programa, tanto si los pagos se efectúan en contraprestación de la utilización de un derecho de autor sobre una aplicación –*software*– para su explotación comercial como si los mismos corresponden a una aplicación –*software*– adquirida para uso empresarial o profesional del comprador, siendo, en este último caso, aplicaciones –software– no absolutamente estándares sino adaptadas de algún modo para el adquirente.

   b) Se entiende que las cantidades de cualquier clase pagadas por el uso o la concesión de uso de noticias serán considerados como derechos de autor sobre obras literarias, teatrales, musicales, artísticas o científicas, comprendidos en la definición del término "regalías".

   c) Se entiende que el término "asistencia técnica" comprende la prestación de servicios independientes por los que el prestador se obliga a proporcionar conocimientos no patentables, que no impliquen la transmisión de información confidencial relativa a experiencias industriales, comerciales o científicas, obligándose con el prestatario a intervenir en la aplicación de dichos conocimientos.

8. Con referencia al Artículo 13:

Se entenderá que las disposiciones del apartado 6 no serán aplicables en relación con bienes sujetos a registro, entendidos como tales las aeronaves automotores y embarcaciones, en cuyo caso aplicará lo dispuesto por el Artículo 22

9. Con referencia al Artículo 14:

Para la aplicación de lo dispuesto en el apartado 1, se entenderá que el término "base fija", a efectos fiscales, tendrá el tratamiento correspondiente a la imposición de un establecimiento permanente.

10. Con referencia al Artículo 17:

Se entenderá que las rentas que un artista o deportista residente de un Estado Contratante obtenga de las actividades personales de dicho residente relacionadas con su reputación como artista o deportista, ejercidas en el otro Estado Contratante, pueden someterse a imposición en ese otro Estado.

11. Con referencia al Artículo 25:

a) Las disposiciones del apartado 3 se aplicarán, en el caso de regalías, en la medida en que los contratos de transferencia de tecnología estén registrados o autorizados de acuerdo con los requisitos previstos en la legislación interna de Argentina.

b) Se entiende que el apartado 3 no prohíbe a un Estado Contratante realizar requerimientos de información adicional en relación con los pagos efectuados a no residentes, dado que su intención es la de garantizar niveles de cumplimiento y de comprobación similares entre los pagos efectuados a residentes y a no residentes.

c) Se entiende que lo dispuesto en el Artículo 21 de la Ley de Impuesto a las Ganancias de Argentina no contraviene lo dispuesto en el apartado 2 del Artículo 25 del Acuerdo.

d) Las disposiciones del apartado 5 se aplicarán únicamente a impuestos federales.

12. Considerando que los objetivos principales del Acuerdo son la eliminación de la doble imposición internacional y la prevención de la evasión fiscal, a fin de eliminar los efectos negativos que éstos generan para el intercambio de bienes y servicios y el libre movimiento de los capitales, las tecnologías y las personas, en el caso que de la aplicación del Acuerdo no resulte en la promoción de sus relaciones económicas, los Estados Contratantes acuerdan que, en cualquier momento después de la expiración de un periodo de tres (3) años desde la fecha de entrada

en vigor del Acuerdo, las Autoridades Competentes podrán reunirse para examinar de manera expedita la necesidad de efectuar posibles cambios respecto del Acuerdo, sobre la base de la experiencia obtenida en su aplicación durante los años precedentes y los cambios introducidos en su legislación impositiva nacional.

En fe de lo cual los signatarios, debidamente autorizados al efecto, han firmado el presente Protocolo.

Hecho en la Ciudad de México, el cuatro de noviembre de dos mil quince, en dos originales en idioma español, siendo ambos textos igualmente auténticos.

POR LOS ESTADOS UNIDOS MEXICANOS

Luis Videgaray Caso
Secretario de Hacienda y Crédito Público

POR LA REPÚBLICA ARGENTINA

Ricardo Daniel Echegaray
Administrador Federal de Ingresos Públicos

[TRANSLATION IN ENGLISH – TRADUCTION EN ANGLAIS]

AGREEMENT BETWEEN THE UNITED MEXICAN STATES AND THE ARGENTINE REPUBLIC FOR THE AVOIDANCE OF DOUBLE TAXATION AND THE PREVENTION OF FISCAL EVASION WITH RESPECT TO TAXES ON INCOME AND ON CAPITAL

The United Mexican States and the Argentine Republic, with the aim to encourage the development of their economic relations and enhance cooperation in tax matters, and desirous of concluding an Agreement for the avoidance of double taxation and the prevention of fiscal evasion with respect to taxes on income and on capital, without creating opportunities for non-taxation or reduced taxation through tax evasion or avoidance (including through treaty-shopping arrangements aimed at obtaining reliefs provided in this Agreement for the indirect benefit of residents of third States),

Have agreed as follows:

SCOPE OF THE AGREEMENT

Article 1. Persons covered

This Agreement shall apply to persons who are residents of one or both of the Contracting States.

Article 2. Taxes covered

1. This Agreement shall apply to taxes on income and on capital imposed on behalf of each Contracting State, irrespective of the manner in which they are levied.

2. There shall be regarded as taxes on income and on capital all taxes imposed on total income, on total capital or on elements of income or of capital, including taxes on gains from the alienation of movable or immovable property, as well as taxes on capital appreciation.

3. The existing taxes to which the Agreement shall apply are in particular:

(a) In the case of Argentina:

(i) The income tax;

(ii) The presumptive minimum income tax;

(iii) The personal assets tax;

(hereinafter referred to as "Argentine tax");

(b) In the case of Mexico:

(i) The federal income tax;

(hereinafter referred to as "Mexican tax").

4. This Agreement shall apply also to any identical or substantially similar taxes which are imposed after the date of signature of this Agreement in addition to, or in place of, the existing taxes.

The competent authorities of the Contracting States shall notify each other of significant changes made to their respective tax laws.

DEFINITIONS

Article 3. General definitions

1. For the purposes of this Agreement, unless the context otherwise requires:
   (a) The terms "a Contracting State" and "the other Contracting State" mean, as the context requires, Mexico or Argentina;
   (b) The term "Argentina" means the territory of the Argentine Republic, defined in accordance with its constitutional and legal norms; and the term "Mexico" means the United Mexican States; used in a geographical sense, it means the territory of the United Mexican States, including the integral parts of the Federation; the islands, including the reefs and cays in the adjacent seas; the islands of Guadalupe and Revillagigedo, the continental shelf, the seabed and the submarine shelves of the islands, cays and reefs; the waters of the territorial seas and internal maritime waters beyond them, and the areas over which, in accordance with international law, Mexico may exercise sovereign rights of exploration and exploitation of the natural seabed resources of the seabed, subsoil and the superjacent waters, and the air space above the territory to the extent and under the conditions prescribed by international law;
   (c) The term "person" includes an individual, a company and any other body of persons;
   (d) The term "company" means any body corporate or any legal entity which is treated as a body corporate for tax purposes;
   (e) The terms "enterprise of a Contracting State" and "enterprise of the other Contracting State" mean, respectively, an enterprise carried on by a resident of a Contracting State and an enterprise carried on by a resident of the other Contracting State;
   (f) The term "international traffic" means any transport by a ship or aircraft operated by an enterprise of a Contracting State, except when the ship or aircraft is operated solely between places in the other Contracting State;
   (g) The term "national" means:
      (i) Any individual possessing the nationality of a Contracting State;
      (ii) Any legal person, partnership or association deriving its status as such from the laws in force in a Contracting State;
   (h) The term "competent authority" means:
      (i) In Argentina, the Ministry of the Treasury and Public Finances, Secretary of the Treasury;
      (ii) In Mexico, the Ministry of Finance and Public Credit.

2. As regards the application of this Agreement at any time by a Contracting State, any term not defined therein shall, unless the context otherwise requires, have the meaning that it has at that time under the laws of that State for the purposes of the taxes to which this Agreement applies, any meaning under the applicable tax laws of that State prevailing over the meaning given to the term under other laws of that State.

Article 4. Resident

1. For the purposes of this Agreement, the term “resident of a Contracting State” means any person who, under the laws of that State, is liable to tax therein by reason of his or her domicile, residence, place of incorporation, place of management or any other criterion of a similar nature, and also includes that State and any political subdivision or local authority thereof. This term, however, does not include any person who is liable to tax in that State in respect only of income from sources in that State or capital situated therein.

2. Where by reason of the provisions of paragraph 1 a person is a resident of both Contracting States, then his or her status shall be determined as follows:

(a) That person shall be deemed to be a resident of the State in which he or she has a permanent home available to him or her; if he or she has a permanent home available to him or her in both States, he or she shall be deemed to be a resident only of the State with which his or her personal and economic relations are closest (centre of vital interests);

(b) If the State in which said person’s centre of vital interests cannot be determined, or if that person does not have a permanent home available in either State, he or she shall be deemed to be a resident only of the Contracting State in which he or she has a habitual abode;

(c) If said person has a habitual abode in both States or in neither of them, that person shall be deemed to be a resident only of the State of which he or she is a national;

(d) If said person is a national of both States or of neither of them, the competent authorities of the Contracting States shall settle the question by mutual agreement.

3. Where by reason of the provisions of paragraph 1 a person other than an individual is a resident of both Contracting States, the competent authorities of the Contracting States shall by mutual agreement endeavour to settle the question and to determine the mode of application of this Agreement to such person. In the absence of a mutual agreement between the competent authorities of the Contracting States, such person shall not be entitled to any relief or exemption from tax provided by this Agreement.

Article 5. Permanent establishment

1. For the purposes of this Agreement, the term “permanent establishment” means a fixed place of business through which the business of an enterprise is wholly or partly carried out.

2. The term “permanent establishment” includes especially:

(a) A place of management;

(b) A branch;

(c) An office;

(d) A factory;

(e) A workshop;

(f) A mine, an oil or gas well, a quarry or any other place related to the exploration, extraction or exploitation of natural resources, including fishing.

3. The term "permanent establishment" also encompasses:

(a) A building site, a construction, assembly or installation project or supervisory activities in connection therewith, but only if such site, project or activities last more than six (6) months;

(b) The furnishing of services, including consultancy services, by an enterprise through employees or other personnel engaged by the enterprise for such purpose, when activities of that nature continue within a Contracting State for a period or periods aggregating more than six (6) months in any 12-month period.

For the purposes of calculating the periods referred to in this paragraph, the activities conducted by an associated enterprise of another company, within the meaning of article 9, shall be considered in aggregate with the period during which the activities are conducted by the associated enterprise, provided that the activities of both enterprises are identical or substantially similar.

4. Notwithstanding the preceding provisions of this article, the term "permanent establishment" shall be deemed not to include:

(a) The use of facilities solely for the purpose of storage or display of goods or merchandise belonging to the enterprise;

(b) The maintenance of a stock of goods or merchandise belonging to the enterprise solely for the purpose of storage or display;

(c) The maintenance of a stock of goods or merchandise belonging to the enterprise solely for the purpose of processing by another enterprise;

(d) The maintenance of a fixed place of business solely for the purpose of purchasing goods or merchandise or of collecting information, for the enterprise;

(e) The maintenance of a fixed place of business solely for the purpose of carrying on, for the enterprise, any other activity of a preparatory or auxiliary character;

(f) The maintenance of a fixed place of business solely for any combination of activities mentioned in subparagraphs (a) to (e), provided that the overall activity of the fixed place of business resulting from this combination is of an auxiliary or preparatory character.

5. Notwithstanding the provisions of paragraphs 1 and 2, where a person, other than an agent of an independent status to whom paragraph 7 applies, is acting in a Contracting State on behalf of an enterprise of the other Contracting State, that enterprise shall be deemed to have a permanent establishment in the first-mentioned Contracting State in respect of any activities which that person undertakes for the enterprise, if such a person:

(a) Has and habitually exercises in that State an authority to conclude contracts in the name of the enterprise, unless the activities of such person are limited to those mentioned in paragraph 4 which, if exercised through a fixed place of business, would not make this fixed place of business a permanent establishment under the provisions of that paragraph; or

(b) Has no such authority, but habitually maintains in the first-mentioned State a stock of goods or merchandise from which she said person regularly delivers goods or merchandise on behalf of the enterprise.

6. Notwithstanding the foregoing provisions of this article, an insurance enterprise of a Contracting State shall be deemed to have a permanent establishment in the other Contracting State if it collects premiums in the territory of that other State or insures risks situated therein through a person other than an independent agent to whom paragraph 7 applies.

7. An enterprise shall not be deemed to have a permanent establishment in a Contracting State merely because it carries on business in that other State through a broker, general commission agent or any other independent agent, provided that such persons are acting in the ordinary course of their business and that, in their commercial or financial relations with that enterprise, conditions are not made or imposed which differ from those generally agreed to by independent agents. However, when activities of such an agent are devoted wholly or almost wholly on behalf of that enterprise, that person shall not be deemed to be an independent agent within the meaning of this paragraph.

8. The fact that a company which is a resident of a Contracting State controls or is controlled by a company which is a resident of the other Contracting State, or which carries out business in that other State (whether through a permanent establishment or otherwise), shall not of itself constitute either company a permanent establishment of the other.

TAXATION OF INCOME

Article 6. Income from immovable property

1. Income derived by a resident of a Contracting State from immovable property (including income from agriculture or forestry) situated in the other Contracting State may be taxed in that other State.

2. The term "immovable property" shall have the meaning which it has under the laws of the Contracting State in which the property in question is situated. The term shall in any case include property accessory to immovable property, livestock and equipment used in agriculture and forestry, rights to which the provisions of general law respecting landed property apply, usufruct of immovable property and rights to variable or fixed payments as consideration for the working of, or the right to work, mineral deposits, sources and other natural resources; ships, boats and aircraft shall not be regarded as immovable property.

3. The provisions of paragraph 1 shall also apply to income derived from the direct use, letting or use in any other form of immovable property.

4. The provisions of paragraphs 1 and 3 shall also apply to the income from immovable property of an enterprise and to income from immovable property used for the performance of independent personal services.

Article 7. Business profits

1. The profits of an enterprise of a Contracting State shall be taxable only in that State unless the enterprise carries out business in the other Contracting State through a permanent establishment situated therein. If the enterprise carries out or has carried out business as aforesaid, the profits of the enterprise may be taxed in the other State but only so much of them as is attributable to that permanent establishment. For these purposes, the profits of the enterprise may be taxed in the other State but only so much of them as is attributable to:

(a) Sales or activities carried out by that permanent establishment;

(b) Sales in that other State of goods or merchandise of the same or similar kind as those sold through that permanent establishment; or

(c) Other business activities carried on in that other State of the same or similar kind as those effected through that permanent establishment.

However, profits derived from the activities described in subparagraphs (b) and (c) shall not be taxable in the other Contracting State if the enterprise establishes that such activities have been carried out for reasons other than obtaining a benefit under this Agreement.

2. Subject to the provisions of paragraph 3, where an enterprise of a Contracting State carries out business in the other Contracting State through a permanent establishment situated therein, there shall in each Contracting State be attributed to that permanent establishment the profits which it might be expected to make if it were a distinct and separate enterprise engaged in the same or similar activities under the same or similar conditions and dealing wholly independently with the enterprise of which it is a permanent establishment.

3. In the determination of the profits of a permanent establishment, there shall be allowed as deductions expenses which are incurred for the purposes of the business of the permanent establishment, including executive and general administrative expenses so incurred, whether in the State in which the permanent establishment is situated or elsewhere. For this purpose, only expenses that are deductible by the permanent establishment in accordance with the provisions of the tax laws of the Contracting State in which the permanent establishment is situated shall be taken into account.

4. Where a permanent establishment plays an active and significant role in the negotiation and conclusion of contracts without material modification by the enterprise, regardless of involvement by other parts of the enterprise in such activities, the share of the profits from such contracts proportional to the contribution made by the permanent establishment to the transactions of the enterprise as a whole shall be attributed to the permanent establishment.

5. Notwithstanding the provisions of paragraph 2, no profits shall be attributed to a permanent establishment by reason of the mere purchase by that permanent establishment of goods or merchandise for the enterprise.

6. For the purposes of the preceding paragraphs, the profits to be attributed to the permanent establishment shall be determined by the same method year by year unless there is good and sufficient reason to the contrary.

7. Where profits include items of income which are dealt with separately in other articles of this Agreement, then the provisions of those articles shall not be affected by the provisions of this article.

Article 8. International transport

1. Profits of an enterprise of a Contracting State derived from the operation of ships or aircraft in international traffic shall be taxable only in that State.

2. For the purposes of this article, profits from the operation of ships or aircraft in international traffic shall include profits from:

(a) Income from the charter or rental on a bareboat basis of ships and aircraft; and

(b) Profits from the use or rental of containers (including trailers and equipment related to the transport of containers) used to transport goods or merchandise;

where such rental or such use, whether in the terms of subparagraph (a) or (b), is incidental to the operation of ships or aircraft in international traffic.

3. Where profits are covered under the provisions of paragraphs 1 and 2 of this article are derived by a resident of a Contracting State from the participation in a pool, a joint business or an international operating company, the profits attributable to that resident shall be taxable only in the Contracting State in which he or she resides.

Article 9. Associated enterprises

1. Where:

(a) An enterprise of a Contracting State participates directly or indirectly in the management, control or capital of an enterprise of the other Contracting State, or

(b) The same persons participate directly or indirectly in the management, control or capital of an enterprise of a Contracting State and an enterprise of the other Contracting State,

and in either case conditions are made or imposed between the two enterprises in their commercial or financial relations which differ from those which would be made between independent enterprises, then any profits which would, but for those conditions, have accrued to one of the enterprises but, by reason of those conditions, have not so accrued, may be included in the profits of that enterprise and taxed accordingly.

2. Where a Contracting State includes in the profits of an enterprise of that State - and taxes accordingly - profits on which an enterprise of the other Contracting State has been charged to tax in that other State and the profits so included are profits which would have accrued to the enterprise of the first-mentioned State if the conditions made between the two enterprises had been those which would have been made between independent enterprises, then that other State shall make an appropriate adjustment to the amount of the tax charged therein on those profits. In determining such adjustment, due regard shall be had to the other provisions of this Agreement and the competent authorities of the Contracting States shall, if necessary, consult each other.

3. The provisions of paragraph 2 shall not apply where judicial, administrative or other legal proceedings have resulted in a final ruling that by actions giving rise to an adjustment of profits in accordance with paragraph 1, one of the enterprises concerned is liable to penalty with respect to fraud, gross negligence or wilful default.

Article 10. Dividends

1. Dividends paid by a company which is a resident of a Contracting State to a resident of the other Contracting State may be taxed in that other State.

2. However, such dividends may also be taxed in the Contracting State of which the company paying the dividends is a resident and according to the laws of that State, but if the beneficial owner of the dividends is a resident of the other Contracting State, the tax so charged shall not exceed:

(a) 10 per cent of the gross amount of the dividends if the beneficial owner is a company which holds at least 25 per cent of the capital of the company paying the dividends; or

(b) 15 per cent of the gross amount of the dividends in all other cases.

This provisions of this paragraph shall not affect the taxation of the company in respect of the profits out of which the dividends are paid.

3. The term "dividends" as used in this article means income from shares, "jouissance" shares or "jouissance" rights, mining shares, founders' shares or other rights, not being debt claims, participating in profits, as well as income from other corporate rights and other income which is subjected to the same taxation treatment as income from shares by the laws of the State of which the company making the distribution is a resident.

4. The provisions of paragraphs 1 and 2 shall not apply if the beneficial owner of the dividends, being a resident of a Contracting State, carries out business in the other Contracting State of which the company paying the dividends is a resident through a permanent establishment situated therein, or performs in that other State independent personal services from a fixed base situated therein, and the holding in respect of which the dividends are paid is effectively connected with such permanent establishment or fixed base. In such case the provisions of article 7 or article 14, as the case may be, shall apply.

5. Where a company which is a resident of a Contracting State derives profit or income from the other Contracting State, that other State may not impose any tax on the dividends paid by the company, except insofar as such dividends are paid to a resident of that other Contracting State or insofar as the holding in respect of which the dividends are paid is effectively connected with a permanent establishment or a fixed base situated in that other Contracting State, nor may that other State subject the company's undistributed profits to a tax on the company's undistributed profits, even if the dividends paid or the undistributed profits consist wholly or partly of profits or income arising in such other State.

6. Notwithstanding any other provision of this Agreement, where an enterprise which is a resident of a Contracting State has a permanent establishment in the other Contracting State, any profits taxable under article 7.1 may be subject to additional tax withholding in the other State, in accordance with its taxation laws when the profits are remitted to the head office, but the withholding shall not exceed 10 per cent of the amount of such profits after deduction therefrom of the corporate tax imposed in that other State.

Article 11. Interest

1. Interest arising in a Contracting State and paid to a resident of the other Contracting State may be taxed in that other State.

2. However, such interest may also be taxed in the Contracting State in which it arises and according to the laws of that State, but if the beneficial owner of the interest is a resident of the other Contracting State, the tax so charged shall not exceed 12 per cent.

3. Notwithstanding the provisions of paragraph 2, the interest referred to in paragraph 1 shall be taxable only in the Contracting State of which the beneficial owner of the interest is a resident if:

(a) The beneficial owner is a Contracting States, a political subdivision or local authority thereof, or the Central Bank of a Contracting State;

(b) The interest is paid by any of the entities mentioned in subparagraph (a);

(c) The interest arises in Argentina and is paid in respect of a loan for a period of not less than three (3) years granted by National Foreign Trade Bank, S.N.C., Nacional Financiera, S.N.C., or the National Bank for Public Works and Services, S.N.C., or by any other institution agreed upon by the competent authorities of the Contracting States; or

(d) The interest arises in Mexico and is paid in respect of a loan for a period of not less than three (3) years granted by the Banco de la Nación Argentina and the Banco de Inversión y Comercio Exterior, or by any other institution agreed upon by the competent authorities of the Contracting States.

4. The term "interest" as used in this article means income from debt claims of every kind, whether or not secured by mortgage, and whether or not carrying a right to participate in the debtor's profits, and in particular, income from government securities and income from bonds or debentures, including premiums and prizes attaching to such securities, bonds or debentures, as well as all other income as assimilated to income from money lent under the taxation laws of the Contracting State in which the interest arises. The term "interest" does not include income considered as dividends in accordance with article 10.3.

5. The provisions of paragraphs 1, 2 and 3 shall not apply if the beneficial owner of the interest, being a resident of a Contracting State, carries out business in the other Contracting State in which the interest arises through a permanent establishment situated therein, or performs in that other State independent personal services from a fixed base situated therein, and the debt claim in respect of which the interest is paid is effectively connected with: (a) such permanent establishment or fixed base; or with (b) business activities referred to in article 7.1 (c). In such case, the provisions of article 7 or article 14, as the case may be, shall apply.

6. Interest shall be deemed to arise in a Contracting State when the payer is a resident of that State. Where, however, the person paying the interest, whether he is a resident of a Contracting State or not, has in a Contracting State a permanent establishment or a fixed base, in connection with which the indebtedness on which the interest is paid was incurred, and such interest is borne by such permanent establishment or fixed base, then such interest shall be deemed to arise in the State in which the permanent establishment or fixed base is situated.

Article 12. Royalties

1. Royalties arising in a Contracting State and paid to a resident of the other Contracting State may be taxed in that other State.

2. However, such royalties may also be taxed in the Contracting State in which they arise and according to the laws of that State, but if the beneficial owner of the royalties is a resident of the other Contracting State, the tax so charged shall not exceed:

(a) 10 per cent of the gross amount paid for the use of, or the right to use, a copyright of any literary, theatrical, musical, artistic or scientific work; or of the gross amount paid for the use of, or the right to use, any patent; design or model; plan; secret formula or process; software; commercial, industrial or scientific equipment; or for information concerning industrial, commercial or scientific experience; or for the provision of technical assistance services; or

(b) 15 per cent of the gross amount of the royalties in all other cases.

Notwithstanding the provisions of article 13, the term "royalties" also includes gains derived from the alienation of any such right or property which are contingent on the productivity, use or disposition thereof.

3. The term "royalties" as used in this article means payments of any kind received as a consideration for the use of, or the right to use, any copyright of literary, musical, theatrical, artistic or scientific work; software; any patent, maker's marks or trademarks, design or model, plan, secret

formula or process; or other intangible property; or for the use of, or the right to use, industrial, commercial or scientific equipment; or for information concerning industrial, commercial or scientific experience, and includes payments for the provision of technical assistance and payments of any kind in respect of cinematograph films, or films or tapes or other means of reproduction used for television broadcasting.

4. The provisions of paragraphs 1 and 2 shall not apply if the beneficial owner of the royalties, being a resident of a Contracting State, carries out business in the other Contracting State in which the royalties arise, through a permanent establishment situated therein, or performs in that other State independent personal services from a fixed base situated therein, and the right or property in respect of which the royalties are paid is effectively connected with: (a) such permanent establishment or fixed base; or with (b) business activities referred to in article 7.1 (c). In such case, the provisions of article 7 or article 14, as the case may be, shall apply.

5. Royalties shall be deemed to arise in a Contracting State when the payer is a resident of that State. Where, however, the person paying the royalties, whether said person is a resident of a Contracting State or not, has a permanent establishment or a fixed base in a Contracting State in connection with which the liability to pay the royalties was incurred, and such royalties are borne by such permanent establishment or fixed base, then such royalties shall be deemed to arise in the State in which the permanent establishment or fixed base is situated.

Article 13. Capital gains

1. Gains derived by a resident of a Contracting State from the alienation of immovable property referred to in article 6 and situated in the other Contracting State may be taxed in that other State.

2. Gains from the alienation of movable property forming part of the business property of a permanent establishment which an enterprise of a Contracting State has in the other Contracting State or of movable property pertaining to a fixed base available to a resident of a Contracting State in the other Contracting State for the purpose of performing independent personal services, including such gains from the alienation of such a permanent establishment (alone or with the whole enterprise) or of such fixed base, may be taxed in that other State.

3. Gains from the alienation of ships or aircraft operated in international traffic, or movable property pertaining to the operation of such ships or aircraft, shall be taxable only in the Contracting State in which the place of effective management of the enterprise is situated.

4. Gains derived by a resident of a Contracting State from the alienation of shares or other participation rights deriving more than 50 per cent of their value directly or indirectly from immovable property situated in the other Contracting State, may be taxed in that other State.

5. Gains, other than those to which paragraph 4 applies, derived from the alienation of shares or the capital stock of a company which is a resident of a Contracting State, may be taxed in that State. However, the tax so charged shall not exceed:

(a) 10 per cent of the gains realized on a direct holding of at least 25 per cent of the capital;

(b) 15 per cent of the gains in all other cases.

6. Gains from the alienation of any property other than that referred to in the preceding paragraphs shall be taxable only in the Contracting State of which the alienator is a resident.

Article 14. Independent personal services

1. Income derived by a resident of a Contracting State in respect of professional services or other activities of an independent character shall be taxable only in that State, except in the following circumstances, when such income may also be taxed in the other Contracting State:

(a) If said person has a fixed base regularly available in the other Contracting State for the purpose of performing those activities; in such case, only the income attributable to that fixed base may be taxed in that other Contracting State; or

(b) If said person's stay in the other Contracting State is for a period or periods amounting to an aggregate 183 days or more in any 12-month period beginning or ending in the fiscal year concerned; in such case, only so much of the income as is derived from activities performed in that other State may be taxed in that other State.

2. The term "professional services" includes especially independent scientific, literary, artistic, educational or teaching activities as well as the independent activities of physicians, lawyers, engineers, architects, dentists and accountants.

Article 15. Dependent personal services

1. Subject to the provisions of articles 16, 18 and 19, salaries, wages and other similar remuneration derived by a resident of a Contracting State in respect of an employment shall be taxable only in that State unless the employment is exercised in the other Contracting State. If the employment is so exercised, such remuneration as is derived therefrom may be taxed in that other State.

2. Notwithstanding the provisions of paragraph 1, remuneration derived by a resident of a Contracting State in respect of an employment exercised in the other Contracting State shall be taxable only in the first-mentioned State if:

(a) The recipient is present in the other State for a period or periods not exceeding in the aggregate 183 days in any 12-month period starting or ending in the fiscal year concerned; and

(b) The remuneration is paid by, or on behalf of, an employer who is not a resident of the other State; and

(c) The remuneration is not borne by a permanent establishment or a fixed base which the employer has in the other State.

3. Notwithstanding the preceding provisions of this article, remuneration derived in respect of an employment exercised aboard a ship or aircraft operated in international traffic may be taxed only in the Contracting State of which the operator of the ships or aircraft is a resident.

Article 16. Directors' fees

Directors' fees and other similar payments derived by a resident of a Contracting State in his or her capacity as a member of the board of directors or management or supervisory board of a company which is a resident of the other Contracting State may be taxed in that other State.

Article 17. Artistes and sportspersons

1. Notwithstanding the provisions of articles 14 and 15, income derived by a resident of a Contracting State as an entertainer, such as a theatre, motion picture, radio or television artiste, or a musician, or as a sportsperson, from his or her personal activities as such exercised in the other Contracting State may be taxed in that other State.

2. Where income in respect of personal activities exercised by an entertainer or a sportsperson in his or her capacity as such accrues not to said entertainer or sportsperson but to another person, that income may, notwithstanding the provisions of articles 7, 14 and 15, be taxed in the Contracting State in which the activities of the entertainer or sportsperson are exercised.

3. Notwithstanding the provisions of paragraphs 1 and 2, income derived by a resident of a Contracting State as an entertainer or sportsperson shall be exempt from tax by the other Contracting State if the visit to that other State is substantially supported by public funds of the first-mentioned State or a political subdivision or local authority thereof.

Article 18. Pensions

Subject to the provisions of article 19.2:

(a) Pensions originating in a Contracting State and paid to a resident of the other Contracting State;

(b) Any type of payment, whether periodical or not, provided for in the social security laws of a Contracting State or scheduled under any type of public scheme intended to provide for social welfare in a Contracting State;

are taxable in both Contracting States. However, the payments referred to in subparagraph (b) shall not be taxable in the Contracting State in which the recipient is a resident if such payments, by their nature, are exempt from tax in the other Contracting State in which they arise.

Article 19. Government service

1. Salaries, wages and other similar remuneration, other than pensions, paid by a Contracting State or a political subdivision or a local authority thereof to an individual in respect of services rendered to that State or subdivision or authority shall be taxable only in that State.

2. However, such salaries, wages and other similar remuneration may be taxable in the other Contracting State if the services are rendered in that other State and the individual is a resident of that State who:

(a) Is a national of that State; or

(b) Did not become a resident of that State solely for the purpose of rendering the services.

3. Notwithstanding the provisions of paragraph 1, pensions and other similar remuneration paid by, or out of funds created by, a Contracting State or a political subdivision or a local authority thereof to an individual in respect of services rendered to that State or subdivision or authority shall be taxable only in that State.

Article 20. Students

Payments which a student or business apprentice who is or was immediately before visiting a Contracting State a resident of the other Contracting State and who is present in the first-mentioned State solely for the purpose of his or her education or training receives for the purpose of his or her maintenance, education or training may not be taxed in that State, provided that such payments arise from sources outside that State.

Article 21. Hydrocarbons

1. The provisions of this article shall apply notwithstanding any other provision of this agreement.

2. Where a resident of one Contracting State carries out business activities consisting of the exploration, production, refining, processing, transport, distribution, storage or trade in hydrocarbons in the other Contracting State, and such activities are carried out for a period or periods aggregating more than 30 days in any 12-month period, such activities shall be treated as though they had been conducted through a permanent establishment situated in that other State.

3. For the purpose of calculating the period referred to in the paragraph above, the activities carried out by a company associated with another company shall be considered as having been carried out by the company with which it is associated if the activities in question are identical or substantially similar to those carried out by the last-mentioned company or are part of the same project. For the purposes of this paragraph, the term "associated company" shall have the meaning assigned to it pursuant to the laws of the State where the activities are carried out.

4. Salaries, wages and similar remuneration derived by a resident of a Contracting State in respect of an employment in connection with the exploration, production, refining, processing, transport, distribution, storage or trade in hydrocarbons situated in the other Contracting State shall be taxable in that other State. However, such remuneration shall be taxed only in the first-mentioned Contracting State if the employment is undertaken for an employer who is not a resident of the other Contracting State, provided that the employment is carried out for a period or periods aggregating not more than 30 days in any 12-month period or periods starting or ending in the fiscal year concerned.

Article 22. Other income

1. Income of a resident of a Contracting State, wherever arising, not dealt with in the foregoing articles of this Agreement shall be taxable only in that State.

2. The provisions of paragraph 1 shall not apply to income, other than income from immovable property as defined in article 6.2, if the recipient of such income, being a resident of a Contracting State, carries out business in the other Contracting State through a permanent establishment situated therein, or performs in that other State independent personal services from a fixed base situated therein, and the right or property in respect of which the income is paid is effectively connected with such permanent establishment or fixed base. In such case, the provisions of article 7 or article 14, as the case may be, shall apply.

3. Notwithstanding the provisions of paragraphs 1 and 2, sources of income of a resident of a Contracting State that are not dealt with in the foregoing articles of this agreement and which arise from the other Contracting State may also be taxed in that other State.

TAXATION OF CAPITAL

Article 23. Capital

1. Capital owned by a resident of a Contracting State and situated in the other Contracting State may be taxed in both States.

2. Notwithstanding the provisions of paragraph 1, capital represented by ships, boats or aircraft operated by a resident of a Contracting State in international traffic, and by movable property pertaining to the operation of such ships, boats or aircraft, shall be taxable only in that State.

METHODS FOR ELIMINATION OF DOUBLE TAXATION

Article 24. Methods for elimination of double taxation

1. In Argentina, double taxation shall be avoided as follows:

Where a resident of Argentina derives income or owns capital which, in accordance with the provisions of this Agreement, may be taxed in Mexico, Argentina shall allow:

(a) As a deduction from the tax on the income of that resident, an amount equal to the income tax paid in Mexico pursuant to this Agreement; and

(b) As a deduction from the tax on the capital of that resident corresponding to property situated in Mexico, an amount equivalent to the tax on the capital paid in Mexico.

Such deduction in either case shall not, however, exceed that part of the income tax or capital tax, as computed before the deduction is given, which is attributable, as the case may be, to the income or to the capital which may be taxed in Mexico.

Where, in accordance with any provision of this Agreement, income derived or capital owned by a resident of Argentina is exempt from tax in Argentina, Argentina may nevertheless, in calculating the amount of tax on the remaining income or capital of such resident, take into account the exempted income or capital.

2. In Mexico, in accordance with the provisions and subject to the limitations established in the laws of Mexico, as may be amended from time to time without changing the general principle hereof, Mexico shall allow its residents as a credit against the Mexican tax:

(a) The Argentine tax paid on income which under this Agreement shall be taxable in Argentina, in an amount not exceeding the tax payable in Mexico on such income; and

(b) In the case of a company owning at least 10 per cent of the capital of a company which is a resident of Argentina and from which the first-mentioned company receives dividends, the Argentine tax paid by the distributing company with respect to the profits out of which the dividends are paid.

SPECIAL PROVISIONS

Article 25. Non-discrimination

1. Nationals of a Contracting State shall not be subject in the other Contracting State to any taxation or any requirement connected therewith which is other or more burdensome than the taxation and connected requirements to which nationals of that other State in the same

circumstances, in particular with respect to residence, are or may be subject. Notwithstanding the provisions of article 1, this provision shall also apply to persons who are not residents of one or both of the Contracting States.

2. The taxation on a permanent establishment which an enterprise of a Contracting State has in the other Contracting State shall not be less favourably levied in that other State than the taxation levied on enterprises of that other State carrying on the same activities. This provision shall not be construed as obliging a Contracting State to grant to residents of the other Contracting State any personal allowances, reliefs and reductions for taxation purposes on account of civil status or family responsibilities which it grants to its own residents.

3. Except where the provisions of article 9.1 apply, interest, royalties and other disbursements paid by an enterprise of a Contracting State to a resident of the other Contracting State shall, for the purpose of determining the taxable profits of such enterprise, be deductible under the same conditions as if they had been paid to a resident of the first-mentioned State.

4. Enterprises of a Contracting State, the capital of which is wholly or partly owned or controlled, directly or indirectly, by one or more residents of the other Contracting State, shall not be subject in the first-mentioned State to any taxation or any requirement connected therewith which is other or more burdensome than the taxation and connected requirements to which other similar enterprises of the first-mentioned State are or may be subject.

5. The provisions of this article shall, notwithstanding the provisions of article 2, apply to taxes of every kind and description.

Article 26. Mutual agreement procedure

1. Where a person considers that the actions of one or both of the Contracting States result or will result for that person in taxation not in accordance with the provisions of this Agreement, she said person may, regardless of the remedies provided by the domestic laws of those States, present a case to the competent authority of the Contracting State of which is the person is a resident or, if the case comes under article 25.1, to that of the Contracting State of which the person is a national. The case must be presented within three (3) years from the first notification of the action resulting in taxation not in accordance with the provisions of this Agreement.

2. The competent authority shall endeavour, if the objection appears justified and if it is not itself able to arrive at a satisfactory solution, to resolve the case by mutual agreement with the competent authority of the other Contracting State, with a view to the avoidance of taxation which is not in accordance with this Agreement, provided that the competent authority of the other Contracting State is notified of the case within four (4) years from the due date or the date of filing of the declaration in that other State, whichever is later.

3. The competent authorities of the Contracting States shall endeavour to resolve by mutual agreement any difficulties or doubts arising as to the interpretation or application of this Agreement.

4. The competent authorities of the Contracting States may communicate with each other directly, including through a joint commission consisting of themselves or their representatives, for the purpose of reaching an agreement in the sense of the preceding paragraphs. The competent authorities, through consultations, may develop appropriate bilateral procedures, conditions, methods and techniques for the implementation of the mutual agreement procedure provided for in this article. In addition, a competent authority may develop appropriate unilateral procedures,

conditions, methods and techniques to facilitate the above-mentioned bilateral actions as well as the implementation of the mutual agreement procedure.

5. Notwithstanding the provisions of any other treaty to which the Contracting States are or may become parties, any dispute over a measure taken by a Contracting State involving a tax covered by article 2, or over any eventual discrimination relating to a taxation measure taken by a Contracting State, including a dispute concerning the applicability of this Agreement, shall be submitted for consideration only to the competent authorities of the Contracting States, which shall endeavour to resolve the case by mutual agreement.

Article 27. Exchange of information

The competent authorities of the Contracting States shall exchange such information as is foreseeably relevant for carrying out the provisions of this Agreement or to the administration or enforcement of the domestic laws, concerning taxes of every kind and description, imposed by the Contracting States. The exchange of information is not restricted by articles 1 and 2.

2. Any information received under paragraph 1 by a Contracting State shall be treated as confidential in the same manner as information obtained under the domestic laws of that State and it shall be disclosed only to persons or authorities (including courts and administrative bodies) concerned with the assessment or collection of, the enforcement or prosecution in respect of, or the determination of appeals in relation to, the taxes referred to in paragraph 1, or the oversight of the above. Such persons or authorities shall use the information only for such purposes. They may disclose the information in public court proceedings or in judicial decisions. Notwithstanding the foregoing, information received by a Contracting State may be used for other purposes when such information may be used for such other purposes under the laws of both States and the competent authority of the supplying State authorizes such use.

3. In no case shall the provisions of paragraphs 1 and 2 be construed so as to impose on a Contracting State the obligation:

(a) To carry out administrative measures at variance with the laws and administrative practice of that or of the other Contracting State;

(b) To supply information which is not obtainable under the laws or in the normal course of the administration of that or of the other Contracting State;

(c) To supply information which would disclose any trade, business, industrial, commercial or professional secret or trade process, or information, the disclosure of which would be contrary to public policy (ordre public).

4. If information is requested by a Contracting State in accordance with this article, the other Contracting State shall use its information gathering measures to obtain the requested information, even though that other State may not need such information for its own tax purposes. The obligation contained in the preceding sentence is subject to the limitations of paragraph 3 but in no case shall such limitations be construed to permit a Contracting State to decline to supply information solely because it has no domestic interest in such information

5. In no case shall the provisions of paragraph 3 be construed to permit a Contracting State to decline to supply information solely because the information is held by a bank, other financial institution, nominee or person acting in an agency or a fiduciary capacity or because it relates to ownership interests in a person.

Article 28. Limitation of relief

1. Except as otherwise provided in this article, a person (other than a natural person) who is a resident of a Contracting State and who derives income from the other Contracting State will be entitled to all the benefits of this Agreement otherwise accorded to residents of a Contracting State only if such person satisfies the requirements of paragraph 2 and meets the other conditions of this Agreement for obtaining such benefits.

2. A person of a Contracting State is a qualified person for a fiscal year only if such resident is either:

(a) A governmental entity; or

(b) A company incorporated in any of the Contracting States, if:

(i) The principal class of its shares is listed on a recognized stock exchange as defined in paragraph 4 of this article and is regularly traded on one or more recognized stock exchanges; or

(ii) At least 50 per cent of the aggregate vote and valuc of thc sharcs of the company is owned directly or indirectly by one or more natural persons resident in any of the Contracting States and/or by other persons incorporated in any of the Contracting States, in which at least 50 per cent of the vote or value of the shares or of the interest in the profits are held directly or indirectly by one or more natural persons resident in any of the Contracting States; or

(c) A partnership or association of persons, in which at least 50 per cent or more of the share in the profits is owned by one or more natural persons resident in any of the Contracting States and/or by other persons incorporated in any of the Contracting States, in which at least 50 per cent of the aggregate vote and value of the shares or of the share in the profits is owned directly or indirectly by one or more natural persons resident in any of the Contracting States; or

(d) A charity or other tax-exempt entity that carries on its main activities in any of the Contracting States.

The persons referred to above shall not be entitled to the benefits of this Agreement if more than 50 per cent of their gross income in the fiscal year in question is paid directly or indirectly to persons who are not residents of either Contracting State in the form of payments which are deductible for the purposes of the taxes covered by this Agreement in that person's State of residence.

3. A resident of a Contracting State shall, nevertheless, be entitled to the benefits of this Agreement if the competent authority of the other Contracting State determines that such resident is actively carrying out business in the other State and that the establishment, acquisition or maintenance of such person and the conduct of its operations did not have as one of its principal purposes the obtaining of benefits under this Agreement.

4. For the purposes of this article, the term "recognized stock exchange" means:

(a) In Argentina, the securities markets that operate under the control of the National Securities Commission;

(b) In Mexico, the Mexican Stock Exchange, and

(c) Any other stock exchange agreed upon by the competent authorities of the Contracting States.

5. The competent authorities of the Contracting States shall consult each other by mutual agreement before a resident of a Contracting State is denied relief from taxation in the other Contracting State by reason of the preceding paragraph. The competent authorities of the Contracting States may also settle the mode of application of this article by mutual agreement.

6. The provisions of this Agreement shall not prevent a Contracting State from applying the provisions regarding thin capitalization and controlled foreign companies (in the case of Mexico, preferential tax regimes) or any anti-abuse rules in force in the domestic laws of the Contracting States.

7. Notwithstanding the other provisions of this Agreement and having regard to all relevant facts and circumstances, a tax benefit shall not be granted under this Agreement in respect of an item of income if it is found that one of the main purposes of any arrangement or transaction was to obtain a benefit, unless the benefit is granted in accordance with the object and purpose of the relevant provisions of this Agreement.

Article 29. Members of diplomatic missions and consular posts

Nothing in this Agreement shall affect the fiscal privileges of members of diplomatic missions or consular posts under the general rules of international law or under the provisions of special agreements.

FINAL PROVISIONS

Article 30. Entry into force

1. Each of the Contracting States shall notify the other through the diplomatic channel of the completion of the procedures required by its laws for the entry into force of this Agreement.

2. This Agreement shall enter into force 30 days after the date of the receipt of the last notification and shall have effect:

(a) In respect of taxes withheld at source, on income derived on or after the first of January of the calendar year following the year in which the Agreement enters into force; and

(b) In respect of other taxes on income and on capital, for fiscal years beginning on or after the first of January in the calendar year following the year in which the Agreement enters into force;

3. The Agreement between the Government of the United Mexican States and the Government of the Argentine Republic for the avoidance of double taxation and the prevention of fiscal evasion with respect to taxes on income from ships and aircrafts operation in international transport, of 26 November 1997, shall be definitively terminated as of the moment this Agreement becomes applicable.

Article 31. Termination

This Agreement shall remain in force until terminated by a Contracting State. Either Contracting State may terminate this Agreement through the diplomatic channel by giving notice of termination at least six (6) months before the end of any calendar year after the expiration of a period of three (3) years from the date of the entry into force. In such case, this Agreement shall cease to have effect:

(a) In respect of taxes withheld at source, on income derived on or after 1 January of the calendar year following the year in which the notice of termination was given; and

(b) In respect of other taxes on income and on capital, for fiscal years commencing on or after 1 January in the calendar year following the notice of termination.

IN WITNESS WHEREOF the undersigned, being duly authorized thereto, have signed this Agreement.

DONE at Mexico City, on 4 November 2015, in two copies in the Spanish language, both texts being equally authentic.

For the United Mexican States:
LUIS VIDEGARAY CASO
Minister of Finance and Public Credit

For the Argentine Republic:
RICARDO DANIEL ECHEGARAY
Federal Administrator of Public Revenues

PROTOCOL TO THE AGREEMENT BETWEEN THE UNITED MEXICAN STATES AND THE ARGENTINE REPUBLIC FOR THE AVOIDANCE OF DOUBLE TAXATION AND THE PREVENTION OF FISCAL EVASION WITH RESPECT TO TAXES ON INCOME AND ON CAPITAL

At the time of signing of the "Agreement between the United Mexican States and the Argentine Republic for the avoidance of double taxation and the prevention of fiscal evasion with respect to taxes on income and on capital", the Contracting States have agreed upon the following provisions, which shall form an integral part of the Agreement:

1. With reference to articles 5 and 7:

For the purposes of article 5.4 (d) and article 7.5, the export of goods or merchandise purchased for the enterprise shall comply with the transfer pricing provisions of this Agreement and the domestic laws of each Contracting State.

2. With reference to article 5.2 (f):

It shall be understood that fishing activities constitute a permanent establishment even without a fixed place of business.

3. With reference to article 5.6:

It is provided that, notwithstanding the provisions of this Agreement, in the case of reinsurance, the domestic laws of each Contracting State shall apply.

4. With reference to article 8:

It shall be understood that the benefits referred to in paragraph 1 do not include those arising from land transport.

5. With reference to article 10:

When a company resident in Argentina pays dividends or distributes profits in excess of the accumulated results taxable at the end of the fiscal year immediately preceding the day of the payment or distribution, determined in accordance with the provisions of the Income Tax Law of Argentina, the limitation under article 10.2 shall not apply with respect to the amount of the withholding, pursuant to the provisions of the aforementioned Income Tax Law of Argentina.

6. With reference to article 12:

   (a) In the case of Argentina, it shall be understood that the limitation on withholding at source shall be applicable provided that the registration, verification and authorization requirements provided for in its domestic laws are met.

   (b) The limitation on the tax imposed in the State in which royalties arise established in paragraph 2 (a) shall apply only, in cases of copyright, where such royalties are paid to the author in person or legitimate heirs.

7. With reference to article 12.3:

   (a) Payments in respect of software shall be understood to fall within the scope of the article when only a part of the rights in the program is transferred, whether the payments are made in consideration of the use of a copyright on an item of software for commercial exploitation or in respect of an item of software acquired for the business or professional use of the purchaser, the latter case being items of software which are not standard but which have been adapted in some way for the purchaser.

(b) It shall be understood that payment of any kind for the use of or right to use news shall be considered as copyright on literary, theatrical, musical, artistic or scientific works, included in the definition of the term "royalties".

(c) The term "technical assistance" shall be understood to include the furnishing of independent services whereby the provider undertakes to supply non-patentable knowledge, not involving the transmission of confidential information concerning industrial, commercial or scientific experience, and undertakes to participate with the provider in the application of such knowledge.

8. With reference to article 13:

It shall be understood that the provisions of paragraph 6 shall not apply in relation to property subject to registration, such as aircraft and motor vehicles, in which case the provisions of article 22 shall apply.

9. With reference to article 14:

For the application of the provisions of paragraph 1, the term "fixed base" shall be treated for tax purposes in the same way as the taxation of a permanent establishment.

10. With reference to article 17:

It shall be understood that items of income derived by an artist or sportsperson who is a resident of a Contracting State from the personal activities of that resident in connection with his or her reputation as an artist or sportsperson, carried on in the other Contracting State, may be subject to taxation in that other State.

11. With reference to article 25:

(a) The provisions of paragraph 3 shall apply, in the case of royalties, provided that technology transfer contracts are registered or authorized in accordance with the requirements of the domestic laws of Argentina.

(b) Paragraph 3 shall be understood not to prohibit a Contracting State from making additional information requirements with respect to payments made to non-residents because such requirements are intended to ensure similar levels of compliance and verification in the case of payments to residents and non-residents.

(c) It shall be understood that the provisions of article 21 of the Income Tax Law of Argentina do not contravene the provisions of article 25.2 of the Agreement.

(d) The provisions of paragraph 5 shall apply only to federal taxes.

12. Considering that the main purposes of the Agreement are the elimination of international double taxation and the prevention of tax evasion, in order to eliminate the negative effects that these have on the trade in goods and services and the free movement of capital, technology and persons, in the event that the application of the Agreement does not result in the promotion of their economic relations, the Contracting States agree that, at any time after the expiration of a period of three (3) years from the date of entry into force of the Agreement, the competent authorities may meet to review, without delay, the need for possible changes to the Agreement, based on the experience obtained in its application during the preceding years and the changes introduced in their national tax laws.

IN WITNESS WHEREOF the undersigned, being duly authorized thereto, have signed this Protocol.

DONE at Mexico City, on 4 November 2015, in two copies in the Spanish language, both texts being equally authentic.

For the United Mexican States:
LUIS VIDEGARAY CASO
Minister of Finance and Public Credit

For the Argentine Republic:
RICARDO DANIEL ECHEGARAY
Federal Administrator of Public Revenues

[TRANSLATION IN FRENCH – TRADUCTION EN FRANÇAIS]

ACCORD ENTRE LES ÉTATS-UNIS DU MEXIQUE ET LA RÉPUBLIQUE ARGENTINE TENDANT À ÉVITER LES DOUBLES IMPOSITIONS ET À PRÉVENIR LA FRAUDE FISCALE EN MATIÈRE D'IMPÔTS SUR LE REVENU ET SUR LA FORTUNE

Les États-Unis du Mexique et la République argentine, afin de promouvoir le développement de leurs relations économiques et leur coopération en matière fiscale, et désireux de conclure un accord tendant à éviter les doubles impositions et à prévenir la fraude fiscale en matière d'impôts sur le revenu et sur la fortune, sans créer de possibilités de non-imposition ou d'imposition réduite par le biais de l'évasion ou de la fraude fiscale (y compris par le biais du chalandage fiscal afin d'obtenir les allégements prévus par le présent Accord au profit indirect de personnes résidentes d'États tiers),

Sont convenus de ce qui suit :

CHAMP D'APPLICATION DE L'ACCORD

Article premier. Personnes visées

Le présent Accord s'applique aux personnes qui sont des résidents d'un État contractant ou des deux États contractants.

Article 2. Impôts visés

1. Le présent Accord s'applique aux impôts sur les revenus et sur la fortune prélevés pour le compte d'un État contractant, quel que soit le système de perception.

2. Sont considérés comme impôts sur le revenu et sur la fortune les impôts perçus sur le revenu total, sur la fortune totale, ou sur des éléments du revenu ou de la fortune, y compris les impôts sur les gains provenant de l'aliénation de biens mobiliers ou immobiliers, ainsi que les impôts sur les plus-values.

3. Les impôts actuels auxquels s'applique le présent Accord sont notamment :

   a) Dans le cas de l'Argentine :

      i) L'impôt sur le revenu ;

      ii) L'impôt sur le revenu minimum présumé ; et

      iii) L'impôt sur la fortune ;

      (ci-après dénommés « impôt argentin ») ;

   b) Dans le cas du Mexique :

      i) L'impôt fédéral sur le revenu ;

      (ci-après dénommé « impôt mexicain »).

4. Le présent Accord s'applique aussi aux impôts de nature identique ou analogue qui seraient établis après la signature de l'Accord et qui s'ajouteraient aux impôts actuels ou qui les remplaceraient. Les autorités compétentes des États contractants se communiquent les modifications significatives apportées à leurs législations fiscales respectives.

DÉFINITIONS

Article 3. Définitions générales

1. Au sens du présent Accord, à moins que le contexte n'exige une interprétation différente :
   a) Les expressions « un État contractant » et « l'autre État contractant » désignent, selon le contexte, le Mexique ou l'Argentine ;
   b) Le terme « Argentine » désigne le territoire de la République argentine, défini conformément à ses règles constitutionnelles et à ses lois, et le terme « Mexique » désigne les États-Unis du Mexique et employé au sens géographique, il désigne le territoire des États-Unis du Mexique, y compris les parties intégrées dans la Fédération, les îles, y compris les récifs et les bancs de sable dans les eaux adjacentes ; les îles de Guadalupe et Revillagigedo ; le plateau continental, les fonds marins et le sous-sol des îles, des bancs de sable et des récifs ; les eaux des mers territoriales ainsi que les eaux intérieures, et, au-delà de celles-ci, les zones sur lesquelles, conformément au droit international, le Mexique peut exercer des droits souverains d'exploration et d'exploitation des ressources naturelles des fonds marins, du sous-sol et des eaux surjacentes ; ainsi que l'espace aérien situé au-dessus du territoire national dans la mesure et selon les conditions établies par le droit international ;
   c) Le terme « personne » comprend les personnes physiques, les sociétés et autres groupements de personnes ;
   d) Le terme « société » désigne toute personne morale ou toute entité qui est considérée comme une personne morale aux fins d'imposition ;
   e) Les expressions « entreprise d'un État contractant » et « entreprise de l'autre État contractant » désignent respectivement une entreprise exploitée par un résident d'un État contractant et une entreprise exploitée par un résident de l'autre État contractant ;
   f) L'expression « trafic international » désigne tout transport effectué par un navire ou un aéronef exploité par un résident d'un État contractant, sauf lorsque le navire ou l'aéronef n'est exploité qu'entre des points situés dans l'autre État contractant ;
   g) Le terme « ressortissant » désigne :
      i) Toute personne physique qui possède la nationalité d'un État contractant ;
      ii) Toute personne morale, société de personnes ou association constituée en vertu de la législation en vigueur d'un État contractant ;
   h) L'expression « autorité compétente » désigne :
      i) Dans le cas de l'Argentine, le Secrétariat du Trésor du Ministère de l'économie et des finances publiques ;
      ii) Dans le cas du Mexique, le Ministère des finances et du crédit public.

2. Pour l'application du présent Accord à tout moment par un État contractant, toute expression ou tout terme qui n'y est pas défini a, à moins que le contexte n'exige une interprétation différente, le sens que lui attribue, à ce moment, le droit de cet État relatif aux impôts auxquels s'applique l'Accord, le sens attribué par le droit fiscal applicable de cet État prévalant sur le sens que lui attribuent les autres branches du droit de cet État.

Article 4. Résident

1. Au sens du présent Accord, l'expression « résident d'un État contractant » désigne toute personne qui, en vertu de la législation de cet État, est assujettie à l'impôt dans cet État, en raison de son domicile, de sa résidence, de son lieu de constitution, de son siège de direction ou de tout autre critère de nature analogue, et s'applique aussi à cet État ainsi qu'à toutes ses subdivisions politiques ou collectivités locales. Toutefois, cette expression ne comprend pas les personnes qui ne sont assujetties à l'impôt dans cet État que pour les revenus de sources situées dans cet État ou pour la fortune qui y est située.

2. Lorsque, selon les dispositions du paragraphe 1, une personne physique est un résident des deux États contractants, sa situation est réglée de la manière suivante :

a) Cette personne est considérée comme résidente seulement de l'État où elle dispose d'un foyer d'habitation permanent ; si elle dispose d'un foyer d'habitation permanent dans les deux États, elle est considérée comme résidente seulement de l'État avec lequel ses liens personnels et économiques sont les plus étroits (centre des intérêts vitaux) ;

b) Si l'État dans lequel cette personne a le centre de ses intérêts vitaux ne peut être déterminé, ou si elle ne dispose d'un foyer d'habitation permanent dans aucun des deux États, elle est considérée comme résidente seulement de l'État contractant où elle séjourne de façon habituelle ;

c) Si cette personne séjourne de façon habituelle dans les deux États ou si elle ne séjourne de façon habituelle dans aucun d'eux, elle est considérée comme résidente seulement de l'État dont elle possède la nationalité ;

d) Si cette personne possède la nationalité des deux États ou si elle ne possède la nationalité d'aucun d'eux, les autorités compétentes des États contractants tranchent la question d'un commun accord.

3. Lorsque, selon les dispositions du paragraphe 1, une personne autre qu'une personne physique est résidente des deux États contractants, les autorités compétentes des États contractants s'efforcent de régler la question et de déterminer les modalités d'application de l'Accord à cette personne. À défaut d'accord entre les autorités compétentes des États contractants, cette personne ne peut bénéficier d'aucun des allègements ou des exonérations d'impôts prévus par le présent Accord.

Article 5. Établissement stable

1. Au sens du présent Accord, l'expression « établissement stable » désigne une installation fixe d'affaires par l'intermédiaire de laquelle une entreprise exerce tout ou partie de son activité.

2. L'expression « établissement stable » comprend notamment :

a) Un siège de direction ;

b) Une succursale ;

c) Un bureau ;

d) Une usine ;

e) Un atelier ;

f) Une mine, un puits de pétrole ou de gaz, une carrière ou tout autre lieu lié à l'exploration, l'exploitation ou l'extraction de ressources naturelles, y compris la pêche.

3. L'expression « établissement stable » comprend également :

a) Un chantier de construction, un projet de montage ou d'installation ou des activités de supervision liées à ce projet, mais seulement si ce chantier de construction, ce projet ou ces activités durent plus de six mois ;

b) La fourniture, par une entreprise, de services, y compris des services de conseil, par l'intermédiaire de salariés ou d'autres membres du personnel engagés par l'entreprise à cette fin, mais seulement lorsque des activités de cette nature se poursuivent dans un État contractant pendant une période ou des périodes totalisant plus de six mois au cours de toute période de 12 mois.

Pour le calcul des périodes visées au présent paragraphe, les activités réalisées par une entreprise associée à une autre entreprise, au sens de l'article 9, sont ajoutées aux périodes pendant lesquelles les activités sont réalisées par l'entreprise à laquelle elle est associée, si les activités des deux entreprises sont identiques ou analogues.

4. Nonobstant les dispositions précédentes du présent article, il est considéré que l'expression « établissement stable » ne comprend pas :

a) L'utilisation d'installations pour le stockage ou l'exposition de biens ou de marchandises appartenant à l'entreprise ;

b) L'exploitation d'un stock de biens et marchandises appartenant à l'entreprise aux seules fins de stockage ou d'exposition ;

c) L'exploitation d'un stock de biens ou de marchandises appartenant à l'entreprise aux seules fins de transformation par une autre entreprise ;

d) L'exploitation d'une installation fixe d'affaires aux seules fins d'acheter des biens ou des marchandises ou de réunir des informations pour l'entreprise ;

e) L'exploitation d'une installation fixe d'affaires aux seules fins d'exercer, pour l'entreprise, toute autre activité de caractère préparatoire ou auxiliaire ;

f) L'exploitation d'une installation fixe d'affaires aux seules fins d'exercice cumulé d'activités mentionnées aux alinéas a) à e), à condition que l'ensemble des activités exercées dans cette installation fixe d'affaires résultant de ce cumul garde un caractère préparatoire ou auxiliaire.

5. Nonobstant les dispositions des paragraphes 1 et 2, lorsqu'une personne autre qu'un agent jouissant d'un statut indépendant auquel s'applique le paragraphe 7, agit dans un État contractant pour le compte d'une entreprise de l'autre État contractant, cette entreprise est considérée comme ayant un établissement stable dans le premier État contractant pour toutes les activités que cette personne entreprend pour l'entreprise, si cette personne :

a) Dispose dans cet État de pouvoirs qu'elle y exerce habituellement lui permettant de conclure des contrats au nom de l'entreprise, à moins que les activités de cette personne ne soient limitées à celles visées au paragraphe 4 et qui, si elles étaient exercées par l'intermédiaire d'une installation fixe d'affaires, ne permettraient pas de considérer cette installation comme un établissement stable selon les dispositions de ce paragraphe ; ou

b) Ne dispose pas de tels pouvoirs, mais exploite habituellement dans le premier État contractant un stock de biens ou de marchandises à partir duquel elle livre régulièrement des biens ou des marchandises pour le compte de l'entreprise.

6. Nonobstant les dispositions précédentes du présent article, une société d'assurances d'un État contractant est considérée comme ayant un établissement stable dans l'autre État contractant si elle perçoit des primes sur le territoire de cet autre État ou si elle y assure contre des risques par l'intermédiaire d'une personne autre qu'un agent jouissant d'un statut indépendant auquel s'applique le paragraphe 7.

7. Une entreprise n'est pas considérée comme ayant un établissement stable dans un État contractant du seul fait qu'elle y exerce une activité par l'entremise d'un courtier, d'un commissionnaire général ou de tout autre agent jouissant d'un statut indépendant, à condition que ces personnes agissent dans le cadre ordinaire de leurs activités et que, dans leurs relations commerciales ou financières avec l'entreprise, les conditions ne soient pas différentes de celles généralement convenues par des agents indépendants. Toutefois, lorsque l'agent agit totalement ou presque totalement pour le compte de cette entreprise, la personne n'est pas considérée comme un agent indépendant au sens du présent paragraphe.

8. Le fait qu'une société qui est résidente d'un État contractant contrôle ou est contrôlée par une société qui est résidente de l'autre État contractant ou qui y exerce son activité (que ce soit par l'intermédiaire d'un établissement stable ou non) ne suffit pas, en lui-même, à faire de l'une quelconque de ces sociétés un établissement stable de l'autre.

IMPOSITION DES REVENUS

Article 6. Revenus immobiliers

1. Les revenus qu'un résident d'un État contractant tire de biens immobiliers (y compris les revenus des exploitations agricoles ou forestières) situés dans l'autre État contractant sont imposables dans cet autre État.

2. L'expression « biens immobiliers » a le sens que lui attribue le droit de l'État contractant où les biens considérés sont situés. L'expression comprend en tout cas les accessoires, le cheptel et le matériel utilisé dans les exploitations agricoles et forestières, les droits auxquels s'appliquent les dispositions du droit privé concernant la propriété foncière, l'usufruit des biens immobiliers et les droits à des paiements variables ou fixes pour l'exploitation ou la concession de l'exploitation de gisements minéraux, sources et autres ressources naturelles ; les navires, bateaux et aéronefs ne sont pas considérés comme des biens immobiliers.

3. Les dispositions du paragraphe 1 s'appliquent aux revenus provenant de l'exploitation directe, de la location ou de l'affermage, ainsi que de toute autre forme d'exploitation des biens immobiliers.

4. Les dispositions des paragraphes 1 et 3 s'appliquent également aux revenus provenant des biens immobiliers d'une entreprise ainsi qu'aux revenus provenant de biens immobiliers servant à l'exercice d'une profession indépendante.

Article 7. Bénéfices des entreprises

1. Les bénéfices d'une entreprise d'un État contractant ne sont imposables que dans cet État, à moins que l'entreprise n'exerce son activité dans l'autre État contractant par l'intermédiaire d'un établissement stable qui y est situé. Si l'entreprise exerce ou a exercé son activité d'une telle façon, les bénéfices de l'entreprise sont imposables dans l'autre État, mais uniquement dans la mesure où ils sont imputables à cet établissement stable. À cette fin, les bénéfices de l'entreprise tirés des activités suivantes sont imputables à l'établissement stable :

a) Ventes effectuées ou activités exercées par cet établissement stable ;

b) Ventes, dans cet autre État, de biens ou de marchandises de nature identique ou similaire à ceux qui sont vendus par l'intermédiaire de l'établissement stable ;

c) Autres activités commerciales exercées dans cet autre État, de nature identique ou similaire à celles exercées par l'intermédiaire de cet établissement stable.

Toutefois, les bénéfices tirés des activités décrites aux alinéas b) et c) ne sont pas imposables dans l'autre État contractant si l'entreprise démontre que ces activités ont été exercées pour des raisons autres que l'obtention d'un avantage au titre du présent Accord.

2. Sous réserve des dispositions du paragraphe 3, lorsqu'une entreprise d'un État contractant exerce son activité dans l'autre État contractant par l'intermédiaire d'un établissement stable qui y est situé, il est imputé à cet établissement stable, dans chaque État contractant, les bénéfices qu'il aurait pu réaliser s'il avait constitué une entreprise distincte exerçant des activités identiques ou analogues dans des conditions identiques ou analogues et traitant en toute indépendance avec l'entreprise dont il constitue un établissement stable.

3. Pour déterminer les bénéfices d'un établissement stable, sont admises en déduction les dépenses relatives aux fins poursuivies par cet établissement stable, y compris les dépenses de direction et les frais généraux d'administration, soit dans l'État où est situé cet établissement stable, soit ailleurs. À cet effet, il n'est tenu compte que des dépenses déductibles par l'établissement stable en vertu des dispositions du droit fiscal de l'État contractant dans lequel est situé l'établissement stable.

4. Lorsqu'un établissement stable joue un rôle important et actif dans la négociation et la conclusion de contrats généralement conclus par l'entreprise, indépendamment de la participation d'autres parties de l'entreprise à ces transactions, la proportion des bénéfices de l'entreprise provenant de ces contrats, qui représente la contribution apportée par l'établissement stable aux transactions de l'entreprise dans son ensemble, est attribuée à cet établissement stable.

5. Nonobstant les dispositions du paragraphe 2, aucun bénéfice n'est imputé à un établissement stable du fait qu'il a simplement acheté des biens ou des marchandises pour l'entreprise.

6. Aux fins des paragraphes précédents, les bénéfices à imputer à l'établissement stable sont déterminés chaque année selon la même méthode, à moins qu'il n'existe des motifs valables et suffisants de procéder autrement.

7. Lorsque les bénéfices comprennent des éléments de revenu traités séparément dans d'autres articles du présent Accord, les dispositions de ces articles ne sont pas affectées par les dispositions du présent article.

Article 8. Trafic international

1. Les bénéfices qu'une entreprise d'un État contractant tire de l'exploitation, en trafic international, de navires ou d'aéronefs, ne sont imposables que dans cet État.

2. Aux fins du présent article, les bénéfices provenant de l'exploitation, en trafic international, de navires ou d'aéronefs incluent les revenus tirés de :

a) La location coque nue de navires ou d'aéronefs ; et

b) L'utilisation ou de la location de conteneurs (y compris les remorques et le matériel connexe servant au transport de conteneurs) utilisés pour le transport de biens ou de marchandises ;

si la location ou l'utilisation citée aux alinéas a) ou b) est accessoire à l'exploitation de navires ou d'aéronefs en trafic international.

3. Les dispositions des paragraphes 1 et 2 du présent article s'appliquent également aux bénéfices qu'un résident d'un État contractant tire de sa participation à un consortium, à une coentreprise ou à un organisme international d'exploitation. Les bénéfices imputables à ce résident ne sont imposables que dans l'État contractant dont il est résident.

Article 9. Entreprises associées

1. Lorsque :

a) Une entreprise d'un État contractant participe directement ou indirectement à la direction, au contrôle ou au capital d'une entreprise de l'autre État contractant ; ou que

b) Les mêmes personnes participent directement ou indirectement à la direction, au contrôle ou au capital d'une entreprise d'un État contractant et d'une entreprise de l'autre État contractant ;

et que, dans l'un et l'autre cas, les deux entreprises sont, dans leurs relations commerciales ou financières, liées par des conditions convenues ou imposées qui diffèrent de celles qui seraient convenues entre des entreprises indépendantes, les bénéfices qui, sans ces conditions, auraient été réalisés par l'une des entreprises, mais n'ont pu l'être en fait à cause de ces conditions, peuvent être inclus dans les bénéfices de cette entreprise et imposés en conséquence.

2. Lorsqu'un État contractant inclut dans les bénéfices d'une entreprise de cet État, et impose en conséquence, des bénéfices sur lesquels une entreprise de l'autre État contractant a été imposée dans cet autre État, et que les bénéfices ainsi inclus sont des bénéfices qui auraient été réalisés par l'entreprise du premier État si les conditions convenues entre les deux entreprises avaient été celles qui auraient été convenues entre des entreprises indépendantes, alors cet autre État procède à un ajustement approprié du montant de l'impôt qui y a été perçu sur ces bénéfices. Pour déterminer cet ajustement, il est tenu compte des autres dispositions du présent Accord et, si nécessaire, les autorités compétentes des États contractants se consultent.

3. Les dispositions du paragraphe 2 ne s'appliquent pas lorsque, à la suite d'une procédure judiciaire, administrative ou légale, une décision finale a établi que, du fait d'actions entraînant un ajustement des bénéfices en vertu du paragraphe 1, une des entreprises en cause est passible d'une pénalité pour fraude, faute grave ou défaillance.

Article 10. Dividendes

1. Les dividendes payés par une société résidente d'un État contractant à un résident de l'autre État contractant sont imposables dans cet autre État.

2. Toutefois, ces dividendes sont aussi imposables dans l'État contractant dont la société qui paie les dividendes est résidente et selon la législation de cet État, mais si le bénéficiaire effectif des dividendes est un résident de l'autre État contractant, l'impôt ainsi établi ne peut excéder :

a) 10 % du montant brut des dividendes si le bénéficiaire effectif est une société qui détient directement au moins 25 % du capital de la société qui paie les dividendes ; ou

b) 15 % du montant brut des dividendes dans tous les autres cas.

Les dispositions du présent paragraphe n'affectent pas l'imposition de la société au titre des bénéfices qui servent au paiement des dividendes.

3. Le terme « dividendes » employé dans le présent article désigne les revenus provenant d'actions, d'actions ou de droits de jouissance, de parts de mines, de parts de fondateur ou d'autres parts bénéficiaires à l'exception des créances, ainsi que les revenus d'autres parts sociales soumis au même régime fiscal que les revenus d'actions par la législation de l'État dont la société distributrice est un résident.

4. Les dispositions des paragraphes 1 et 2 ne s'appliquent pas lorsque le bénéficiaire effectif des dividendes, résident d'un État contractant, exerce dans l'autre État contractant dont la société qui paie les dividendes est résidente, soit une activité industrielle ou commerciale par l'intermédiaire d'un établissement stable qui y est situé, soit une profession indépendante au moyen d'une base fixe qui y est située, et que la participation génératrice des dividendes s'y rattache effectivement. Dans ce cas, les dispositions de l'article 7 ou de l'article 14, selon le cas, sont applicables.

5. Lorsqu'une société résidente d'un État contractant tire des bénéfices ou des revenus de l'autre État contractant, cet autre État ne peut percevoir aucun impôt sur les dividendes payés par la société, sauf dans la mesure où ces dividendes sont payés à un résident de cet autre État ou dans la mesure où la participation génératrice des dividendes se rattache effectivement à un établissement stable ou à une base fixe situés dans cet autre État, ni prélever aucun impôt, au titre de l'imposition des bénéfices non distribués, sur les bénéfices non distribués de la société, même si les dividendes payés ou les bénéfices non distribués consistent en tout ou partie en bénéfices ou revenus provenant de cet autre État.

6. Nonobstant toute autre disposition du présent Accord, lorsqu'une société qui est résidente d'un État contractant a un établissement stable dans l'autre État contractant, les bénéfices imposables en vertu du paragraphe 1 de l'article 7 peuvent être assujettis à un impôt supplémentaire prélevé dans cet autre État, conformément à sa législation fiscale lorsque les bénéfices sont payés au siège, mais le prélèvement ne peut excéder 10 % du montant de ces bénéfices, après déduction de l'impôt sur les sociétés prélevé dans cet autre État.

Article 11. Intérêts

1. Les intérêts provenant d'un État contractant et payés à un résident de l'autre État contractant sont imposables dans cet autre État.

2. Toutefois, ces intérêts sont aussi imposables dans l'État contractant d'où ils proviennent et selon la législation de cet État, mais si le bénéficiaire effectif des intérêts est un résident de l'autre État contractant, l'impôt ainsi établi ne peut excéder 12 %.

3. Nonobstant les dispositions du paragraphe 2, les intérêts visés au paragraphe 1 ne sont imposables que dans l'État contractant dont le bénéficiaire effectif des intérêts est résident si :

a) Le bénéficiaire effectif est un des États contractants, l'une de ses subdivisions politiques ou collectivités locales ou la Banque centrale d'un État contractant ;

b) Les intérêts sont payés par l'une des entités mentionnées à l'alinéa a) ;

c) Les intérêts proviennent de l'Argentine et sont payés à l'égard d'un prêt d'une durée d'au moins trois ans accordé par la Banque nationale de commerce extérieure S.N.C., la Nacional Financiera S.N.C. ou la Banque nationale de travaux et services publics S.N.C., ou par toute autre institution convenue par les autorités compétentes des États contractants ; ou

d) Les intérêts proviennent du Mexique et sont payés à l'égard d'un prêt d'une durée d'au moins trois ans accordé par la Banque de la nation argentine et par la Banque d'investissement et de commerce extérieur, ou par toute autre institution convenue par les autorités compétentes des États contractants.

4. Le terme « intérêts » employé dans le présent article désigne les revenus des créances de toute nature, assorties ou non de garanties hypothécaires ou d'une clause de participation aux bénéfices du débiteur, et notamment les revenus des fonds publics et des obligations d'emprunts, y compris les primes et lots attachés à ces titres, ainsi que tout autre revenu considéré comme des revenus de sommes prêtées par la législation de l'État contractant d'où les revenus proviennent. Le terme « intérêts » ne comprend pas les revenus considérés comme des dividendes au sens du paragraphe 3 de l'article 10.

5. Les dispositions des paragraphes 1, 2 et 3 ne s'appliquent pas lorsque le bénéficiaire effectif des intérêts, résident d'un État contractant, exerce, dans l'autre État contractant d'où proviennent les intérêts, soit une activité industrielle ou commerciale par l'intermédiaire d'un établissement stable qui y est situé, soit une profession indépendante au moyen d'une base fixe qui y est située, et que la créance génératrice des intérêts se rattache effectivement : a) à cet établissement stable ou à cette base fixe, ou b) à des activités industrielles ou commerciales visées à l'alinéa c) du paragraphe 1 de l'article 7. Dans ce cas, les dispositions de l'article 7 ou de l'article 14, selon le cas, s'appliquent.

6. Les intérêts sont considérés comme provenant d'un État contractant lorsque le débiteur est un résident de cet État. Toutefois, lorsque le débiteur des intérêts, qu'il soit ou non résident d'un État contractant, a dans un État contractant un établissement stable ou une base fixe pour lesquels la dette donnant lieu au paiement des intérêts a été contractée et qui supportent la charge de ces intérêts, ceux-ci sont considérés comme provenant de l'État où l'établissement stable, ou la base fixe, est situé.

Article 12. Redevances

1. Les redevances générées dans un État contractant et payées à un résident de l'autre État contractant sont imposables dans cet autre État.

2. Toutefois, ces redevances sont également imposables dans l'État contractant de la source et selon la législation de cet État, mais si le bénéficiaire effectif de ces redevances est un résident de l'autre État contractant, l'impôt ainsi établi ne peut excéder :

a) 10 % du montant brut payé pour l'usage ou la concession de l'usage d'un droit d'auteur sur une œuvre littéraire, théâtrale, musicale, artistique ou scientifique ; pour l'usage ou la concession de l'usage d'un brevet, d'un dessin ou d'un modèle, d'un plan ; d'une formule ou d'un procédé secret, d'un logiciel, d'un équipement commercial, industriel ou scientifique, ainsi que pour les informations ayant trait à une expérience acquise dans le domaine industriel, commercial ou scientifique et les honoraires de service technique ; ou

b) 15 % du montant brut des redevances dans tous les autres cas.

Nonobstant les dispositions de l'article 13, le terme « redevances » comprend également les gains provenant de l'aliénation d'un de ces biens ou droits déterminés en fonction de la productivité, de l'usage ou de la cession ultérieure de ces droits ou biens.

3. Le terme « redevances » employé dans le présent article désigne les rémunérations de toute nature payées pour l'usage ou la concession de l'usage d'un droit d'auteur sur une œuvre littéraire, musicale, théâtrale, artistique ou scientifique, d'un logiciel, d'un brevet, d'une marque de fabrique ou d'une marque déposée, d'un dessin ou d'un modèle, d'un plan, d'une formule ou d'un procédé secret, ou d'autres biens incorporels, ou pour l'usage ou la concession de l'usage de tout équipement industriel, commercial ou scientifique, ou pour des informations ayant trait à l'expérience acquise dans les domaines industriel, commercial ou scientifique, et comprend les paiements relatifs à la fourniture d'une assistance technique et les paiements de toute nature concernant des films cinématographiques, des films, des bandes ou tout autre moyen de reproduction utilisé pour la diffusion télévisée.

4. Les dispositions des paragraphes 1 et 2 ne s'appliquent pas lorsque le bénéficiaire effectif des redevances, résident d'un État contractant, exerce dans l'autre État contractant d'où proviennent les redevances, soit une activité industrielle ou commerciale par l'intermédiaire d'un établissement stable qui y est situé, soit une profession indépendante au moyen d'une base fixe qui y est située, et que le droit ou le bien générateur des redevances se rattache effectivement : a) à l'établissement stable ou à la base fixe en question, ou b) aux activités visées à l'alinéa c) du paragraphe 1 de l'article 7. Dans ce cas, les dispositions de l'article 7 ou de l'article 14, selon le cas, sont applicables.

5. Les redevances sont considérées comme provenant d'un État contractant lorsque le débiteur est un résident de cet État. Toutefois, lorsque le débiteur des redevances, qu'il soit ou non résident d'un État contractant, a dans un État contractant un établissement stable ou une base fixe pour lesquels l'engagement donnant lieu aux redevances a été contracté et qui supportent la charge de ces redevances, celles-ci sont considérées comme provenant de l'État contractant où l'établissement stable ou la base fixe sont situés.

Article 13. Gains en capital

1. Les gains qu'un résident d'un État contractant tire de l'aliénation de biens immobiliers visés à l'article 6 et situés dans l'autre État contractant sont imposables dans cet autre État.

2. Les gains issus de l'aliénation de biens meubles qui font partie de l'actif d'un établissement stable qu'une entreprise d'un État contractant a dans l'autre État contractant ou de biens meubles qui appartiennent à une base fixe dont un résident d'un État contractant dispose dans l'autre État contractant pour l'exercice d'une profession indépendante, y compris de tels gains dégagés par l'aliénation de cet établissement stable (seul ou avec l'ensemble de l'entreprise) ou de cette base fixe, sont imposables dans cet autre État.

3. Les gains issus de l'aliénation de navires ou d'aéronefs exploités en trafic international, ou de biens meubles affectés à l'exploitation de ces navires ou aéronefs, ne sont imposables que dans l'État contractant où le siège de direction effective de l'entreprise est situé.

4. Les gains qu'un résident d'un État contractant tire de l'aliénation d'actions ou d'autres titres de participation dont plus de 50 % de la valeur provient directement ou indirectement de biens immobiliers situés dans l'autre État contractant sont imposables dans cet autre État.

5. Les gains issus de l'aliénation de parts ou d'actions en capital d'une société résidente d'un État contractant, autres que ceux visés au paragraphe 4 sont imposables dans cet État. Toutefois, l'impôt ainsi établi ne peut excéder :

a) 10 % des gains en cas de participation directe d'au moins 25 % du capital ;

b) 15 % des gains dans les autres cas.

6. Les gains tirés de l'aliénation de tous biens autres que ceux visés aux paragraphes précédents ne sont imposables que dans l'État contractant dont le cédant est résident.

Article 14. Professions indépendantes

1. Les revenus qu'un résident d'un État contractant tire d'une profession libérale ou d'autres activités de caractère indépendant ne sont imposables que dans cet État ; toutefois, ces revenus sont également imposables dans l'autre État contractant dans les cas suivants :

a) Si ce résident dispose de façon habituelle, dans l'autre État contractant, d'une base fixe pour l'exercice de ses activités ; dans ce cas, seule la fraction des revenus qui est imputable à ladite base fixe est imposable dans l'autre État contractant ; ou

b) Si son séjour dans l'autre État contractant s'étend sur une période ou des périodes d'une durée totale égale ou supérieure à 183 jours au cours de toute période de 12 mois commençant ou s'achevant pendant l'exercice fiscal considéré ; dans ce cas, seule la fraction des revenus qui est tirée des activités exercées dans cet autre État est imposable dans cet autre État.

2. L'expression « profession indépendante » se rapporte notamment aux activités indépendantes d'ordre scientifique, littéraire, artistique, éducatif ou pédagogique, ainsi qu'aux activités indépendantes des médecins, avocats, ingénieurs, architectes, dentistes et comptables.

Article 15. Professions salariées

1. Sous réserve des dispositions des articles 16, 18 et 19, les salaires, traitements et autres rémunérations similaires qu'un résident d'un État contractant reçoit au titre d'un emploi salarié ne

sont imposables que dans cet État, à moins que l'emploi ne soit exercé dans l'autre État contractant. Si l'emploi y est exercé, les rémunérations reçues à ce titre sont imposables dans cet autre État.

2. Nonobstant les dispositions du paragraphe 1, les rémunérations qu'un résident d'un État contractant reçoit au titre d'un emploi salarié exercé dans l'autre État contractant ne sont imposables que dans le premier État si :

a) Le bénéficiaire séjourne dans l'autre État pendant une période ou des périodes n'excédant pas au total 183 jours au cours de toute période de 12 mois commençant ou s'achevant durant l'exercice fiscal concerné ; et

b) Les rémunérations sont payées par un employeur ou pour le compte d'un employeur qui n'est pas un résident de l'autre État ; et

c) La charge des rémunérations n'est pas supportée par un établissement stable ou une base fixe que l'employeur a dans l'autre État.

3. Nonobstant les dispositions précédentes du présent article, les rémunérations reçues au titre d'un emploi exercé à bord d'un navire ou d'un aéronef exploité en trafic international ne sont imposables que dans l'État contractant dont l'entreprise qui exploite le navire ou l'aéronef est résident.

Article 16. Tantièmes

Les tantièmes, jetons de présence et autres rémunérations qu'un résident d'un État contractant reçoit en sa qualité de membre du conseil de direction, du conseil d'administration ou de gestion d'une société résidente de l'autre État contractant sont imposables dans cet autre État.

Article 17. Artistes et sportifs

1. Nonobstant les dispositions des articles 14 et 15, les revenus qu'un résident d'un État contractant tire de ses activités personnelles exercées dans l'autre État contractant en tant qu'artiste du spectacle, tel qu'un artiste de théâtre, de cinéma, de la radio ou de la télévision, ou musicien, ou en tant que sportif, sont imposables dans cet autre État.

2. Lorsque les revenus d'activités qu'un artiste du spectacle ou un sportif exerce personnellement et en cette qualité sont attribués non pas à l'artiste ou au sportif lui-même, mais à une autre personne, ces revenus sont, nonobstant les dispositions des articles 7, 14 et 15, imposables dans l'État contractant où les activités de l'artiste ou du sportif sont exercées.

3. Sous réserve des dispositions des paragraphes 1 et 2, les revenus perçus par un résident d'un État contractant en qualité d'artiste ou de sportif sont exonérés d'impôt dans l'autre État contractant si son séjour dans cet autre État est substantiellement financé par des fonds publics du premier État ou par l'une de ses subdivisions politiques ou collectivités locales.

Article 18. Pensions

Sous réserve des dispositions du paragraphe 2 de l'article 19 :

a) Les pensions provenant d'un État contractant et payées à un résident de l'autre État contractant ;

b) Tous types de paiements, périodiques ou non, visés dans la législation sur la sécurité sociale d'un État contractant ou prévu par tout type de régime public destiné à assurer le bien-être social dans un État contractant ;

sont imposables dans les deux États contractants. Toutefois, les paiements visés à l'alinéa b) ne sont pas imposables dans l'État contractant dont le bénéficiaire est un résident si les paiements concernés sont, par nature, exonérés d'impôt dans l'autre État d'où ils proviennent.

Article 19. Fonction publique

1. Les salaires, traitements et autres rémunérations similaires, autre que les pensions, payés par un État contractant ou l'une de ses subdivisions politiques ou collectivités locales à une personne physique au titre de services fournis à cet État ou à cette subdivision ou collectivité, ne sont imposables que dans cet État.

2. Toutefois, ces traitements, salaires et autres rémunérations similaires ne sont imposables que dans l'autre État contractant si les services sont exécutés dans cet autre État et si la personne physique est un résident de cet État qui :

a) Possède la nationalité de cet État ; ou

b) N'est pas devenu un résident de cet État à seule fin de fournir les services en question.

3. Nonobstant les dispositions du paragraphe 1, les pensions et autres rémunérations similaires payées par un État contractant ou l'une de ses subdivisions politiques ou collectivités locales, soit directement soit par prélèvement sur des fonds qu'ils ont constitués, à une personne physique au titre de services fournis à cet État ou à cette subdivision ou collectivité, ne sont imposables que dans cet État.

Article 20. Étudiants

Les sommes qu'un étudiant ou un stagiaire qui est ou qui était immédiatement avant de se rendre dans un État contractant un résident de l'autre État contractant et qui séjourne dans le premier État à seule fin d'y poursuivre ses études ou sa formation, reçoit pour couvrir ses frais d'entretien, d'études ou de formation ne sont pas imposables dans cet État, à condition qu'elles proviennent de sources situées en dehors de cet État.

Article 21. Hydrocarbures

1. Les dispositions du présent article s'appliquent nonobstant toute autre disposition du présent Accord.

2. Lorsqu'une personne résidente d'un État contractant exerce dans l'autre État contractant des activités industrielles ou commerciales liées à l'exploration, la production, le raffinage, la transformation, le transport, la distribution, le stockage ou le commerce d'hydrocarbures, et que ces activités sont exercées pendant une ou plusieurs périodes d'une durée totale supérieure à 30 jours au cours de toute période de 12 mois, ces activités sont considérées avoir été exercées par l'intermédiaire d'un établissement stable situé dans cet autre État.

3. Pour le calcul de la période visée au précédent paragraphe, les activités exercées par une entreprise associée à une autre entreprise sont considérées comme ayant été exercées par l'entreprise avec laquelle elle est associée, si les activités en question sont identiques ou substantiellement

similaires à celles exercées par cette dernière entreprise, ou font partie du même projet. Au sens du présent paragraphe, l'expression « entreprise associée » a le sens qui lui est attribué par la législation de l'État où les activités sont exercées.

4. Les salaires, traitements et rémunérations similaires qu'un résident d'un État contractant reçoit au titre d'un emploi salarié en rapport avec l'exploration, la production, le raffinage, la transformation, le transport, la distribution, le stockage ou le commerce d'hydrocarbures situés dans l'autre État contractant sont imposables dans cet autre État. Toutefois, ces rémunérations ne sont imposables que dans le premier État contractant si l'emploi est exercé pour un employeur qui n'est pas un résident de l'autre État contractant, à condition que l'emploi soit exercé pendant une ou plusieurs périodes n'excédant pas au total 30 jours au cours de toute période de 12 mois commençant ou s'achevant pendant l'exercice fiscal considéré.

Article 22. Autres revenus

1. Les éléments de revenu d'un résident d'un État contractant, d'où qu'ils proviennent, qui ne sont pas traités dans les articles précédents du présent Accord ne sont imposables que dans cet État.

2. Les dispositions du paragraphe 1 ne s'appliquent pas aux revenus, autres que les revenus provenant des biens immeubles tels que définis au paragraphe 2 de l'article 6, lorsque le bénéficiaire de tels revenus, résident d'un État contractant, exerce dans l'autre État contractant soit une activité industrielle ou commerciale par l'intermédiaire d'un établissement stable qui y est situé soit une profession indépendante au moyen d'une base fixe qui y est située, et que le droit ou le bien générateur des revenus se rattache effectivement à cet établissement stable ou à cette base fixe. Dans ce cas, les dispositions de l'article 7 ou de l'article 14, selon le cas, sont applicables.

3. Nonobstant les dispositions des paragraphes 1 et 2, les éléments du revenu d'un résident d'un État contractant qui ne sont pas traités dans les articles précédents du présent Accord et qui proviennent de l'autre État contractant sont aussi imposables dans cet autre État.

IMPÔT SUR LA FORTUNE

Article 23. Fortune

1. La fortune que possède un résident d'un État contractant et qui est située dans l'autre État contractant est imposable dans les deux États.

2. Nonobstant les dispositions du paragraphe 1, la fortune constituée par des navires, des bateaux ou des aéronefs exploités en trafic international par un résident d'un État contractant en trafic international, ainsi que par des biens meubles affectés à l'exploitation de ces navires, bateaux ou aéronefs, n'est imposable que dans cet État.

ÉLIMINATION DES DOUBLES IMPOSITIONS

Article 24. Élimination des doubles impositions

1. En Argentine, les doubles impositions sont évitées comme suit :

Lorsqu'un résident de l'Argentine reçoit des revenus ou possède de la fortune qui, conformément aux dispositions du présent Accord, sont imposables au Mexique, l'Argentine autorise :

a) Sur l'impôt qu'elle perçoit sur les revenus de ce résident, la déduction d'un montant égal à l'impôt sur le revenu payé au Mexique, conformément aux dispositions du présent Accord ;

b) Sur l'impôt qu'elle perçoit sur la fortune de ce résident correspondant aux biens situés au Mexique, la déduction d'un montant égal à l'impôt sur la fortune payé au Mexique.

Dans l'un et l'autre cas, cette déduction ne peut toutefois excéder la fraction de l'impôt sur le revenu ou de l'impôt sur la fortune, calculé avant déduction, correspondant selon le cas aux revenus ou à la fortune imposables au Mexique.

Lorsque, conformément à une disposition quelconque du présent Accord, les revenus qu'un résident de l'Argentine reçoit, ou la fortune qu'il possède, sont exonérés d'impôt en Argentine, l'Argentine peut néanmoins, pour calculer le montant de l'impôt sur le reste des revenus ou de la fortune de ce résident, tenir compte des revenus ou de la fortune exonérés.

2. Conformément aux dispositions et sous réserve des limitations de la législation du Mexique, telle qu'elle peut être amendée de temps à autre sans que ses principes généraux ne s'en trouvent modifiés, le Mexique permet à ses résidents de déduire de l'impôt mexicain :

a) L'impôt argentin payé sur les revenus imposables en Argentine en vertu du présent Accord, à concurrence d'un montant ne dépassant pas l'impôt dû au Mexique sur ces revenus ; et

b) Dans le cas d'une société détenant au moins 10 % du capital d'une autre société qui est un résident de l'Argentine et qui verse des dividendes à la première, l'impôt argentin payé par la société distributrice de ces dividendes sur les bénéfices qui servent au paiement des dividendes.

Dispositions particulières

Article 25. Non-discrimination

1. Les ressortissants d'un État contractant ne sont soumis dans l'autre État contractant à aucune imposition ou obligation correspondante qui est autre ou plus lourde que celles auxquelles sont ou pourraient être assujettis les ressortissants de cet autre État qui se trouvent dans la même situation, notamment au regard de la résidence. La présente disposition s'applique aussi, nonobstant les dispositions de l'article premier, aux personnes qui ne sont pas des résidents d'un État contractant ou des deux États contractants.

2. L'imposition d'un établissement stable qu'une entreprise d'un État contractant a dans l'autre État contractant n'est pas établie dans cet autre État d'une façon moins favorable que l'imposition des entreprises de cet autre État qui exercent la même activité. La présente disposition ne peut être interprétée comme obligeant un État contractant à accorder aux résidents de l'autre État contractant les déductions personnelles, abattements et réductions d'impôt en fonction de la situation ou des charges de famille qu'il accorde à ses propres résidents.

3. À moins que les dispositions du paragraphe 1 de l'article 9 ne soient applicables, les intérêts, redevances et autres montants payés par une entreprise d'un État contractant à un résident de l'autre État contractant sont déductibles, pour la détermination des bénéfices imposables de cette entreprise, dans les mêmes conditions que s'ils avaient été payés à un résident du premier État.

4. Les entreprises d'un État contractant dont le capital est en totalité ou en partie, directement ou indirectement, détenu ou contrôlé par un ou plusieurs résidents de l'autre État contractant, ne

sont soumises dans le premier État à aucune imposition ou obligation correspondante, qui est autre ou plus lourde que celles auxquelles sont ou pourraient être assujetties les autres entreprises similaires du premier État.

5. Les dispositions du présent article s'appliquent, nonobstant les dispositions de l'article 2, aux impôts de toute nature ou dénomination.

Article 26. Procédure amiable

1. Lorsqu'une personne estime que les mesures prises par un État contractant ou par les deux États contractants entraînent ou entraîneront pour elle une imposition non conforme aux dispositions du présent Accord, elle peut, indépendamment des recours prévus par le droit interne de ces États, soumettre son cas à l'autorité compétente de l'État contractant dont elle est résidente ou, si sa situation relève du paragraphe 1 de l'article 25, à celle de l'État contactant dont elle est ressortissante. Le cas doit être soumis dans un délai de trois ans à partir de la première notification de la mesure entraînant une imposition non conforme aux dispositions du présent Accord.

2. L'autorité compétente s'efforce, si la réclamation lui paraît fondée et si elle n'est pas elle-même en mesure d'y apporter une solution satisfaisante, de résoudre le cas par voie d'accord amiable avec l'autorité compétente de l'autre État contractant, en vue d'éviter une imposition non conforme au présent Accord, à condition que l'autorité compétente de l'autre État contractant soit avertie de l'affaire dans les quatre ans suivant la date d'échéance ou la date de dépôt de la déclaration de retour dans cet autre État, la date la plus tardive étant retenue.

3. Les autorités compétentes des États contractants s'efforcent, par voie d'accord amiable, de résoudre les difficultés ou de dissiper les doutes auxquels peuvent donner lieu l'interprétation ou l'application de l'Accord.

4. Les autorités compétentes des États contractants peuvent communiquer entre elles directement, y compris au sein d'une commission mixte composée de ces autorités ou de leurs représentants, en vue de parvenir à un accord au sens des paragraphes précédents. Les autorités compétentes élaborent, par voie de consultations, des procédures, des conditions, des méthodes et des techniques bilatérales appropriées pour mettre en œuvre la procédure amiable prévue au présent article. En outre, une autorité compétente peut concevoir des procédures, conditions, méthodes et techniques unilatérales appropriées pour faciliter les actions bilatérales susmentionnées et la mise en œuvre de la procédure amiable.

5. Nonobstant les dispositions de tout autre traité auquel les États contractants sont ou pourraient devenir parties, tout différend relatif à une mesure prise par un État contractant concernant un impôt visé à l'article 2, ou toute discrimination relative à une mesure fiscale prise par un État contractant, y compris un différend concernant l'applicabilité du présent Accord, est soumis à l'examen des seules autorités compétentes des États contractants, qui s'efforcent de résoudre le cas par voie d'accord amiable.

Article 27. Échange de renseignements

1. Les autorités compétentes des États contractants échangent les renseignements vraisemblablement pertinents pour appliquer les dispositions du présent Accord ou celles de la législation interne relative aux impôts de toute nature ou dénomination perçus par les États contractants. L'échange de renseignements n'est pas limité par les articles premier et 2.

2. Les renseignements reçus en vertu du paragraphe 1 par un État contractant sont tenus secrets de la même manière que les renseignements obtenus en application de la législation interne de cet État, et ne sont communiqués qu'aux personnes ou autorités (y compris les tribunaux et organes administratifs) concernées par l'établissement ou le recouvrement des impôts mentionnés au paragraphe 1, par les procédures ou poursuites concernant ces impôts, ou par les décisions sur les recours relatifs à ces impôts, ou par le contrôle de ce qui précède. Ces personnes ou autorités n'utilisent les renseignements qu'à ces fins. Elles peuvent faire état de ces renseignements dans le cadre d'audiences publiques de tribunaux ou dans des décisions judiciaires. Nonobstant ce qui précède, les renseignements reçus par un État contractant peuvent être utilisés à d'autres fins si la législation des deux États l'autorise et si l'autorité compétente de l'État qui fournit ces renseignements autorise cette utilisation.

3. Les dispositions des paragraphes 1 et 2 ne peuvent en aucun cas être interprétées comme imposant à un État contractant l'obligation :

a) De prendre des mesures administratives dérogeant à sa législation et à sa pratique administrative ou à celles de l'autre État contractant ;

b) De fournir des renseignements qui ne pourraient être obtenus sur la base de sa législation ou dans le cadre de sa pratique administrative normale ou de celles de l'autre État contractant ;

c) De fournir des renseignements qui révéleraient un secret commercial, industriel, professionnel ou un procédé commercial ou des renseignements dont la communication serait contraire à l'ordre public.

4. Si des renseignements sont demandés par un État contractant conformément aux dispositions du présent article, l'autre État contractant utilise ses mesures de collecte de renseignements pour obtenir les renseignements demandés, quand bien même il n'aurait pas besoin de ces renseignements à ses propres fins fiscales. L'obligation énoncée dans la phrase précédente est soumise aux limitations prévues au paragraphe 3, mais en aucun cas ces limitations ne doivent être interprétées comme autorisant un État contractant à refuser de fournir des renseignements au seul motif qu'il ne détient aucun intérêt national dans de tels renseignements.

5. Les dispositions du paragraphe 3 ne peuvent en aucun cas être interprétées comme permettant à un État contractant de refuser de communiquer des renseignements uniquement parce que ceux-ci sont détenus par une banque, une autre institution financière, un mandataire ou une personne agissant en tant qu'agent ou à titre fiduciaire, ou parce que ces renseignements concernent les droits de propriété d'une personne.

Article 28. Limitation des avantages

1. Sauf disposition contraire du présent article, une personne (autre qu'une personne physique) qui est un résident d'un État contractant et qui tire un revenu de l'autre État contractant ne peut bénéficier de tous les avantages qui seraient autrement prévus pour les résidents d'un État contractant que si cette personne satisfait aux conditions du paragraphe 2 et remplit les autres conditions du présent Accord pour bénéficier de ces avantages.

2. Une personne d'un État contractant est une personne qui répond aux conditions pour la durée d'un exercice fiscal uniquement si ce résident est :

a) Une entité gouvernementale ; ou

b) Une société constituée dans l'un des États contractants, si :

i) La principale catégorie de ses actions est cotée sur un ou plusieurs marchés boursiers reconnus au sens du paragraphe 4 du présent article et sont régulièrement négociées sur un ou plusieurs marchés boursiers ; ou

ii) Au moins 50 % du total des droits de vote et de la valeur des actions de la société sont détenus directement ou indirectement par une ou plusieurs personnes physiques résidentes de l'un des États contractants et/ou par d'autres personnes constituées dans l'un des États contractants, dans lesquels au moins 50 % des droits de vote ou de la valeur des actions ou de la participation aux bénéfices sont détenus directement ou indirectement par une ou plusieurs personnes physiques résidentes de l'un des États contractants ; ou

c) Une société de personnes ou une association de personnes dont au moins 50 % de la participation aux bénéfices est détenue par une ou plusieurs personnes physiques résidentes de l'un des États contractants et/ou par d'autres personnes constituées dans l'un des États contractants, dont au moins 50 % des droits de vote et de la valeur des actions ou de la participation aux bénéfices sont détenus directement ou indirectement par une ou plusieurs personnes physiques résidentes de l'un des États contractants ; ou

d) Une association caritative ou autre entité exonérée d'impôt qui exerce ses principales activités dans l'un des États contractants.

Les personnes visées précédemment n'ont pas droit aux avantages du présent Accord si plus de 50 % de leurs revenus bruts au cours de l'exercice fiscal considéré sont versés, directement ou indirectement, à des personnes qui ne sont pas des résidents de l'un des États contractants, sous forme de paiements déductibles aux fins des impôts visés par le présent Accord dans l'État de résidence de la personne.

3. Un résident d'un État contractant a néanmoins droit aux avantages du présent Accord si l'autorité compétente de l'autre État contractant détermine que ce résident exerce activement une activité industrielle ou commerciale dans l'autre État et que la création, l'acquisition ou l'exploitation de cette personne et la conduite de ces opérations n'avaient pas pour but principal l'obtention d'avantages en vertu de l'Accord.

4. Aux fins du présent article, l'expression « bourse de valeurs reconnue » désigne :

a) En Argentine, les marchés boursiers qui fonctionnent sous le contrôle de la Commission nationale des valeurs mobilières ;

b) Au Mexique, la Bourse mexicaine ; et

c) Toute autre marché boursier convenue par les autorités compétentes des États contractants.

5. Avant qu'un résident d'un État contractant ne se voie refuser un allègement fiscal dans l'autre État contractant en vertu du précédent paragraphe, les autorités compétentes des États contractants se consultent. Les autorités compétentes des États contractants peuvent régler d'un commun accord les modalités d'application du présent article.

6. Les dispositions du présent Accord n'empêchent pas un État contractant d'appliquer les dispositions relatives à la sous-capitalisation et aux entreprises étrangères contrôlées (dans le cas du Mexique, les régimes fiscaux préférentiels) ou toute règle de lutte contre les abus en vigueur dans le droit interne des États contractants.

7. Nonobstant les autres dispositions du présent Accord et compte tenu de tous les faits et circonstances pertinents, un avantage au titre du présent Accord n'est pas accordé à l'égard d'un

élément de revenu s'il est constaté que l'un des principaux objectifs d'une structure ou d'une transaction était d'obtenir cet avantage, à moins qu'il ne soit établi que l'octroi de cet avantage est conforme à l'objet et au but des dispositions pertinentes du présent Accord.

Article 29. Membres de missions diplomatiques et de postes consulaires

Les dispositions du présent Accord ne portent pas atteinte aux privilèges fiscaux dont bénéficient les membres des missions diplomatiques ou des postes consulaires en vertu soit des règles générales du droit international, soit des dispositions d'accords particuliers.

DISPOSITIONS FINALES

Article 30. Entrée en vigueur

1. Les États contractants se notifient mutuellement, par la voie diplomatique, l'accomplissement des procédures requises par leur droit interne pour l'entrée en vigueur du présent Accord.

2. Le présent Accord entre en vigueur 30 jours après la date de réception de la dernière de ces notifications et s'applique :

a) En ce qui concerne les impôts retenus à la source, sur les montants payés à partir du 1er janvier de l'année civile suivant celle de l'entrée en vigueur du présent Accord ; et

b) À l'égard des autres impôts sur le revenu et sur la fortune, pour les exercices fiscaux qui commencent à partir du 1er janvier de l'année civile suivant celle de l'entrée en vigueur de l'Accord.

3. L'Accord entre le Gouvernement des États-Unis du Mexique et le Gouvernement de la République argentine tendant à éviter la double imposition et à prévenir l'évasion fiscale en matière d'impôts sur le revenu en provenance de l'opération des navires et des aéronefs dans le transport international, daté du 26 novembre 1997, sera définitivement abrogé lorsque le présent Accord entrera en vigueur.

Article 31. Dénonciation

Le présent Accord demeure en vigueur jusqu'à ce qu'il soit dénoncé par un État contractant. Chaque État contractant peut le dénoncer moyennant une notification de dénonciation adressée par voie diplomatique au moins six mois avant la fin de toute année civile, après l'expiration d'une période de trois ans à compter de la date d'entrée en vigueur. Dans ce cas, l'Accord cesse de produire ses effets :

a) En ce qui concerne les impôts retenus à la source, à l'égard des montants payés à partir du 1er janvier de l'année civile suivant celle de la notification de dénonciation ; et

b) En ce qui concerne les autres impôts sur le revenu et sur la fortune, pour les exercices fiscaux qui commencent à partir du 1er janvier de l'année civile suivant celle de la notification de dénonciation.

EN FOI DE QUOI, les soussignés, à ce dûment autorisés, ont signé le présent Accord.

FAIT à Mexico, le 4 novembre 2015, en deux exemplaires originaux en langue espagnole, les deux textes faisant également foi.

Pour les États-Unis du Mexique :

LUIS VIDEGARAY CASO
Ministre des finances et du crédit public

Pour la République argentine :

RICARDO DANIEL ECHEGARAY
Administrateur fédéral des revenus publics

PROTOCOLE À L'ACCORD ENTRE LES ÉTATS-UNIS DU MEXIQUE ET LA RÉPUBLIQUE ARGENTINE TENDANT À ÉVITER LES DOUBLES IMPOSITIONS ET À PRÉVENIR LA FRAUDE FISCALE EN MATIÈRE D'IMPÔTS SUR LE REVENU ET SUR LA FORTUNE

Au moment de la signature de l'« Accord entre les États-Unis du Mexique et la République argentine tendant à éviter les doubles impositions et à prévenir la fraude fiscale en matière d'impôts sur le revenu et sur la fortune », les États contractants sont convenus des dispositions suivantes, qui font partie intégrante de l'Accord :

1. En ce qui concerne les articles 5 et 7 :

Aux fins de l'alinéa d) du paragraphe 4 de l'article 5 et du paragraphe 5 de l'article 7, l'exportation de biens ou de marchandises achetés pour l'entreprise doit respecter les dispositions relatives aux prix de transfert conformément au présent Accord et à la législation nationale de chaque État contractant.

2. En ce qui concerne l'alinéa f) du paragraphe 2 de l'article 5 :

Il est entendu que la pêche constitue un établissement stable, même en l'absence d'une base fixe.

3. En ce qui concerne le paragraphe 6 de l'article 5 :

Nonobstant les dispositions de l'Accord, le droit interne de chaque État contractant s'applique en cas de réassurance.

4. En ce qui concerne l'article 8 :

Il est entendu que les bénéfices visés au paragraphe 1 n'incluent pas les bénéfices provenant des transports routiers intérieurs.

5. En ce qui concerne l'article 10 :

Lorsqu'une entreprise résidente de l'Argentine paie des dividendes ou distribue des bénéfices supérieurs aux résultats cumulés imposables à la fin de l'exercice fiscal précédant immédiatement la date du paiement ou de la distribution, déterminé conformément aux dispositions de la loi argentine sur l'impôt sur le revenu, la limitation prévue au paragraphe 2 de l'article 10 ne s'applique pas au montant de la retenue correspondante en vertu des dispositions de la loi argentine susmentionnée sur l'impôt sur le revenu.

6. En ce qui concerne l'article 12 :

   a) Dans le cas de l'Argentine, il est entendu que la limitation concernant la retenue à la source s'applique si les conditions concernant l'enregistrement, la vérification et l'autorisation prévues dans sa législation nationale sont remplies ;

   b) La limite de l'impôt à payer dans l'État d'où proviennent les redevances, établie à l'alinéa a) du paragraphe 2, ne s'applique que dans le cas des droits d'auteur, lorsque ces redevances sont versées à l'auteur lui-même ou à ses ayants droit légitimes.

7. En ce qui concerne le paragraphe 3 de l'article 12 :

   a) Il est entendu que les paiements relatifs aux applications informatiques (logiciels) relèvent du champ d'application de l'article lorsqu'une partie seulement des droits du logiciel est transférée, que les paiements soient réalisés en contrepartie de l'usage d'un droit d'auteur sur un logiciel acheté pour une exploitation commerciale ou pour un usage professionnel ou commercial de l'acheteur ; dans ce dernier cas, il s'agit de logiciels qui ne sont pas totalement standard et ont été adaptés d'une façon ou d'une autre pour l'acheteur ;

b) Il est entendu que les montants de toute nature payés pour l'usage ou la concession de l'usage d'informations sont considérés comme des droits d'auteur sur des œuvres littéraires, théâtrales, musicales, artistiques ou scientifiques, y compris dans la définition du terme « redevances » ;

c) L'expression « assistance technique » inclut la fourniture de services indépendants par lesquels le prestataire s'engage à fournir des connaissances non brevetables et ne comprenant pas la transmission d'informations confidentielles ayant trait à une expérience acquise dans le domaine industriel, commercial ou scientifique, et s'engage à participer à l'application de ces connaissances.

8. En ce qui concerne l'article 13 :

Il est entendu que les dispositions du paragraphe 6 ne s'appliquent pas aux biens soumis à immatriculation, tels que les aéronefs, les véhicules à moteur et les bateaux, auquel cas les dispositions de l'article 22 s'appliquent.

9. En ce qui concerne l'article 14 :

Pour l'application des dispositions du paragraphe 1, l'expression « base fixe » est considérée, aux fins d'imposition, de la même manière que l'imposition d'un établissement stable.

10. En ce qui concerne l'article 17 :

Il est entendu que les éléments de revenu d'un artiste ou d'un sportif résident d'un État contractant provenant d'activités personnelles exercées par lui en relation avec sa réputation en tant qu'artiste ou sportif et exercées dans l'autre État contractant sont imposables dans cet autre État.

11. En ce qui concerne l'article 25 :

a) Les dispositions du paragraphe 3 s'appliquent aux redevances si les contrats de transfert de technologies sont enregistrés ou autorisés conformément aux exigences de la législation interne de l'Argentine ;

b) Il est entendu que le paragraphe 3 n'interdit pas un État contractant d'exiger des renseignements complémentaires à propos de paiements effectués à des non-résidents, puisque l'intention est d'assurer les mêmes niveaux de conformité et de vérification aux paiements versés aux résidents et aux non-résidents ;

c) Il est entendu que les dispositions de l'article 21 de la loi argentine relative à l'impôt sur le revenu ne contreviennent pas aux dispositions du paragraphe 2 de l'article 25 du présent Accord ;

d) Les dispositions du paragraphe 5 s'appliquent uniquement aux impôts fédéraux.

12. Considérant que les principaux objectifs de l'Accord sont d'éliminer les doubles impositions internationales et de prévenir la fraude fiscale, afin d'éliminer leurs effets négatifs sur l'échange de biens et de services et la libre circulation des capitaux, des technologies et des personnes, si la mise en œuvre de l'Accord ne conduit pas à la promotion de leurs relations économiques, les États contractants conviennent que, à tout moment après l'expiration d'une période de trois ans suivant la date d'entrée en vigueur du présent Accord, les autorités compétentes peuvent se réunir pour examiner rapidement la nécessité d'apporter d'éventuelles modifications à l'Accord, en tenant compte de l'expérience acquise dans sa mise en œuvre au cours des années précédentes et des modifications apportées à leur législation fiscale interne.

EN FOI DE QUOI, les soussignés, à ce dûment autorisés, ont signé le présent Protocole.

FAIT à Mexico, le 4 novembre 2015, en deux exemplaires originaux en langue espagnole, les deux textes faisant également foi.

Pour les États-Unis du Mexique :
LUIS VIDEGARAY CASO
Ministre des finances et du crédit public

Pour la République argentine :
RICARDO DANIEL ECHEGARAY
Administrateur fédéral des revenus publics

No. 54784

Turkey and Tunisia

Protocol of cooperation between the Government of the Republic of Tunisia and the Government of the Republic of Turkey in the area of civil registration. Tunis, 6 June 2013

Entry into force: *28 July 2017, in accordance with article 7*

Authentic texts: *Arabic, English and Turkish*

Registration with the Secretariat of the United Nations: *Turkey, 20 November 2017*

Turquie et Tunisie

Protocole de coopération entre le Gouvernement de la République tunisienne et le Gouvernement de la République turque en matière d'enregistrement des faits d'état civil. Tunis, 6 juin 2013

Entrée en vigueur : *28 juillet 2017, conformément à l'article 7*

Textes authentiques : *arabe, anglais et turc*

Enregistrement au Secrétariat de l'Organisation des Nations Unies : *Turquie, 20 novembre 2017*

المادة السابعة: بدأ التنفيذ والإنهاء

1- يدخل هذا البروتوكول حيز التنفيذ بعد ثلاثين (30) يومًا من استلام أخر إشعار مكتوب والذي من خلاله يعلم الأطراف بعضهما البعض عن استيفاء إجراءاتهم القانونية الداخلية اللازمة للدخول في حيز التنفيذ.

2- يظل البروتوكول ساري المفعول لمدة عشر (10) سنوات قابل للتجديد تلقائيًا لمدة خمس (5) سنوات بعد ذلك إن لم يخطر أحد الأطراف المتعاقدة الطرف الآخر برغبته في إنهائه بإخطار مكتوب في مدة لا تقل عن 3 أشهر من إنتهائه.

3- يحق للأطراف إنهاء هذا البروتوكول في أي وقت عن طريق إرسال إخطار نصي مسبق للطرف الآخر بهذا الصدد عن طريق السلك الدبلوماسي. يصبح الانهاء ساري المفعول بعد تسعين (90) يومًا من تاريخ استلام هذا الإخطار.

حرر هذا البروتوكول في تونس يوم 6 جوان 2013 في نسختين أصليتين كلا منهما باللغة التركية والعربية والإنجليزية مع توثيق كل النسخ. يتم العمل بالنسخة الإنجليزية في حالة وجود اختلافات في التأويل.

حكومة الجمهورية التركية	حكومة الجمهورية التونسية
أحمد داود أوغلو	لطفي بن جدو
وزير الشؤون الخارجية	وزير الداخلية

المادة الرابعة: مبادئ التعاون

1- يجب على الأطراف التعاون وفقا لقانونهم الوطني بالإضافة إلى الاتفاقيات الدولية التي ينضم إليها كل منهما مع الأخذ بعين الإعتبار مبادئ حماية البيانات الشخصية.
2- يجب على الأطراف التعاون فيما يخص تبادل المعلومات في مجالات التنسيق والتنظيم وتطبيق برامج التدريب.
3- يجب على الأطراف تحديد أسم أنشطة التعاون المذكورة في هذا البروتوكول وإطارها وطرق تطبيقها ووقتها ومكانها من خلال مناقشات ومراسلات متبادلة.
4- على البلد المضيف توفير خدمات الترجمة خلال أنشطة التعاون.
5- على البلد المضيف توفير مناخ عمل مناسب لتطبيق البرامج.
6- يجب تعزيز التعاون الفني والإداري من خلال زيارات متبادلة.

المادة الخامسة: الأمور التنظيمية والإدارية

1- تعتبر السلطات الوطنية المسؤولة عن تطبيق هذا البروتوكول هي وزارة الداخلية للجمهورية التركية و وزارة الداخلية للجمهورية التونسية.
2- تتحمل البلدان المعنية كل التكاليف المتعلقة بتنمية هذا التعاون وفقا لهذا النمط: يتحمل الطرف المضيف كل تكاليف الأمور التنظيمية المتعلقة بمكان العمل والبرنامج ومصاريف الإقامة، في حين يتحمل الطرف المستضاف التكاليف الخاصه به فيما يتعلق بسفر وفده.
3- على الأطراف في كل الأحوال قبل تنظيم أية زيارة،الأخذ بعين الاعتبار دراسة خيار إقامة مداولات هاتفية في المقام الأول لتجنب أعباء مالية إضافية على ميزانية الوزارات وفقا للتشريعات الوطنية.
4- لدى الأطراف الحق في إعادة النظر في دراسة الأمور ذات الاهتمام المشترك الموجودة في إطار هذا البروتوكول.

المادة السادسة: تسوية النزاعات

يجب حل النزاع الذي قد ينشأ عن تأويل هذه الإتفاقية أو تنفيذها عن طريق تشاور الأطراف

[TEXT IN ARABIC – TEXTE EN ARABE]

بروتوكول تعاون بين حكومة الجمهورية التركية

وحكومة الجمهورية التونسية في مجال التسجيل المدني

اتفقت حكومتي الجمهورية التركية والجمهورية التونسية المشار إليهما فيما يلي "بالأطراف" في إطارتعزيزالعلاقات الودية بين البلدين تطلعًا إلى تطوير التعاون فيما بعد على ما يلي:

المادة الأولى: الهدف

يهدف البروتوكول إلى تطوير التعاون في القضايا الفنية والإدارية فيما يخص التسجيل المدني.

المادة الثانية: الإطار

يشمل هذا البروتوكول تبادل المعلومات والخبرات في المجالات المذكورة أسفله والتي تخضع لأحكام التشريعات الوطنية والالتزامات الدولية.

المادة الثالثة: مجالات التعاون

يتعاون الأطراف في القضايا الفنية والإدارية المتعلقة بالتسجيل المدني والتي تخضع لأحكام التشريعات الوطنية ذات الصلة. وفي إطار هذا التعاون، تم تصور الزيارات التدريبية وبرامج التعليم وتبادل الخبرات والمعلومات، ما لم تشكل تهديدًا على المصالح العامة والأمن الوطني للأطراف ويجب تنظيمها كما يلي:

أ. تأسيس هيكلا للحالة المدنية وتنفيذه وصيانته وتوفير الأمان به.

ب. توفير دراسة التكلفة حول المتطلبات التشغيلية المشتركة وإمكانيات أنظمة التسجيل المدني ذات الصلة.

ج. الصيانة الالكترونية للمعلومات المتعلقة بالعناوين.

د. التكنولوجيا التي تم تنفيذها في بطاقات التعريف بالإضافة إلى الممارسات الإدارية المتعلقة بها.

ه. الأدوات التكنولوجية المستخدمة والممارسات الإدارية التي تم تنفيذها خلال تسجيل بيانات المواطنين ووضعها.

[TEXT IN ENGLISH – TEXTE EN ANGLAIS]

PROTOCOL OF COOPERATION BETWEEN THE GOVERNMENT OF THE REPUBLIC OF TUNUSIA AND THE GOVERNMENT OF THE REPUBLIC OF TURKEY IN THE AREA OF CIVIL REGISTRATION

The Government of the Republic of Tunisia and the Government of the Republic of Turkey hereinafter referred to as the "Parties", wishing to strengthen the friendly relations between the two countries and with the view to further promote their cooperation, have agreed as follows:

Article 1
Purpose

The purpose of this Protocol is to enhance the cooperation on technical and administrative issues regarding civil registration.

Article 2
Scope

This Protocol covers the exchange of information and experience in the areas stated below, subject to the provisions of national legislation and international obligations.

Article 3
Cooperation areas

The Parties shall cooperate in technical and administrative issues related to civil registration subject to relevant national legislation provisions. Training visits, educational programs and exchange of best practices and information, are envisaged in the context of this cooperation, when these do not constitute a threat to the public interest and national security of the Parties and shall be organized with regard to:

a) Establishment, execution, maintenance and security of the civil registration architectures,
b) Feasibility study on the interoperability requirements and capabilities of the relevant civil registration systems.
c) Electronic maintenance of address information,
d) The technology implemented for identity cards as well as the respective administrative practices,
e) Technological tools used and administrative practices implemented while recording and elaborating citizens' data,

Article 4

Cooperation Principles

1- The Parties shall cooperate in accordance with their national legislation, as well as international agreements to which they are parties, concerning the principles of personal data protection.

2- The Parties shall cooperate regarding the exchange of information in the areas of cooperation and organisation and application of training programs.

3- The Parties shall determine the name, scope, application method, time and place of the cooperation activities mentioned in this Protocol by mutual discussion and correspondence.

4- Translation services during the cooperation activities shall be provided by the host country.

5- Working environment for the application of the programs shall be provided by the host country.

6- Technical and administrative cooperation shall be strengthened with mutual visits.

Article 5

Organizational and Financial Matters

1- The national authorities responsible for the implementation of the present Protocol shall be the Ministry of Interior of the Republic of Turkey and the Ministry of Interior of the Tunisia Republic.

2 - All expenditure related to the development of this cooperation shall be borne by the Parties, in the following pattern: The host party covers the expenditure for all organizational matters concerning the working place, accommodation and program whereas the visiting party covers its own expenditure concerning travelling.

3 - In any case, before organizing any visit, both parties should first and foremost examine/consider the option of teleconference so as to avoid additional financial surcharge on the Ministries' budgets, according to national legislation.

4- Both parties have the possibility to further examine matters of mutual interest which fall within the scope of this Protocol.

Article 6

Settlement of Disputes

Differences concerning the interpretation or the implementation of this Protocol shall be settled amicably by negotiations by the Parties.

Article 7
Entry into Force and Termination

This Protocol shall enter into force thirty (30) days after the date of receipt of the last written notification by which the Parties shall inform each other on the fulfillment of their internal legal procedures required for its entry into force.

This Protocol shall remain in force for a period of ten (10) years. Any Party may notify the other Party at any time in writing through diplomatic channels of its intention to terminate the Protocol. The termination shall become effective 90 days after the date of the receipt of this notification. It shall be renewed automatically for successive periods of 5 years, unless one of the Parties notifies the other in writing through diplomatic channels of its intention to terminate the Protocol three (3) months prior to its expiration.

Done in Tunisia, on 06 June 2013 in two originals, each in Turkish, Arabic and English languages, all texts being equally authentic. In case of divergence in interpretation, the English text shall prevail.

FOR THE GOVERNMENT OF THE REPUBLIC OF TURKEY	FOR THE GOVERNMENT OF THE REPUBLIC OF TUNISIA
[signature]	[signature]
AHMET DAVUTOĞLU MINISTER OF FOREIGN AFFAIRS	LOTFI BEN JEDDOU MINISTER OF INTERIOR

[TEXT IN TURKISH – TEXTE EN TURC]

TÜRKİYE CUMHURİYETİ HÜKÜMETİ İLE TUNUS CUMHURİYETİ HÜKÜMETİ ARASINDA NÜFUS İŞLERİ ALANINDA İŞBİRLİĞİ PROTOKOLÜ

Bundan sonra "Taraflar" olarak anılacak olan Türkiye Cumhuriyeti Hükümeti ile Tunus Cumhuriyeti Hükümeti, dostluk bağlarını geliştirmek ve Taraflar arasındaki işbirliğini sürdürmek amacıyla aşağıda belirtilen hususlarda mutabakata varmışlardır.

Madde 1

Amaç

Bu Protokol'ün amacı, Taraflar arasında nüfus işlerine ilişkin teknik ve idari konularda işbirliğini geliştirmektir.

Madde 2

Kapsam

Bu Protokol, ulusal mevzuat ve uluslararası yükümlülüklerin hükümlerine tabi olmak kaydıyla, aşağıda belirlenen alanlarda bilgi ve deneyim paylaşımını kapsamaktadır.

Madde 3

İşbirliği alanları

Taraflar, ulusal mevzuat hükümlerine tabi olmak kaydıyla, nüfus işleriyle ilgili teknik ve idari alanlarda işbirliği yapacaklardır. Bu işbirliği kapsamında, Tarafların kamu yararı ve ulusal güvenliğine karşı tehdit oluşturmadığı sürece, aşağıda belirtilen konularda inceleme ziyaretleri, eğitim programları ve en iyi uygulamaların ve bilginin değişimi öngörülmektedir:

a) Nüfus kayıt düzenlerin kurulması, işletilmesi, sürdürülmesi ve güvenliği,
b) İlgili nüfus kayıt sistemlerinin karşılıklı çalışabilirlik gereklerine ve yeterliliklerine ilişkin fizibilite çalışması,
c) Adres bilgilerinin elektronik ortamda tutulması,
d) Kimlik kartlarında ve karşılıklı olarak idari uygulamalarda kullanılan teknoloji,
e) Vatandaşlara ilişkin verilerin kaydedilmesi ve işlenmesi sırasında kullanılan teknolojik araçlar ve yürütülen idari uygulamalar.

Madde 4

İşbirliği ilkeleri

1- Taraflar, kişisel verilerin korunması ilkelerine ilişkin, ulusal hukukun yanında, taraf oldukları uluslararası andlaşmalara uygun olarak işbirliği yapacaktır.

2- Taraflar işbirliği alanlarında bilgi paylaşımı ile eğitim programlarının düzenlenmesi ve uygulanmasına yönelik işbirliği yapacaktır.

3- Taraflar bu Protokol'de belirtilen işbirliği faaliyetlerinin adı, kapsamı, uygulama şekli, zamanı ve yerini karşılıklı görüşme ve yazışma yoluyla belirleyecektir.

4- İşbirliği faaliyetleri sırasında tercüme hizmetleri ev sahibi ülke tarafından karşılanacaktır.

5- Programların uygulanması için çalışma ortamı ev sahibi ülke tarafından sağlanacaktır.

6- Teknik ve idari işbirliği karşılıklı ziyaretlerle güçlendirilecektir.

Madde 5

Organizasyona İlişkin ve Mali Meseleler

1- Türkiye Cumhuriyeti İçişleri Bakanlığı ve Tunus Cumhuriyeti İçişleri Bakanlığı bu Protokol'ün uygulanmasından sorumlu ulusal makamlardır.

2- Bu işbirliğinin geliştirilmesine yönelik her türlü gider aşağıda gösterilen şekilde karşılanacaktır. Ev sahibi ülke, çalışma yeri, konaklama ve programa ilişkin her türlü organizasyon masrafını karşılarken, misafir ülke kendi heyetinin seyahat masrafını karşılar.

3- Her durumda, herhangi bir ziyaret düzenlenmeden önce, taraflar öncelikle, ulusal mevzuat uyarınca Bakanlıkların bütçelerinde oluşabilecek ek mali yükü önlemek amacıyla telekonferans seçeneğini değerlendirmeli/göz önünde bulundurmalıdır.

4- Taraflar, bu Protokol'ün kapsamına giren karşılıklı çıkar meselelerini ayrıntılı inceleme olanağına sahiptir.

Madde 6

Anlaşmazlıkların Halli

İşbu Protokolün yorumlanması ya da uygulanmasından doğan farklılıklar dostane bir şekilde Taraflar arasındaki görüşmeler ile çözümlenecektir.

Madde 7

Yürürlük ve Sona Erdirme

1- Bu Protokol, Tarafların, Protokol'ün yürürlüğe girmesi için gerekli kendi iç yasal prosedürlerinin tamamlandığına dair son yazılı bildirimin alınmasını takiben otuz (30) gün sonra yürürlüğe girecektir.

2- Bu Protokol on (10) yıl yürürlükte kalacaktır. Taraflardan biri Protokolü sona erdirme niyetini herhangi bir zamanda diplomatik yollar ile diğer tarafa yazılı olarak bildirebilir. Protokol'ün sona ermesi, söz konusu bildirimin yapıldığı tarihten itibaren doksan (90) gün sonra geçerli olacaktır. Taraflardan biri Protokol'ü sona erdirme niyetini, yürürlük süresi dolmadan üç (3) ay önce karşı Tarafa diplomatik kanallardan yazılı olarak bildirmediği sürece 5 yılda bir otomatik olarak yenilenecektir.

Bu Protokol 6 Haziran .2013 günü Tunus'da, iki asıl nüsha halinde, her bir metin aynı derecede geçerli olmak üzere Türkçe, Arapça ve İngilizce olarak imzalanmıştır. Anlaşmazlık durumunda Protokol'ün İngilizce versiyonu geçerli olacaktır.

TÜRKİYE CUMHURİYETİ HÜKÜMETİ ADINA

AHMET DAVUTOĞLU

DIŞİŞLERİ BAKANI

TUNUS CUMHURİYETİ HÜKÜMETİ ADINA

LOTFI BEN JEDDOU

İÇİŞLERİ BAKANI

[TRANSLATION IN FRENCH – TRADUCTION EN FRANÇAIS]

PROTOCOLE DE COOPÉRATION ENTRE LE GOUVERNEMENT DE LA RÉPUBLIQUE TUNISIENNE ET LE GOUVERNEMENT DE LA RÉPUBLIQUE TURQUE EN MATIÈRE D'ENREGISTREMENT DES FAITS D'ÉTAT CIVIL

Le Gouvernement de la République tunisienne et le Gouvernement de la République turque, ci-après dénommés les « Parties », désireux de renforcer les relations amicales entre leurs deux pays et en vue de promouvoir davantage leur coopération, sont convenus de ce qui suit :

Article premier. Objectif

L'objectif du présent Protocole est de renforcer la coopération sur les questions techniques et administratives liées à l'enregistrement des faits d'état civil.

Article 2. Champ d'application

Le présent Protocole couvre l'échange d'informations et d'expériences dans les domaines indiqués ci-dessous, sous réserve des dispositions de la législation interne des Parties et des obligations internationales.

Article 3. Domaines de coopération

Les Parties coopèrent sur les questions techniques et administratives relatives à l'enregistrement des faits d'état civil, sous réserve des dispositions pertinentes en la matière de leur législation interne. Dans le cadre de cette coopération, des visites de formation, des programmes éducatifs ainsi que des échanges de meilleures pratiques et d'informations sont envisagés, s'ils ne constituent pas une menace pour l'intérêt public et la sécurité nationale des Parties, et portent sur les thèmes suivants :

a) L'établissement, la mise en œuvre, l'entretien et la sécurité des dispositifs d'enregistrement des faits d'état civil ;

b) L'étude préalable des exigences et capacités d'interopérabilité des systèmes d'enregistrement des faits d'état civil concernés ;

c) La gestion électronique des informations relatives aux adresses ;

d) La technologie utilisée pour les cartes d'identité ainsi que les pratiques administratives associées ;

e) Les outils technologiques employés et les pratiques administratives adoptées dans le cadre de l'enregistrement et de l'élaboration de données sur les citoyens.

Article 4. Principes de coopération

1. Les Parties coopèrent au sujet des principes de protection des données à caractère personnel, conformément à leur législation interne ainsi qu'aux accords internationaux auxquels elles sont parties.

2. Les Parties coopèrent en matière d'échange d'informations dans les domaines de la coordination, de l'organisation et de la mise en œuvre de programmes de formation.

3. Les Parties discutent et correspondent afin de déterminer l'intitulé, la portée ainsi que la méthode, le moment et le lieu des activités de coopération mentionnées dans le présent Protocole.

4. Les services de traduction fournis pendant les activités de coopération sont assurés par le pays d'accueil.

5. Le pays d'accueil fournit un cadre de travail adéquat pour la mise en œuvre des programmes.

6. La coopération technique et administrative est renforcée par des visites mutuelles.

Article 5. Organisation et financement

1. Les autorités nationales chargées de l'application du présent Protocole sont le Ministère de l'intérieur de la République turque et le Ministère de l'intérieur de la République tunisienne.

2. Les Parties prennent en charge l'ensemble des dépenses liées à la mise en place de leur coopération selon la répartition suivante : la Partie d'accueil couvre tous les frais d'organisation relatifs au lieu d'activité, à l'hébergement et au programme, tandis que la Partie en visite assume ses propres frais de déplacement.

3. Dans tous les cas, avant d'organiser une visite, les deux Parties devraient tout d'abord examiner/envisager la possibilité de se réunir en téléconférence afin d'éviter de faire peser une charge supplémentaire sur les budgets des Ministères, conformément à leur législation interne.

4. Les deux Parties ont la possibilité d'examiner plus avant les questions d'intérêt commun qui relèvent du champ d'application du présent Protocole.

Article 6. Règlement des différends

Les différends concernant l'interprétation ou l'application du présent Protocole sont réglés à l'amiable par voie de négociations entre les Parties.

Article 7. Entrée en vigueur et dénonciation

Le présent Protocole entre en vigueur 30 jours après la date de réception de la dernière des notifications écrites par lesquelles les Parties s'informent de l'accomplissement de leurs procédures juridiques internes nécessaires à cet effet.

Le présent Protocole reste en vigueur pour une durée de 10 ans. Une Partie peut à tout moment notifier à l'autre Partie son intention de dénoncer le Protocole au moyen d'une notification écrite transmise par la voie diplomatique. La dénonciation prend effet 90 jours après la date de réception de cette notification. Le présent Protocole est automatiquement renouvelé pour des périodes successives de cinq ans, à moins que l'une des Parties ne fasse part de son intention de le dénoncer en adressant une notification écrite par la voie diplomatique à l'autre Partie trois mois avant l'expiration de la période concernée.

FAIT en Tunisie, le 6 juin 2013, en deux exemplaires originaux, chacun en langues turque, arabe et anglaise, tous les textes faisant également foi. En cas de divergence d'interprétation, le texte anglais prévaut.

Pour le Gouvernement de la République turque :

AHMET DAVUTOĞLU
Ministre des affaires étrangères

Pour le Gouvernement de la République tunisienne :

LOTFI BEN JEDDOU
Ministre de l'intérieur

No. 54785

Turkey
and
Brunei Darussalam

Agreement on economic, trade and technical cooperation between the Government of the Republic of Turkey and the Government of Brunei Darussalam. Ankara, 10 April 2012

Entry into force: *3 July 2017 by notification, in accordance with article XIV*

Authentic texts: *English and Turkish*

Registration with the Secretariat of the United Nations: *Turkey, 24 November 2017*

Turquie
et
Brunéi Darussalam

Accord de coopération économique, commerciale et technique entre le Gouvernement de la République turque et le Gouvernement du Brunéi Darussalam. Ankara, 10 avril 2012

Entrée en vigueur : *3 juillet 2017 par notification, conformément à l'article XIV*

Textes authentiques : *anglais et turc*

Enregistrement au Secrétariat de l'Organisation des Nations Unies : *Turquie, 24 novembre 2017*

[TEXT IN ENGLISH – TEXTE EN ANGLAIS]

AGREEMENT ON ECONOMIC, TRADE AND TECHNICAL COOPERATION BETWEEN THE GOVERNMENT OF THE REPUBLIC OF TURKEY AND THE GOVERNMENT OF BRUNEI DARUSSALAM

PREAMBLE

The Government of the Republic of Turkey (hereinafter referred as "Turkey") and the Government of Brunei Darussalam (hereinafter referred to as Brunei Darussalam), also referred to individually as a "Party" or collectively as the "Parties",

Desiring to promote friendly relations and develop economic, trade and technical cooperation between the two countries on the basis of equality and mutual respect;

Reaffirming that the economic cooperation will provide a useful framework for enhanced bilateral trade and investment relations and serve the common interests of the Parties;

Recognizing that the two countries are members of the World Trade Organization (WTO);

Considering that bilateral consultation may encourage dialogue, exchanges and implementation of cooperative activities.

Have agreed as follows:

ARTICLE I

MOST FAVOURED NATION TREATMENT (MFN)

The Parties (in conformity with the GATT/WTO obligations) shall grant each other the most-favoured-nation treatment with respect to customs duties and other charges in connection with the imports and exports of goods between two countries.

The provision of this Article shall not apply to any existing or future privileges and advantages granted to third countries within the framework of free trade areas, customs union, other regional agreements and special arrangements with developing countries and border trade.

ARTICLE II

OBJECTIVES

The objectives of this Agreement shall be to;

a) establish a framework for promoting and encouraging bilateral economic and technical cooperation and exchanges between the Parties, in the areas of cooperation set out in this Agreement;

b) strengthen linkages between the relevant ministries and agencies for dialogue and exchanges;
c) promote the interaction and cooperation of the business sectors of the respective Parties.
d) create effective procedures for the implementation of this Agreement.

ARTICLE III

TRADE AND ECONOMIC COOPERATION AREAS

The Parties shall consider ways and means to promote the facilitation and liberalization of trade in accordance with the laws and regulations of the respective Parties in areas of mutual interest and benefit, including:

a) economic, commercial and technical areas;
b) bilateral trade and investment;
c) financial services;
d) air services;
e) energy;
f) information and communications technology;
g) transportation;
h) construction;
i) agriculture and agrifood;
j) industry;
k) culture;
l) sports;
m) tourism cooperation and promotion.

ARTICLE IV

FORMS OF COOPERATION

The forms of cooperation shall include:

a) exchange of information and experience;
b) sharing of best practices and procedures;
c) collaboration of initiatives and projects of mutual benefit and interest;
d) organizing meetings, seminars, workshops and conferences;
e) promoting linkages and exchange of visits between officials and experts in the areas of cooperation mutually identified between the Parties;
f) promoting private sector participation in relevant areas of cooperation; and
g) participating in fairs and exhibitions in the respective countries of the Parties.

The implementation of agreed projects relating to the economic and commercial cooperation within the framework of the present Agreement shall be realized on the basis of contracts or arrangements to be signed between the interested enterprises, organizations or public institutions of the two countries.

ARTICLE V

MODE OF PAYMENT

All payments for goods and services to be exchanged between the two countries shall be made in freely convertible currencies, in accordance with the foreign exchange laws and regulations in force in each respective country.

ARTICLE VI

TEMPORARY IMPORTATION

The Parties, in accordance with their national legislation in force, agree to exempt from customs duties the goods and equipments imported temporarily for use in trade promotional events such as fairs, exhibitions, missions and seminars, provided that such goods and equipment are not subject to commercial transaction and will be re-exported after exhibition.

ARTICLE VII

SHARING OF INFORMATION

The Parties, aiming to improve and diversify the bilateral trade and develop economic cooperation between the two countries, agree to facilitate and accelerate the exchange of information, particularly concerning their respective legislations and economic programmes, to encourage contacts between their companies and organizations involved in trade and economic cooperation.

ARTICLE VIII

IMPLEMENTATION MECHANISM

1. The Parties shall establish a Joint Commission on Economic, Trade and Technical Cooperation (hereinafter referred to as "the Joint Commission") at the Ministerial level to ensure the effective implementation of this Agreement.

2. The Joint Commission shall:

a) facilitate the implementation of the agreed activities and programmes;
b) monitor and review the implementation of this Agreement;
c) make recommendations for promoting cooperation in the areas mentioned in this Agreement;
d) encourage and facilitate direct contacts between the public and private sectors of the two countries.
e) establish committees and call upon experts and advisors to attend the meetings of the Committees. The committees shall report their activities to the Joint Commission.
f) be chaired jointly by Ministers or their representatives from the Ministry of Economy of the Republic of Turkey and the Ministry of Foreign Affairs and Trade of Brunei Darussalam.
g) meet at such venues and times as may be agreed by the Parties.

ARTICLE IX

CONFIDENTIALITY

1. The Parties shall keep confidential and shall not, without the prior written consent of the other Party, disclose or distribute to any third party the documents, information or data acquired as a result of or pursuant to this Agreement.

2. The provisions of this Article shall continue to apply notwithstanding the termination of this Agreement.

ARTICLE X

RELATION TO OTHER AGREEMENTS

This Agreement is without prejudice to the domestic laws and regulations of either Party and any other international agreement to which it is a party.

ARTICLE XI

SETTLEMENT OF DISPUTES

Any dispute between the Parties relating to the interpretation or implementation of the present Agreement shall be resolved amicably without unreasonable delay, by friendly consultations and negotiations between the Parties.

ARTICLE XII

COMMUNICATIONS

Any notice or other communication shall be made in writing and transmitted through diplomatic channels.

ARTICLE XIII

AMENDMENT AND REVIEW

Any amendment or modification to the present Agreement shall be made through diplomatic channels and approved by the Parties. Amendments shall be made in accordance with the procedures in Article 8 and enter into force in accordance with Article 14. Such an amendment shall be deemed as an integral part of this Agreement.

ARTICLE XIV

ENTRY INTO FORCE, DURATION AND TERMINATION

Entry into Force

This agreement shall enter into force on the date of the receipt of the last written notification by which the Parties notify each other, through diplomatic channels, of the completion of their internal legal procedures required for the entry into force of the concerned document.

Validity of the Agreement

The present Agreement shall remain in force for a period of five (5) years and thereafter its validity shall be automatically extended for successive periods of one (1) year, unless a written notice of termination is given by either Party six (6) months prior to its expiration.

Termination

This Agreement may be terminated by either Party giving six (6) months advance written notice to the other Party. The termination of this Agreement shall not affect the activities and projects already in progress or executed according to the provisions of any separate protocol, contract or agreement concluded in respect of the present Agreement, unless the Parties agree otherwise.

In witness whereof, the undersigned being duly authorized by their respective Governments, have signed the present Agreement.

Done and signed in Ankara on April 10, 2012, in duplicate copies in Turkish and English languages, each being equally authentic. In case of any divergence in the texts, the English version shall prevail.

FOR THE GOVERNMENT OF THE REPUBLIC OF TURKEY

Ahmet Yakıcı
Undersecretary of the Ministry of Economy

FOR THE GOVERNMENT OF BRUNEI DARUSSALAM

Dato Mohd Roselan Mohd Daud
Permanent Secretary at the Prime Minister's Office

[TEXT IN TURKISH – TEXTE EN TURC]

TÜRKİYE CUMHURİYETİ HÜKÜMETİ İLE BRUNEİ SULTANLIĞI HÜKÜMETİ ARASINDA EKONOMİK, TİCARET VE TEKNİK İŞBİRLİĞİ ANLAŞMASI

DİBACE

Türkiye Cumhuriyeti Hükümeti (bundan sonra "Türkiye" olarak anılacaktır) ve Brunei Sultanlığı Hükümeti (bundan sonra "Brunei Sultanlığı" olarak anılacaktır), bundan sonra ayrı ayrı "Taraf" ya da birlikte "Taraflar" olarak anılacaktır,

Dostluk ilişkilerini güçlendirmeyi ve iki ülke arasındaki ekonomik, ticari ve teknik işbirliğini eşitlik ve karşılıklı saygı temelinde geliştirmeyi arzu ederek;

Ekonomik işbirliğinin, ikili ticaret ve yatırım ilişkilerinin güçlendirilmesi için yararlı bir çerçeve oluşturacağının ve Tarafların ortak çıkarlarına hizmet edeceğinin tekrar onaylayarak;

İki ülkenin de Dünya Ticaret Örgütü (DTÖ) üyesi olduklarını tanıyarak;

İkili danışmanın, diyalog, değişim ve işbirliği faaliyetlerinin uygulanmasını teşvik edeceğini göz önünde bulundurarak;

aşağıdaki hususlarda karar almıştır:

I. MADDE

EN ÇOK KAYRILAN ULUS MUAMELESİ

Taraflar (GATT/DTÖ yükümlülüklerine uygun olarak), gümrük vergileri ve iki ülke arasındaki mal ithalatı ve ihracatı ile ilgili diğer masraflar konusunda birbirlerine en çok kayrılan ülke muamelesi yapacaklardır.

Bu Madde hükmü, serbest ticaret alanları, gümrük birliği ve diğer bölgesel düzenlemeler ile gelişmekte olan ülkeler ve sınır ticareti ile ilgili özel düzenlemeler çerçevesinde sağlanan ya da gelecekte sağlanacak olan ayrıcalıklara ilişkin olarak uygulanamaz.

II. MADDE

AMAÇLAR

Bu Anlaşmanın amaçları şunlardır;

a) Bu Anlaşma ile belirlenen işbirliği alanlarında, Taraflar arasında ikili ekonomik ve teknik işbirliğini ve karşılıklı değişimleri geliştirecek ve teşvik edecek bir çerçeve kurmak;
b) Diyalog ve değişim için ilgili bakanlıklar ve kuruluşlar arasındaki bağları güçlendirmek;
c) Tarafların iş çevreleri arasındaki işbirliği ve etkileşimi teşvik etmek;
d) Bu Anlaşmanın uygulanması için etkili prosedürler oluşturmak.

III. MADDE

TİCARET VE EKONOMİK İŞBİRLİĞİ ALANLARI

Taraflar, karşılıklı çıkar ve faydanın sözkonusu olduğu alanlarda Tarafların karşılıklı yasa ve düzenlemelerine uygun olarak, aşağıdakiler dâhil olmak üzere ticaretin kolaylaştırılması ve serbestleştirilmesini teşvik edecek yollar ve araçları dikkate alacaktır;

a) Ekonomik, ticari ve teknik alanlar;
b) İkili ticaret ve yatırım;
c) Finansal hizmetler;
d) Hava hizmetleri;
e) Enerji;
f) Bilgi ve iletişim teknolojileri;
g) Ulaştırma;
h) İnşaat;
i) Tarım ve tarımsal gıda;
j) Sanayi;
k) Kültür;
l) Spor;
m) Turizm işbirliği ve teşviki.

IV. MADDE

İŞBİRLİĞİ BİÇİMLERİ

İşbirliği,

a) Bilgi ve tecrübe değişimini;
b) En iyi uygulama ve prosedürlerin paylaşılmasını;
c) Karşılıklı yarar ve çıkara dayalı girişim ve projelerde işbirliğini;
d) Toplantılar, seminerler, çalıştaylar ve konferanslar düzenlenmesini;
e) Taraflar arasında karşılıklı olarak belirlenen işbirliği alanlarında, yetkililer ve uzmanlar arasında bağlantıların ve karşılıklı ziyaretlerin teşvik edilmesini;
f) İlgili işbirliği alanlarında özel sektörün katılımının teşvik edilmesini ve
g) Tarafların ülkelerinde düzenlenen fuar ve sergilere karşılıklı katılım sağlanmasını

içerecektir.

Bu Anlaşma çerçevesinde ekonomik ve ticari işbirliğine ilişkin olarak kararlaştırılan projelerin uygulanması, iki ülkenin ilgili şirketleri, örgütleri ya da kamu kuruluşları arasında imzalanacak sözleşmeler ya da düzenlemeler temelinde gerçekleştirilecektir.

V. MADDE

ÖDEME ŞEKLİ

İki ülke arasında ticarete konu olacak mal ve hizmetlere ilişkin tüm ödemeler, her iki ülkede yürürlükte olan kambiyo kanunlarına ve düzenlemelerine uygun şekilde, serbestçe çevrilebilir para birimleri üzerinden yapılacaktır.

VI. MADDE

GEÇİCİ İTHALAT

Taraflar, yürürlükteki ulusal mevzuatlarına uygun olarak, ticari işleme tabi olmamak ve sergiden sonra geri ihraç edilmek koşuluyla, fuar, sergi, ticaret heyeti ve seminer gibi ticareti geliştirici faaliyetlerde kullanılmak üzere geçici olarak ithal edilen mal ve teçhizat üzerindeki gümrük vergilerinden birbirlerini muaf tutmayı kararlaştırır.

VII. MADDE

BİLGİ PAYLAŞIMI

Taraflar, iki ülke arasındaki ikili ticareti geliştirmek ve çeşitlendirmek ve ekonomik işbirliğini geliştirmek amacıyla, ticari ve ekonomik işbirliği yapan şirket ve kuruluşlararasındaki iletişimi teşvik etmek için başta mevzuat ve ekonomik programları hakkında bilgi değişiminin kolaylaştırılması ve hızlandırılmasıhususunda mutabık kalırlar.

VIII. MADDE

UYGULAMA MEKANİZMASI

1. Taraflar, bu Anlaşmanın etkin bir şekilde uygulanmasını sağlamak üzere Bakanlar düzeyinde bir Ekonomik, Ticaret ve Teknik İşbirliği Karma Komisyonu (bundan sonra "Karma Komisyon" olarak anılacaktır) kuracaklardır.

2. Karma Komisyon,

   a) Kararlaştırılan faaliyet ve programların uygulanmasını kolaylaştıracaktır;
   b) Bu Anlaşmanın uygulanmasınıtakip edecek ve gözden geçirecektir;
   c) Bu Anlaşmada bahsi geçen alanlarda işbirliğini teşvik etmek üzere tavsiyelerde bulunacaktır;
   d) İki ülkenin özel ve kamu sektörleri arasında doğrudan iletişimi kolaylaştıracak ve teşvik edecektir;
   e) Komiteler kuracak ve komite toplantılarına katılmak üzere uzmanları ve danışmanları davet edecektir. Komiteler faaliyetlerini Karma Komisyon'a rapor edecektir;
   f) Bakanlar ya da onların Türkiye Cumhuriyeti Ekonomi Bakanlığı ve Brunei Sultanlığı Dışişleri ve Ticaret Bakanlığı'ndan belirleyecekleri temsilcilerin eşbaşkanlığında toplanacaktır;
   g) Taraflarca kararlaştırılacak yer ve zamanlarda toplanacaktır.

IX. MADDE

GİZLİLİK

1. Taraflar, diğer Tarafın yazılı rızasını almadan önce, bu Anlaşma neticesinde yahut çerçevesinde edinilmiş belge, bilgi ya da verileri gizli tutacaktır ve üçüncü kişilere açıklamayacak ya da dağıtmayacaktır.

2. Bu Maddenin hükümleri, bu Anlaşma feshedilse bile uygulanmaya devam edecektir.

X. MADDE

DİĞER ANLAŞMALAR İLE İLİŞKİSİ

Bu Anlaşma, iki Tarafın ulusal mevzuat ve düzenlemeleri ile taraf olduğu diğer uluslararası anlaşmalara halel getirmez.

XI. MADDE

ANLAŞMAZLIKLARIN HALLİ

Bu Anlaşmanın yorumlanması ve uygulanmasına ilişkin Taraflar arasındaki herhangi bir anlaşmazlık, makul olmayan bir gecikmeye mahal vermeksizin, Taraflar arasında dostane danışma ve müzakereler ile çözümlenecektir.

XII. MADDE

İLETİŞİM

Bildirimler yahut diğer iletişim yazılı olarak yapılacak ve diplomatik yollardan iletilecektir.

XIII. MADDE

DEĞİŞİKLİK VE GÖZDEN GEÇİRME

Bu Anlaşmaya ilişkin herhangi bir değişiklik ya da tadilat diplomatik yollarla yapılacaktır ve Taraflarca onaylanacaktır. Değişiklikler 8. Madde'deki usullere uygun olarak yapılacak ve 14. Madde'ye uygun olarak yürürlüğe girecektir. Bu şekilde yapılan bir değişiklik, Anlaşmanın ayrılmaz bir parçası olarak kabul edilecektir.

XIV. MADDE

YÜRÜRLÜĞE GİRME, SÜRE VE FESİH

Yürürlüğe Girme

Bu Anlaşma, ilgili belgenin yürürlüğe girmesi için gerekli iç hukuk prosedürlerinin tamamlandığını Tarafların diplomatik kanallardan birbirlerine ilettikleri son yazılı bildirimin alındığı tarihte yürürlüğe girecektir.

Anlaşmanın Geçerliliği

Bu Anlaşma beş (5) yıl süreyle yürürlükte kalacaktır ve bu sürenin sonundan itibaren, Taraflardan herhangi biri Anlaşmanın süresi dolmadan altı (6) ay önce yazılı bir fesih bildirimi yapmadığı sürece geçerliliği otomatik olarak müteakip bir (1) yıllık sürelerle uzatılacaktır.

Fesih

Bu Anlaşma, her bir Tarafın altı (6) ay önceden diğer Tarafa yazılı bildirimde bulunması ile feshedilebilir. Bu Anlaşmanın feshi, Taraflar aksi şekilde kararlaştırmadığı sürece, bu Anlaşma çerçevesinde yapılmış farklı bir sözleşme ya da anlaşmanın hükümlerine uygun olarak halen yürütülen ya da hâlihazırda gerçekleştirilmiş faaliyet ve projeleri etkilemeyecektir.

İşbu keyfiyeti teyiden, bu Anlaşma, ilgili Hükümetler tarafından usulüne uygun olarak yetkilendirilenler tarafından imzalanmıştır.

10 Nisan 2012 tarihinde Ankara'da, her ikisi de eşit derecede geçerli Türkçe ve İngilizce iki nüsha olarak düzenlenmiştir ve imzalanmıştır. Metinler üzerinde anlaşmazlık olması durumunda İngilizce nüsha esas alınacaktır.

TÜRKİYE CUMHURİYETİ HÜKÜMETİ ADINA	**BRUNEİ SULTANLIĞI HÜKÜMETİ ADINA**
Ahmet Yakıcı **Ekonomi Bakanlığı Müsteşarı**	**Dato Mohd Roselan Mohd Daud** **Başbakanlık Daimi Müsteşarı**

[TRANSLATION IN FRENCH – TRADUCTION EN FRANÇAIS]

ACCORD DE COOPÉRATION ÉCONOMIQUE, COMMERCIALE ET TECHNIQUE ENTRE LE GOUVERNEMENT DE LA RÉPUBLIQUE TURQUE ET LE GOUVERNEMENT DU BRUNÉI DARUSSALAM

Préambule

Le Gouvernement de la République turque (ci-après dénommée « Turquie ») et le Gouvernement du Brunéi Darussalam (ci-après dénommé « Brunéi Darussalam »), ci-après dénommés individuellement la « Partie » ou collectivement les « Parties »,

Désireux de promouvoir les relations amicales et de développer la coopération économique, commerciale et technique entre les deux pays sur la base de l'égalité et du respect mutuel,

Réaffirmant que la coopération économique fournira un cadre utile au renforcement des relations bilatérales en matière de commerce et d'investissement et servira les intérêts communs des Parties,

Reconnaissant que les deux pays sont membres de l'Organisation mondiale du commerce (OMC),

Considérant que la consultation bilatérale peut favoriser le dialogue, les échanges et la mise en œuvre d'activités de coopération,

Sont convenus de ce qui suit :

Article premier. Régime de la nation la plus favorisée

Les Parties [conformément aux obligations de l'Accord général sur les tarifs douaniers et le commerce (GATT) et de l'OMC] s'accordent le régime de la nation la plus favorisée en ce qui concerne les droits de douane et autres frais au titre des importations et exportations de biens entre les deux pays.

Les dispositions du présent article ne s'appliquent pas aux privilèges et avantages existants ou futurs accordés à des pays tiers dans le cadre de zones de libre-échange, d'unions douanières, d'autres accords régionaux et d'arrangements spéciaux avec les pays en développement et dans le cadre du commerce frontalier.

Article II. Objectifs

Les objectifs du présent Accord sont les suivants :

a) Établir un cadre destiné à promouvoir et à encourager la coopération et les échanges économiques et techniques bilatéraux entre les Parties, dans les domaines de coopération énoncés au présent Accord ;

b) Renforcer les liens entre les ministères et organismes compétents pour le dialogue et les échanges ;

c) Promouvoir l'interaction et la coopération des secteurs commerciaux de chacune des Parties ;

d) Créer des procédures efficaces en vue de la mise en œuvre du présent Accord.

Article III. Domaines de coopération commerciale et économique

Les Parties envisagent les moyens de promouvoir la facilitation et la libéralisation du commerce conformément à leurs lois et règlements respectifs dans les domaines d'intérêt et d'avantage mutuels, notamment :

a) Les domaines économiques, commerciaux et techniques ;

b) Le commerce et l'investissement bilatéraux ;

c) Les services financiers ;

d) Les services aériens ;

e) L'énergie ;

f) Les technologies de l'information et des communications ;

g) Les transports ;

h) La construction ;

i) L'agriculture et l'agroalimentaire ;

j) L'industrie ;

k) La culture ;

l) Les sports ;

m) La coopération touristique et la promotion du tourisme.

Article IV. Formes de coopération

Les formes de coopération incluent :

a) L'échange de renseignements et d'expériences ;

b) Le partage de meilleures pratiques et de procédures ;

c) La collaboration à des initiatives et des projets présentant des intérêts et des avantages mutuels ;

d) L'organisation de réunions, de séminaires, d'ateliers et de conférences ;

e) La promotion des liens et des échanges de visites entre les fonctionnaires et les experts dans les domaines de coopération définis d'un commun accord entre les Parties ;

f) La promotion de la participation du secteur privé dans les domaines de coopération pertinents ;

g) La participation à des foires et expositions dans les pays respectifs des Parties.

La mise en œuvre des projets convenus en matière de coopération économique et commerciale dans le cadre du présent Accord est réalisée sur la base de contrats ou d'arrangements signés par les entreprises, les organisations ou les institutions publiques intéressées des deux pays.

Article V. Mode de paiement

Tous les paiements relatifs aux biens et services échangés entre les deux pays sont effectués dans des devises librement convertibles, conformément aux lois et règlements sur le change en vigueur dans chaque pays.

Article VI. Importation temporaire

Les Parties, conformément à leur législation interne en vigueur, conviennent d'exempter de droits de douane les biens et équipements importés temporairement pour des événements commerciaux promotionnels tels que des foires, des expositions, des missions et des séminaires, à condition que ces biens et équipements ne fassent pas l'objet de transactions commerciales et soient réexportés après l'exposition.

Article VII. Échange de renseignements

Les Parties, afin d'améliorer et de diversifier leurs relations commerciales bilatérales et de développer la coopération économique entre les deux pays, conviennent de faciliter et d'accélérer l'échange de renseignements, notamment en ce qui concerne leurs législations et programmes économiques respectifs, en vue d'encourager les contacts entre leurs entreprises et organisations engagées dans la coopération commerciale et économique.

Article VIII. Mécanisme de mise en œuvre

1. Les Parties établissent une Commission mixte sur la coopération économique, commerciale et technique (ci-après dénommée la « Commission mixte ») au niveau ministériel afin d'assurer la mise en œuvre effective du présent Accord.

2. La Commission mixte :

a) Facilite la mise en œuvre des activités et programmes convenus ;

b) Surveille et examine la mise en œuvre du présent Accord ;

c) Émet des recommandations concernant la promotion de la coopération dans les domaines mentionnés dans le présent Accord ;

d) Encourage et facilite les contacts directs entre les secteurs public et privé des deux pays ;

e) Établit des comités et fait appel à des experts et à des conseillers afin que ces derniers assistent aux réunions desdits comités. Les comités rendent compte de leurs activités à la Commission mixte ;

f) Est présidée conjointement par les Ministres ou leurs représentants du Ministère de l'économie de la République turque et du Ministère des affaires étrangères et du commerce du Brunéi Darussalam ;

g) Se réunit aux lieux et aux dates convenus par les Parties.

Article IX. Confidentialité

1. Les Parties respectent le caractère confidentiel des documents, renseignements ou données acquis du fait ou en vertu du présent Accord, et ne divulguent ni ne transmettent à aucune tierce partie lesdits documents, renseignements ou données sans le consentement écrit préalable de l'autre Partie.

2. Les dispositions du présent article restent applicables nonobstant la dénonciation du présent Accord.

Article X. Rapport avec d'autres accords

Le présent Accord est conclu sans préjudice des lois et règlements internes de chacune des Parties ainsi que de tout autre accord international auquel l'une des Parties est partie.

Article XI. Règlement des différends

Tout différend entre les Parties relatif à l'interprétation ou à la mise en œuvre du présent Accord est réglé à l'amiable, sans retard déraisonnable, par voie de consultations et négociations amiables entre les Parties.

Article XII. Communications

Toute notification ou autre communication est formulée par écrit et transmise par la voie diplomatique.

Article XIII. Amendement et révision

Tout amendement ou modification du présent Accord est effectué par la voie diplomatique et approuvé par les Parties. Les amendements sont effectués conformément aux procédures définies à l'article 8 du présent Accord et entrent en vigueur conformément à l'article 14 du présent Accord. Ces amendements sont considérés comme faisant partie intégrante du présent Accord.

Article XIV. Entrée en vigueur, durée et dénonciation

ENTREE EN VIGUEUR

Le présent Accord entre en vigueur à la date de réception de la dernière des notifications écrites par lesquelles les Parties s'informent mutuellement, par la voie diplomatique, de l'accomplissement de leurs procédures juridiques internes nécessaires à cette fin.

VALIDITE DE L'ACCORD

Le présent Accord reste en vigueur pour une durée de cinq ans et est reconduit automatiquement pour des périodes successives d'un an, à moins que l'une des Parties n'informe par écrit l'autre Partie de son intention de dénoncer l'Accord six mois avant son expiration.

DENONCIATION

Le présent Accord peut être dénoncé par l'une des Parties au moyen d'un préavis écrit adressé à l'autre Partie six mois à l'avance. La dénonciation du présent Accord est sans incidence sur les activités et les projets déjà en cours ou exécutés conformément aux dispositions de tout protocole, contrat ou accord distinct conclu dans le cadre du présent Accord, à moins que les Parties n'en conviennent autrement.

EN FOI DE QUOI, les soussignés, à ce dûment autorisé par leurs Gouvernements respectifs, ont signé le présent Accord.

FAIT et SIGNÉ à Ankara, le 10 avril 2012, en double exemplaire, chacun en langues turque et anglaise, tous les textes faisant également foi. En cas de divergence entre les textes, le texte anglais prévaut.

Pour le Gouvernement de la République turque :

AHMET YAKICI
Sous-secrétaire du Ministère de l'économie

Pour le Gouvernement du Brunéi Darussalam :

DATO MOHD ROSELAN MOHD DAUD
Secrétaire permanent au Cabinet du Premier Ministre

No. 54786

Turkey and Uganda

Agreement between the Government of the Republic of Turkey and the Government of the Republic of Uganda on cooperation in the field of tourism. Kampala, 1 June 2016

Entry into force: *19 May 2017 by notification, in accordance with article 12*

Authentic texts: *English and Turkish*

Registration with the Secretariat of the United Nations: *Turkey, 20 November 2017*

Turquie et Ouganda

Accord entre le Gouvernement de la République turque et le Gouvernement de la République de l'Ouganda relatif à la coopération dans le domaine du tourisme. Kampala, 1er juin 2016

Entrée en vigueur : *19 mai 2017 par notification, conformément à l'article 12*

Textes authentiques : *anglais et turc*

Enregistrement au Secrétariat de l'Organisation des Nations Unies : *Turquie, 20 novembre 2017*

[TEXT IN ENGLISH – TEXTE EN ANGLAIS]

AGREEMENT
BETWEEN
THE GOVERNMENT OF THE REPUBLIC OF TURKEY

AND

THE GOVERNMENT OF THE REPUBLIC OF UGANDA
ON COOPERATION IN THE FIELD OF TOURISM

PREAMBLE

The Government of the Republic of Turkey and the Government of the Republic of Uganda hereinafter referred to as "the Parties"

Desiring to strengthen their existing friendly relations;

Recognizing the importance of tourism as an important factor of development of mutual understanding as well as means for further cultivating the ties and understanding between their peoples,

Desiring to improve mutual brotherhood ties between the people of the two countries,

Striving to develop cooperation in tourism in order to promote the goals of sustainable development and to contribute to social and economic development;

The Parties have agreed upon the following;

ARTICLE 1
Purpose

The Parties shall promote, develop and increase cooperation in the field of tourism within their respective jurisdiction on the basis of equality and mutual benefit.

ARTICLE 2
Tourism Investment

1. The Parties shall encourage, improve and support the efforts and activities of institutions, professionals and other bodies in their countries in the field of tourism, in order to promote mutual entrepreneurship and investment in tourism.
2. The Parties shall inform potential investors about the opportunities in tourism in

both countries.

3. The Parties shall share experiences in financing and building capacities of small and medium sized enterprises in the field of tourism.

ARTICLE 3
Tourism Marketing and Promotion

The Parties shall cooperate for providing technical support to the tourism marketing organizations.

ARTICLE 4
Improving the Quality of Accommodation

1. The Parties shall share experiences in the area of classification and quality control of tourist accommodation facilities.
2. The Parties shall cooperate for utilization of the experiences of vocational training experts, organization of seminars for raising awareness in tourism, improvement and implementation of training programs for personnel of accommodation and food & beverage sectors.

ARTICLE 5
Tourism Research and Development

1. Within the framework of sustainable tourism, the Parties shall cooperate within the framework of a special subtitle, decided unanimously.
2. The Parties shall cooperate for building capacity in the areas of data collection, analysis and dissemination.

ARTICLE 6
Improvement of Rural and Cultural Tourism

1. The Parties shall cooperate for maximizing the benefit of economic development of local people via rural tourism.
2. The Parties shall cooperate for community based tourism projects, cultural and heritage tourism.

ARTICLE 7
Tourism Events and Cultural Exchange

1. Parties shall exchange data on culture and tourism and information on the forthcoming tourism events and festivals to take place in their country.
2. The Parties will support special groups, individual tourists and tourist groups of their country, to participate in music, theatre festivals and also exhibitions, symposiums and congresses in the field of tourism.
3. Mutual workshops about travel industry shall be planned in both countries.
4. Tour operators, journalists, film crews, airline representatives, travel writers, opinion leaders etc. shall be hosted by the Parties to increase mutual tourism demand in both countries.

ARTICLE 8
Expert and Information Exchange

1. The Parties shall organize training programs regarding the related basic proficiency fields like tourism marketing and sustainable tourism development for officers of the two countries. Accommodation and other running expenses of these experts shall be covered by the host country. Educational training and mutual exchange programs shall be organized for the expert staff. Undergraduate and graduate programs on tourism in both countries and share of experience shall be improved. Close cooperation between tourism institutions of the two countries shall be improved.

2. Parties shall share information in the field of tourism as follows :
a) Tourism legislation and management organization development strategy,
b) Management experiences like hotel management, management of facilities and other institutions contributing to tourism,
c) Classification and certification of touristic facilities throughout quality assessment standards, identification of environmental consciousness standards,
d) Directing investments in line with innovation and sustainable tourism principles.

3. The Parties shall share information on current or new tourism products, and any new technology both in the domestic and international tourism arena to enhance and promote tourism.

ARTICLE 9
Coordination and Cooperation

The Parties shall coordinate cooperation in the field of tourism between their respective administrations and other related international organizations via mutual counselling. Also the Parties shall improve cooperation within the framework of United Nations World Tourism Organization and other international organizations.

ARTICLE 10
Joint Committee

The Parties agree to establish a joint technical committee for the implementation of this Agreement and prepare necessary programs for the development of tourism relations between the two countries.

The composition of the joint committee and the schedule of meetings shall be agreed upon by the Parties through the diplomatic channel.

ARTICLE 11
The Competent Authorities

The competent authorities responsible for the implementation of this agreement are:

a) For the Government of the Republic of Turkey, the Ministry of Culture and Tourism;

b) For the Government of the Republic of Uganda, the Ministry of Tourism, Wildlife and Antiquities.

ARTICLE 12
Entry into Force

This Agreement shall enter into force on the date of the receipt of the last notification by the Contracting Parties, in writing and through diplomatic channels, of the completion of the respective internal legal procedures necessary to that effect.

ARTICLE 13
Validity and Postponement

1. This Agreement shall remain in force for a period of five (5) years and shall be automatically renewed for successive five year periods unless terminated in terms of sub article two (2).
2. This Agreement may be terminated by either Party giving six (6) months written notice in advance through the diplomatic channel to the other Party of its intention to terminate this Agreement.
3. The termination of this Agreement shall not affect any existing projects established under the terms of this Agreement. Such projects shall continue until completion.

ARTICLE 14
Amendments

This Agreement may be amended by written mutual consent of the Parties through diplomatic channels. The amendments shall enter in force according to the Article 12 of this Agreement.

ARTICLE 15
Settlement of Disputes

Any dispute between the Parties arising out of the interpretation or implementation of this Agreement shall be settled amicably through mutual consultation or negotiation.

In witness, whereof, the undersigned being duly authorized by their respective Governments have signed this Agreement in two originals in the Turkish and English languages, both texts being equally authentic. In case of any divergency, the English text shall prevail.

Signed on 1st of June, 2016 in Kampala.

For the Government of
the Republic of Turkey

Nihat ZEYBEKCİ
Minister of Economy

For the Government of
the Republic of Uganda

Maria LUBEGA MUTAGAMBA
Minister of Tourism, Wildlife and Antiquities

[TEXT IN TURKISH – TEXTE EN TURC]

TÜRKİYE CUMHURİYETİ HÜKÜMETİ
İLE
UGANDA CUMHURİYETİ HÜKÜMETİ
ARASINDA
TURİZM ALANINDA İŞBİRLİĞİ ANLAŞMASI

GİRİŞ

Türkiye Cumhuriyeti Hükümeti ile Uganda Cumhuriyeti Hükümeti (bundan böyle "Taraflar" olarak anılacaktır)

Mevcut dostluk ilişkilerini güçlendirmek arzusuyla;

Turizmin hem iki ülke halkları arasındaki dostluk ve işbirliğini güçlendirmede, hem de karşılıklı anlayışı geliştirmede önemli bir araç olduğunun farkında olarak,

İki ülke halkları arasında karşılıklı kardeşlik bağlarını geliştirmeyi dileyerek,

Sürdürülebilir gelişmenin hedeflerine ulaşmak, sosyal ve ekonomik gelişmeye katkıda bulunmak amacıyla turizmde işbirliğinin gelişmesine gayret ederek,

Taraflar aşağıdaki hususlarda anlaşmışlardır:

MADDE 1
Amaç

Taraflar eşitlik ve karşılıklı menfaat ilkelerine bağlı kalarak kendi yetkileri çerçevesinde turizm alanında işbirliğini arttıracak, geliştirecek ve teşvik edeceklerdir.

MADDE 2
Turizm Yatırımı

1. Taraflar, turizm alanında karşılıklı yatırımı ve girişimciliği desteklemek amacıyla, ülkelerinde turizm alanında faaliyet gösteren kuruluşların, profesyonellerin ve diğer organların gayretlerini ve faaliyetlerini teşvik edecek, geliştirecek ve destekleyeceklerdir.
2. Taraflar her iki ülkedeki potansiyel yatırımcıları turizm olanakları konusunda bilgilendireceklerdir.
3. Taraflar turizm alanındaki küçük ve orta ölçekli işletmelerin kapasitelerinin geliştirilmesi ile bunların finansmanı konusunda deneyimlerini paylaşacaklardır.

MADDE 3

Turizm Pazarlaması ve Tanıtımı

Taraflar, turizm pazarlama kuruluşlarına teknik destek sağlamak amacıyla işbirliği yapacaklardır.

MADDE 4

Konaklama Kalitesinin Arttırılması

1. Taraflar, turist konaklama tesislerinin sınıflandırılması ve kalite kontrolü alanındaki deneyimlerini paylaşacaklardır.
2. Taraflar mesleki turizm eğitimi konusunda uzman kişilerin deneyimlerinden yararlanılması, turizm bilincinin oluşturulması amacıyla seminerler gerçekleştirilmesi, konaklama ve yeme-içme işletmelerinde çalışan personele yönelik olarak mesleki turizm eğitim programlarının geliştirilmesi ve düzenlenmesi konularında işbirliği yapacaktır.

MADDE 5

Turizme Yönelik Araştırma ve Geliştirme

1. Sürdürülebilir turizm çerçevesinde, taraflar ortaklaşa kararlaştırılacak özel bir alt başlık çerçevesinde işbirliği yapacaklardır.

2. Taraflar veri toplanması, analizi ve yayınlanması alanlarında kapasite oluşturma hususunda işbirliği yapacaklardır.

MADDE 6

Kırsal ve Kültürel Turizmin Geliştirilmesi

1. Taraflar kırsal turizm aracılığıyla yerel halkın ekonomik gelişimine yönelik faydanın en üst düzeye çıkarılması amacına yönelik işbirliğinde bulunacaklardır.
2. Taraflar toplum temelli turizm projeleri, kültürel ve miras turizmi konularında işbirliğinde bulunacaklardır.

MADDE 7

Turizm Faaliyetleri ve Kültürel Değişim

1. Taraflar, kültür ve turizm verileri ile ülkelerinde düzenlenecek turizm faaliyetleri ve festivalleri hakkında bilgi değişiminde bulunacaklardır.

2. Taraflar ülkelerinden turist kişi veya grupların; spor faaliyetleri, müzik ve tiyatro festivalleri ile turizm alanında sergi, sempozyum ve kongrelere katılımlarını destekleyeceklerdir.

3. Her iki ülkede seyahat sektörüne yönelik karşılıklı olarak çalıştaylar düzenlenmesi planlanacaktır.

4. Her iki ülke arasında karşılıklı turizm talebinin artırılması amacıyla; seyahat yazarları, gazeteciler, film ekipleri, tur operatörleri, havayolu temsilcileri, kanaat önderleri vb. kişilerin Taraflarca ağırlanması sağlanacaktır.

MADDE 8

Uzman ve Bilgi Değişimi

1. Taraflar, her iki ülkenin resmi görevlileri için, turizm pazarlaması, turizmin sürdürülebilir gelişimi ve ilgili alanları içeren temel yeterlilik konularında eğitim programları düzenleyeceklerdir. Görevlendirilecek uzman personelin konaklama masrafları ile diğer zaruri giderleri ev sahibi ülke tarafından karşılanacaktır. Uzman personeller için mesleki eğitim ve karşılıklı değişim programları oluşturacaklardır. Her iki ülkedeki turizm lisans ve yüksek lisans programları geliştirilecek ve bu konuda deneyim paylaşımı gerçekleştirilecektir. Her iki ülkenin turizm kuruluşları arasındaki yakın işbirliğini geliştireceklerdir.

2.Taraflar turizm alanında aşağıdaki konuları içeren hususlarda bilgi paylaşımında bulunacaklardır:

a) Turizm mevzuatı ve idari organizasyon gelişme stratejisi,
b) Otel yönetimi ve ilgili diğer tesislerin yönetimi ve turizme katkıda bulunan diğer kuruluşların yönetimi alanlarındaki deneyimleri,
c) Turistik tesislerin nitelik değerlendirme ölçütleri çerçevesinde sınıflandırılması, belgelendirilmesi, çevreye duyarlılık ölçütlerinin belirlenmesi,
d) Yatırımların, yenilikçilik ve sürdürülebilir turizm ilkeleri doğrultusunda yönlendirilmesi.

3.Taraflar turizmi teşvik etmek ve geliştirmek için yeni veya mevcut turizm ürünleri ile hem yerli hem de uluslararası turizm alanındaki herhangi bir yeni teknoloji ile ilgili bilgi paylaşımında bulunacaklardır.

MADDE 9

Koordinasyon ve İşbirliği

Taraflar, kendi yönetimleriyle diğer ilgili uluslararası örgütler arasında turizm alanında işbirliğini karşılıklı istişare yoluyla koordine edeceklerdir. Ayrıca Taraflar Birleşmiş Milletler Dünya Turizm Örgütü ve diğer uluslararası organizasyonlar çerçevesinde işbirliğini geliştireceklerdir.

MADDE 10

Ortak Komite

Taraflar İşbu Anlaşma'nın yürütülmesi için ve iki ülke arasındaki turizm ilişkilerinin geliştirmesi için gerekli programları hazırlamak amacıyla bir ortak teknik komite kurma hususunda anlaşmışlardır.

Ortak komitenin oluşumu ve toplantıların tarihleri diplomatik kanallar yolu ile Taraflarca kararlaştırılacaktır.

MADDE 11

Yetkili Makamlar

İşbu Anlaşmanın yürütülmesinden sorumlu olan yetkili makamlar:

a) Türkiye Cumhuriyeti Hükümeti nezdinde Kültür ve Turizm Bakanlığı,
b) Uganda Cumhuriyeti Hükümeti nezdinde Turizm, Doğal Hayat ve Tarihi Eserler Bakanlığı olacaktır.

MADDE 12

Yürürlüğe Giriş

İşbu Anlaşma, Tarafların, anılan belgenin yürürlüğe girmesi için gerekli iç yasal usulleri tamamladıklarını, birbirlerine yazılı olarak, diplomatik yollarla bildirdikleri son yazılı bildirimin alındığı tarihte yürürlüğe girecektir

MADDE 13

Geçerlilik ve Erteleme

1. İşbu Anlaşma, beş (5) yıllık bir dönem için yürürlükte kalacak ve alt madde iki (2)'de belirtilen durum dışında sona erdirilmediği sürece takip eden beşer(5) yıllık dönemler için kendiliğinden yenilenecektir.
2. İşbu Anlaşma, Taraflardan herhangi birinin diğerine İşbu Anlaşmanın sonlandırılmasına yönelik niyetini altı (6) ay önce diplomatik kanallar yoluyla yazılı olarak bildirdiği sürece feshedilebilir.
3. İşbu Anlaşmanın feshi bu Anlaşma'nın maddelerine dayanarak yürütülmekte olan mevcut projeleri etkilemeyecektir. Bu projeler tamamlanana kadar devam edecektir.

MADDE 14
Değişiklikler

İşbu Anlaşma, Tarafların karşılıklı yazılı onayıyla, diplomatik kanallar aracılığıyla değiştirilebilir. Değişiklikler İşbu Anlaşmanın 12. maddesine göre yürürlüğe girecektir.

MADDE 15
Uyuşmazlıkların Giderilmesi

Taraflar arasında İşbu Anlaşmanın yorumlanmasından veya yürütülmesinden kaynaklanacak herhangi bir uyuşmazlık karşılıklı müzakere ve görüşme yoluyla dostça çözülecektir.

İşbu Anlaşma kendi Hükümetleri tarafından usulünce yetkilendirilmiş olan aşağıda imzası bulunanların tanıklığında, Türkçe ve İngilizce dillerinde, her iki metinde eşit derecede geçerli olmak üzere iki orijinal nüsha halinde imzalanmıştır. Herhangi bir uyuşmazlık durumunda İngilizce metin esas alınacaktır.

1 Haziran 2016 tarihinde Kampala'da imzalanmıştır.

Türkiye Cumhuriyeti
Hükümeti Adına

Nihat ZEYBEKCİ
Ekonomi Bakanı

Uganda Cumhuriyeti
Hükümeti Adına

Maria LUBEGA MUTAGAMBA
Turizm, Vahşi Hayat
ve Tarihi Eserler Bakanı

[TRANSLATION IN FRENCH – TRADUCTION EN FRANÇAIS]

ACCORD ENTRE LE GOUVERNEMENT DE LA RÉPUBLIQUE TURQUE ET LE GOUVERNEMENT DE LA RÉPUBLIQUE DE L'OUGANDA RELATIF À LA COOPÉRATION DANS LE DOMAINE DU TOURISME

Préambule

Le Gouvernement de la République turque et le Gouvernement de la République de l'Ouganda, ci-après dénommés « Parties »,

Désireux de renforcer les relations amicales qui existent entre leurs pays,

Reconnaissant l'importance du tourisme, en tant que facteur essentiel au renforcement de la compréhension mutuelle et moyen de resserrer les liens et d'améliorer la compréhension entre leurs peuples,

Désireux de renforcer les liens de fraternité mutuelle entre les peuples des deux pays,

S'efforçant de favoriser la coopération dans le domaine du tourisme afin de promouvoir les objectifs en matière de développement durable et de participer au développement économique et social,

Sont convenus de ce qui suit :

Article premier. Objectif

Les Parties entendent promouvoir, enrichir et renforcer la coopération dans le domaine du tourisme au sein de leur territoire respectif sur la base des principes d'égalité et des avantages mutuels.

Article 2. Investissement dans le tourisme

1. Les Parties encouragent, améliorent et soutiennent les efforts et les activités des institutions, des professionnels et des autres organismes de leurs pays dans le domaine du tourisme, afin de promouvoir l'entrepreneuriat et les investissements mutuels dans ce domaine.

2. Les Parties informent les éventuels investisseurs des possibilités qu'offre le tourisme dans les deux pays.

3. Les Parties partagent leurs expériences en matière de financement et de renforcement des capacités des petites et moyennes entreprises opérant dans le domaine du tourisme.

Article 3. Marketing touristique et promotion du tourisme

Les Parties coopèrent afin de fournir un appui technique aux organisations spécialisées dans le marketing touristique.

Article 4. Amélioration de la qualité des hébergements

1. Les Parties partagent leurs expériences dans le domaine de la classification et du contrôle de la qualité des installations d'hébergement touristique.

2. Les Parties coopèrent pour mettre à profit l'expérience d'experts en formation professionnelle, organiser des séminaires de sensibilisation au tourisme et améliorer et mettre en œuvre des programmes de formation pour le personnel des secteurs de l'hébergement et de la restauration.

Article 5. Recherche et développement dans le domaine du tourisme

1. S'agissant du tourisme durable, les Parties coopèrent dans le cadre d'un sous-titre spécial convenu à l'unanimité.

2. Les Parties coopèrent pour renforcer les capacités dans les domaines de la collecte, de l'analyse et de la diffusion de données.

Article 6. Amélioration du tourisme rural et culturel

1. Les Parties coopèrent en vue de tirer le meilleur parti des avantages du développement économique des populations locales par l'intermédiaire du tourisme rural.

2. Les Parties coopèrent sur des projets de tourisme communautaire, ainsi que dans les domaines du tourisme culturel et du tourisme de patrimoine.

Article 7. Événements touristiques et échanges culturels

1. Les Parties s'échangent des données concernant la culture et le tourisme ainsi que des renseignements sur les prochains événements et festivals touristiques qui auront lieu dans leur pays.

2. Les Parties aideront les groupes spéciaux, les touristes individuels et les groupes de touristes de leur pays à participer aux festivals de musique et de théâtre, ainsi qu'aux expositions, colloques et congrès liés au tourisme.

3. Des ateliers mutuels sur l'industrie du voyage sont organisés dans les deux pays.

4. Les Parties accueillent des voyagistes, des journalistes, des équipes de tournage, des représentants de compagnies aériennes, des auteurs de récits de voyage, des personnalités influentes, etc., afin d'accroître la demande touristique mutuelle dans les deux pays.

Article 8. Échange de renseignements et d'experts

1. Les Parties organisent des programmes de formation dans des domaines de compétence de base connexes, tels que le marketing touristique et le renforcement du tourisme durable, à l'intention des agents des deux pays. L'hébergement et les autres frais liés aux activités de ces experts sont couverts par le pays hôte. Des programmes de formation et d'échanges mutuels sont organisés pour le personnel expert. Les programmes de premier et de deuxième cycle universitaire sur le tourisme dans les deux pays et le partage d'expérience doivent être améliorés. La coopération étroite entre les institutions touristiques des deux pays est encouragée.

2. Les Parties partagent des informations relevant du domaine du tourisme :
   a) Sur la stratégie de développement de l'organisation de la gestion du tourisme et de la législation relative au tourisme ;
   b) Sur les expériences en matière de gestion comme la gestion hôtelière et la gestion des installations et autres institutions contribuant au tourisme ;
   c) Sur la classification et la certification des installations touristiques grâce à des normes d'évaluation de la qualité et sur le recensement des normes de sensibilisation à l'environnement ;
   d) Sur l'orientation des investissements en fonction de l'innovation et des principes du tourisme durable.

3. Les Parties s'échangent des informations sur les produits touristiques actuels ou les nouveaux produits touristiques, ainsi que sur toute nouvelle technologie relevant du tourisme national ou international afin de favoriser et de promouvoir le tourisme.

Article 9. Coordination et coopération

Les Parties coordonnent la coopération dans le domaine du tourisme entre leurs administrations respectives et d'autres organisations internationales connexes en s'échangeant des conseils. En outre, les Parties renforcent leur coopération dans le cadre de l'Organisation mondiale du tourisme des Nations Unies et d'autres organisations internationales.

Article 10. Comité mixte

Les Parties conviennent de créer un comité technique mixte responsable de la mise en œuvre du présent Accord, ainsi que de préparer les programmes nécessaires à l'approfondissement des relations touristiques entre les deux pays.

La composition du comité mixte ainsi que le calendrier de ses réunions sont convenus par les Parties par la voie diplomatique.

Article 11. Autorités compétentes

Les autorités compétentes responsables de la mise en œuvre de l'Accord sont :

a) Pour le Gouvernement de la République turque, le Ministère de la culture et du tourisme ;

b) Pour le Gouvernement de la République de l'Ouganda, le Ministère du tourisme, de la faune et des antiquités.

Article 12. Entrée en vigueur

Le présent Accord entre en vigueur à la date de réception de la dernière des notifications par lesquelles les Parties contractantes s'informent, par écrit et par la voie diplomatique, de l'accomplissement de leurs procédures juridiques internes respectives nécessaires à cet effet.

Article 13. Validité et report

1. Le présent Accord est conclu pour une période de cinq ans et est automatiquement renouvelé pour des périodes successives de cinq ans, à moins qu'il ne soit dénoncé conformément aux dispositions du paragraphe 2.

2. L'une ou l'autre des Parties peut dénoncer le présent Accord en adressant un préavis écrit de six mois, par la voie diplomatique, à l'autre Partie, l'informant de son intention d'y mettre fin.

3. La dénonciation du présent Accord ne porte pas atteinte aux projets en cours lancés en vertu des dispositions du présent Accord. Lesdits projets se poursuivent jusqu'à leur terme.

Article 14. Amendements

Le présent Accord peut être amendé par consentement mutuel écrit des Parties signifié par la voie diplomatique. Ces amendements entrent en vigueur conformément aux dispositions de l'article 12 du présent Accord.

Article 15. Règlement des différends

Tout différend entre les Parties découlant de l'interprétation ou de l'application du présent Accord est réglé à l'amiable au moyen de consultations ou de négociations.

EN FOI DE QUOI, les soussignés, dûment autorisés par leurs Gouvernements respectifs, ont signé le présent Accord en double exemplaire en langues turque et anglaise, les deux textes faisant également foi. En cas de divergence, le texte anglais prévaut.

SIGNÉ le 1er juin 2016 à Kampala.

Pour le Gouvernement de la République turque :

NIHAT ZEYBEKCI
Ministre de l'économie

Pour le Gouvernement de la République de l'Ouganda :

MARIA LUBEGA MUTAGAMBA
Ministre du tourisme, de la faune et des antiquités

No. 54787

Turkey and Qatar

Security Cooperation Protocol in education and training between the Government of the Republic of Turkey and the Government of the State of Qatar. Doha, 2 December 2015

Entry into force: *18 January 2017 by notification, in accordance with article 14*

Authentic texts: *Arabic, English and Turkish*

Registration with the Secretariat of the United Nations: *Turkey, 24 November 2017*

Turquie et Qatar

Protocole de coopération en matière de sécurité relatif à l'éducation et à la formation entre le Gouvernement de la République turque et le Gouvernement de l'État du Qatar. Doha, 2 décembre 2015

Entrée en vigueur : *18 janvier 2017 par notification, conformément à l'article 14*

Textes authentiques : *arabe, anglais et turc*

Enregistrement au Secrétariat de l'Organisation des Nations Unies : *Turquie, 24 novembre 2017*

وإشهاداً على ما تقدم قام الموقعان ادناه المفوضان تماما بذلك من قبل حكوماتهم بالتوقيع و الختم على هذا البرتوكول.

وقع هذا البرتوكول في مدينة الدوحة بدولة قطر بتاريخ .../2015/12(الموافق.../.../1437 هجرية) في نسختين اصليتين باللغات العربية والتركية والإنجليزية، ولكل نص منها ذات الحجية، وفي حال الاختلاف في التفسير يرجح النص المحرر باللغة الإنجليزية.

عن حكومة جمهورية تركيا

أفكان آلا

وزير الداخلية

عن حكومة دولة قطر

الي الشيخ/ عبد الله بن ناصر آل ثاني

رئيس مجلس الوزراء وزير الداخلية

مــــادة (10)

أي خلاف قد ينشأ عن تفسير أحكام هذا البرتوكول تتم تسويته بواسطة التشاور والمفاوضات عبر الطرفين.

مــادة (11)

السلطات المختصة المسئولة عن تنفيذ أحكام هذا البروتوكول هي :

بالنسبة لحكومة دولة قطر :

- **وزارة الداخلية (إدارة التعاون الدولي).**

بالنسبة لحكومة جمهورية تركيا :

- **وزارة الداخلية .**

مــادة (12)

يجوز تعديل أحكام هذا البروتوكول، أو أي نص من نصوصه باتفاق الأطراف كتابةً ، دون المساس بالتشريعات الوطنية و الإجراءات القانونية المعمول بها في كلا البلدين.

مــادة (13)

يستخدم كل من الطرفين لغة دولته في حالات التعاون ضمن إطار هذا البرتوكول مع ترجمة مصدقة باللغة الانجليزية.

مــادة (14)

يدخل هذا البرتوكول حيز النفاذ اعتبارا من تاريخ آخر إخطار بإتمام الإجراءات التشريعية والقانونية المعمول بها في كلا البلدين، ويسري لمدة (3) ثلاث سنوات، ويمدد تلقائياً لمدة أو لمدد أخرى مماثلة، مالم يخطر أحد الطرفين الطرف الآخر كتابة عبر القنوات الدبلوماسية برغبته في إنهائه وذلك قبل (6) ستة اشهر على الأقل من تاريخ إنهائه أو انتهاء مدة سريانه.

2- يتم تقديم الطلبات الخاصة بهذا البرتوكول كتابةً، مباشرة أو عبر القنوات الدبلوماسية لدى الطرف المقدم له الطلب، ويرسل الطلب بالبريد، أو بالفاكس، أو بأي طريقة أخرى يتم الاتفاق عليها من قبل السلطات المختصة.

3- يتضمن الطلب البيانات الضرورية لتنفيذه، ، وكذلك صور من الوثائق المتعلقة بالموضوع التي يجب أن توقع وتختم من قبل السلطة المختصة لدى الطرف الطالب .

4- في الحالات الطارئة، يجوز تقديم الطلب شفاهه على أن يتم تأكيده كتابةً خلال (48) ساعة، ويمكن طلب معلومات إضافية عند الضرورة حول تنفيذ الطلب.

5- وعندما لا يكون تنفيذ الطلب في مجال اختصاص السلطات المختصة لدى الطرف المطلوب منه المساعدة وفقاً لهذا البرتوكول، على ذلك الطرف أن يقوم بتحويل الطلب للسلطة المختصة المعنية بالتنفيذ، ويتم إخطار السلطة المختصة لدى الطرف الطالب بهذا الإجراء .

مـــادة (6)

يلتزم كل طرف بخصوصية وسرية المعلومات والوثائق والمواد التي يتلقاها من الطرف الآخر، وعدم نقلها إلى أي طرف ثالث إلا بموجب تفويض مكتوب من الطرف مقدم المعلومة، ويجب أن يتم أي طلب للمعلومات أو الوثائق السرية كتابة، و أن يتضمن أي طلب للمعلومة وصفاً مختصراً للأسباب التي تبرر الطلب.

مـــادة (7)

سيتم تحديد تكاليف أي نشاط أو برنامج تدريبي بين الطرفين كتابة في عقود ثنائية منفصلة، على أن يتم التوقيع عليها من قبل الطرفين.

مـــادة (8)

في حالة إنهاء أو إبطال هذا البرتوكول وفقاً لأحكام المادة (14) ، لا يجوز تعليق أو إيقاف أي نشاط تم البدء فيه وفقا لأحكام هذا البروتوكول دون موافقة من قبل الطرفين.

مـــادة (9)

لا تخل أحكام هذا البرتوكول بالحقوق والالتزامات المستمدة من الاتفاقيات والمعاهدات الدولية أو الثنائية التي تكون إحدى الدولتين طرفاً فيها.

مـــادة (4)

يجب على الطرف الثاني أن يقوم بتحديد كافة الضوابط والشروط والمقابل المادي لكل دورة من الدورات التدريبية التي يرغب الطرف الأول التعاقد على تنفيذها وذلك وفقاً لما يلي:-

1- عنوان ووصف شامل عن الدورة، بما في ذلك بيان مفصل عن موضوعاتها وأهدافها ونتائج مخرجاتها.
2- السيرة الذاتية والعلمية ومدة الخبرة العملية للمدربين (للمساعدة في اختيار المشاركين)
3- مكان التدريب ، الأسلوب التدريبي (متنقل/ في موقع)، مكان السكن و الطعام، والعدد الأقصى للمتدربين.
4- مدة النشاط التدريبي بحسب أيام التدريب والأيام التقويمية.
5- متطلبات خاصة بالدورة، كغرف الاجتماعات ، الوسائل التدريبية، الكتب، الوثائق، المواد، المعدات، و التقدير و التقييم اللازمين للتعليم أو الزيارات الميدانية.
6- أعضاء الفريق العلمي.
7- تكلفة الدورة والتجهيزات ذات الصلة، لتحديد المقدرة التشغيلية.
8- التاريخ المقترح لوصول المدربين إلى موقع التدريب وتاريخ بدء التدريب .
9- تحديد كيفية سداد الرسوم والتكلفة الإجمالية لكل دورة على حده وذلك بالتنسيق بين الطرفين وفقاً للإجراءات التنظيمية المتبعة لدى الطرفين.
10- يجب على الطرف الموفد أن يقوم بتوفير تأمين صحي لمنسوبيه من المتدربين وعائلاتهم وذلك أثناء مدة تدريبهم في بلد الطرف الثاني.
11- يجب علي المتدربين الالتزام بالقوانين والأنظمة المعمول بها في بلد الطرف الثاني، واعتبارهم أحد منسوبي الطرف الثاني فيما يتعلق بالتشريعات التأديبية والعقابية، وفي حال الغاء الدورة من قبل الطرف الأول كمغادرة المتدربين أو استدعائهم أو قيامهم بالاستراحة أو في حالة الوفاة، تدفع تكاليف الدورة من قبل الطرف المرسل.

مادة (5)

1- التعاون في إطار هذا البرتوكول يتم وفقاً لطلبات تقدم من السلطات المختصة .

3- يجب أن يعمل الطرفان في مشاريع البحوث الأمنية والاستفادة من تقنيات الاتصال عن بعد لعقد المحاضرات العلمية للطلاب.

جـ- إلحاق وانتداب العاملين:-

- يجوز لأي من الطرفين إلحاق وانتداب بعض من منسوبيهم للاستفادة من تجارب الطرف الآخر.

د- إعارة العاملين:-

- يجوز للطرفين طلب إعارة مختصين بغرض المشاركة في مجالات أمنية معينة تحدد بعقود منفصلة.

هـ- تبادل الزيارات:-

- لكل من الطرفين زيارة بلد الطرف الآخر لغرض دراسة المجالات الممكنة للتعاون والتدريب وتبادل الخبرات والمعلومات الفنية.

و- الاستشارات

- يجوز للطرفين تسمية مستشارين يتمتعون بصفة البعثة الدائمة لدى الطرف الآخر، وذلك من أجل تبادل المعرفة و الخبرة في المسائل التعليمية والتدريبية و الفنية واللوجستية.

مـــادة (3)

1) تجتمع اللجنة المشتركة بين البلدين مرة كل عام في أوقات يتم الاتفاق عليها ولها أن تعقد اجتماعات أخرى إذا دعت الحاجة لذلك .

2) علي اللجنة متابعة التقدم الحاصل في النشاطات والمشروعات المتفق عليها وإعطاء التوجيهات والحلول العملية اللازمة.

3) على اللجنة مناقشة الموضوعات التي تحقق المصلحة الأمنية المشتركة للبلدين.

4) للجنة العمل المشتركة الحق في تشكيل سكرتارية مشتركة لعمل الدعم اللازم للجنة ، ولها أن تضم في عضويتها أحد الأعضاء إذا استجدت أوجه تعاون أو أنشطة أو دعت الحاجة لذلك.

5) لا يجوز لأي من الطرفين أن يضم إلى عضوية اللجنة المشتركة بين البلدين طرفاً ثالثاً من خارج وزارتي الداخلية للطرفين إلا بموافقة كتابية من الطرف الآخر.

[TEXT IN ARABIC – TEXTE EN ARABE]

بروتوكول للتعاون الأمني في مجالات التدريب والتعليم
بين حكومة جمهورية تركيا وحكومة دولة قطر

إن حكومة دولة قطر ، وتمثلها وزارة الداخلية ، الطرف الأول .
وحكومة جمهورية تركيا ، وتمثلها وزارة الداخلية، الطرف الثاني .
والمشار إليهما فيما بعد بـ " الطرفان " ،

رغبة منهما في توطيد علاقات الصداقة والتعاون بينهما،
واقتناعا منهما بأهمية التعاون الأمني في مجالات التدريب والتعليم وتبادل الخبرات ، واتخاذ الخطوات الضرورية لتحقيق ذلك، ورفع مستوى التعاون بين ادارات الأمن وادارات تنفيذ القانون لدى الطرفين ،
واستناداً للاتفاقية الأمنية الموقعة بين البلدين عام 2001م، و علي وجه الخصوص، المادة رقم (6) من الاتفاقية، اتفق الطرفان على الآتي:-

مادة (1)

يتعاون الطرفان فيما بينهما، في إطار أحكام هذا البروتوكول، في مجالات التعاون الأمني والتدريب والتعليم وتبادل الخبرات وتعزيز القدرات المشتركة، وذلك بما لا يتعارض مع التشريعات الوطنية لدولتيهما.

مادة (2)

أ- التدريب:-

يجوز للطرفين ابتعاث منسوبي الوزارة للالتحاق وحضور الدورات في الأكاديميات أو المؤسسات التدريبية و الوحدات التابعة للطرف الآخر.

ب- الجانب الأكاديمي:-

1- يجوز للطرف الأول ابتعاث منسوبيه لحضور و دراسة الدرجات التدريبية الأولي لقادة الشرطة، و درجات الماجستير و الدكتوراه، وذلك بأكاديمية الشرطة الوطنية التركية، شريطة استيفائهم لمعايير ومتطلبات الأكاديمية.

2- تبادل الخبرات من خلال عقد ورش عمل وندوات في العديد من مجالات العلوم الأمنية والشرطية، على أن يستفيد الطرف الأول من خبرة أكاديمية الشرطة الوطنية التركية والوحدات التدريبية التابعة لمؤسسات تنفيذ القانون في مجالات التطوير والتخطيط الاستراتيجي.

[TEXT IN ENGLISH – TEXTE EN ANGLAIS]

SECURITY COOPERATION PROTOCOL IN EDUCATION AND TRAINING BETWEEN THE GOVERNMENT OF THE REPUBLIC OF TURKEY AND THE GOVERNMENT OF THE STATE OF QATAR

Whereas, The Government of the Republic of Turkey (Second Party) :

The Government of the State of Qatar, (First Party):

Hereinafter jointly referred to as the "Two Parties",

Aiming to further enhance and develop mutual friendly relations and cooperation;

Believing in the importance of security cooperation in the fields of training, education and exchange of expertise, the importance of undertaking the necessary procedures to this end and enhancing cooperation among security and law enforcement departments within the Parties;

Taking into consideration the Security Cooperation Agreement signed by and between the two States in the year 2001 and with special reference to Article 6 thereof;

Now therefore, the Two Parties have agreed as follows:

Article 1

The Two Parties shall cooperate within the framework of this Protocol and without prejudice to the national legislations of the States thereof, in the fields of security, training, education, exchange of expertise and mutual capacity building.

Article 2

A.Training:

The Two Parties may send the employees thereof to join and attend courses at the academies or training institutions and unions of the other Party.

B.Academics:

1. The first party may send the employees thereof to attend and read for First Grade Training Of Police Chiefs, Master's and PhD degrees at the Turkish National Police Academy, given that they satisfy the criteria of the Academy.
2. Workshops and seminars in different fields of police and security sciences shall be held for exchange of expertise and for the first Party to benefit from the experience of the Turkish National Police Academy and Law Enforcement Training Units in development and strategic planning.
3. The Two Parties, shall work on security research projects and benefit from distance communication technologies in holding lectures for the students.

C. **Attachment and Assignment:**

Each Party may attach or assign any of the employees thereof to benefit from the experience of the other Party

D. **Secondment:**

The Parties may request the secondment of experts for the purpose of participating in specific security fields to be defined in accordance with separate protocols.

E. **Exchange of Visits:**

Each Party may visit the state of the Other Party for the purpose of discussing potential fields for cooperaiton, training, exchange of expertise and technical knowledge.

F. **Counseling:**

The Parties may appoint consultants in permanent mission status in the other Party in order to exchange knowledge and experience on education-training and technical-logistical issues.

Article 3

1. The Joint Committee shall hold one annual meeting on the time to be agreed upon and shall have the right to hold additional meetings whenever deemed necessary.
2. The Committee shall follow up the progress of and give proper guidance and practical solutions on the activities and projects agreed upon
3. The Committee shall discuss the subjects serving the mutual security interests of the two States
4. The joint working committee shall have the right to form a loint secretariat to mobilize necessary support to the joint working group and shall have the right to amend the membership of such secretariat to accommodate the different fields of cooperation.
5. Neither Party shall have the right to include a third party in the membership of the joint working committee from outside the Ministiries of Interior of both Parties without the written consent of the other Party.

Article 4

The second party shall set all regulations, rules and fees for each training course, the fist party expresses interest in, according to the following:

1. Title and full description of the course including detailed description of the subjects, aims and expected results thereof

2. Resume of the trainers including the academic and practical experiences thereof (to aid in selecting the participants)
3. Training location, training methods (mobile/on-site), board and lodging location and the maximum number of trainee
4. Duration of the training activity in terms of training days and calendar days
5. Course requirements such as meeting rooms, training aid, books, documents, material, equipment, assessment and evaluation needed in education or field visits
6. Members of the scientific team
7. Costs of the course and relevant fixturess; to determine the operational capacity
8. Suggested start date and arrival date of trainers at the training location
9. Payment method of fees and total costs of each course independently; to be coordinated between the Two Parties as per the applicable organisational procedures thereof
10. Trainee personnel and their relatives shall be insured with a health insurance with international validity by the Sending Party before the courses start.
11. Trainee personnel shall be subject to the laws and regulations in force in the Receiving Party when they stay in the Receiving Party. The trainee personnel shall be considered as the personnel of the Receiving Party in respect of penal and disciplinary legislation. The costs of leaving the course, calling back, relaxation and decease shall be paid by the Sending Party.

Article 5

1. Cooperation as per this Protocol shall be based on applications by the competent authorities
2. Applications in accordance with this Protocol shall be made in writing, either directly or through diplomatic channels to the receiving Party, and shall be sent by mail, fax or any other means to be agreed upon by the competent authorities.
3. The application shall include all the data necessary for the processing thereof, including without limitation copies of relevant documents signed and sealed by the competent authority (ies) of the requesting Party.

4. In case of urgency, the application may be made verbally provided it shall be confirmed in writing within a maximum of 48 hours; additional information may be requested, when necessary, for the processing of the application.

5. In case processing the application is not under the jurisdiction of the authority of the authority of the receiving Party under this Protocol, such Party shall forward the application to the competent authority(ies) for execution and shall inform the competent authority of the requesting Party of such action.

Article 6

Each Party shall maintain the secrecy and confidentiality of the information, document and material received thereby from the other Party and shall not transfer such information to any third party without the written consent of one of the Parties. The classified information and document shall be requested in writing and any request of information shall include a brief justification.

Article 7

Cost of each training activity/programme will be determined separately according to bilateral consent in writing.

Article 8

In case of termination or annulment of this Protocol in accordance with the provisions of Article 14 there of, no activity that has been started under this Protocol prior to the date of termination or annulment shall be suspended or abandoned in accordance hereto, without the approval of both Parties

Article 9

The provisions of this Protocol shall not prejudice the rights and obligations of any of the two State Parties thereto under any bilateral or international treaties or agreements to which such state is a party.

Article 10

Any disputes arising from or with relevance to the interpretation of the provisions of this Protocol shall be settled by way of consultation and negotiation between the Two Parties.

Article 11

The competent authorities for executing the provisions of this Protocol:

- In the Government of the Republic of Turkey
  (Ministry of Interior)
- In the State of Qatar:
  Ministry of Interior (International Cooperation Department)

Article 12

Any amendment to the provisions of this Protocol shall be made in writing by agreement by and between the Parties and without prejudice to the applicable national legislations and legal procedures in both states.

Article 13

Each Party shall use the language of the state thereof in any cooperation activity under this Protocol with certified English translation.

Article 14

This Protocol shall enter into force as of the date of the last notification of consummation of necessary legislative and legal procedures in both states and shall be valid for three (3) automatically renewable years unless one Party notifies the other Party in writing through diplomatic channels with desire thereof to terminate this Protocol (6) six months at least prior to the end date thereof or validity date thereof.

In witness whereof, the authorised signatories commissioned by the states thereof have signed and sealed this Protocol.

This Protocol has been signed in the city of Doha in the State of Qatar on this day 02/12/2015 in two original counterparts in the Turkish, Arabic and English languages each, with each text having the same authenticity, in case of discrepancy the English text shall prevail.

For The Goverment of the Republic of Turkey

Efkan ALA
Minister of Interior

For The Goverment of the State of Qatar

H.H Sheikh
Abdullah Bin Nasser Al Thani
Prime Minister and Minister Of Interior

[TEXT IN TURKISH – TEXTE EN TURC]

TÜRKİYE CUMHURİYETİ HÜKÜMETİ İLE KATAR DEVLETİ HÜKÜMETİ ARASINDA EĞİTİM VE ÖĞRETİM KONULU GÜVENLİK İŞBİRLİĞİ PROTOKOLÜ

Bundan böyle müştereken 'İki Taraf olarak anılacak olan Türkiye Cumhuriyeti Hükümeti (İkinci Taraf) ve 'Katar Devleti Hükümeti (Birinci Taraf) ;

Karşılıklı dostane ilişkileri ve işbirliğini daha da ilerletip geliştirmeyi amaç edinerek;

Eğitim, öğretim ve uzmanlık teatisi alanlarında güvenlik işbirliğinin önemine, bu amaca yönelik olarak gerekli prosedürlerin uygulanmasının ve İki Tarafın güvenlik ile kanun uygulama kurumları arasında işbirliğinin artırılmasının mühim olduğuna inanarak;

İki Devlet arasında 2001 yılında imzalanan Güvenlik İşbirliği Anlaşmasını göz önünde bulundurarak ve 6. Maddeye özellikle atıfta bulunarak;

Taraflar olarak aşağıdaki hususlarda anlaşmaya varmışlardır:

Madde 1

İki Taraf, işbu Protokol çerçevesinde, devletlerin ulusal mevzuatlarına halel getirmeksizin güvenlik, eğitim, öğretim, uzmanlık teatisi ve karşılıklı kapasite artırımı alanlarında işbirliğinde bulunacaktır.

Madde 2

A. Eğitim:

İki Taraf, diğer Tarafın akademilerinde ya da eğitim kurumlarında kurslara katılım sağlamaları için çalışanlarını gönderebilir.

B. Akademik Alan:

1. Birinci Taraf, Akademinin kriterlerini karşılamaları durumunda, Türk Polis Akademisi'nde Polis Şefleri Birinci Kademe Eğitimi, Yüksek Lisans ve Doktora eğitimlerine iştirak edip bu eğitimleri almaları için çalışanlarını gönderebilir.
2. Gelişim ve stratejik planlama alanında Türk Polis Akademisi'nin ve Kanun Uygulama Eğitim Birimlerinin haiz olduğu tecrübelerden yararlanmak üzere Birinci Taraf için uzmanlık teatisi amacıyla polis ve güvenlik bilimlerinin farklı alanlarında çalıştay ve seminerler düzenlenecektir.
3. İki Taraf, güvenlik araştırma projeleri üzerinde çalışmalar gerçekleştirecek ve öğrenciler için ders verilmesinde uzaktan muhabere teknolojilerinden yararlanacaktır.

C. Atama ve Görevlendirme

Her bir Taraf, diğer Tarafın tecrübesinden yararlanılması için çalışanlarını atayıp görevlendirme yapabilirler.

D. Geçici Görevlendirme

Taraflar, münferit protokoller uyarınca belirlenecek olan belli başlı güvenlik alanlarına katılmaları amacıyla uzmanların geçici görevlendirilmesini talep edebilirler.

E. **Ziyaret Mübadelesi**

Her bir Taraf, işbirliği, eğitim, uzmanlık ve teknik bilgi teatisi için potansiyel işbirliği alanlarını görüşmek amacıyla diğer Tarafın Devletini ziyaret edebilir.

F. **Danışmanlık**

Taraflar, Eğitim-öğretim ve teknik-lojistik konularında bilgi ve tecrübe tebdili yapılabilmesi amacıyla, diğer Tarafta daimi misyon statüsü çerçevesinde danışmanlar tayin edebilirler.

Madde 3

1.Ortak Komite, üzerinde anlaşmaya varılacak zamanlarda yıllık bir toplantı düzenleyecektir ve gerekli olarak addedilirse ek toplantılar düzenleme hakkına da sahip olacaktır.
2. Komite, üzerinde anlaşmaya varılan faaliyet ve projelere ilişkin süreci takip edecek ve bunlara yönelik gerekli yönlendirmeyi ve pratik çözümleri temin edecektir.
3. Komite, iki Devletin karşılıklı güvenlik çıkarlarına hizmet eden konuları ele alacaktır.
4. Ortak Çalışma Komitesi, ortak çalışma grubuna gerekli desteğin verilmesi için ortak bir sekretarya oluşturma hakkına ve bu gibi bir sekretaryanın üyeliğini farklı işbirliği alanlarına uyacak şekilde tadil etme hakkına sahip olacaktır.
5. Taraflardan hiçbirisi, diğer Tarafın yazılı rızası olmaksızın, iki Tarafın İçişleri Bakanlıkları dışından üçüncü taraf bir üyeliği ortak çalışma komitesine dâhil etme hakkına sahip olmayacaktır.

Madde 4

İkinci Taraf, aşağıda yer alan hususlar uyarınca, Birinci Tarafın ilgisi olduğunu belirttiği her bir eğitim için tüm yönetmelik, kural ve ücretleri belirleyecektir:
1. Konu, amaç ve beklenilen sonuçların ayrıntılı tanımlaması da dâhil olmak üzere kursun başlığı ve tam tanımı
2. İlgili olan akademik ve pratik tecrübeleri dâhil olmak üzere eğitimcilerin özgeçmişleri (katılımcıların seçilmesinde yardım sağlamak üzere)
3. Eğitim yeri, eğitim yöntemleri (mobil/yerinde), iaşe ve ibate yerleri ve azami kursiyer sayısı
4. Eğitim günleri ve takvim günleri bağlamında eğitim faaliyetinin süresi
5. Toplantı odaları, eğitim yardımı, kitap, doküman, materyal, ekipman, eğitimde ya da saha ziyaretlerinde gerekli olan ölçme-değerlendirme gibi kurs gereklilikleri
6. Bilim ekibinin üyeleri
7. Operasyonel yeterliliği belirlemek üzere kursa ve ilgili tamamlayıcı parçalara ilişkin ücretler
8. Önerilen başlama tarihi ve eğitimcilerin eğitim yerine varış zamanları
9. Ücretlerin ödenme şekli ve münferit olarak her bir kursa dair toplam maliyet. Uygulanabilir olan teşkilat prosedürlerine göre iki Taraf arasında koordine edilecektir.
10. Kursiyer personel ve yakınları, kurs başlamadan evvel Gönderen Tarafça uluslararası bir geçerliliği olan sağlık sigortası ile sigortalı hale getirilecektir.

11. Kursiyer personel, Kabul Eden Tarafta kaldıkları sürece, Kabul Eden Tarafın yürürlükte olan kanun ve yönetmeliklerine tabi olacaktır. Kursiyer personel, ceza ve disiplin mevzuatı bağlamında Kabul Eden Tarafın personeli olarak göz önünde bulundurulacaktır. Kurstan ayrılma, geri çağrılma, istirahat ve ölüm masrafları Gönderen Tarafça karşılanacaktır.

Madde 5

1. İşbu Protokol uyarınca işbirliği, yetkili makamların müracaatlarına dayanacaktır.
2. Bu Protokol uyarınca müracaatlar yazılı şekilde, direkt olarak ya da diplomatik kanallar aracılığıyla Alıcı Tarafa yapılacaktır ve elektronik posta, faks ya da yetkili makamlarca üzerinde anlaşmaya varılan diğer şekillerde gönderilecektir.
3. Müracaat, Talep eden Tarafın yetkili makamı (makamları) tarafından imzalanıp mühürlenen ilgili belgelerin sınırlı olmayan kopyaları dâhil olmak üzere ilgili süreç için gerekli olan tüm verileri içerecektir.
4. Acil durumda, azami 48 saat içerisinde yazılı olarak teyit edilmesi kaydıyla müracaat sözlü olarak yapılabilir; müracaata yönelik işlem yapılmasında gerekli olduğunda ek bilgi talep edilebilir.
5. Müracaata yönelik işlem yapılması bu Protokol uyarınca Kabul eden Tarafın yetkisi dâhilinde değilse bu Taraf, işlem yapılması için müracaatı yetkili makama/makamlara iletecektir ve talep eden Tarafın yetkili makamını bu işlemden haberdar edecektir.

Madde 6

Her bir Taraf, diğer Taraftan aldığı bilginin hususiyetini ve gizliliğini muhafaza edecektir ve bu gibi bilgileri, diğer Tarafın yazılı izni olmaksızın üçüncü bir Tarafa iletmeyecektir; her türlü bilgi talebi kısa bir gerekçe içermelidir.

Madde 7

Her bir eğitim faaliyetinin/programının masrafı karşılıklı ve yazılı rıza uyarınca münferiden belirlenecektir.

Madde 8

İşbu Protokolün ilgili 14. Maddesinin hükümleri uyarınca; fesih ya da iptal edilmesi durumunda her iki Tarafın da rızası olmadan Protokol uyarınca sonlanma ya da iptal tarihinden önce başlayan hiçbir faaliyet askıya alınmayacak ya da iptal edilmeyecektir.

Madde 9

İşbu Protokolün hükümleri, Devletlerin taraf oldukları herhangi bir ikili ya da uluslararası antlaşma veya anlaşma uyarınca mevcut olan hakları ve yükümlülüklerine halel getirmeyecektir.

Madde 10

İşbu Protokol hükümlerinin yorumlanmasından ya da yorumlanmasına ilişkin olarak ortaya çıkan herhangi bir anlaşmazlık iki Taraf arasındaki istişare ve müzakereler yoluyla çözümlenecektir.

Madde 11

İşbu Protokol hükümlerinin yerine getirilmesinden sorumlu olan yetkili makamlar şu şekildedir:

- Türkiye Cumhuriyeti Hükümeti'nde
  (İçişleri Bakanlığı)

- Katar Devleti'nde
  İçişleri Bakanlığı (Uluslararası İlişkiler Dairesi)

Madde 12

Protokolün hükümlerine ilişkin herhangi bir değişiklik, Taraflar arasındaki anlaşma ile yazılı olarak ve her iki devletin uygulanabilir olan ulusal mevzuatlarına ve dâhili prosedürlerine halel getirmeksizin yapılacaktır.

Madde 13

Her bir Taraf, bu Protokol uyarınca herhangi bir işbirliği faaliyetinde onaylı İngilizce tercümesi ile birlikte kendi devletlerinin lisanını kullanacaktır.

Madde 14

İşbu Protokol, iki Devlette de gerekli olan yasal ve hukuki prosedürlerin tamamlandığına ilişkin son bildirimin alındığı tarih itibariyle yürürlüğe girecektir. Taraflardan herhangi birisi bu Protokolü sonlandırmaya ilişkin isteğini diplomatik kanallar aracılığıyla, ilgili sonlanma tarihi ya da geçerlilik tarihi öncesinde en az altı (6) ay içerisinde yazılı olarak diğer Tarafa bildirmediği sürece otomatik olarak yenilenen üç (3) yıl için geçerli olacaktır.

Yukarıdaki hususlar muvacehesinde; Devletleri tarafından görevlendirilen imza yetkilileri bu Protokolü imzalamış ve mühürlemişlerdir.

İşbu Protokol, 02/12/2015 tarihinde, Katar Devletinin Doha şehrinde, her biri eşit derecede geçerli olmak üzere Türkçe, Arapça ve İngilizce dillerinde iki orijinal nüsha halinde tanzim edilmiştir. Yorumlamadan doğan farklılıklarda İngilizce metin esas alınacaktır.

Türkiye Cumhuriyeti Hükümeti Adına	Katar Devleti Hükümeti Adına
Efkan ALA **İçişleri Bakanı**	**H.H. Sheikh** **Abdullah Bin Nasser Al Thani** **Başbakan ve İçişleri Bakanı**

[TRANSLATION IN FRENCH – TRADUCTION EN FRANÇAIS]

PROTOCOLE DE COOPÉRATION EN MATIÈRE DE SÉCURITÉ RELATIF À L'ÉDUCATION ET À LA FORMATION ENTRE LE GOUVERNEMENT DE LA RÉPUBLIQUE TURQUE ET LE GOUVERNEMENT DE L'ÉTAT DU QATAR

Le Gouvernement de la République turque (deuxième Partie),

Le Gouvernement de l'État du Qatar (première Partie),

Ci-après dénommés conjointement les « deux Parties »,

Désireux de renforcer et d'améliorer les relations amicales et la coopération,

Convaincus de l'importance de la coopération en matière de sécurité dans les domaines de la formation, de l'éducation et de l'échange d'expertise, de l'importance d'entreprendre les procédures nécessaires à cette fin et de renforcer la coopération entre les services chargés de la sécurité et de l'application de la loi au sein des Parties,

Tenant compte de l'Accord de coopération en matière de sécurité signé par et entre les deux États en 2001 et se référant particulièrement à son article 6,

Les deux Parties sont convenues de ce qui suit :

Article premier

Les deux Parties coopèrent dans le cadre du présent Protocole, sans préjudice de la législation interne de leurs États, dans les domaines de la sécurité, de la formation, de l'éducation, de l'échange d'expertise et du renforcement mutuel de capacités.

Article 2

A. Formation :

Les deux Parties peuvent envoyer leurs employés suivre des cours dans les universités ou les institutions de formation et les syndicats de l'autre Partie.

B. Universitaires :

1. La première Partie peut envoyer ses employés suivre et donner des cours de premier cycle pour former des responsables de services de police, ainsi que des cours de maîtrise et de doctorat à l'École nationale de police turque, à condition qu'ils répondent aux critères de l'École.

2. Des ateliers et des séminaires dans différents domaines des sciences de la police et de la sécurité sont organisés pour permettre un échange d'expertise et pour que la première Partie bénéficie de l'expérience de l'École nationale de police turque et des services de formation des forces de l'ordre en matière de développement et d'élaboration de stratégies.

3. Les deux Parties travaillent sur des projets de recherche en matière de sécurité et bénéficient de technologies de communication à distance pour la tenue de conférences à l'intention des étudiants.

C. Rattachement et affectation :

Chaque Partie peut rattacher ou affecter les employés de son choix pour bénéficier de l'expérience de l'autre Partie.

D. Détachement :

Les Parties peuvent demander le détachement d'experts afin de coopérer dans des domaines de sécurité spécifiques à définir conformément à des protocoles séparés.

E. Échange de visites :

Chaque Partie peut se rendre sur le territoire de l'autre Partie afin de discuter des domaines potentiels de coopération, de formation, d'échange d'expertise et de connaissances techniques.

F. Conseil :

Les Parties peuvent nommer des consultants en mission permanente dans l'autre Partie afin d'échanger des connaissances et des données d'expériences sur les questions en matière d'éducation, de formation, de technique et de logistique.

Article 3

1. Le Comité mixte organise une réunion annuelle à une date à définir et a le droit d'en organiser d'autres chaque fois que cela est jugé nécessaire.

2. Le Comité suit l'état d'avancement des activités et des projets convenus, donne des conseils appropriés et propose des solutions pratiques.

3. Le Comité discute des sujets servant les intérêts de sécurité mutuels des deux États.

4. Le Comité de travail mixte a le droit de constituer un secrétariat conjoint pour mobiliser l'appui nécessaire au groupe de travail mixte et a le droit de modifier la composition de ce secrétariat pour tenir compte des différents domaines de coopération.

5. Aucune des Parties n'a le droit d'inclure dans la composition du Comité de travail mixte une tierce partie extérieure au Ministère de l'intérieur des deux Parties sans le consentement écrit de l'autre Partie.

Article 4

La deuxième Partie établit l'ensemble des règlements, des règles et des frais pour chaque cours de formation pour lequel la première Partie exprime de l'intérêt, selon les éléments suivants :

1. Titre et description complète du cours, y compris une description détaillée des sujets, des objectifs et des résultats escomptés ;

2. Curriculum vitae des formateurs, y compris leurs expériences académiques et pratiques (pour faciliter la sélection des participants) ;

3. Lieu de formation, méthodes de formation (mobile/sur site), lieu d'hébergement et de restauration et nombre maximal de stagiaires ;

4. Durée de la formation en nombre de jours de formation et de jours calendaires ;

5. Besoins liés aux cours, tels que les salles de réunion, les aides à la formation, les livres, les documents, le matériel, l'équipement, l'appréciation et l'évaluation nécessaires à l'enseignement ou aux visites sur le terrain ;

6. Membres de l'équipe scientifique ;

7. Coûts de la formation et des aménagements pertinents, pour déterminer la capacité opérationnelle ;

8. Dates suggérées pour le début de la formation et l'arrivée des formateurs sur le lieu de formation ;

9. Mode de paiement des frais et coût total de chaque cours indépendamment ; à coordonner entre les deux Parties conformément aux procédures organisationnelles applicables en la matière ;

10. La Partie d'envoi assure le personnel stagiaire et les membres de leur famille à l'aide d'une assurance maladie valable à l'international avant le début des cours ;

11. Le personnel stagiaire est soumis aux lois et règlements en vigueur dans la Partie d'accueil lors de son séjour dans la Partie d'accueil. Le personnel stagiaire est considéré comme le personnel de la Partie d'accueil au regard de la législation pénale et disciplinaire. Les frais relatifs à l'abandon de la formation, au rappel, à la rétractation et au décès sont à la charge de la Partie d'envoi.

Article 5

1. La coopération au titre du présent Protocole est fondée sur les demandes des autorités compétentes.

2. Les demandes présentées conformément au présent Protocole sont adressées par écrit, soit directement, soit par la voie diplomatique, à la Partie destinataire, et sont envoyées par courrier, par télécopie ou par tout autre moyen à convenir entre les autorités compétentes.

3. La demande comprend toutes les données nécessaires à son traitement, y compris, sans s'y limiter, les copies des documents pertinents signés et cachetés par les autorités compétentes de la Partie requérante.

4. En cas d'urgence, la demande peut être adressée verbalement à condition d'être confirmée par écrit dans un délai maximum de 48 heures ; un complément d'informations peut être demandé, si nécessaire, pour le traitement de la demande.

5. Dans le cas où le traitement de la demande ne relève pas de la compétence de l'autorité de la Partie destinataire en vertu du présent Protocole, cette Partie transmet la demande à l'autorité ou aux autorités compétentes pour exécution et informe l'autorité compétente de la Partie requérante de cette action.

Article 6

Chacune des Parties maintient le secret et la confidentialité des informations, des documents et du matériel reçus de l'autre Partie et ne les transfère à aucun tiers sans le consentement écrit de l'une des Parties. Les informations et documents classifiés sont demandés par écrit et toute demande d'information comporte une brève justification.

Article 7

Le coût de chaque activité/programme de formation sera déterminé séparément, dans le cadre d'un accord bilatéral écrit.

Article 8

En cas de dénonciation ou d'annulation du présent Protocole conformément aux dispositions de son article 14, aucune activité entreprise dans le cadre du présent Protocole avant la date de dénonciation ou d'annulation ne peut être suspendue ou abandonnée sans l'accord des deux Parties.

Article 9

Les dispositions du présent Protocole ne portent pas atteinte aux droits et obligations de l'un quelconque des deux États Parties en vertu de tout traité ou accord bilatéral ou international auquel cet État est partie.

Article 10

Tout différend découlant de l'interprétation des dispositions du présent Protocole, ou lié à celle-ci, est réglé par voie de consultations et de négociations entre les deux Parties.

Article 11

Les autorités compétentes chargées de l'exécution du présent Protocole sont :

- Pour le Gouvernement de la République turque :
  (Ministère de l'intérieur)
- Pour le Gouvernement de l'État du Qatar :
  Ministère de l'intérieur (Service de la coopération internationale)

Article 12

Tout amendement des dispositions du présent Protocole doit être effectué par écrit, par accord entre les Parties et sans préjudice de la législation et des procédures juridiques internes applicables dans les deux États.

Article 13

Chaque Partie utilise la langue de son État dans toute activité de coopération menée au titre du présent Protocole, avec une traduction anglaise certifiée.

Article 14

Le présent Protocole entre en vigueur à la date de la dernière notification de l'accomplissement des procédures législatives et juridiques nécessaires dans les deux États et reste valable pour une période de trois ans, renouvelable automatiquement, à moins qu'une Partie ne notifie par écrit à l'autre Partie, par la voie diplomatique, son désir de dénoncer le présent Protocole six mois au moins avant la date d'expiration ou de validité de celui-ci.

EN FOI DE QUOI, les signataires autorisés mandatés par leurs États ont signé le présent Protocole et y ont apposé leur sceau.

FAIT à Doha (État du Qatar), le 2 décembre 2015, en deux exemplaires originaux en langues turque, arabe et anglaise, chaque texte faisant également foi. En cas de divergence, le texte anglais prévaut.

Pour le Gouvernement de la République turque :

EFKAN ALA
Ministre de l'intérieur

Pour le Gouvernement de l'État du Qatar :

ABDULLAH BIN NASSER AL THANI
Premier Ministre et Ministre de l'intérieur

No. 54788

Turkey
and
Benin

Memorandum of Understanding between the Government of the Republic of Turkey and the Government of the Republic of Benin on agricultural cooperation. Ankara, 9 July 2012

Entry into force: *3 March 2017 by notification, in accordance with article 8*

Authentic texts: *English, French and Turkish*

Registration with the Secretariat of the United Nations: *Turkey, 20 November 2017*

Turquie
et
Bénin

Protocole d'Accord entre le Gouvernement de la République de Turquie et le Gouvernement de la République du Bénin dans le domaine de la coopération agricole. Ankara, 9 juillet 2012

Entrée en vigueur : *3 mars 2017 par notification, conformément à l'article 8*

Textes authentiques : *anglais, français et turc*

Enregistrement au Secrétariat de l'Organisation des Nations Unies : *Turquie, 20 novembre 2017*

[TEXT IN ENGLISH – TEXTE EN ANGLAIS]

MEMORANDUM OF UNDERSTANDING BETWEEN THE GOVERNMENT OF THE REPUBLIC OF TURKEY AND THE GOVERNMENT OF THE REPUBLIC OF BENIN ON AGRICULTURAL COOPERATION

The Government of the Republic of Turkey and the Government of the Republic of Benin (hereinafter referred to as "the Contracting Parties");

Desiring to enhance the existing amicable relations between the two countries through the development of cooperation in the field of agriculture,

Within the framework of the prevailing laws and regulations in their respective countries;

Have agreed as follows:

ARTICLE 1
OBJECTIVES

The objective of the Memorandum of Understanding is to promote and encourage economic, scientific and technical cooperation in the field of agriculture among economic, scientific, technical, training units and other organizations in agriculture.

ARTICLE 2
AREAS AND FORM OF COOPERATION

The Contracting Parties shall develop cooperation in the following areas:

a) Technical cooperation in the field of plant production, seed production and aquaculture, and the mutual training of the staff,
b) Exchange of the research results of the Contracting Parties published in the related research institutions.
c) Exchange of materials of plant and animal origin,
d) Exchange of information and experts in the fields of animal diseases, veterinary and public health,
e) Organization of training programs, seminars, conferences and meetings in both countries,
f) Establishment of joint studies among the related research institutions of the Contracting Parties,

g) Promoting the establishment of cooperation and joint investments among private sector enterprises on agriculture and agricultural products both in the Contracting Parties and in other markets.

ARTICLE 3

EXECUTIVE AUTHORITIES

The Executive Authorities responsible for the implementation of this Memorandum of Understanding are:

The Ministry of Food, Agriculture and Livestock on behalf of the Government of the Republic of Turkey; and,

The Ministry of Agriculture, Livestock and Fisheries on behalf of the Government of the Republic of Benin.

ARTICLE 4
THE ESTABLISHMENT OF THE STEERING COMMITTEE

1. The Contracting Parties agree to establish an Agricultural Steering Committee (hereinafter referred to as "the Committee") to monitor and review the implementation of the cooperation under this Memorandum of Understanding.
2. The Committee consists of 5 members from each country including the delegation heads on the level of Deputy Undersecretary.
3. The Committee shall meet annually or at a time as mutually agreed, alternately in Turkey and the Republic of Benin;
4. This Committee shall be responsible for:

   - Analyzing the implementation of the cooperation programs as mutually agreed upon;
   - Submitting proposals on the further development and improvement of cooperation forms;
   - Recommending possible solutions to overcome difficulties arising from the cooperation activities.

ARTICLE 5
EXPENSES

The Contracting Parties shall exchange experts on matters mutually agreed upon by the Parties in order to realize the cooperation stated in Article 2 of this Memorandum of Understanding. The international travel expenses of the Steering Committee members and experts shall be borne by the sending Party, whereas the local expenses shall be assumed by the receiving country.

The receiving country shall be informed of the intended visits at least two months prior to the date of arrival.

ARTICLE 6
SETTLEMENT OF DISPUTES

Any dispute or differences arising out of the interpretation or implementation of this Memorandum of Understanding shall be settled amicably through consultation or negotiation between the Contracting Parties.

ARTICLE 7
AMENDMENTS

This Memorandum of Understanding may be amended by mutual written consent of the Contracting Parties.

Such amendments shall be made through following the same legal procedure specified in Article 8 of the Memorandum and shall be an integral part of this Memorandum.

ARTICLE 8

ENTRY INTO FORCE, DURATION AND TERMINATION

This Memorandum of Understanding shall enter into force on the date of the last written notification by which the Parties notify each other through diplomatic channels, of the completion of their internal legal procedures required for the entry into force of the Memorandum of Understanding.

This Memorandum of Understanding shall remain into force for a period of at least five years from the date of its entry into force and shall be extended automatically for successive periods of five years, unless one of the Contracting Parties notifies the other in writing through diplomatic channels of its intention to terminate the Memorandum of Understanding at least 6 months prior to its expiration.

IN WITNESS WHEREOF, the undersigned, being dully authorized by their respective Governments have signed this Memorandum of Understanding.

Done in Ankara on 07 / 09 /2012 in original copies in Turkish, French and English languages, all texts being equally authentic. In case of any divergence of interpretation, the English text shall prevail.

On Behalf of the
Government of the Republic of
Turkey

Taner YILDIZ

The Minister of Energy and
Natural Resources

On Behalf of the
Government of the Republic of
Benin

Nassirou BAKO-ARIFARI

Minister of Foreign Affairs, African Integration,
Francophonie and Beninese of Diaspora.

[TEXT IN FRENCH – TEXTE EN FRANÇAIS]

PROTOCOLE D'ACCORD
ENTRE
LE GOUVERNEMENT DE LA REPUBLIQUE DE TURQUIE
ET
LE GOUVERNEMENT DE LA REPUBLIQUE DU BENIN
DANS LE DOMAINE DE LA
COOPERATION AGRICOLE

Le gouvernement de la République de Turquie et le Gouvernement de la République du Bénin (ci-après dénommés les « parties contractantes ») ;

Désireux de renforcer les relations amicales existantes entre les deux pays à travers le développement d'une coopération dans le domaine de l'agriculture,

Dans le cadre des lois et des règlements en vigueur dans leurs pays respectifs ;

Sont convenus de ce qui suit :

ARTICLE 1
OBJECTIFS

Le Protocole d'Accord vise à promouvoir et encourager la coopération économique, scientifique et technique dans le domaine de l'agriculture entre les unités de formation économique, scientifique et technique et autres organisations agricoles.

ARTICLE 2
DOMAINES ET FORME DE COOPERATION

Les parties contractantes développent une coopération dans les domaines suivants :

a) La coopération technique dans le domaine de la production végétale, la production de semences et l'aquaculture, et la formation mutuelle du personnel,
b) L'échange de résultats de recherche des Parties Contractantes publiés dans les institutions de recherche y relatives,
c) L'échange de matériels d'origine végétale et animale,
d) L'échange d'informations et d'experts dans les domaines de maladies des animaux, vétérinaire et de santé publique,
e) L'organisation de programmes de formation, séminaires, conférences et réunions dans les deux pays,
f) Conduite d'études conjointes entre les institutions de recherche y relatives des Parties Contractantes,
g) La promotion de la création de coopération et d'investissements entre les entreprises du secteur privé dans le domaine de l'agriculture et des produits agricoles au niveau des Parties Contractantes ainsi que d'autres marchés.

ARTICLE 3
LES AUTORITES EXECUTIVES

Les Autorités Exécutives responsables de la mise en œuvre du présent Protocole d'Accord sont :

Le Ministère de l'Alimentation, de l'Agriculture et de l'Elevage au nom du Gouvernement de la République de Turquie ; et,

Le Ministère de l'Agriculture, de l'Elevage et des Pêches au nom du Gouvernement de la République du Bénin.

ARTICLE 4
LA CREATION DU COMITE DIRECTEUR

1. Les Parties Contractantes acceptent de créer un Comité Directeur Agricole (ci-après dénommé « le Comité ») pour suivre de près et pour réviser la mise en œuvre de la coopération dans le cadre du présent Protocole d'accord.
2. Le Comité consiste en 5 membres venant de chaque pays y compris les chefs de délégation du niveau de Sous-secrétaire Adjoint.
3. Le Comité se réunit chaque année ou à une période convenue d'accord partie, alternativement en Turquie et en République du Bénin ;
4. Ce Comité est chargé de :

    - L'analyse de la mise en œuvre des programmes de la coopération tel que mutuellement convenu;

    - La soumission de propositions pour le développement et l'amélioration des formes de la coopération;

    - La recommandation de solutions possibles pour surmonter les difficultés survenant des activités de coopération.

ARTICLE 5
DEPENSES

Les Parties Contractantes échangent les experts sur les questions convenues d'accord partie afin de réaliser la coopération stipulée dans l'Article 2 du présent Protocole d'Accord. Les frais de déplacements internationaux des membres du Comité Directeur et des experts seront supportés par la Partie qui envoie, tandis que les dépenses locales seront assumées par le pays qui reçoit.

Le pays qui reçoit devra être informé des visites prévues au moins deux mois avant le jour d'arrivée.

ARTICLE 6
REGLEMENT DES DIFFERENDS

Toute dispute ou tout différend découlant de l'interprétation ou de la mise en œuvre du présent Protocole d'Accord sera réglé à l'amiable par voie de consultation ou de négociation entre les Parties Contractantes.

ARTICLE 7
AMENDEMENTS

Le présent Protocole d'Accord sera amendé par consentement mutuel écrit des Parties Contractantes.

De tels amendements seront faits suivant la même procédure juridique spécifiée à l'Article 8 du Protocole et seront une part intégrale du présent Protocole.

ARTICLE 8
ENTREE EN VIGUEUR, DUREE ET FIN

Le présent Protocole d'Accord entrera en vigueur à la date de la dernière notification écrite par laquelle les Parties se notifient par voie diplomatique, pour l'aboutissement de leurs procédures légales internes exigées pour l'entrée en vigueur du Protocole d'Accord.

Le présent Protocole d'Accord restera en vigueur durant une période d'au moins cinq ans, à compter de sa date de mise en œuvre et sera renouvelée automatiquement pour des périodes successives de cinq ans, à moins que l'une des Parties Contractantes informe l'autre par écrit et par voie diplomatique de sa volonté de résilier le Protocole d'Accord six mois au moins avant sa date d'expiration.

En foi de quoi, les soussignés, étant dument autorisés par leurs Gouvernements respectifs ont signé le présent Protocole d'Accord.

Fait à ………….. le …………en copies originales en langues Turque, Française et Anglaise, les textes faisant foi. En cas de divergence d'interprétation, le texte Anglais prime.

Au nom du Gouvernement de la République de Turquie

Taner YILDIZ

Ministre de l'Énergie
Et Ressources Naturelles

Au nom du Gouvernement de la République du Bénin

Nassirou BAKO ARIFARI

Ministère des Affaires Etrangères, de l'Intégration Africaine, de la Francophonie et des Béninois de l'Extérieur

[TEXT IN TURKISH – TEXTE EN TURC]

TÜRKİYE CUMHURİYETİ HÜKÜMETİ İLE BENİN CUMHURİYETİ HÜKÜMETİ ARASINDA TARIM ALANINDA İŞBİRLİĞİ KONULU MUTABAKAT ZAPTI

Türkiye Cumhuriyeti Hükümeti ile Benin Cumhuriyeti Hükümeti (bundan böyle "Akit Taraflar" olarak anılacaklardır);

Tarım alanındaki işbirliğini geliştirerek iki ülke arasında mevcut dostane ilişkileri artırmak isteği ile;

İlgili ülkelerdeki mevcut kanunlar ve yönetmelikler çerçevesinde;

Aşağıdaki hususlarda mutabakata varmışlardır.

MADDE 1
AMAÇLAR

İşbu Mutabakat Zaptı'nın amacı, tarım alanındaki ekonomik, teknik, bilimsel birimler ve eğitim birimleri ile diğer kurumlar arasında tarım alanındaki ekonomik, bilimsel ve teknik işbirliğini desteklemek ve geliştirmektir.

MADDE 2
İŞBİRLİĞİ ŞEKLİ VE ALANLARI

Akit Taraflar aralarında aşağıdaki alanlarda işbirliği gerçekleştirirler.

a) Bitkisel üretim, tohumluk ve su ürünleri yetiştiriciliği konularında teknik işbirliği ve personelin karşılıklı olarak eğitilmesi,

b) Tarafların ilgili araştırma kuruluşlarında yayınlanan araştırma sonuçlarının mübadelesi,

c) Bitkisel ve hayvansal materyal mübadelesi,

d) Hayvan hastalıkları ve veteriner halk sağlığı konularında karşılıklı bilgi ve uzman değişimi,

e) Her iki ülkede eğitimler, seminerler, konferanslar ve toplantılar düzenlenmesi,

f) Tarafların ilgili araştırma kuruluşları arasında ortak çalışmaların tesisi,

g) Her iki ülkede ve diğer pazarlarda tarım ve tarımsal ürünler konusunda, özel sektör kuruluşları arasında işbirliği ve ortak yatırımların tesisinin teşvik edilmesi,

MADDE 3

UYGULAMAYA YETKİLİ ORGANLAR

Akit Tarafların işbu Mutabakat Zaptının uygulanmasından sorumlu olan yetkili organları;
Türkiye Cumhuriyeti Hükümeti adına Gıda, Tarım ve Hayvancılık Bakanlığı; ve
Benin Cumhuriyeti Hükümeti adına Tarım, Hayvancılık ve Balıkçılık Bakanlığı'dır.

MADDE 4

YÜRÜTME KOMİTESİNİN KURULMASI

1. Akit Taraflar, işbu Mutabakat Zaptı kapsamındaki işbirliğinin uygulanmasını izlemek ve değerlendirmek amacıyla bir Yürütme Komitesinin (bundan sonra "Komite" olarak anılacaktır) kurulmasını kararlaştırmıştır.
2. Komite, Müsteşar Yardımcısı düzeyindeki heyet başkanları da dahil olmak üzere her ülkeden beşer üyeden oluşur.
3. Komite yıllık olarak veya karşılıklı mutabakata varılan bir zamanda dönüşümlü olarak Türkiye ve Benin Cumhuriyeti'nde toplanır.
4. Bu Komite aşağıdaki görevlerden sorumludur:
 - Karşılıklı olarak mutabakata varılan işbirliği programlarının uygulanmasının analizi;
 - İşbirliği şeklinin daha da geliştirilmesi ve iyileştirilmesi konusunda teklifler sunulması;
 - İşbirliği faaliyetlerinden kaynaklanan güçlüklerin aşılması için olası çözümler tavsiye edilmesi.

MADDE 5

MASRAFLAR

Bu Mutabakat Zaptının 2. Maddesinde yer alan işbirliğini gerçekleştirmek için Taraflar, üzerinde mutabık kalınan konularda uzman mübadelesi yaparlar. Tarım Yürütme Komitesi üyelerinin ve uzmanların iki ülke arasındaki yolculuk masrafları gönderen ülke, dahili masrafları ise ev sahibi ülke tarafından karşılanır.

Ev sahibi ülke, ziyaret tarihinden en az iki ay önce planlanan ziyaret hakkında bilgilendirilir.

MADDE 6

ANLAŞMAZLIKLARIN ÇÖZÜMÜ

İşbu Mutabakat Zaptının yorumlanması veya uygulanmasından doğabilecek her türlü anlaşmazlık veya görüş ayrılığı, Akit Taraflar arasında karşılıklı istişare ve müzakere yoluyla dostça çözüme kavuşturulur.

MADDE 7

DEĞİŞİKLİKLER

Bu Mutabakat Zaptı, istenildiği zaman Akit Tarafların karşılıklı yazılı onayıyla değiştirilebilir. Değişiklikler, bu Mutabakat Zaptının 8. Maddesi ile belirlenen aynı yasal prosedür izlenerek yapılır ve bu Mutabakat Zaptının bütünleyici bir parçasını teşkil eder.

MADDE 8

YÜRÜRLÜĞE GİRİŞ, SÜRE VE SONA ERME

İşbu Mutabakat Zaptı, Tarafların birbirlerine diplomatik kanallar yoluyla Mutabakat Zaptının yürürlüğe konulması için gerekli olan iç yasal prosedürlerin tamamlandığını bildirdikleri son yazılı bildirimin alındığı tarihten itibaren yürürlüğe girecektir.

İşbu Mutabakat Zaptı yürürlüğe girdiği tarihten itibaren beş yıl süreyle yürürlükte kalır ve Akit Taraflardan biri, bitiminden en az 6 ay önceden diplomatik kanallar aracılığıyla diğer tarafa sona erdirmek istediğini yazılı tebligatla bildirmedikçe, birbirini takip eden beş yıllık sürelerde otomatik olarak süresi uzatılır.

YUKARIDAKİ HUSUSLAR MUVACEHESİNDE, Hükümetleri tarafından usulüne uygun olarak yetkilendirilen aşağıdaki imza sahipleri, işbu Mutabakat Zaptını imzalamışlardır.

09 / 07 / 2012 tarihinde Ankara'da her biri aynı derecede geçerli ikişer orijinal nüsha halinde, Türkçe, Fransızca ve İngilizce dillerinde imzalanmıştır. Yorumlamada farklılıklar olması durumunda, İngilizce metin geçerlidir.

Türkiye Cumhuriyeti
Hükümeti adına

Taner YILDIZ
Enerji ve Tabii Kaynaklar Bakanı

Benin Cumhuriyeti
Hükümeti adına

Nassirou BAKO-ARIFARI
Dışişleri, Afrika Bütünleşmesi, Frankofoni ve Benin Diasporası Bakanı

No. 54789

Turkey
and
Russian Federation

Treaty between the Republic of Turkey and the Russian Federation on mutual legal assistance in criminal matters and extradition. Ankara, 1 December 2014

Entry into force: *21 August 2017, in accordance with article 38*

Authentic texts: *English, Russian and Turkish*

Registration with the Secretariat of the United Nations: *Turkey, 24 November 2017*

Turquie
et
Fédération de Russie

Traité entre la République turque et la Fédération de Russie relatif à l'entraide judiciaire en matière pénale et à l'extradition. Ankara, 1er décembre 2014

Entrée en vigueur : *21 août 2017, conformément à l'article 38*

Textes authentiques : *anglais, russe et turc*

Enregistrement au Secrétariat de l'Organisation des Nations Unies : *Turquie, 24 novembre 2017*

[TEXT IN ENGLISH – TEXTE EN ANGLAIS]

TREATY
BETWEEN
THE REPUBLIC OF TURKEY AND
THE RUSSIAN FEDERATION
ON MUTUAL LEGAL ASSISTANCE IN
CRIMINAL MATTERS AND EXTRADITION

The Republic of Turkey and the Russian Federation (hereinafter referred to as the "Parties"),

Desirous of further promoting friendly relations and arranging mutual legal assistance in criminal matters and extradition on the basis of the principals of national sovereignty, equality of rights and of non-interference in the internal affairs of the Parties,

Aiming at facilitation of application between the Parties of the European Convention on Extradition of 13 December 1957 and of the European Convention on Mutual Assistance in Criminal Matters of 20 April 1959,

Have decided to conclude the Treaty on Mutual Legal Assistance in Criminal Matters and Extradition and have agreed as follows:

CHAPTER I
GENERAL PROVISIONS

ARTICLE 1
Central and competent authorities

1. In order to provide for the appropriate cooperation of the Parties in the framework of this Treaty. Central Authorities for the Parties shall be appointed.

2. For the purposes of mutual legal assistance the Central Authority for the Turkish Party shall be the Ministry of Justice of the Republic of Turkey.

For the purposes of mutual legal assistance the Central Authorities for the Russian Party shall be:

The Ministry of Justice of the Russian Federation for purposes connected with the proceedings of the courts of the Russian Federation, as well as for the purposes of Article 2 of this Treaty;

The General Prosecutor's Office for all other purposes of granting legal assistance.

3. For the purposes of extradition the Central Authority for the Turkish Party shall be the Ministry of Justice of the Republic of Turkey, for the Russian Party the General Prosecutor's Office of the Russian Federation.

4. The competent authorities are the authorities of the Parties participating in implementation of this Treaty.

5. The Central Authorities of the Parties shall counteract directly or, if necessary, through diplomatic channels.

6. The Parties shall promptly notify each other through diplomatic channels in case of any change of their Central Authorities and their competences.

7. The Central Authorities of the Parties shall directly transmit and receive all requests provided for in this Treaty and responses to them.

ARTICLE 2

Exchange of information

The Central Authorities of the Parties shall, upon request, give information to each other on their laws in force or repealed and judicial practices with regard to legal matters that constitute subject to this Treaty.

ARTICLE 3

Languages

Request for legal assistance or for extradition, its supporting documents and additional information forwarded in accordance with this Treaty shall be accompanied by certified translation into the language of the Requested Party.

ARTICLE 4

Validity of the documents

1. Documents transmitted pursuant to this Treaty and attested to by the official seal of competent or Central Authority of the transmitting Party are admissible in evidence without further authorization or any other form of certification.

At the request of the Requesting Party, the documents transmitted within the framework of this Treaty, may be certified in any other form, as indicated in the request provided that is not contrary to the legislation of the Requested Party.

2. For the purposes of this Treaty the documents which are recognised as official in the territory of one Party shall be recognised as such in the territory of the other Party.

ARTICLE 5

Confidentiality and the limitations of use of information

1. The Requested Party upon request of the Central Authority of the Requesting Party shall provide in accordance with its legislation for the confidentiality of the fact of the receipt of the request for legal assistance, of its contents or any action taken pursuant to the request, excluding the cases when the breach of confidentiality of the request is necessary for its execution.

If the execution of the request makes it necessary to remove this limitation, the Requested Party shall in writing seek the permission of the Requesting Party, without which the request will not be executed.

2. The Requesting Party shall not use the information or evidence obtained under this Treaty without the prior permission of the Requested Party for purposes other than those indicated in the request for legal assistance.

3. In cases where the Requesting Party needs to disclose and use fully or in part the information or evidence for purposes other than those stated in the request, it shall seek the consent of the Requested Party, which may either agree or refuse, fully or partially, such permission.

CHAPTER II
MUTUAL LEGAL ASSISTANCE IN CRIMINAL MATTERS

ARTICLE 6
Obligation to provide legal assistance

1. The Parties shall undertake to afford each other mutual legal assistance in connection with investigation, prosecution and other procedural acts on criminal matters (hereinafter referred to as "legal assistance") in accordance with provisions of this Treaty.

2. The Requested Party may grant legal assistance in case the offence, in connection with which the request was received, is not criminally punishable under its legislation.

3. The purpose of this Treaty is granting legal assistance by one Party to the other Party. The provisions of this Treaty shall not give rise to a right for a natural or legal person to obtain or exclude any evidence or to prevent the execution of a request.

4. This Treaty does not grant to competent authorities of one Party the right to exercise in the territory of the other Party powers which fall exclusively within the competence of that other Party.

5. This Treaty shall apply to requests for legal assistance, presented after the entry into force of this Treaty even if the corresponding act or omission took place before this date.

ARTICLE 7

Scope of application

Legal assistance shall include:

(1) Service of documents;

(2) Taking evidence and statements of persons and obtaining other evidence;

(3) Location and identification of persons and objects;

(4) Invitation of witnesses, victims and experts for their voluntary appearance before the competent authority of the Requesting Party;

(5) Temporary transfer of persons in custody or serving sentences of imprisonment to participate in criminal proceedings in the territory of the Requesting Party as witnesses and victims or for the purpose of other criminal proceedings indicated in the request;

(6) Taking measures on search, restrain, forfeiture, confiscation and return of proceeds of crime and the instruments of crime;

(7) Transfer of documents, objects and other evidence;

(8) Granting permission to the persons specified in the request of the competent authorities of the Requesting Party to be present at the execution of the request;

(9) Execution of requests for criminal prosecution in respect of nationals of the Requested Party and stateless persons permanently living on its territory;

(10) Search and seizure;

(11) Any other forms of legal assistance consistent with the objects of this Treaty and not inconsistent with the law of the Requesting Party.

ARTICLE 8

Form and contents of request

1. A request for legal assistance shall be made in writing.

2. The Requested Party shall immediately receive the request for the execution upon its delivering by facsimile, electronic mail or other such type of communication and the original of the request shall be submitted promptly thereafter by the Requesting Party. The Requested Party shall inform the Requesting Party of the results of the execution of the request only with the condition that it receives the original of the request.

3. A request for legal assistance shall include;

a) The name of the requesting competent authority.
b) The purpose of the request and description of the requested legal assistance.
c) A description of the act in connection with which the investigation or the proceedings are being conducted, its legal qualification, extracts from the texts of the relevant laws of the Requesting Party necessary for execution of the request, full names of the suspects, accused or sentenced persons, information on their domicile or residence, nationality and profession and where possible, places and dates of birth and names of parents, for legal persons – title, legal and actual address,
d) If relevant, the indication of the cost of damage occurred as a result of the offence,
e) Reasons for use and a description of any particular procedures that the Requesting Party wishes to be followed in execution of the request;
f) Data identifying witnesses or victims;
g) Any time limit within which compliance with the request is desired by the Requesting Party;
h) Full names and addresses and also if possible telephone numbers of the persons who are to be notified and their connection to the investigation or proceedings in progress;
i) Indication of the location and description of the place, where inspection and search is required, and of the objects to be seized;

j) Questions to be asked in order to gather evidence in the Requested Party;

k) In case of an indication that the presence of persons indicated by the competent authorities of the Requesting Party is desired, their full names and official designations as well as grounds for their presence;

l) The need, if any, for confidentiality of the fact that the request was received of its contents and/or of any action undertaken in connection with the request;

m) Any other information that might be useful to the Requested Party in order to execute the request.

4. If the Requested Party considers that the information contained in the request is insufficient for its execution, that Party may request additional information.

ARTICLE 9

Execution of request

1. Requests for legal assistance shall be executed in accordance with the laws of the Requested Party and the provision of this Treaty. However, upon the request of Requesting Party, the law of the latter may be applied to the extent that it is not contrary to the law of the Requested Party.

2. The Central Authorities of the Parties shall execute the request for legal assistance directly or transmit it to the competent authority for execution. If a Central Authority transmits the request for execution to a competent authority, it shall ensure prompt and appropriate execution of this request by the competent authority.

3. If the Requesting Party seeks the presence of the persons indicated by its Competent Authorities during the execution of a request, the Requested Party will inform the Requesting Party about its decision. In case of a positive decision, the Requesting Party will be informed beforehand of the time and the place of the execution of the request.

4. The Central Authority of the Requested Party, following the execution of the request, shall send the information and the documents concerning the execution of the request to the Central Authority of the Requesting Party.

5. In case of inability to execute the request, the Central Authority of the Requested Party shall inform the Central Authority of the Requesting Party of this fact, as well as of the reasons preventing execution of the request.

ARTICLE 10

Refusal or postponement of legal assistance

1. Requests for the legal assistance may be refused if:

a) The Requested Party is of the opinion that the request would prejudice its sovereignty, security, public order or other essential interests,

b) The Requested Party has substantial reasons to believe that the request was submitted in order to prosecute the person on grounds of race, gender, faith, citizenship, ethnic origin or political convictions, or the position of that person may be prejudiced because of any of these causes,

c) The execution of the request is regarded by the Requested Party as being incompatible with its law and the provisions of this Treaty,

d) The request relates to a crime under military law that is not a crime under general criminal law;

e) The request relates to the offence for which the person accused of criminal offence in the Requesting Party was convicted or acquitted in the Requested Party in connection with the same offence, or for which the limitation period elapsed in accordance with the laws of the Requested Party.

2. Bank secrecy or confidentiality of taxation may not be invoked as the absolute ground for refusal to grant legal assistance.

3. Legal assistance may be postponed or refused by the Requested Party if execution of the request would damage or impede an ongoing investigation or proceedings in the Requested Party.

4. Before making a decision to postpone or refuse the execution of the request the Requested Party shall consider whether legal assistance may be granted subject to such conditions, as it deems necessary. If the Requesting Party accepts legal assistance subject to these conditions, it is obliged to comply with them.

5. If the Requested Party decides to postpone execution of, or refuse to grant, a request it shall promptly inform the Requesting Party via its Central Authority and give reasons for that decision.

ARTICLE 11

Appearance of witness, victims and expert and safe conduct

1. If the Requesting Party submits a request for personal appearance to produce evidence, carry out expert examination or for other procedural measures in its territory, the Requested Party informs that person of the invitation to appear before competent authorities of the Requesting Party.

2. The request for the person to appear shall contain information on the conditions and requirements to cover cost and the expenses related to the appearance of the summoned person, as well as the list of guarantees which will be provided to the person under paragraphs 5 and 6 of this Article.

3. The invitations stated in the first paragraph shall not contain any threat to use coercive measures or penalty in case of a failure of the person to appear in the territory of the Requesting Party.

4. The summoned person will take the decision to appear voluntarily. The Central Authority of the Requested Party shall promptly inform the Central Authority of the Requesting Party of the person's response.

5. A person present before the competent authority in the Requesting Party, whatever his/her nationality, shall not be prosecuted or detained or subjected to any other restriction of his/her personal liberty in the territory of that Party for committing any act or on the basis of any conviction anterior to his/her departure from the territory of the Requested Party.

6. The summoned person shall not be forced to present evidence on any other case than that indicated in the request.

7. The summoned person shall lose the right to inviolability provided for in this Article if the person, being free to leave the territory of the Requesting Party, has not left it within a period of 15 days after being notified in writing that the person's attendance is no longer required by the relevant competent authority or, having left that territory, has voluntarily returned.

ARTICLE 12

Temporary transfer of detained persons (including those serving punishment in the form of imprisonment)

1. A person in custody (including a person serving a sentence in the form of imprisonment) notwithstanding citizenship whose personal appearance as a witness or a victim or to assist in other proceedings indicated in the request is requested by the Requesting Party may be temporarily transferred to the territory of the Requesting Party, provided that he shall be sent back within the period stipulated by the Requested Party and subject to the paragraphs 5 and 6 of the Article 11 of this Treaty in so far as these are applicable.

Initial term for which the person may be transmitted shall not exceed 90 days. Upon the request of the Central Authority of the Requesting Party, based on substantial

grounds, the term of stay of the transferred person may be extended by the Central Authority of the Requested Party.
The order and the conditions of transfer and return of the person shall be coordinated by the Central Authorities of the Parties.

2. Transfer may be refused:

a) If the person in custody does not consent,

b) If his/her presence is necessary at proceedings pending in the territory of the Requested Party,

c) If transfer is liable to prolong his/her detention,

d) If there are other good grounds for not transferring him to the territory of the Requesting Party.

3. The transferred person shall remain in custody in the territory of the Requesting Party on the ground and in accordance with its legislation and in so far as the decision of the competent authority of the Requesting Party to hold that person in custody is in force. In case of release of the person in custody upon the decision of the Requested Party, the Requesting Party shall use the provisions of the paragraphs 5 and 6 of the Article 11 and the Article 21 of this Treaty in relation to that person.

4. The period of custody of the person outside the territory of the Requested Party is regarded as part of being in custody.

5. If the person in custody does not consent to appear before the Requesting Party that person by reason thereof shall not be liable to any measure of compulsion or penalty.

ARTICLE 13

Protection of the person appearing upon request or transferred to the territory of the Requesting Party

If necessary, the Requesting Party shall provide for the protection of the person appearing upon request or transferred to its territory in accordance with Articles 11 and 12 of this Treaty.

ARTICLE 14

Service of documents

1. The Requested Party shall effect service of documents accompanied by certified translations prepared in the language of Requested Party in the manner provided for by its own law.

2. The Requesting Party shall transmit a request for the service of a document pertaining to a response or appearance in the territory of the Requesting Party within a reasonable time, before the scheduled response or appearance, normally not later than 60 days before appearance.

3. The known address of the addressee and the nature of the document shall be indicated in a request for the service of documents.

4. Execution of such request shall be confirmed by the document of service indicating the date and signature of the addressee or the statement of the competent authority of the Requested Party, confirming the fact, date and means of service.

5. The Requesting Party shall be promptly informed of the service of documents or impossibility of service.

ARTICLE 15

Request for prosecution

1. Upon the request and accordance with their law, each Party shall undertake to proceed against their nationals and stateless persons having permanent residence in its territory who committed an offence falling under the jurisdiction of the other Party.

Upon receipt of the said request, the Requested Party transfers the received case-file to its competent authorities for taking decision as to initiate criminal prosecution in accordance with the legislation of that Party.

2. A request for prosecution shall include:

a) The name of the requesting competent authority;
b) Full name of the person, who suspectedly committed a crime, information on his/her nationality, and as far as possible, information on the domicile or residence, a description of his/her or her appearance, a photograph, fingerprints or any other data necessary to identify the person;
c) A description and legal classification of the conduct, in connection with which the request for prosecution is forwarded;
d) A precise, to the extent possible, specification of the time and place of the offence;
e) If necessary, a request to return the original documents and objects of physical evidence.

3. Request for prosecution shall be supported by the following documents:
a) Investigation documents or certified copies thereof, including evidence available,
b) The text of applicable criminal law and, if necessary, of the other laws of the Requesting Party which are essential for the prosecution,
c) If applicable, to the extent possible, data on the amount of damage,
d) Applications of victims for instituting prosecution, if it is required in accordance with the laws of the Requested Party.

4. With a view to securing the legitimate rights of third persons, the Requested Party, upon completion of procedural acts, shall return, upon request of the Requesting Party, the original documents and objects of physical evidence.

5. The Requested Party shall notify the Requesting Party of the measures taken in connection with the request of the latter, of the result of the criminal prosecution and shall forward a copy of the final decision.

6. Where a request had been received, and a decision of a judicial authority of the Requested Party was delivered on the person indicated in the request and the said decision entered into legal force, the competent authorities of the Requesting Party may not prosecute the said person for the same offence.

7. Where the Requested Party has taken the decision not to grant the request or to terminate the case or an out-of-court settlement has been reached not to institute proceedings the case files and objects of physical evidence transferred by the Requesting Party shall be promptly returned to it.

ARTICLE 16

Taking of evidence in the Requested Party

1. The Requested Party shall in its territory take evidence and expert opinions or produce documents, objects and evidence indicated in the request and transmit it to the Requesting Party.

2. The persons indicated by the Requesting Party that are present at the execution of the request shall be allowed to formulate questions that may be put to the corresponding person through the representative of the competent authority of the Requested Party.

3. The Requesting Party shall observe any conditions imposed by the Requested Party in relation to any documents and objects which may be delivered to it, including conditions for the protection of third party interests in any such documents and objects.

4. Upon a request by the Requested Party, the Requesting Party shall, as soon as possible, return the originals of documents and objects delivered to it in accordance with Paragraph 1 of this Article.

ARTICLE 17

Provision of information, documents and objects

1. The Requested Party shall provide the Requesting Party with copies of documents and information of Governmental authorities, which under its laws are publicly available.

2. The Requested Party may, subject to its laws, provide the Requesting Party with any information, documents and objects in possession of a governmental authority but not publicly available, to the same extent and under the same conditions as they would be available to its own law enforcement and judicial authorities.

3. Each Party may provide the other Party with the information or documents which, in its opinion, might be used for criminal prosecution of natural or legal persons or for initiation of relevant proceedings in respect of legal persons in connection with commission of crimes by natural persons.

ARTICLE 18

Search and seizure

1. The Requested Party shall, in so far as its law permits, carry out requests for search, seizure and delivery of documents and objects to the Requesting Party which are relevant to an investigation or other proceedings in relation to the pending criminal matter in the Requesting Party, provided that the request includes information enough to justify such action under the laws of the Requested Party.

2. The Requested Party shall provide such information as may be required by the Requesting Party concerning the result of any search, the place of seizure, the circumstances of seizure and the subsequent custody of the documents and objects seized.

3. The Requesting Party shall observe any conditions imposed by the Requested Party in relation to any seized documents and objects which are delivered to the Requesting Party.

ARTICLE 19

Location and identification of persons and objects

The competent authorities of the Requested Party shall use its best efforts as provided for by its law to ascertain the location and identity of persons and objects specified in the request.

ARTICLE 20

Performance of measures on search, restrain, forfeiture, confiscation and return of proceeds and instruments of crime

1. The Parties, in accordance with their laws, shall assist each other in locating, freezing, restraining, forfeiting and confiscating proceeds and instruments of crime.

For the purposes of this Treaty, "proceeds of crime" mean monetary funds or other property received as a result of crime, income and other benefits received from these proceeds, or property into which the proceeds of crime were converted or transformed, or property to which the proceeds of crime were adjoined.

2. The Requested Party shall, upon request, endeavour to ascertain whether any proceeds of crime or instruments of crime are located within its jurisdiction, notify the Requesting Party of the results of its inquiries. In making the request, the Requesting Party shall notify the Requested Party of the basis of its belief that such proceeds or instruments may be located in its jurisdiction.

3. Where, pursuant to paragraph 2 of this Article, suspected proceeds or instruments of crime are found, the Requested Party shall upon request give effect to a restraining order made by a competent authority of the Requesting Party or take such measures as are permitted by its law to prevent any dealing in, transfer or disposal of those suspected proceeds or instruments of crime, pending a final determination in respect of those proceeds or instruments by a court of the Requesting Party or the Requested Party.

4. The Requested Party shall, to the extent permitted by its law, give effect to a final order made by a competent authority of the Requesting Party on forfeiture or confiscation of the proceeds of crime or of the instruments of crime.

5. In the application of this Article, the rights of bona fide third parties shall be respected under the law of the Requested Party.

6. At the request of the Requesting Party, the Requested Party may, to the extent permitted by its laws and under any terms and conditions agreed to by the Central authorities of the Parties, transfer the proceeds or instruments of crime to the Requesting Party.

7. The provisions of this Article shall not affect any rights and obligations of the Parties arising from other multilateral international treaties to which they are both parties.

ARTICLE 21

Expenses

1. The Requested Party shall bear the regular expenses incurred for the execution of legal assistance request, except that the Requesting Party shall bear:

a) The expenses associated with the travel of persons to and from its territory in accordance with Article 11 and 12 of this Treaty and their presence in that territory, as well as other payments due to those persons;
b) The expenses and fees of experts;
c) The expenses associated with the travel and presence of the persons indicated by the competent authorities of the Requesting Party at the execution of the request in accordance with paragraph 3 of Article 9 of this Treaty;
d) The expenses associated with the transition of transmitted objects from the territory of the Requested Party to the territory of the Requesting Party and back.

2. In case the expenses of provision of judicial assistance requires expenses of substantial or extraordinary nature, the Central Authorities of the Parties shall consult to determine the terms and conditions under which the requested assistance can be provided, as well as the order of expenses regulation.

CHAPTER III
EXTRADITION

ARTICLE 22
Obligation to extradite

1. Within the framework of the provisions of this Treaty, the Parties shall agree to extradite to the other, upon request, persons present in their territory and wanted by the Requesting Party for a criminal proceedings or the enforcement of a sentence for crimes entailing extradition.

2. Extradition for criminal proceedings shall be granted only for the offences punishable by imprisonment for a term of at least 12 months or by a more severe penalty under the laws of both Parties.

3. Extradition of a person for the execution of a sentence shall be granted only for the offences punishable by imprisonment and in case the person sought has been punished by imprisonment for a term of at least 4 months to be served or by a more severe penalty under the laws of both Parties.

4. If the request for extradition comprises several separate offences, each of which is punishable by imprisonment under the laws of both Parties but some of which do not fulfill the conditions provided in the paragraphs 2 and 3 of this Article, the Requested Party may also grant extradition for the latter offences.

5. Any differences in the legal terminology shall not hinder fulfillment of the request for extradition, if the act, for which extradition is requested, is a penal act as defined in applicable laws of both Parties.

6. Where the offence has been committed outside the territory of the Requesting Party, extradition shall be granted where the law of the Requested Party provides for the punishment of an offence committed outside its territory in similar circumstances.

7. This Treaty shall apply to requests for extradition, made upon commencement hereof, even if they relate to any crimes committed prior to such commencement.

ARTICLE 23
Refusal of extradition

1. Extradition shall not be granted, if:

a) If the act, for which extradition is requested, is not an extraditable offence pursuant to this Treaty;
b) The person sought is a national of the Requested Party,
c) No criminal case may be initiated or the judgment can no longer be executed because of the lapse of time or of another reason provided in the law of the Requested Party,
d) The person sought is the subject of criminal proceedings, a pending trial or a finalized court judgment or of a judgment of non-prosecution by the competent authority of the Requested Party for the same offence for which extradition is sought.
e) The Requested Party has substantial grounds to assume that a request for extradition is made with the aim to persecute or punish a person due to his/her race, sex, religion, citizenship, ethnic origin or in connection with his/her political or other beliefs;
f) The Requested Party considers that the extradition of the person would impair its sovereignty, security, public order or other essential interests;
g) The offence, for which extradition is requested, is subject to capital punishment pursuant to applicable laws of the requesting Party, unless such Party presents sufficient material, in the opinion of the requested Party to guarantee that the person, sought for extradition, will not incur capital punishment.

2. Any request for extradition may be rejected if any offence, for which extradition is requested, pursuant to applicable laws of the requested Party, was committed fully or partially in the territory of that Party.

3. Where the Requested Party does not extradite the person sought in accordance with subparagraph "b" of Paragraph 1 or paragraph 2 of this Article, it shall, upon request of the Requesting Party, deliver all received materials to its competent authorities for considering criminal prosecution of such person pursuant to its laws. To do so, relevant files, information and other evidence regarding the offence shall be submitted by the Requesting Party to the Requested Party. All materials of the case, received in connection with the investigation completed in the Requesting Party, may be used in criminal proceedings in the Requested Party. The Requesting Party shall be informed of the results of this consideration and of the criminal proceedings.

The Requesting Party shall not use any witnesses, statements or objects provided according to this Treaty for performance of investigations or procedural acts other than specified in the request, unless the Central Authority of the Requested Party gives its consent on it.

ARTICLE 24

Provisional arrest

1. In case of urgency the Central Authority of the Requesting Party may apply for provisional arrest of the person sought. The Central Authority of the Requested Party shall decide the matter in accordance with its law.

2. The application for provisional arrest shall state that arrest warrant or final sentence in respect of the person sought exists and that it is intended to send a request for extradition. It shall also state for what offence extradition will be requested and when and where such offence was committed and shall so far as possible give a description of the person sought.

3. An application for provisional arrest shall be sent to the Central Authority of the Requested Party either through the diplomatic channel or direct by post or facsimile or

through the International Criminal Police Organisation (INTERPOL) or by any other means affording evidence in writing or accepted by the Requested Party.

4. The Requesting Party shall be informed of the result of its application without delay.

5. Provisional arrest may be terminated if, within a period of 18 days after arrest, the Requested Party has not received the request for extradition and arrest warrant or final sentence in respect of the person sought. It shall not, in any event, exceed 40 days from the date of such arrest. The possibility of provisional release at any time is not excluded, but the Requested Party shall take any measures which it considers necessary to prevent the escape of the person sought.

6. Release shall not prejudice re-arrest and extradition if a request for extradition is received subsequently.

ARTICLE 25

Request and supporting documents

1. A request for extradition shall be made in writing and sent by the Central Authority of either Party to the Central Authority of the other Party. It shall contain the name of the competent authority of the Requesting Party, full name of the person, sought for extradition, the nationality and physical description to the extent possible, information on residence or domicile and accompanied by photograph and fingerprints of the person sought if possible.

2. A request for extradition submitted for the purpose of any criminal proceedings shall be accompanied by a certified copy of the arrest warrant, a statement defining the act constituting offence and the full text of relevant articles of the law applicable to the offence, as well as lapse of time. In case of a pecuniary damage occurred as a result of the offence, the amount of damage shall be mentioned as accurate as possible.

3. A request submitted for the purpose of enforcement of any sentence shall be accompanied by certified copy of the final judgment and full text of relevant articles

of the law applicable to the offence, as well as lapse of time, and statement of the term of sentence served.

4. The Requested Party shall immediately receive the request for extradition upon its delivering by facsimile, electronic mail or other such type of communication and the original of the request shall be submitted promptly thereafter by the Requesting Party.

ARTICLE 26

Supplementary information

1. If a request for extradition does not include all the necessary information, the Requested Party may ask for supplementary information. To do so, the Requested Party may set a time-limit not exceeding 30 days. In exceptional cases, the specified time limit may be extended upon agreement of the Central Authorities of the Parties, for the term not exceeding 30 days.

2. If the person whose extradition is requested is in custody and the supplementary information furnished is not found sufficient or is not received within the time specified in paragraph 1 of this Article, the person may be released from custody. Such release shall not preclude the Requesting Party from making a new request for the extradition of the person and taking custody over that person.

3. Where the person is released from custody in accordance with paragraph 2 of this Article, the Requested Party shall promptly notify the Requesting Party of this.

ARTICLE 27

Conflicting requests

If the extradition of the person either for the same offence or for different offences is requested by more than one State, the Requested Party shall determine to which one is to be granted extradition taking into consideration all circumstances, especially, gravity and place of such offence, dates of requests, international treaties on extradition, nationality and principal place of residence of the person sought for extradition.

ARTICLE 28

Notification of the decision on the request

1. The Requested Party shall inform the Requesting Party of its decision on the request for extradition.

2. In case of any complete or partial refusal of the request for extradition, reasons thereof shall be communicated to the Requesting Party.

ARTICLE 29

Surrender of a person

1. If the request is agreed to, the competent authorities of the Parties shall agree upon the place and date of surrender of the person. The Requested Party informs the Requesting Party of the term, for which such person was detained by virtue of such request for extradition, with a view to taking this term into account while determining the total term of imprisonment for this person.

2. In case of a favourable decision regarding extradition, the Requesting Party shall receive such surrendered person within 30 days from the day of notification of such decision. If no taking over by the Requesting Party takes place within such period, such person shall be released from detention.

3. If either Party is unable, for any circumstances beyond its control, to surrender or receive the person, subject to extradition, it shall inform the other Party thereof, and the term of surrender may be extended for not more than 15 days. If no surrender takes place within the set term, such person shall be released from detention.

4. In case transportation of the person, subject to extradition, to the territory of the requesting Party may pose any risk to his/her life or health the surrender shall be postponed until according to the Central Authority of the Requested Party his/her state of health allows to effect such surrender.

ARTICLE 30

Postponed or conditional surrender

1. The Requested Party may, after making its decision on the request for extradition, postpone the surrender of a person sought, in order that he may be proceeded against by that Party or, if he has already been convicted, in order that he may serve his/her sentence in the territory of that Party for an offence other than that for which extradition is requested.

2. In case the deferral of extradition stipulated for in paragraph 1 of this Article may incur lapse of time or affect the investigation of a crime, the Requested Party may surrender the person sought to the Requesting Party for the term up to 90 days. The person, thus surrendered, shall be kept in custody in the territory of the Requesting Party and sent back to the territory of the Requested Party after the completion of the procedural actions in respect of that person in accordance with the conditions agreed by the Parties. If necessary, this term may be prolonged upon written agreement of the Parties up to 90 days.

ARTICLE 31

Rule of specialty

A person who has been extradited shall not be detained in custody, proceeded against, or subjected to any punishment or the serving of a sentence or transferred to a third country, nor shall he/she be for any reason restricted in his/her personal freedom for an offence committed prior to surrender and other than that for which extradition was granted, except in the following cases:

a) When the Requested Party consents upon request. In this case, the Requesting Party shall submit to the Requested Party the information and the documents mentioned in the Article 25 herein, necessary for taking the decision on granting such consent.

b) When that person, having had an opportunity to leave the territory of the Party to which he has been surrendered, has not done so within 30 days of his/her final discharge, or has returned to that territory after leaving it. The time period that prevents the extradited person from leaving the territory of the Requesting Party freely for reasons beyond his/her control shall be exempted.

ARTICLE 32

Handing over of objects

1. If the extradition request is granted, to the extent admissible by applicable laws of the Requested Party, and with due consideration of third persons' rights, objects, located in the territory of the Requested Party, which have been acquired as a result of the offence or those that might constitute evidence for criminal proceedings shall be delivered to the Requesting Party. Objects may be handed over, even if extradition cannot be carried out owing to the death or escape of the person sought.

2. The Requested Party may temporarily postpone the delivery of the objects, mentioned in Paragraph 1 of this Article if it is considered that objects would be necessary for any other proceedings.

3. If so required by applicable laws of the Requested Party or protection of third persons' rights, any objects, handed over in such manner, shall be gratuitously returned to the Requested Party on its request as soon as possible upon completion of such proceedings.

ARTICLE 33

Transit

1. Each Party shall, upon request of the other Party including necessary documents and information laid out in the Article 25 of this Treaty, as well as a copy of the decision on extradition, may grant transit through its territory for a person to be extradited to a third State by the latter.

2. The competent authorities of the Parties shall agree on the type, route and other conditions of the transit in each case.

3. The permit mentioned in paragraph 1 of this Article is not required, if such transit transportation is carried out by air and no landing in the territory of the other Party is expected.

4. In case of an unforeseen landing of an aircraft, the request for transit made in accordance with paragraph 1 of this Article shall be submitted. Before the request for transit is received, the Party on which territory the landing took place, may detain the person, subject to extradition, for 24 hours on request of the accompanying officer till the request for transit, made pursuant to Paragraph 1 of this Article, is received. Further detention of the person subject to extradition is performed in accordance with the laws of that Party.

5. Such request for transit may be rejected in cases, specified in Paragraphs 1 and 2 of Article 23 of this Treaty.

ARTICLE 34
Communication of information

The Parties shall exchange information on the results of the criminal proceedings initiated against extradited persons, their escape, as well as of their re-extradition of the person to a third state. In addition, upon request, the Parties shall transmit each other the copy of final decision concluding criminal proceedings against extradited person.

ARTICLE 35
Expenses

1. The Requested Party shall meet the costs of any proceedings in its jurisdiction arising out of a request for extradition.

2. The Requested Party shall bear the costs incurred in its territory in connection with the arrest and detention of the person whose extradition is sought, or the seizure and transfer of property.

3. In case the costs connected with the seizure and transfer of property, have extreme character, the Central Authorities of the Parties hold consultations with the purpose of their distribution.

4. The Requesting Party shall bear the costs on returning property to the Requested Party under paragraph 3 of Article 32 of this Treaty.

5. The Requesting Party shall bear the costs incurred in conveying the person on whose extradition there is consent from the territory of the Requested Party and the costs of transit.

CHAPTER IV
FINAL PROVISIONS

ARTICLE 36
Consultations and settlement of disputes

1. The Central Authorities of the Parties at the request of either of them shall consult on interpretation or application of this Treaty.

2. Disputed issues resulting from interpretation or application of this Treaty shall be resolved through diplomatic negotiations.

ARTICLE 37
Amendments to the treaty

Additional provisions may be inserted to this Treaty or amendments may be made with a separate protocol upon the mutual consent of the Contracting Parties. Additions and amendments shall enter into force in accordance with the procedures in the Article 38 of this Treaty.

ARTICLE 38

Entry into force and termination

1. This Treaty shall enter into force 30 days after the last date of which the Parties have notified each other through diplomatic channels that their respective domestic legal requirements for the entry into force of this Treaty have been complied with.

2. The present Treaty shall terminate 180 days after the date either of the Parties has received through diplomatic channels a written notification by the other Party of its intention to terminate it.

3. Termination of this Treaty shall not be the ground for non-execution of any request for legal assistance or extradition received prior to the date of receipt of the notification mentioned in paragraph 2 of this Article.

Done at Ankara on 1 December 2014, in two duplicates, each in the Turkish, Russian and English languages, all texts having the same force. In case of difference in the interpretation, the English text shall be used.

For THE REPUBLIC OF TURKEY	For THE RUSSIAN FEDERATION
Bekir BOZDAĞ	Aleksandr KONOVALOV
MINISTER OF JUSTICE	MINISTER OF JUSTICE

[TEXT IN RUSSIAN – TEXTE EN RUSSE]

ДОГОВОР
между Турецкой Республикой и Российской Федерацией
о взаимной правовой помощи по уголовным делам и выдаче

Турецкая Республика и Российская Федерация (в дальнейшем именуемые «Сторонами»),

желая укрепить дружеские отношения и организовать взаимное оказание правовой помощи по уголовным делам и выдачу на основе принципов национального суверенитета, равенства в правах и невмешательства во внутренние дела Сторон,

имея целью облегчение применения между Сторонами Европейской конвенции о выдаче от 13 декабря 1957 г. и Европейской конвенции о взаимной правовой помощи по уголовным делам от 20 апреля 1959 г.,

решили заключить настоящий Договор о взаимной правовой помощи по уголовным делам и выдаче и с этой целью договорились о следующем:

Глава I
Общие положения

Статья 1
Центральные и компетентные органы

1. В целях обеспечения надлежащего сотрудничества Сторон в рамках настоящего Договора назначаются центральные органы Сторон.

2. По вопросам, связанным с оказанием взаимной правовой

помощи по уголовным делам, центральным органом с Турецкой Стороны является Министерство юстиции Турецкой Республики.

По вопросам, связанным с оказанием взаимной правовой помощи по уголовным делам, центральными органами с Российской Стороны являются:

Министерство юстиции Российской Федерации – по вопросам, связанным с деятельностью судов Российской Федерации, а также в целях реализации статьи 2 настоящего Договора;

Генеральная прокуратура Российской Федерации – по всем иным вопросам оказания правовой помощи.

3. По вопросам, связанным с выдачей, центральным органом с Турецкой Стороны является Министерство юстиции Турецкой Республики, с Российской Стороны является Генеральная прокуратура Российской Федерации.

4. Компетентными органами являются органы Сторон, участвующие в реализации настоящего Договора.

5. Центральные органы Сторон контактируют напрямую или при необходимости по дипломатическим каналам.

6. Стороны незамедлительно уведомляют друг друга по дипломатическим каналам в случае любых изменений своих центральных органов и сферы их компетенции.

7. Центральные органы Сторон непосредственно направляют и получают запросы, предусмотренные настоящим Договором, и ответы на них.

Статья 2
Обмен информацией

Центральные органы Сторон предоставляют друг другу по запросу информацию о действующих или действовавших на их территориях законодательстве и судебной практике по правовым вопросам, являющимся предметом настоящего Договора.

Статья 3
Языки

Запрос о правовой помощи или о выдаче, прилагаемые к нему документы и дополнительная информация, направляемые в соответствии
с настоящим Договором, сопровождаются удостоверенным переводом на язык запрашиваемой Стороны.

Статья 4
Действительность документов

1. Документы, направленные в рамках настоящего Договора и удостоверенные официальной печатью компетентного или центрального органа направляющей Стороны, имеют доказательную силу без их легализации или иной формы заверения.

По запросу запрашивающей Стороны документы, направляемые
в рамках настоящего Договора, могут быть заверены иным образом, указанным в запросе, если это не противоречит законодательству запрашиваемой Стороны.

2. Для целей настоящего Договора документы, которые являются официальными на территории одной Стороны, признаются таковыми и на территории другой Стороны.

Статья 5
Конфиденциальность и ограничения в использовании информации

1. Запрашиваемая Сторона по запросу центрального органа запрашивающей Стороны обеспечивает в соответствии со своим законодательством конфиденциальность в отношении факта получения запроса о правовой помощи, его содержания или любого действия, предпринятого в связи с запросом, за исключением тех случаев, когда огласка запроса является необходимой для его исполнения.

Если при исполнении запроса возникает необходимость снятия этого ограничения, запрашиваемая Сторона в письменной форме запрашивает разрешение запрашивающей Стороны, без которого запрос не исполняется.

2. Запрашивающая Сторона без предварительного разрешения запрашиваемой Стороны не использует информацию или доказательства, полученные в рамках настоящего Договора, для иных целей, кроме указанных в запросе.

3. В случае если запрашивающей Стороне необходимо предать огласке и использовать полностью или частично полученные информацию или доказательства для иных целей, кроме указанных в запросе, она запрашивает разрешение запрашиваемой Стороны, которая может согласиться или отказать полностью или частично в таком разрешении.

Глава II
Взаимная правовая помощь по уголовным делам

Статья 6
Обязательство предоставления правовой помощи

1. Стороны обязуются взаимно оказывать правовую помощь в связи с расследованием, уголовным преследованием и другими процессуальными действиями по уголовным делам (далее – правовая помощь) в соответствии с положениями настоящего Договора.

2. Запрашиваемая Сторона может оказать правовую помощь в случае, если деяние, в связи с которым поступил запрос о правовой помощи, не является уголовно наказуемым по ее законодательству.

3. Целью настоящего Договора является оказание правовой помощи одной Стороной другой Стороне. Положения настоящего Договора не ведут к возникновению у каких-либо физических и юридических лиц права получать или исключать доказательства либо препятствовать исполнению запроса о правовой помощи.

4. Настоящий Договор не предоставляет компетентным органам одной из Сторон права осуществлять на территории другой Стороны полномочия, которые отнесены исключительно к компетенции органов другой Стороны.

5. Настоящий Договор применяется в отношении запросов о правовой помощи, поступивших после вступления настоящего Договора в силу, даже если соответствующее действие или бездействие было совершено до этой даты.

Статья 7
Сфера действия Договора

Правовая помощь включает:

1) вручение документов;

2) получение показаний, заявлений лиц и других доказательств;

3) установление местонахождения и идентификацию лиц и предметов;

4) вызов свидетелей, потерпевших и экспертов для их добровольной явки в компетентный орган запрашивающей Стороны;

5) передачу на время лиц, содержащихся под стражей или отбывающих наказание в виде лишения свободы, для участия в уголовном судопроизводстве на территории запрашивающей Стороны в качестве свидетелей и потерпевших или для производства иных процессуальных действий, указанных в запросе;

6) осуществление мер по розыску, изъятию, аресту, конфискации
и возврату доходов, полученных в результате преступной деятельности,
и средств совершения преступления;

7) передачу документов, предметов и иных доказательств;

8) предоставление разрешения на присутствие при исполнении запроса лиц, указанных в запросе компетентных органов запрашивающей Стороны;

9) исполнение запросов по осуществлению уголовного преследования в отношении граждан запрашиваемой Стороны и лиц без гражданства, постоянно проживающих на ее территории;

10) обыск и изъятие;

11) другие виды правовой помощи, соответствующие целям настоящего Договора, не противоречащие законодательству запрашиваемой Стороны.

Статья 8
Форма и содержание запроса

1. Запрос о правовой помощи составляется в письменной форме.

2. Запрашиваемая Сторона принимает к исполнению запрос о правовой помощи немедленно по его получении по факсу, электронной почте или другому подобному виду связи, при этом запрашивающая Сторона в возможно короткий срок представляет оригинал запроса. Запрашиваемая Сторона информирует запрашивающую Сторону о результатах исполнения запроса только при условии получения его оригинала.

3. В запросе о правовой помощи указываются:

a) наименование запрашивающего компетентного органа;

b) цель запроса и описание запрашиваемой правовой помощи;

c) описание деяния, в связи с которым проводится расследование или судебное разбирательство, его юридическая квалификация, выписки из текстов применимых законодательных актов запрашивающей Стороны, необходимых для исполнения запроса, полные имена подозреваемых, обвиняемых и осужденных, информация об их месте жительства или пребывания, их гражданстве и профессии и по возможности их месте и дате рождения, имена их родителей, а для юридических лиц – наименование, юридический и фактический адреса;

d) указание на размер ущерба, причиненного в результате

совершения преступления, если это применимо;

e) обоснование применения и описание особых процедур, соблюдение которых желает запрашивающая Сторона при исполнении запроса;

f) данные о свидетелях или потерпевших;

g) желаемый для запрашивающей Стороны срок исполнения запроса;

h) полные имена и адреса, а также по возможности номера телефонов лиц, которые должны быть уведомлены, и их отношение к ведущемуся расследованию или судебному разбирательству;

i) указание на расположение и описание места, где необходимо произвести осмотр и обыск, а также предметов, подлежащих изъятию;

j) вопросы, которые необходимо задать для получения показаний
в запрашиваемой Стороне;

k) в случае указания на необходимость присутствия лиц, определенных компетентными органами запрашивающей Стороны – их полные имена, должности и обоснование необходимости их присутствия;

l) в случае необходимости – просьба о соблюдении конфиденциальности факта поступления запроса, его содержания и (или) любого действия, предпринятого в связи с запросом;

m) любая другая информация, которая может быть полезной запрашиваемой Стороне для исполнения запроса.

4. Если запрашиваемая Сторона считает, что сведения, указанные
в запросе о правовой помощи, не достаточны для его исполнения, эта Сторона может запросить дополнительную информацию.

Статья 9
Исполнение запроса

1. Исполнение запросов о правовой помощи осуществляется в соответствии с законодательством запрашиваемой Стороны и положениями настоящего Договора. Однако по просьбе запрашивающей Стороны может применяться ее законодательство в той мере, в которой это не противоречит законодательству запрашиваемой Стороны.

2. Центральные органы Сторон исполняют запрос о правовой помощи непосредственно или направляет его для выполнения компетентному органу. Если центральный орган направляет запрос для исполнения компетентному органу, он содействует оперативному
и надлежащему исполнению запроса этим компетентным органом.

3. Если запрашивающая Сторона обращается с просьбой о присутствии лиц, определенных ее компетентными органами, при исполнении запроса о правовой помощи, запрашиваемая Сторона уведомляет запрашивающую Сторону о своем решении. В случае положительного решения запрашивающая Сторона заблаговременно уведомляется о времени и месте исполнения запроса.

4. По завершении исполнения запроса центральный орган запрашиваемой Стороны направляет информацию и документы об исполнении запроса центральному органу запрашивающей Стороны.

5. В случае невозможности исполнения запроса центральный орган запрашиваемой Стороны информирует центральный орган запрашивающей Стороны об этом, а также о причинах, препятствующих исполнению запроса.

Статья 10
Отказ или отсрочка оказания правовой помощи

1. В оказании правовой помощи может быть отказано, если:

a) запрашиваемая Сторона считает, что исполнение запроса может нанести ущерб ее суверенитету, безопасности, публичному порядку или другим существенным интересам;

b) запрашиваемая Сторона имеет веские основания полагать, что запрос представлен с целью преследования лица по признаку расы, пола, вероисповедания, гражданства, этнического происхождения или по политическим убеждениям либо положению этого лица может быть нанесен ущерб по любой из этих причин;

c) запрашиваемая Сторона считает, что исполнение запроса противоречит ее законодательству и положениям настоящего Договора;

d) запрос касается преступления против военной службы, которое не является преступлением по общему уголовному законодательству;

e) запрос касается деяния, за которое лицо, привлекаемое к уголовной ответственности в запрашивающей Стороне, было осуждено или оправдано в запрашиваемой Стороне в связи с тем же деянием, или по которому истек срок давности в соответствии с законодательством запрашиваемой Стороны.

2. Ссылка на банковскую или налоговую тайны не может служить основанием для отказа в оказании правовой помощи.

3. Запрашиваемая Сторона может отсрочить или отказать в правовой помощи, если исполнение запроса может нанести ущерб или затруднить расследование или судебное разбирательство, проводимое

в запрашиваемой Стороне.

4. Перед принятием решения об отсрочке или отказе в исполнении запроса запрашиваемая Сторона рассматривает вопрос о том, может ли правовая помощь быть оказана на условиях, которые она считает необходимыми. Если запрашивающая Сторона соглашается на оказание правовой помощи на таких условиях, она обязуется соблюдать их.

5. Если запрашиваемая Сторона принимает решение об отказе в оказании правовой помощи или ее отсрочке, она уведомляет об этом запрашивающую Сторону через ее центральный орган с указанием причины такого решения.

Статья 11
Вызов свидетелей, потерпевших и экспертов, гарантии, предоставляемые вызываемому лицу

1. Если запрашивающая Сторона представляет запрос о вызове лица для дачи показаний, проведения экспертизы или иных процессуальных действий на своей территории, запрашиваемая Сторона сообщает этому лицу о приглашении явиться в компетентный орган запрашивающей Стороны.

2. Запрос о вызове лица должен содержать сведения об условиях
и порядке оплаты расходов, связанных с явкой вызываемого лица, а также перечень гарантий, которые предоставляются ему в соответствии
с пунктами 5 и 6 настоящей статьи.

3. Приглашение, указанное в пункте 1 настоящей статьи, не

должно содержать угрозу применения принуждения или наказания в случае неявки этого лица на территорию запрашивающей Стороны.

4. Вызванное лицо добровольно принимает решение о явке. Центральный орган запрашиваемой Стороны незамедлительно информирует центральный орган запрашивающей Стороны о решении этого лица.

5. Лицо, явившееся в компетентный орган запрашивающей Стороны, независимо от его гражданства не может быть подвергнуто уголовному преследованию, аресту либо иным ограничениям личной свободы на территории этой Стороны за совершение деяния или на основании приговора, имевшего место до его выезда с территории запрашиваемой Стороны.

6. Вызванное лицо не может быть принуждено к даче показаний по делу, не указанному в запросе о вызове лица.

7. Вызванное лицо лишается гарантий, предусмотренных в настоящей статье, в том случае, если оно, имея возможность покинуть территорию запрашивающей Стороны, не сделало этого в течение 15 суток со дня его письменного уведомления о том, что его присутствие перестало быть необходимым для соответствующего компетентного органа, или покинуло эту территорию и затем добровольно вернулось.

Статья 12
Передача на время лиц, содержащихся под стражей
(в том числе отбывающих наказание в виде лишения свободы)

1. Лицо независимо от его гражданства, которое содержится под стражей (в том числе, отбывающее наказание в виде лишения свободы)

и в отношении которого запрашивающая Сторона запросила личное присутствие в качестве свидетеля или потерпевшего либо для производства иных процессуальных действий, указанных в запросе, может быть передано на время на территорию запрашивающей Стороны, если такое лицо будет возвращено запрашиваемой Стороне в сроки, указанные запрашиваемой Стороной, и при соблюдении условий, указанных в пунктах 5 и 6 статьи 11 настоящего Договора, в той мере, насколько это применимо.

Первичный срок, на который лицо может быть передано, не может превышать 90 дней. По обоснованному ходатайству центрального органа запрашивающей Стороны срок пребывания переданного лица может быть продлен центральным органом запрашиваемой Стороны.

Порядок и условия передачи и возврата лица согласовываются центральными органами.

2. В передаче лица может быть отказано:

a) если лицо, содержащееся под стражей, не дает письменного согласия на это;

b) если необходимо присутствие этого лица в судопроизводстве, осуществляемом на территории запрашиваемой Стороны;

c) если передача продлит срок его содержания под стражей;

d) если имеются иные веские основания не передавать лицо на территорию запрашивающей Стороны.

3. Переданное лицо содержится под стражей на территории запрашивающей Стороны на основании и в соответствии с ее законодательством, пока остается в силе решение компетентного органа запрашиваемой Стороны о его содержании под стражей. В

случае освобождения переданного лица из-под стражи по решению запрашиваемой Стороны, запрашивающая Сторона применяет к этому лицу положения пунктов 5 и 6 статьи 11 и статьи 21 настоящего Договора.

4. Время содержания под стражей переданного лица вне территории запрашиваемой Стороны засчитывается в общий срок его содержания под стражей.

5. Если содержащееся под стражей лицо не дает согласия прибыть на территорию запрашивающей Стороны, оно не подвергается мерам принуждения или наказанию.

Статья 13
Защита лица, явившегося по вызову или переданного на территорию запрашивающей Стороны

В случае необходимости запрашивающая Сторона обеспечивает защиту лица, явившегося по вызову или переданного на ее территорию в соответствии со статьями 11 и 12 настоящего Договора.

Статья 14
Вручение документов

1. Запрашиваемая Сторона осуществляет вручение документов, сопровождаемых удостоверенными переводами на язык запрашиваемой Стороны, в соответствии со своим законодательством.

2. Запрашивающая Сторона передает запрос о вручении

документов относительно ответа или явки на территорию запрашивающей Стороны в разумные сроки до намеченного ответа или явки, как правило, не позднее чем за 60 дней до даты явки.

3. В запросе о вручении документов должны быть указаны известный адрес получателя и название вручаемого документа.

4. Исполнение запроса о вручении документов подтверждается документом о вручении с указанием даты и подписью адресата или заявлением компетентного органа запрашиваемой Стороны, в котором подтверждаются факт, дата и порядок вручения.

5. О вручении документов или о невозможности их вручения незамедлительно информируется запрашивающая Сторона.

Статья 15
Запрос об осуществлении уголовного преследования

1. Каждая из Сторон по запросу и в соответствии со своим законодательством осуществляет уголовное преследование в отношении своих граждан и постоянно проживающих на ее территории лиц без гражданства, совершивших преступление, подпадающее под юрисдикцию запрашивающей Стороны.

По получении указанного запроса запрашиваемая Сторона передает полученные материалы уголовного дела своим компетентным органам для принятия решения об осуществлении уголовного преследования в соответствии с законодательством этой Стороны.

2. Запрос об осуществлении уголовного преследования содержит:

а) наименование запрашивающего компетентного органа;

b) полное имя лица, предположительно совершившего преступление, информацию о его гражданстве и по возможности информацию о его месте жительства или пребывания, описание его внешности, фотографию, отпечатки пальцев и другие данные, позволяющие идентифицировать это лицо;

c) описание и правовую квалификацию деяния, в связи с которым направляется запрос об осуществлении уголовного преследования;

d) возможно более точное указание времени и места совершения деяния;

e) если необходимо, требование о возврате оригиналов документов
и предметов, являющихся вещественными доказательствами.

3. К запросу об осуществлении уголовного преследования прилагаются:

a) материалы расследования или их заверенные копии, в том числе имеющиеся доказательства;

b) тексты уголовно-правовых норм, а при необходимости – и других норм законодательства запрашивающей Стороны, имеющих существенное значение для уголовного судопроизводства;

c) если применимо и при наличии возможности – данные о размере причиненного ущерба;

d) ходатайства потерпевших о возбуждении уголовного преследования, если это требуется в соответствии с законодательством запрашиваемой Стороны.

4. В целях обеспечения законных прав третьих лиц запрашиваемая Сторона по завершении процессуальных действий по требованию запрашивающей Стороны возвращает оригиналы

документов и предметы, являющиеся вещественными доказательствами.

5. Запрашиваемая Сторона уведомляет запрашивающую Сторону о принятых в связи с ее запросом об осуществлении уголовного преследования мерах, о результатах уголовного преследования и высылает копию вынесенного по уголовному делу решения.

6. Если после получения запроса об осуществлении уголовного преследования в отношении указанного в нем лица вынесено и вступило в законную силу решение судебного органа запрашиваемой Стороны, то компетентные органы запрашивающей Стороны не могут осуществлять уголовное преследование в отношении этого лица за то же деяние.

7. В случае если запрашиваемой Стороной принято решение не принимать мер в отношении запроса об осуществлении уголовного преследования или отказать в его принятии либо принято внесудебное решение об отказе в возбуждении уголовного дела или о его прекращении, запрашивающей Стороне незамедлительно возвращаются переданные ею материалы уголовного дела и вещественные доказательства.

Статья 16
Получение доказательств на территории запрашиваемой Стороны

1. Запрашиваемая Сторона получает на своей территории показания свидетелей и потерпевших, заключения экспертов, документы, предметы и доказательства, указанные в запросе, и передает их запрашивающей Стороне.

2. Присутствующим при исполнении запроса о правовой помощи лицам, определенным запрашивающей Стороной, разрешается формулировать вопросы, которые могут быть заданы соответствующему лицу через представителя компетентного органа запрашиваемой Стороны.

3. Запрашивающая Сторона соблюдает любые условия, установленные запрашиваемой Стороной в отношении передаваемых ей документов и предметов, в том числе касающиеся защиты прав третьих лиц на такие документы и предметы.

4. Запрашивающая Сторона по требованию запрашиваемой Стороны возвращает в возможно короткий срок оригиналы документов и предметы, переданные ей в соответствии с пунктом 1 настоящей статьи.

Статья 17
Предоставление информации, документов и предметов

1. Запрашиваемая Сторона представляет запрашивающей Стороне копии документов и информацию государственных органов, которые по ее законодательству являются общедоступными.

2. Запрашиваемая Сторона может в соответствии со своим законодательством представить запрашивающей Стороне любую информацию, документы, предметы, находящиеся во владении государственного органа, не являющиеся общедоступными, в той степени и на тех же условиях, как они были бы доступны ее собственным правоохранительным и судебным органам.

3. Каждая Сторона может представить другой Стороне информацию или документы, которые, по ее мнению, могут быть использованы с целью уголовного преследования физических или юридических лиц или начала соответствующего производства в

отношении юридических лиц в связи
с преступлениями физических лиц.

Статья 18
Обыск и изъятие

1. Запрашиваемая Сторона в такой мере, в какой позволяет ее законодательство, исполняет запросы об обыске, изъятии и передаче запрашивающей Стороне документов и предметов, имеющих отношение
к расследованию или иным процессуальным действиям в связи
с производством по уголовному делу в запрашивающей Стороне, при условии, что запрос включает в себя достаточно информации, чтобы в соответствии с законодательством запрашиваемой Стороны такие действия были обоснованными.

2. Запрашиваемая Сторона предоставляет информацию, необходимую запрашивающей Стороне, относительно результатов любого обыска, места изъятия, обстоятельств изъятия и последующего хранения изъятых документов и предметов.

3. Запрашивающая Сторона соблюдает любые условия, установленные запрашиваемой Стороной в отношении любых изъятых документов и предметов, передаваемых запрашивающей Стороне.

Статья 19
Установление местонахождения и идентификация лиц и предметов

Компетентные органы запрашиваемой Стороны предпринимают всевозможные предусмотренные ее законодательством меры для установления местонахождения и идентификации лиц и предметов, указанных в запросе.

Статья 20
Осуществление мер по розыску, изъятию, аресту, конфискации и возврату доходов, полученных в результате преступной деятельности, и средств совершения преступления

1. Стороны в соответствии со своим законодательством оказывают взаимную правовую помощь в выявлении, замораживании, аресте, изъятии и конфискации доходов, полученных в результате преступной деятельности, и средств совершения преступления.

В целях настоящего Договора под доходами, полученными в результате преступной деятельности, понимаются денежные средства или иное имущество, полученное в результате совершения преступления, выручка и другие выгоды, полученные от таких доходов, от имущества, в которое они были превращены или преобразованы, или от имущества, к которому были приобщены доходы, полученные в результате преступной деятельности.

2. По запросу запрашиваемая Сторона принимает меры к установлению того, находятся ли доходы, полученные в результате преступной деятельности, и средства совершения преступления под ее юрисдикцией, информирует запрашивающую Сторону о результатах такого розыска. В запросе о проведении указанных действий запрашивающая Сторона информирует запрашиваемую Сторону об основаниях, позволяющих полагать, что такие доходы и средства совершения преступления могут находиться в пределах юрисдикции запрашиваемой Стороны.

3. В случае обнаружения в соответствии с пунктом 2 настоящей статьи доходов, полученных в результате преступной деятельности,
и средств совершения преступления, запрашиваемая Сторона по запросу исполняет решение о наложении ареста, вынесенное компетентным органом запрашивающей Стороны, или принимает такие меры
в соответствии со своим законодательством в целях предотвращения любых действий с такими доходами и средствами совершения преступления, передачи или распоряжения ими до принятия окончательного решения в их отношении судом запрашивающей или запрашиваемой Стороны.

4. Запрашиваемая Сторона в соответствии со своим законодательством обеспечивает исполнение вступившего в силу решения, вынесенного компетентным органом запрашивающей Стороны, об изъятии или конфискации доходов, полученных в результате преступной деятельности, или средств совершения преступления.

5. При реализации положений настоящей статьи должны соблюдаться права добросовестных приобретателей – третьих лиц в соответствии с законодательством запрашиваемой Стороны.

6. На основании запроса запрашивающей Стороны запрашиваемая Сторона в соответствии со своим законодательством и согласованными центральными органами Сторон условиями передает запрашивающей Стороне доходы, полученные в результате преступной деятельности, или средства совершения преступления.

7. Положения настоящей статьи не затрагивают прав и обязательств Сторон, вытекающих из многосторонних

международных договоров, участниками которых являются обе Стороны.

Статья 21
Расходы

1. Запрашиваемая Сторона несет обычные расходы, связанные с исполнением запроса о правовой помощи, за исключением следующих расходов, которые несет запрашивающая Сторона:

a) расходы, связанные с проездом лиц на ее территорию и обратно
в соответствии со статьями 11 и 12 настоящего Договора и их пребыванием на этой территории, а также иные выплаты, полагающиеся этим лицам;

b) расходы и гонорары экспертов;

c) расходы, связанные с проездом, пребыванием и присутствием определенных компетентными органами запрашивающей Стороны лиц при исполнении запроса в соответствии с пунктом 3 статьи 9 настоящего Договора;

d) расходы по перевозке переданных предметов с территории запрашиваемой Стороны на территорию запрашивающей Стороны и их возвращению.

2. Если исполнение запроса о правовой помощи требует существенных или чрезвычайных расходов, центральные органы Сторон проводят консультации с целью определения условий, на которых может быть исполнен запрос о правовой помощи, и порядка покрытия расходов.

Глава III
Выдача

Статья 22
Обязательство выдачи

1. Стороны обязуются в соответствии с положениями настоящего Договора выдавать по запросу друг другу лиц, находящихся на их территории и разыскиваемых запрашивающей Стороной для целей уголовного преследования или для исполнения приговора за совершение преступлений, влекущих выдачу.

2. Выдача для привлечения к уголовной ответственности производится только в случае преступлений, за которые в соответствии

с законодательством обеих Сторон предусматривается наказание в виде лишения свободы на срок не менее 12 месяцев или другое более тяжкое наказание.

3. Выдача лица для исполнения приговора осуществляется только за преступления, которые считаются таковыми в соответствии

с законодательством обеих Сторон, и только если данное лицо осуждено

к лишению свободы сроком свыше 4 месяцев или другому более тяжкому наказанию.

4. Если запрос о выдаче касается нескольких не зависящих друг от друга преступлений, каждое из которых в соответствии с законодательством обеих Сторон влечет за собой лишение свободы, но некоторые из них не отвечают условиям, предусмотренным пунктами 2 и 3 настоящей статьи, то

запрашиваемая Сторона может согласиться на выдачу за эти преступления.

5. Различия в юридической терминологии не препятствуют исполнению запроса о выдаче, если деяние, в связи с которым поступил запрос, является уголовно наказуемым по законодательству обеих Сторон.

6. Если преступление было совершено за пределами территории запрашивающей Стороны, выдача осуществляется, если законодательство запрашиваемой Стороны предусматривает наказание за преступление, совершенное вне его территории при аналогичных обстоятельствах.

7. Настоящий Договор применяется к запросам о выдаче, направленным после его вступления в силу, даже если они связаны с преступлениями, совершенными до его вступления в силу.

Статья 23
Отказ в выдаче

1. Выдача не производится, если:

a) деяние, в связи с которым поступил запрос о выдаче, не является преступлением, влекущим выдачу в соответствии с настоящим Договором;

b) лицо, выдача которого запрашивается, является гражданином запрашиваемой Стороны;

c) уголовное дело не может быть возбуждено или приговор не может быть приведен в исполнение вследствие истечения срока давности или по другим основаниям, предусмотренным законодательством запрашиваемой Стороны;

d) в отношении лица, выдача которого запрашивается, компетентным органом запрашиваемой Стороны в связи с тем же преступлением ведется уголовное преследование, судебное разбирательство, или был вынесен вступивший в силу приговор, или было принято решение об отказе в уголовном преследовании;

e) запрашиваемая Сторона имеет веские основание полагать, что запрос о выдаче представлен с целью преследования или наказания лица, по признаку расы, пола, вероисповедания, гражданства, этнического происхождения или по политическим или иным убеждениям;

f) запрашиваемая Сторона считает, что выдача лица может нанести ущерб ее суверенитету, безопасности, публичному порядку или иным существенным интересам;

g) преступление, в связи с которым запрашивается выдача, влечет за собой наказание в виде смертной казни по законодательству запрашивающей Стороны, если только эта Сторона не предоставит заверений, которые запрашиваемая Сторона сочтет достаточными, о том, что к запрашиваемому лицу не будет применена смертная казнь.

2. В выдаче может быть отказано, если преступление, в связи с которым запрашивается выдача, рассматривается по законодательству запрашиваемой Стороны как совершенное полностью или частично на ее территории.

3. Если запрашиваемая Сторона отказывает в выдаче на основании подпункта «b» пункта 1 или пункта 2 настоящей статьи, то запрашиваемая Сторона по запросу запрашивающей Стороны

передает полученные материалы своим компетентным органам для рассмотрения вопроса об осуществлении уголовного преследования против этого лица
в соответствии со своим законодательством. С этой целью запрашивающая Сторона направляет запрашиваемой Стороне соответствующие документы, информацию и другие доказательства, касающиеся преступления. Материалы дела, которые были получены в связи с проведенным расследованием в запрашивающей Стороне, могут быть использованы
в уголовном судопроизводстве в запрашиваемой Стороне. Запрашивающая Сторона информируется о результатах рассмотрения и уголовного преследования.

Запрашивающая Сторона не использует никаких показаний, заявлений или предметов, предоставленных согласно настоящему Договору, при проведении иных расследований или других процессуальных действий, чем те, которые указаны в запросе о выдаче, без предварительного согласия центрального органа запрашиваемой Стороны.

Статья 24
Временное задержание

1. В случае, не терпящем отлагательства, центральный орган запрашивающей Стороны может обратиться с ходатайством о временном задержании разыскиваемого лица. Центральный орган запрашиваемой Стороны принимает решение по данному вопросу в соответствии с ее законодательством.

2. В ходатайстве о временном задержании сообщается о наличии постановления суда о взятии лица, выдача которого запрашивается, под стражу или вступившего в силу приговора в

отношении него и намерении направить запрос о выдаче. В нем также указывается, в связи с каким преступлением будет направлен запрос о выдаче, где и когда такое преступление было совершено, и приводится по возможности описание разыскиваемого лица.

3. Ходатайство о временном задержании направляется центральным органом запрашиваемой Стороны по дипломатическим каналам, или непосредственно по почте или факсимильной связи, или через Международную организацию уголовной полиции (Интерпол), или

с помощью любых других средств, обеспечивающих письменное подтверждение или приемлемых для запрашиваемой Стороны.

4. Запрашивающая Сторона безотлагательно информируется о результатах рассмотрения ходатайства.

5. Временное задержание может быть отменено, если в течение 18 дней после задержания запрашиваемая Сторона не получила запрос

о выдаче и постановление суда о взятии указанного в ходатайстве лица под стражу или вступивший в силу приговор в отношении него. В любом случае этот период не превышает 40 дней с даты такого задержания. Возможность временного освобождения в любое время не исключается, однако запрашиваемая Сторона принимает любые меры, которые она считает необходимыми, для предотвращения побега разыскиваемого лица.

6. Освобождение не препятствует повторному задержанию и выдаче, если впоследствии получен запрос о выдаче.

Статья 25
Запрос и прилагаемые документы

1. Запрос о выдаче составляется в письменной форме,

направляется центральным органом одной Стороны центральному органу другой Стороны. Он содержит наименование компетентного органа запрашивающей Стороны, полное имя лица, выдача которого запрашивается, сведения о его гражданстве и по возможности описание внешности, информацию о месте проживания или пребывания, а также сопровождается по возможности фотографией и отпечатками пальцев.

2. Запрос о выдаче для привлечения к уголовной ответственности должен сопровождаться заверенной копией постановления суда о взятии под стражу, описанием фактических обстоятельств преступного деяния и полным текстом соответствующих статей применимого закона, квалифицирующего преступление и касающегося применимого срока давности. Если в результате преступления нанесен материальный ущерб, то по возможности точно следует указать его размер.

3. Запрос для исполнения приговора должен сопровождаться заверенной копией приговора, вступившего в законную силу, полным текстом соответствующих статей применимого закона, квалифицирующего преступление и касающегося применимого срока давности, и заявлением относительно отбытой части наказания.

4. Запрашиваемая Сторона принимает к исполнению запрос о выдаче немедленно по его получении по факсу, электронной почте или другому подобному виду связи, при этом запрашивающая Сторона в возможно короткий срок представляет оригинал запроса.

Статья 26
Дополнительная информация

1. Если запрос о выдаче не содержит всю необходимую информацию, то запрашиваемая Сторона может запросить дополнительную информацию. Для предоставления такой информации запрашиваемая Сторона может установить срок, который не должен превышать 30 дней. В исключительных случаях этот срок может быть продлен не более чем на 30 дней по согласованию центральных органов Сторон.

2. Если лицо, выдача которого запрашивается, находится под стражей, но предоставленная дополнительная информация признана запрашиваемой Стороной недостаточной или не получена в течение срока, указанного в пункте 1 настоящей статьи, то такое лицо может быть освобождено из-под стражи. Освобождение этого лица не препятствует повторному обращению запрашивающей Стороны с запросом о выдаче этого лица и взятии его под стражу.

3. Если это лицо освобождено из-под стражи в соответствии с пунктом 2 настоящей статьи, запрашиваемая Сторона в возможно короткий срок уведомляет об этом запрашивающую Сторону.

Статья 27
Конкурирующие запросы

Если несколько государств запрашивают выдачу лица за совершение одного и того же преступления или за совершение разных преступлений, запрашиваемая Сторона принимает решение о том, какой из этих запросов о выдаче будет удовлетворен, учитывая все обстоятельства, в особенности тяжесть и место совершения преступления, даты запросов, наличие международных договоров о выдаче, гражданство и основное место жительства лица, выдача которого запрашивается.

Статья 28
Уведомление о результатах рассмотрения запроса о выдаче

1. Запрашиваемая Сторона сообщает запрашивающей Стороне о своем решении в отношении запроса о выдаче.

2. В случае полного или частичного отказа в выдаче причины такого решения доводятся до сведения запрашивающей Стороны.

Статья 29
Передача лица

1. В случае согласия удовлетворить запрос компетентные органы Сторон договариваются о месте и дате передачи выдаваемого лица. Запрашиваемая Сторона информирует запрашивающую Сторону о сроке,
в течение которого лицо было лишено свободы в связи с запросом о выдаче, с тем чтобы этот срок был засчитан в срок лишения свободы данного лица.

2. В случае положительного решения вопроса о выдаче запрашивающая Сторона принимает выданное лицо в срок не позднее 30 дней со дня, когда она была уведомлена о таком решении. Если передача не состоится в указанный срок, данное лицо освобождается из-под стражи.

3. В случае если одна из Сторон по не зависящим от нее причинам не может передать или принять лицо, подлежащее выдаче, она уведомляет об этом другую Сторону и срок передачи может быть продлен на период не более 15 дней. Если передача не состоится в указанный срок, лицо освобождается из-под стражи.

4. В случае если перевозка лица, подлежащего выдаче, на

территорию запрашивающей Стороны может угрожать его жизни и здоровью, передача может быть отложена до тех пор, пока состояние его здоровья, по мнению запрашиваемой Стороны, не позволит осуществить эту передачу.

Статья 30
Отсрочка в выдаче и выдача на время

1. Запрашиваемая Сторона, приняв решение по запросу о выдаче, может отсрочить передачу соответствующего лица с тем, чтобы осуществить в отношении него уголовное преследование или чтобы это лицо отбыло на его территории наказание за совершение преступления, не являющегося основанием для запроса о выдаче.

2. Если отсрочка в выдаче лица, предусмотренная пунктом 1 настоящей статьи, может повлечь за собой истечение срока давности уголовного преследования или причинить ущерб расследованию преступления, запрашиваемая Сторона может передать запрашивающей Стороне такое лицо на срок не более 90 дней. Переданное таким образом лицо содержится под стражей на территории запрашивающей Стороны и должно быть возвращено на территорию запрашиваемой Стороны после завершения процессуальных действий в отношении этого лица в соответствии с условиями, согласованными обеими Сторонами. В случае необходимости этот срок может быть продлен по письменному согласию Сторон на срок до 90 дней.

Статья 31
Правило конкретности

Выданное лицо не может быть заключено под стражу, преследоваться в уголовном порядке, подвергаться наказанию или отбыванию приговора, быть выдано третьему государству, и его личная свобода ни по каким иным причинам не может быть ограничена в связи с преступлением, совершенным до его выдачи и не являющимся преступлением, обусловившим выдачу, за исключением следующих случаев:

а) если запрашиваемая Сторона по запросу дает согласие на это.

В таком случае запрашивающая Сторона представляет запрашиваемой Стороне информацию и документы, указанные в статье 25 настоящего Договора, необходимые для решения вопроса о даче такого согласия;

b) если это лицо, имея возможность покинуть территорию Стороны, которой оно было выдано, не сделало этого в течение 30 дней после своего окончательного освобождения или, покинув ее территорию, вернулось туда. В этот срок не включается время, в течение которого выданное лицо не могло покинуть территорию запрашивающей Стороны по независящим от него обстоятельствам.

Статья 32
Передача предметов

1. Если имеется согласие на выдачу, то в пределах, допускаемых законодательством запрашиваемой Стороны, и с учетом прав третьих лиц находящиеся на территории запрашиваемой Стороны предметы, которые были приобретены в результате преступления или могут являться доказательствами по уголовному делу, передаются запрашивающей Стороне. Передача может быть

произведена, даже если выдача не может быть осуществлена вследствие смерти или побега лица, выдача которого запрашивается.

2. Запрашиваемая Сторона может отложить передачу предметов, указанных в пункте 1 настоящей статьи, если она сочтет, что они необходимы для производства по другому делу.

3. Если того требует законодательство запрашиваемой Стороны или защита прав третьих лиц, любые переданные в соответствии с настоящей статьей предметы безвозмездно возвращаются запрашиваемой Стороне по ее запросу в возможно короткий срок после окончания производства по делу.

Статья 33
Транзитная перевозка

1. Каждая из Сторон по запросу на транзит другой Стороны, содержащему необходимые информацию и документы, указанные в статье 25 настоящего Договора, а также копию решения о выдаче, может разрешить перевозку по своей территории лиц, выданных этой Стороной третьему государству.

2. Компетентные органы Сторон согласуют в каждом конкретном случае способ, маршрут и другие условия транзита.

3. Указанного в пункте 1 настоящей статьи разрешения не требуется, если используется воздушный способ перевозки и посадка на территории другой Стороны не предусматривается.

4. В случае непредвиденной посадки воздушного судна направляется запрос на транзит, составленный в соответствии с пунктом 1 настоящей статьи. До получения запроса на транзит Сторона, на территории которой произведена посадка, может содержать выдаваемое лицо под стражей

в течение 24 часов по запросу сопровождающего его должностного лица до получения запроса на транзит, составленного в соответствии с пунктом 1 настоящей статьи. Дальнейшее содержание выданного лица под стражей осуществляется в соответствии с законодательством этой Стороны.

5. В разрешении на транзит может быть отказано в случаях, указанных в пунктах 1 и 2 статьи 23 настоящего Договора.

Статья 34
Предоставление информации

Стороны взаимно информируют друг друга о результатах уголовного преследования выданных лиц, об их побеге, выдаче третьему государству. Стороны направляют также друг другу по запросу копию вступившего в законную силу решения в отношении выданного лица.

Статья 35
Расходы

1. Запрашиваемая Сторона несет расходы по любым процессуальным действиям в пределах своей юрисдикции, вытекающим из запроса о выдаче.

2. Запрашиваемая Сторона принимает на себя расходы, возникающие на ее территории в связи с задержанием и содержанием под стражей лица, выдача которого запрашивается, а также арестом, изъятием и передачей предметов.

3. В случае если расходы, связанные с изъятием и передачей предметов, носят чрезвычайный характер, центральные органы

Сторон проводят консультации с целью их распределения.

4. Расходы по возвращению запрашиваемой Стороне предметов
в соответствии с пунктом 3 статьи 32 настоящего Договора несет запрашивающая Сторона.

5. Запрашивающая Сторона принимает на себя расходы, связанные
с доставкой лица, на выдачу которого имеется согласие, с территории запрашиваемой Стороны, и расходы, связанные с транзитной перевозкой.

Глава IV
Заключительные положения

Статья 36
Консультации и разрешение споров

1. Центральные органы Сторон по запросу одного из них проводят консультации по вопросам толкования и применения настоящего Договора.

2. Спорные вопросы, возникающие при толковании и применении настоящего Договора, разрешаются путем дипломатических переговоров.

Статья 37
Внесение изменений в Договор

По взаимному согласию Сторон в настоящий Договор могут быть внесены дополнения и изменения, которые оформляются отдельными протоколами. Такие дополнения и изменения вступают в силу в соответствии с порядком, установленным в статье 38 настоящего Договора.

Статья 38

Вступление в силу и прекращение действия

1. Настоящий Договор вступает в силу по истечении 30 дней с даты уведомления Сторонами друг друга по дипломатическим каналам
о выполнении ими внутригосударственных процедур, необходимых для его вступления в силу.

2. Настоящий Договор прекращает свое действие по истечении 180 дней с даты получения по дипломатическим каналам одной Стороной письменного уведомления другой Стороны о ее намерении прекратить его действие.

3. Прекращение действия настоящего Договора не является основанием для неисполнения запросов о правовой помощи и о выдаче, поступивших до даты получения уведомления, указанного в пункте 2 настоящей статьи.

Совершено в г. Анкара 1 декабря 2014 г. в двух экземплярах, каждый на турецком, русском и английском языках, причем все тексты имеют одинаковую силу. В случае разногласия для целей толкования используется текст на английском языке.

За Турецкую Республику	**За Российскую Федерацию**
Бекир БОЗДАГ	**Александр Коновалов**
Министр юстиции	**Министр юстиции**

[TEXT IN TURKISH – TEXTE EN TURC]

TÜRKİYE CUMHURİYETİ
İLE
RUSYA FEDERASYONU
ARASINDA
CEZAİ KONULARDA KARŞILIKLI ADLİ YARDIMLAŞMA VE SUÇLULARIN İADESİ ANLAŞMASI

Türkiye Cumhuriyeti ve Rusya Federasyonu, (bundan sonra "Taraflar" olarak anılacaktır)

Dostane ilişkileri geliştirmek ve cezai konularda ve suçluların iadesi hakkında adli işbirliğini, ulusal egemenlik, hakların eşitliği ve Tarafların içişlerine karışmama ilkeleri temelinde düzenleme arzusuyla,

13 Aralık 1957 tarihli Suçluların İadesine dair Avrupa Sözleşmesi ile 20 Nisan 1959 tarihli Ceza İşlerinde Karşılıklı Yardım Avrupa Sözleşmesi'nin taraflar arasında uygulamasının kolaylaştırılması amacıyla,

Cezai Konularda ve Suçluların İadesi Hakkında Karşılıklı Adli Yardımlaşma Anlaşmasını imzalamaya karar vermiş ve aşağıdaki konularda mutabık kalmıştır:

BÖLÜM I
GENEL HÜKÜMLER

MADDE 1
Merkezi ve yetkili makamlar

1. İşbu Anlaşma kapsamında Tarafların uygun işbirliğini sağlamalarını temin etmek amacıyla, Tarafların Merkezi Makamları belirlenir.

2. Karşılıklı adli yardımlaşma kapsamında, Türkiye Tarafının Merkezi Makamı, Türkiye Cumhuriyeti Adalet Bakanlığı'dır.

Karşılıklı adli yardımlaşma kapsamında Rusya Tarafının Merkezi makamı:
Rusya Federasyonu mahkemelerinin yargı işlemleriyle bağlantılı olan konularda ve işbu Anlaşmanın 2. maddesi kapsamındaki konularda, Rusya Federasyonu Adalet Bakanlığı;
Diğer tüm konularda adli yardımlaşma kapsamında Başsavcılık.

3. Suçluların iadesi kapsamında, Türkiye Tarafının Merkezi Makamı, Türkiye Cumhuriyeti Adalet Bakanlığı, Rusya Tarafının Merkezi Makamı, Rusya Federasyonu Başsavcılığı'dır.

4. Yetkili makamlar, Tarafların işbu Anlaşmanın uygulamasına dâhil olan makamlarıdır.

5. Tarafların Merkezi Makamları, doğrudan ya da gerekli olması durumunda diplomatik kanallar yoluyla iletişim kurar.

6. Taraflar, Merkezi Makamlarının ya da bu Makamların yetkilerinin değişmesi halinde, birbirlerini derhal diplomatik kanallarla bilgilendirir.

7. Tarafların Merkezi Makamları, işbu Anlaşmada öngörülen tüm talepleri ve bunların cevaplarını doğrudan gönderir ve alır.

MADDE 2

Bilgi paylaşımı

Tarafların Merkezi Makamları, talep üzerine, işbu Anlaşmanın konusunu oluşturan adli meselelere ilişkin yürürlükte olan ya da kaldırılmış mevzuatları ve adli uygulamalarına dair birbirlerine bilgi temin eder.

MADDE 3

Diller

İşbu Anlaşma uyarınca gönderilen adli yardım ve iade taleplerine, destekleyici belgelere ve ek bilgilere, Talep Edilen Tarafın dilinde onaylanmış çevirileri eklenir.

MADDE 4

Belgelerin geçerliliği

1. İşbu Anlaşma uyarınca gönderilen ile gönderen Tarafın yetkili ya da Merkezi Makamının resmi mührüyle tasdik edilmiş olan belgeler, başka bir yetkilendirmeye ya da herhangi başka bir sertifikaya gerek duyulmaksızın açıkça kabul edilir.

Talep Eden Tarafın talebi üzerine, işbu Anlaşma kapsamında gönderilen belgeler, Talep Edilen Tarafın mevzuatına aykırı olmaması koşuluyla talepte belirtilen diğer biçimlerde de onaylanabilir.

2. İşbu Anlaşma kapsamında, bir Taraf ülkesinde resmi olarak kabul edilen belgeler, diğer Taraf ülkesinde de bu şekilde kabul edilir.

MADDE 5

Gizlilik ve bilgi kullanımının kısıtlamaları

1. Talep Edilen Taraf, Talep Eden Tarafın Merkezi Makamının talebi üzerine, talebin gizliliğinin ihlalinin talebin yerine getirilmesi için gerekli olduğu durumlar hariç olmak üzere, adli yardımlaşma talebinin unsurlarının, talebin içeriğinin ya da talep uyarınca yerine getirilen her türlü faaliyetin gizliliğini kendi mevzuatı uyarınca sağlar.

Talebin yerine getirilmesinin, bu kısıtlamayı ortadan kaldırmayı gerektirmesi durumunda, Talep Edilen Taraf, Talep Eden Tarafın iznini yazılı olarak ister ve bu izin olmaksızın talep yerine getirilemez.

2. Talep Eden Taraf, adli yardımlaşma talebinde belirtilen maksatlar dışında Talep Edilen Tarafın ön iznini almaksızın işbu Anlaşma uyarınca elde edilen bilgileri ya da delilleri kullanamaz.

3. Talep Eden Tarafın, talepte belirtilen amaçlar dışında bilginin ya da delilin tamamını ya da bir kısmını ifşa etmesi ve kullanması gereken durumlarda, koşullara

göre tamamen ya da kısmen bu izni vermeyi kabul etme ya da reddetme yetkisi olan Talep Edilen Tarafın rızası aranır.

BÖLÜM II
CEZAİ KONULARDA KARŞILIKLI ADLİ YARDIMLAŞMA

MADDE 6
Adli yardımda bulunma yükümlülüğü

1. Taraflar, işbu Anlaşmanın hükümleri uyarınca cezai konularda yürütülen soruşturma, kovuşturma ve diğer usule dair eylemlerle bağlantılı olarak birbirlerine karşılıklı adli yardımlaşmada (bundan sonra "adli yardımlaşma" olarak anılacaktır) bulunacaklarını taahhüt eder.

2. Talep Edilen Taraf, ulaşan taleple bağlantılı olarak, suçun cezai olarak kendi mevzuatı uyarınca cezalandırılabilir olmaması halinde adli yardımlaşmayı kabul edebilir.

3. İşbu Anlaşmanın amacı, bir Tarafın diğer Tarafa adli yardımda bulunmasıdır. İşbu Anlaşmanın hükümleri, gerçek ya da tüzel bir kişinin, herhangi bir delili elde etmesi ya da hariç tutma veya talebin infazını engelleme hakkını elde etmesine neden olmaz.

4. İşbu Anlaşma, Taraflardan birinin yetkili makamına, münhasıran diğer Tarafın yetkisi kapsamına giren yetkileri o Taraf ülkesinde kullanma hakkını vermez.

5. İşbu Anlaşma, adli yardımlaşma kapsamına giren eylem ya da ihmal bu tarihten önce gerçekleşmiş olsa bile, Anlaşmanın yürürlüğe girdiği tarihten sonra sunulan adli yardımlaşma taleplerine uygulanır.

MADDE 7
Uygulama kapsamı

Adli yardımlaşma şunları kapsar:

(1) Tebligatı;

(2) Kişilerden delil elde edilmesi ile kişilerin ifadelerinin alınmasını ve diğer delillerin toplanmasını;
(3) Kişilerin ve eşyaların tespit edilmesini ve tanımlanmasını;
(4) Talep Eden Tarafın yetkili makamlarının huzurunda hazır bulunmaları amacıyla tanıkların, mağdurların ve bilirkişilerin davet edilmesini;
(5) Talep Eden Tarafta görülen ceza yargılamasına tanık ve mağdur olarak katılmaları ya da ceza yargılamasına ilişkin talepte belirtilen diğer amaçlarla gözaltında bulunan ya da hapis cezasını çekmekte olan kişinin geçici naklini;
(6) Suç araçlarının ve gelirlerinin aranması, muhafaza altına alınması, bunlara el konulması, bunların müsadere edilmesi ve iadesi amaçlı tedbirler alınmasını;
(7) Belgelerin, eşyaların ve diğer delillerin naklini;
(8) Talep Eden Tarafın yetkili makamlarının talebinde belirtilen kişilerin talebin yerine getirilmesi sırasında hazır bulunması için izin verilmesini;
(9) Talep Edilen Tarafın vatandaşları ile o Taraf ülkesinde sürekli olarak yaşayan vatansız kişilere ilişkin ceza muhakemesi taleplerinin yerine getirilmesini;
(10) Arama ve el koymayı;
(11) İşbu Anlaşmanın amaçlarıyla ve Talep Tarafın kanunlarıyla uyumlu diğer adli yardımlaşma biçimlerini.

MADDE 8

Talebin biçimi ve içeriği

1. Adli yardım talebi yazılı yapılır.

2. Talep Edilen Taraf, talebin faks, elektronik posta ya da diğer iletişim araçlarıyla gönderilmesi üzerine yerine getirilecek talebi o an almış olur ve talebin aslı bunun hemen ardında Talep Eden Tarafça iletilir. Talep Edilen Taraf, talebin aslının eline geçmesi koşuluyla, Talep Eden Tarafı talebin yerine getirilme sonuçlarına dair bilgilendirir.

3. Adli yardımlaşma talebinde aşağıdakiler belirtilir:
a) Talep eden yetkili makamın adı.
b) Talebin amacı ve talep edilen adli yardımlaşmanın tanımı.

c) Yürütülen soruşturma ya da yargılamayla bağlantılı olan eylemlerin tanımı ve hukuki nitelemesi, talebin yerine getirilmesi için Talep Eden Tarafın ilgili kanun metinleri, şüphelilerin, sanıkların ya da hükümlülerin tam isimleri, bu kişilerin ikametgâhlarına ya da adreslerine dair bilgi, kişilerin milliyeti ile meslekleri ve mümkünse doğum yerleri ve tarihleri, anne baba adları, tüzel kişiler için de isim, yasal ve fiili adresleri,

d) İlgisi bulunuyorsa, suçun neden olduğu zararın miktarının göstergesi,

e) Talep Eden Tarafın talebin yerine getirilmesi sırasında takip edilmesini istediği her türlü belirli usulün tanımı ile kullanım nedenleri,

f) Tanıkları ya da mağdurları tanımlayan veriler,

g) Talep Eden Tarafın talebin yerine getirilmesini istediği süre kısıtlaması,

h) Bilgilendirilmesi gereken kişilerin tam isimleri, adresleri ve mümkünse telefon numaraları ile devam etmekte olan soruşturma ya da yargılamayla olan bağlantıları,

i) İncelenmesi ya da aranması gereken yer ile el koyulacak eşyaların konumu ve tanımı,

j) Talep Edilen Tarafta elde edilmesi gereken delillere ulaşılması için sorulması istenen sorular,

k) Talep Eden Tarafın yetkili makamlarında hazır bulunması istenen kişilerin belirtilmesi durumunda, bu kişilerin tam adları, resmi sıfatları ve hazır bulunma nedenleri,

l) Talebin içeriğiyle birlikte ulaştığına ve/veya taleple bağlantılı olarak yerine getirilmiş eylemlere dair bilgilendirmenin gerekli ise gizliliğinin ihtiyacı,

m) Talep Edilen Tarafın talebi yerine getirirken faydalanabileceği diğer tüm bilgiler.

4. Talep Edilen Tarafın, talepte bulunan bilgilerin talebin yerine getirilmesi için yetersiz olduğu kanaatine varması durumunda, bu Taraf ek bilgi talep edebilir.

MADDE 9

Talebin yerine getirilmesi

1. Adli yardımlaşma talepleri, Talep Edilen Tarafın kanunları ve işbu Anlaşmanın hükümleri uyarınca yerine getirilir. Ancak, Talep Eden Tarafın talebi üzerine, Talep Eden Tarafın kanunları, Talep Edilen Tarafın kanunlarına aykırı olmadığı ölçüde uygulanabilir.

2. Tarafların Merkezi Makamları, adli yardımlaşma talebini doğrudan yerine getirirler ya da yerine getirilmesi için yetkili makamlarına gönderirler. Merkezi bir makamın, talebi yerine getirilmesi amacıyla yetkili makamına göndermesi halinde, Merkezi Makam, yetkili makamının talebi hızlı ve uygun bir şekilde yerine getirmesini sağlar.

3. Talep Eden Tarafın, talebin yerine getirilmesi sırasında yetkili makamlarının belirttiği kişilerin hazır bulunmasını istemesi durumunda, Talep Edilen Taraf, Talep Eden Tarafı kararına dair bilgilendirir. Kararın olumlu olması durumunda, Talep Eden Taraf, talebin yerine getirileceği yer ve zaman bakımından önceden bilgilendirilir.

4. Talep Edilen Tarafın Merkezi Makamı, talebin yerine getirilmesinin ardından, talebin yerine getirilmesine ilişkin bilgi ve belgeleri Talep Eden Tarafın Merkezi Makamına gönderir.

5. Talebin yerine getirilememesi durumunda, Talep Edilen Tarafın Merkezi Makamı, Talep Eden Tarafın Merkezi Makamını bu durum ve talebin yerine getirilmesini engelleyen nedenler hakkında bilgilendirir.

MADDE 10

Adli yardımlaşmanın reddi ya da ertelenmesi

1. Adli yardımlaşma talepleri şu durumlarda reddedilebilir:

a) Talep Edilen Taraf, talebin kendi egemenliğini, güvenliğini, kamu düzenini ya da diğer gerekli çıkarlarını tehlikeye atacağı görüşündeyse,

b) Talep Edilen Tarafın, talebin, kişiyi ırk, cinsiyet, inanç, milliyet, etnik köken ya da siyasi mahkûmiyetler nedeniyle takibat amacıyla iletildiğine veya bu kişinin konumunun tüm bu nedenlerle tehlikeye atılacağına inanmak için ciddi gerekçeleri varsa,

c) Talep Edilen Tarafın, talebin yerine getirilmesini kendi kanunlarına ya da işbu Anlaşmanın hükümlerine aykırı olarak değerlendiriyorsa,

d) Talep, askeri kanunlara göre suç sayılan, ancak genel ceza kanununda suç teşkil etmeyen bir suça ilişkinse ,

e) Talebin konusunu oluşturan kişi, Talep Eden Devlette kendisine isnat edilen suça ilişkin olarak Talep Edilen Devlette mahkûm edilmiş ya da beraat etmişse ya da suça ilişkin zaman aşımı Talep Edilen Tarafın kanunları uyarınca dolmuşsa.

2. Bankacılık sırları ya da vergi mahremiyeti, adli yardımlaşma talebinin reddedilmesine ilişkin mutlak bir neden olarak kullanılmayabilir.

3. Talebin yerine getirilmesinin, Talep Edilen Devlette devam eden bir soruşturma ya da yargılamaya zarar verebileceği ya da sekteye uğratabileceği durumlarda, adli yardımlaşma talebi ertelenebilir ya da reddedilebilir.

4. Talep Edilen Devlet, talebin yerine getirilmesinin ertelenmesine ya da reddedilmesine dair bir karara varmadan önce, adli yardımlaşmanın gerekli olan bu koşullara tabi olarak kabul edilip edilemeyeceğini değerlendirir. Talep Eden Tarafın, bu koşullara tabi olarak adli yardımlaşmanın yerine getirilmesini kabul etmesi durumunda, Talep Eden Taraf bu koşullara uymakla yükümlüdür.

5. Talep Edilen Taraf, talebin yerine getirilmesini ertelemeye ya da reddetmeye karar vermesi durumunda, Talep Eden Tarafı Merkezi Makamı aracılığıyla derhal bilgilendirir ve bu karara dair nedenlerini belirtir.

MADDE 11

Tanıkların, mağdurların bilirkişilerin hazır bulunması ve güvenli geçiş

1. Talep Eden Taraf, kişinin delil sunması, bilirkişinin inceleme yapması ya da kendi ülkesindeki diğer usule dair tedbirler amacıyla hazır bulunma talebi sunarsa, Talep Edilen Taraf, o kişiyi Talep Eden Tarafın yetkili makamlarının huzurunda hazır bulunması davetine ilişkin bilgilendirir.

2. Bu kişinin hazır bulunması talebi, davet edilen kişinin hazır bulunmasına ilişkin masraf giderlerinin karşılanmasına dair koşullara ve gerekliliklere ilişkin bilgiyle birlikte işbu maddenin 5 ve 6. fıkraları uyarınca kişiye temin edilecek garantilerin bir listesini içerir.

3. Kişinin Talep Eden Taraf ülkesinde hazır bulunamaması durumunda, ilk fıkrada belirtilen davetiyeler, herhangi bir zorlayıcı tedbir kullanımını ya da ceza verilmesi tehlikesini içermez.

4. Davet edilen kişi, hazır bulunma kararını gönüllü olarak alır. Talep Edilen Tarafın Merkezi Makamı, Talep Eden Tarafın Merkezi Makamını kişinin cevabına dair derhal bilgilendirir.

5. Talep Eden Tarafın yetkili makamı huzurunda hazır bulunan kişi, milliyeti ne olursa olsun, Talep Edilen Tarafın ülkesinden ayrılmadan önce işlemiş olduğu herhangi bir eylem ya da hakkında verilen herhangi bir mahkûmiyet kararına ilişkin olarak Talep Eden Taraf ülkesinde takibata maruz bırakılamaz, tutuklanamaz ya da kişisel hürriyetini bağlayıcı herhangi başka bir kısıtlamaya tabi tutulamaz.

6. Davet edilen kişi, talepte belirtilen dışında herhangi başka bir davada delil sunmaya zorlanamaz.

7. Davet edilen kişiye ilgili yetkili makam tarafından hazır bulunmasının artık gerekli olmadığını yazılı olarak bildirilmesinden 15 gün sonraki süre içinde, davet edilen kişi, Talep Eden Taraf ülkesinden özgürce ayrılma imkanı olmasına rağmen ayrılmazsa ya da ayrılmasının ardından isteyerek geri dönmüşse, işbu maddede öngörülen dokunulmazlık hakkını kaybeder.

MADDE 12

Tutuklu kişilerin geçici nakli
(hapis cezası halihazırda infaz edilen kişi de dahil)

1. Milliyetine bakılmaksızın, Talep Eden Tarafın tanık ya da mağdur olarak ya da talepte belirtilen diğer işlemlere yardımcı olması için hazır bulunmasını talep ettiği tutuklu bulunan kişi (Hapis Cezası Halihazırda İnfaz Edilen Kişi de Dahil), Talep Edilen Tarafın belirttiği sürede geri gönderilmesi ve uygulanabilir olduğu ölçüde işbu Anlaşmanın 11. maddesinin 5 ve 6. fıkralarına tabi olması koşuluyla, geçici olarak Talep Eden Devlet ülkesine nakledilebilir.

Kişinin nakledilmesi için öngörülen başlangıç süresi 90 günü geçemez. Talep Eden Tarafın Merkezi Makamının talebi üzerine, önemli gerekçelere dayanmak koşuluyla, nakledilmiş kişinin kalış süresi, Talep Edilen Tarafın Merkezi Makamı tarafından uzatılabilir.

Kişinin nakline ve geri dönüşüne dair düzen ve koşullar, Tarafların Merkezi Makamı tarafından koordine edilir.

2. Transfer şu durumlarda reddedilebilir:

a) Tutuklu kişinin rızasının olmaması,

b) Kişinin hazır bulunmasının Talep Edilen Tarafta devam eden yargılamada gerekli olması,

c) Transferin, kişinin tutukluluğunu uzatacak olması,

d) Kişiyi Talep Eden Tarafa nakletmemek için diğer önemli gerekçelerin bulunması.

3. Nakledilen kişi, Talep Eden Tarafın mevzuatı temelinde ve uyarınca, Talep Eden Tarafın yetkili makamının aldığı kişinin tutuklu kalması kararı yürürlükte kaldığı süre boyunca Talep Eden Taraf ülkesinde tutuklu kalır. Talep Edilen Tarafın kararı üzerine kişinin tutukluluktan salıverilmesi durumunda, Talep Eden Taraf, bu kişi hakkında işbu Anlaşmanın 11. maddesinin 5. ve 6. fıkraları ile ve 21. maddesinin hükümlerini kullanır.

4. Talep Edilen Taraf ülkesinin dışında kişinin tutuklu kaldığı süre, tutuklu kaldığı süre olarak değerlendirilir.

5. Tutuklu bulunan kişinin Talep Eden Taraf makamları huzurunda hazır bulunmaya rıza göstermemesi durumunda, bu nedenle bu kişi herhangi bir zorunlu tedbire ya da cezaya tabi tutulamaz.

MADDE 13

Talep üzerine hazır bulunan ya da Talep Eden Taraf ülkesine nakledilen kişinin korunması

Gerekli olması durumunda, Talep Eden Taraf, talep üzerine hazır bulunan ya da işbu Anlaşmanın 11 ve 12. maddeleri uyarınca nakledilen kişinin korunmasını sağlar.

MADDE 14

Tebligat

1. Talep Edilen Taraf, kendi kanunlarının öngördüğü şekilde, Talep Edilen Tarafın diline yapılmış onaylı çevirilerle birlikte belgeleri tebliğ eder.

2. Talep Eden Taraf, Talep Eden Taraf ülkesinde hazır bulunmaya ya da bir cevaba ilişkin belgenin tebliğine ilişkin talebini, tarihi belirlenmiş cevap ya da hazır bulunma tarihinden önce, normalde hazır bulunma tarihinden 60 günden az olmayacak makul bir süre içinde iletir.

3. Muhatabın bilinen adresi ve belgenin niteliği, tebligat talebinde belirtilir.

4. Bu taleplerin yerine getirilmesi, tebligatın tarihi ve muhatabın imzası ya da Talep Edilen Tarafın yetkili makamının tebligatı, tarihi ve tebligat yöntemini doğrulayan ifadesini gösteren tebligat mazbatasıyla onaylanır.

5. Talep Eden Taraf, tebligatın yerine getirilmesi ya da tebligatın yerine getirilmesinin mümkün olmaması durumlarına dair derhal bilgilendirilir.

MADDE 15

Kovuşturma talebi

1. Her bir Tarafın talebi üzerine ve Tarafların kanunları uyarınca, Taraflar, diğer Tarafın yargı yetkisine giren bir suç işlemiş olan vatandaşları ya da ülkelerinde ikametgâhı bulunan vatansız kişiler hakkında işlem başlatmayı taahhüt ederler.

Bahsi geçen talebin ulaşması üzerine, Talep Edilen Taraf, o Tarafın mevzuatı uyarınca ceza kovuşturması başlatmaya ilişkin karar alınması için dava dosyasını yetkili makamlarına iletir.

2. Kovuşturma talebi şunları içerir:

a) Talep eden yetkili makamın adı;

b) Suç işlediği şüphesi bulunan kişinin tam adı, kişinin milliyetine dair bilgi ve mümkünse ikametgâhına ya da sürekli adresine dair bilgi, eşkâlinin tarifi, bir fotoğraf, parmak izleri ya da kişinin belirlenmesi için gerekli olan diğer veriler;

c) Kovuşturma talebine konu olan eylemin tanımı ve hukuki sınıflandırması;

d) Mümkün olduğu ölçüde, tam olarak suçun işlendiği zaman ve yer;

e) Gerekliyse, fiziksel delillere dair eşyalar ve belgelerin asıllarının iade edilmesine dair talep.

3. Kovuşturma talebi, aşağıdaki belgelerle desteklenir:

a) Mevcut deliller dâhil olmak üzere, soruşturma belgeleri ya da bunların onaylı nüshaları,

b) Uygulanan ceza kanunu ve zorunlu olması durumunda kovuşturma için gerekli olan Talep Eden Tarafın diğer kanun metinleri,

c) Uygulanabilir ise, mümkün olduğu ölçüde, zarar miktarı bilgisi,

d) Talep Edilen Tarafın kanunları uyarınca gerekli olması durumunda, soruşturmanın başlatılması için mağdur başvuruları.

4. Üçüncü kişilerin yasal haklarını güvence altına almak adına, Talep Edilen Taraf, usule dair işlemlerin tamamlanmasının ardından, Talep Eden Tarafın talebi üzerine, belgelerin aslını ve fiziksel delil teşkil eden eşyaları iade eder.

5. Talep Edilen Taraf, Talep Eden Tarafı talebiyle bağlantılı alınan tedbirler ile ceza muhakemesinin sonuçlarına dair bilgilendirir ve nihai kararın bir nüshasını iletir.

6. Talep ulaşıp, Talep Edilen Tarafın adli makamının kararı talepte belirtilen kişiye tebliğ edildiğinde ve bahsi geçen karar kesinleştiğinde, Talep Eden Tarafın yetkili makamları, bahsi geçen kişiyi aynı suçtan dolayı kovuşturamaz.

7. Talep Edilen Tarafın, talebi yerine getirmeyi reddetme ya da davayı sonlandırma kararı almış veya yargılamaya başlamama konusunda mahkeme dışı uzlaşmaya varılmış olması durumunda, Talep Eden Tarafın ilettiği dava dosyası ile fiziksel delillere ait eşyalar, derhal Talep Eden Devlete iade edilir.

MADDE 16

Talep Edilen Tarafta delil toplanması

1. Talep Edilen Taraf kendi ülkesinde, delilleri ve bilirkişi görüşlerini toplar ya da talepte belirtilen belgeleri, eşyaları ve delilleri temin eder ve bunları Talep Eden Tarafa iletir.

2. Talebin yerine getirilmesi sırasında Talep Eden Tarafın hazır bulunmasını istediği yetkililerin, Talep Edilen Tarafın yetkili makamının temsilcileri aracılığıyla ilgili kişiye sorulması için soru oluşturmalarına izin verilir.

3. Talep Eden Taraf, belgeler ve eşyalara ilişkin üçüncü tarafların çıkarlarının korunmasına dair koşullar dâhil olmak üzere, teslim edilebilecek tüm belge ve eşyalara ilişkin Talep Edilen Tarafın belirleyeceği tüm koşulları dikkate alır.

4. Talep Edilen Tarafın talebi üzerine, Talep Eden Taraf, işbu maddenin 1. fıkrası uyarınca teslim edilmiş olan belgelerin asıllarını ve eşyaları mümkün olan en kısa sürede iade eder.

MADDE 17

Bilgi, evrak ve eşyaların verilmesi

1. Talep Edilen Taraf, kanunlarına göre halka açık olan. Hükümet makamlarının evrak ve bilgilerinin nüshalarını Talep Eden Tarafa verir.

2. Talep Edilen Taraf, kanunlarına bağlı olmak üzere, Hükümet makamlarının kullanımında ve fakat halka açık olmayan bilgi, evrak ve eşyaları kendi kolluk kuvvetleri ve adli makamlarına sunulduğu aynı ölçü ve şartlar etrafında Talep eden Tarafa sunabilir.

3. Taraflardan herhangi biri. kendisine göre. gerçek şahısların işlemiş olduğu suçlarla bağlantılı olarak tüzel kişiler hakkında yargılama sürecinin başlatılmasında ve gerçek

veya tüzel kişiler hakkındaki ceza muhakemelerinde kullanılması muhtemel bilgi ve belgeleri diğer tarafa sunabilir.

MADDE 18

Arama ve el koyma

1. Talep Edilen Taraf, Talep Eden Tarafta devam etmekte olan cezai bir konuyla ilgili soruşturma veya yargılamaya konu evrak ve eşyaların arama, el koyma ve teslim etme taleplerini, bu talebin Talep Edilen Tarafın kanunları kapsamında böylesi bir eylemin yapılabilmesini meşru kılacak ölçüde bilgi içermesi şartıyla ve kendi kanunları izin verdiği ölçüde yerine getirir.

2. Talep Edilen Taraf, aramanın sonucu, el koymanın yapıldığı yer, el koyma şartları ve el koyulan eşya ve evrakların müteakip muhafazasıyla ilgili olarak Talep Eden Tarafça istenebilecek tüm bilgiyi sağlar.

3. Talep Eden Taraf, kendisine teslim edilen el konulmuş evrak ve eşyalarla bağlantılı olarak Talep Edilen Tarafça konulan tüm şartlara riayet eder.

MADDE 19

Kişi ve eşyaların yerlerinin belirlenmesi ve tespiti

Talep Edilen Tarafın ilgili makamları, talepte belirtilen kişi ve eşyaların yerlerinin belirlenmesi ve tespit edilmesinde kanunlarının izin verdiği ölçüde elinden geleni yapar.

MADDE 20

Suç gelirleri ve araçlarının aranması, muhafaza altına alma, el koyma, müsaderesi ve iadesi hakkındaki tedbirlerin uygulanması

1. Taraflar, kanunlarına uygun olarak, suç gelirleri ve araçlarının yerlerinin tespit edilmesinde, dondurulmasında, muhafaza altına alınmasında, el konulmasında ve müsaderesinde birbirine yardım eder.

İşbu Anlaşmanın amaçları doğrultusunda, "suç gelirleri" ifadesi, işlenen bir suç neticesinde elde edilen sermaye veya servet, bu gelirlerden elde edilen kazanç ve menfaatler veya suç gelirlerinin değiştirildiği veya dönüştürüldüğü mal veya suç gelirlerinin de içine dâhil olduğu servet anlamına gelir.

2. Talep Edilen Taraf, talep edilmesi halinde, herhangi bir suç geliri veya aracının kendi yargı alanında bulunup bulunmadığını tespit etmek üzere çaba gösterir ve Talep Eden Tarafı yapmış olduğu araştırmaların sonucu hakkında bilgilendirir. Talep yapılırken, Talep Eden Taraf bu gelir ve araçların Talep Edilen Tarafın yargı alanında bulunabileceği yönündeki inancına temel oluşturan dayanağı Talep Edilen Tarafa bildirir.

3. İşbu maddenin 2. paragrafı uyarınca, şüphe duyulan suç gelirleri ve araçlarının bulunduğu hallerde, Talep Edilen Taraf, talep edilmesi halinde Talep Eden Tarafın yetkili makamı tarafından verilmiş muhafaza altına alma emrini yerine getirir veya kendi kanunlarının izin verdiği ölçüde, Talep eden veya Talep Edilen Tarafın bir mahkemesi tarafından hakkında verilecek nihai kararı beklemede olan, şüphe duyulan bu suç gelirleri veya eşyalarının muamelesi, nakli veya imhasıyla ilgili gerekli tedbirler alır.

4. Talep Edilen Taraf, kendi kanunları izin verdiği ölçüde, suç gelirleri veya araçlarının el konulması veya müsaderesiyle ilgili olarak Talep Eden Tarafın yetkili makamı tarafından verilen nihai emri yerine getirir.

5. İşbu maddenin uygulanmasında, hüsnüniyetli üçüncü tarafların haklarına Talep Edilen Tarafın kanunları uyarınca saygı gösterilecektir.

6. Talep Eden Tarafın talebinde, Talep Edilen Taraf kendi kanunları izin verdiği ölçüde ve Tarafların Merkezi makamları tarafından uzlaşılan koşul ve şartlar etrafında, Talep Eden Tarafa suç gelirlerini veya araçlarını aktarabilir.

7. İşbu madde hükümleri, her iki tarafın da taraf olduğu diğer çok taraflı uluslararası Anlaşmalardan doğan hak ve yükümlülüklerini etkilemez.

MADDE 21

Masraflar

1. Talep Edilen Taraf, adli yardım talebinin uygulanmasından doğan olağan masrafları karşılar. Bunların dışında, aşağıda sıralanan masraflar Talep Eden Tarafça karşılanır:

a) İşbu Anlaşmanın 11 ve 12. maddelerine uygun olarak, sınırlarına giren ve çıkan kişilerin seyahat ve ikametleriyle alakalı masraflar ile bu kişilerin neden olduğu diğer ödemeler;

b) Bilirkişi masraf ve ücretleri;

c) İşbu Anlaşmanın 9. maddesinin 3. Paragrafına uygun olarak talebin yerine getirilmesinde Talep Eden Tarafın yetkili makamları tarafından belirtilmiş olan, insanların seyahat ve ikametleriyle alakalı masraflar;

d) Talep Edilen Tarafın sınırlarından Talep Eden Tarafın sınırlarına ve oradan tekrar nakledilen eşyaların nakliyle alakalı masraflar.

2. Adli yardımın sağlanmasıyla alakalı masrafların hatırı sayılır yahut olağandışı ölçekte masraf yapmayı gerektirmesi halinde, Tarafların Merkezi Makamları, talep edilen yardımın sağlanabileceği koşul ve şartları ve masraf düzenlemesini görüşür.

BÖLÜM III

İADE

MADDE 22

İade yükümlülüğü

1. İşbu Anlaşma hükümleri çerçevesinde, Taraflar, ceza muhakemesi yahut iadeyi gerektiren işlenmiş bir suçtan ötürü verilen cezanın infazı için, sınırlarında bulunan ve Talep Eden Tarafça istenen kişileri, talep edilmesi halinde, birbirine iade etmeyi kabul ederler.

2. Suçlunun bir ceza muhakemesi için iadesi, her iki tarafın da kanunları kapsamında en az 12 ay veya daha fazla bir süre hapis cezası ile cezalandırılabilir suçlar için sağlanır.

3. Bir kişinin, cezasının infaz edilebilmesi için iade edilmesi, yalnızca hapis cezasıyla cezalandırılacak suçlarda ve aranan kişinin taraflardan her ikisinin de kanunları kapsamında en az 4 ay veya daha fazla hapis cezasına çarptırılmış olması halinde sağlanır.

4. İade talebi, her bir suçun taraflardan her ikisinin de kanunlarına göre hapis cezasını gerektiren birtakım ayrı suçları da kapsıyor, ancak bunlardan bazıları işbu maddenin 2 ve 3. paragraflarında belirtilen şartları taşımıyorsa, Talep Edilen Taraf bahsedilen bu diğer suçlar için de suçlunun iadesini sağlayabilir.

5. Hukuki terminolojide olabilecek herhangi bir farklılık, iade talebine konu eylemin taraflardan her ikisinin de uygulanabilir kanunlarında tanımlandığı ölçüde cezai bir eylem olması halinde iade talebinin yerine getirilmesine herhangi bir engel teşkil etmez.

6. Suçun Talep Eden Tarafın sınırları dışında işlenmiş olması halinde, Talep Edilen Tarafın kanunlarının da, benzeri koşullarda kendi sınırları dışında işlenmiş olan bir suç için ceza verilmesini öngörmesi halinde iadeye izin verilir.

7. İşbu Anlaşma, yürürlük kazanmasından önce işlenmiş suçları da kapsamak üzere, suçluların iade taleplerinde uygulanır.

<u>MADDE 23</u>

Suçlunun iadesine yönelik talebin geri çevrilmesi

1. Suçlunun iadesine şu hallerde izin verilmez:

a) İadeye konu eylemin işbu Anlaşma uyarınca suçlunun iade edilmesini gerektiren bir suç olmaması halinde;

b) Aranan kişinin Talep Edilen Tarafın vatandaşı olması halinde,

c) Zamanaşımı veya Talep Edilen Tarafın kanunlarında bulunan herhangi bir sebepten ötürü artık cezai bir davanın açılamaması veya hükmün infaz edilememesi hallerinde.

d) Aranan kişinin, iadenin talep edildiği aynı suçtan ötürü Talep Edilen Tarafın yetkili makamı tarafından bir ceza takibatı, devam eden bir duruşma veya nihai mahkeme kararı veya takipsizlik kararına konu olması halinde,

e) Talep Edilen Tarafın, iade talebinin, bu kişiyi ırkı, cinsi, dini, tabiiyeti, etnik kökeni ve siyasi veya diğer görüşleri sebebiyle cezalandırmak veya ona zulmetmek amacıyla yapıldığına kanaat getirecek ölçüde sağlam dayanağının olması halinde;

f) Talep Edilen Tarafın, kişinin iadesinin kendi bağımsızlığına, güvenliğine, kamu düzenine veya diğer hayati çıkarlarına zarar vereceğini düşünmesi halinde;

g) İadenin talep edilmesine konu suçun, Talep Eden Tarafın uygulanabilir kanunlarına göre ölüm cezasına tabi olması ve Talep Eden Tarafın da, iadesi yapılacak kişinin, ölüm cezasına çarptırılmayacağını garanti edecek yeterli oranda materyali Talep Edilen Tarafa sunmaması halinde.

2. İadenin talep edildiği herhangi bir suçun, Talep Edilen Tarafın uygulanabilir kanunlarına göre tamamen veya kısmen bu Tarafın sınırları içerisinde işlenmiş olması halinde her türlü iade talebi geri çevrilebilir.

3. Talep Edilen Tarafın, işbu maddenin 1. paragrafının "b" bendi ile 2. paragrafına uygun olarak iadesi istenen kişiyi iade etmemesi halinde, Talep Eden Tarafın talebi doğrultusunda kendisine iletilen tüm materyalleri, kendi kanunlarına göre bir ceza takibatı yapılmasını mülahaza etmek üzere kendi yetkili makamlarına iletir. Bunun yapılabilmesi için, ilgili dosyalar, bilgiler ve suçla ilgili diğer deliller Talep Eden Taraftan Talep Edilen Tarafa sunulur. Talep Eden Tarafta tamamlanmış olan soruşturmayla bağlantılı olarak davayla ilgili alınan tüm materyaller, Talep Edilen Tarafın ceza muhakemesi işlemlerinde kullanılabilir. Talep Eden Taraf bu bağlamda çıkacak sonuçlar ile ceza muhakemesi hakkında bilgilendirilir.

Talep Eden Taraf, Talep Edilen Tarafın Merkezi Makamının buna rıza göstermemesi halinde, soruşturma veya adli işlemlerin uygulanabilmesi için işbu Anlaşmaya göre talepte belirtilmiş olanların dışında bir tanık, ifade veya eşya kullanamaz.

MADDE 24

Geçici tutuklama

1. Acil durumlarda, Talep Eden Tarafın Merkezi Makamı, aranan kişinin geçici tutuklanması yoluna gidebilir. Talep Edilen Tarafın Merkezi Makamı, konuyu kendi kanunlarına uygun olarak değerlendirir.

2. Geçici tutuklama başvurusu, aranılan kişi hakkındaki tutuklama müzekkeresi veya nihai hükmün bulunduğunu ve iade talebi gönderilmesinin amaçlandığını belirtir. Ayrıca iadenin hangi suç için talep edildiği, suç yeri ve tarihi ile aranan kişinin mümkün olduğunca tarifi de belirtilir.

3. Geçici tutuklama başvurusu, diplomatik kanallardan veya doğrudan posta veya faksla yahut Uluslararası Polis Teşkilatı (Interpol) yoluyla veya yazılı olarak delil sunan veya Talep Edilen Tarafın kabul ettiği diğer yollarla Talep edilen makamın Merkezi Makamına gönderilir.

4. Talep Eden Tarafın makamlarına talep başvurusunun sonucu hakkında gecikmeksizin bilgi verilir.

5. İade talebi ve tutuklama müzekkeresi veya aranan kişiye yönelik nihai hükmün tutuklamayı takiben 18 günlük bir süre içerisinde Talep Edilen Tarafa ulaşmaması halinde geçici tutuklama sonlandırılabilir. Geçici tutuklama, herhangi bir durumda 40 günü aşamaz. Şartlı tahliye olasılığı her zaman için ihtimal dâhilinde olmakla beraber Talep Edilen Taraf, aranan kişinin kaçmasını önlemek için gerekli gördüğü tüm tedbirleri alır.

6. İade talebi daha sonra ulaşmışsa, şahsın tahliye edilmiş olması, yeniden tutuklama yapmaya ve şahsın iade edilmesine halel getirmez.

MADDE 25

Talep ve destekleyici belgeler

1. Bir iade talebi, taraflardan birinin Merkezi Makamından bir diğerininkine yazılı olarak gönderilir. Talepte, Talep Eden Tarafın yetkili makamının tam adı, iadesi istenen kişinin tam adı, uyruğu, mümkün olduğunca fiziksel olarak tarifi, ikamet adresi bilgileri ve eğer mümkünse bu kişinin fotoğrafı ve parmak izi yer alır.

2. Herhangi bir ceza takibatı amacıyla yapılan bir iade talebinde, suça sebep olan eylemi tanımlayan bir açıklamanın yer aldığı onaylanmış tutuklama müzekkeresi

nüshası ve bu suça yönelik uygulanabilir ilgili kanun maddelerinin tam metni ile zamanaşımı bilgileri yer alır. Suçun maddi hasara sebep olması halinde, zarar miktarı mümkün olduğunca tam olarak belirtilir.

3. Herhangi bir cezanın infaz edilmesi amacıyla sunulan bir talepte, nihai kararın onaylanmış bir nüshası, bu suça yönelik uygulanabilir ilgili kanun maddelerinin tam metni, zamanaşımı bilgileri ile ceza infaz süresinin açıklaması yer alır.

4. İade talebi, faks, elektronik posta ve bu türde iletişim araçlarıyla yapılan iletimin hemen ardından Talep Edilen Tarafa gönderilir. Daha sonra ise talebin aslı Talep Eden Tarafça derhal sunulur.

MADDE 26

Ek bilgi

1. İade talebinin gerekli tüm bilgileri içermemesi halinde, Talep Edilen Taraf ek bilgi talep edebilir. Bunu yapabilmek için, Talep Edilen Taraf 30 günü aşmamak üzere bir süre sınırlaması koyabilir. Bazı durumlar istisna olmak üzere, belirtilen süre sınırlaması, 30 günlük bir süreyi aşmamak üzere tarafların Merkezi Makamlarının mutabakatıyla uzatılabilir.

2. İadesi istenen kişinin gözaltına alınmış olması ve sağlanan ek bilgilerin yetersiz olması yahut işbu maddenin 1. paragrafında belirtilen süre içerisinde ulaşmamış olması halinde, kişi gözaltındayken serbest bırakılabilir. Ancak bu durum, Talep Eden Tarafı, kişinin iadesi için yeni bir talepte bulunmasına veya bu kişinin gözaltına alınmasına engel teşkil etmez.

3. Kişinin işbu maddenin 2. paragrafına uygun olarak gözaltındayken serbest bırakılması halinde, Talep Edilen Taraf bu durumla ilgili olarak Talep Eden Tarafı derhal bilgilendirir.

MADDE 27

Yarışan talepler

Kişinin iadesinin, birden fazla Devlet tarafından aynı veya farklı suçlardan dolayı talep edilmesi halinde, Talep Edilen Taraf, özellikle bu suçun ağırlığı ve işlendiği yer, talep tarihleri, uluslararası iade anlaşmaları, iadesi istenen kişinin uyruğu ve başlıca ikamet adresi gibi tüm koşulları göz önünde bulundurarak bu suçlardan hangisi için iade kararı verilebileceğini belirler.

MADDE 28

Talep hakkındaki kararın bildirilmesi

1. Talep Edilen Taraf, iade talebi hakkındaki kararını Talep Eden Tarafa bildirir.

2. İade talebinin tamamen veya kısmen geri çevrilmesi halinde, bunun sebepleri Talep Eden Tarafa bildirilir.

MADDE 29

Bir kişinin teslim edilmesi

1. Eğer talepte mutabık kalınırsa, tarafların yetkili makamları bu kişinin teslim yeri ve tarihi konusunda anlaşmaya varırlar. Talep Edilen Taraf, bu kişi için toplam hapis cezası süresi belirlenirken, bu kişinin iade edilmek üzere tutuklu kaldığı süre hakkında da Talep Eden Tarafı bilgilendirir.

2. İadeyle ilgili olarak olumlu bir kararın verilmesi halinde, kişi bu kararın bildirilmesinden itibaren 30 gün içerisinde Talep Eden Tarafa teslim edilir. Bu süre zarfında Talep Eden Tarafça herhangi bir devralma gerçekleşmezse, kişi serbest bırakılır.

3. Taraflardan herhangi birinin, kontrolü dışındaki herhangi bir durumdan dolayı, iadesi yapılacak kişiyi teslim edememesi veya alamaması halinde, diğer tarafı bilgilendirir ve teslim süresi de 15 günlük bir süreyi aşmamak üzere uzatılabilir. Belirlenen süre zarfında teslim gerçekleşmezse, kişi serbest bırakılır.

4. İadesi yapılacak kişinin, Talep Eden Tarafın sınırlarına naklinin, bu kişinin yaşamını veya sağlığını riske sokacağı bir durum varsa, teslim, Talep Edilen Tarafın Merkezi Makamına göre bu kişinin sağlığının böylesi bir teslimin gerçekleşebilmesine elverecek ölçüde iyi olduğuna kanaat getirdiği tarihe kadar ertelenir.

MADDE 30

Ertelenmiş veya şartlı teslim

1. Talep Edilen Taraf, iade talebi hakkındaki kararını verdikten sonra, Talep Edilen Tarafın bu kişi hakkında bir takibat yapması, veya kişinin halihazırda işlemiş olduğu bir suçtan ötürü mahkum olmuş olması ve buna mukabil iadesine konu suç dışında işlemiş olduğu bu suçtan ötürü cezasını çekmek üzere bu kişinin teslimini erteleyebilir.

2. İşbu maddenin 1. Paragrafında şart koşulan durumla ilgili olarak suçlunun iadesinin ertelenmesi, zamanaşımına neden olur veya ceza soruşturmasını etkilerse, Talep Edilen Taraf, iadesi istenen kişiyi 90 günlük bir süre için teslim edebilir. Bu sayede teslim edilmiş olan kişi, Talep Eden Tarafın sınırlarında gözaltında tutulur ve tarafların uzlaşmaya varmış oldukları koşullara uygun olarak bu kişi bakımından yapılan usulü işlemlerin tamamlanmasını müteakip Talep Edilen Tarafın sınırlarına tekrar gönderilir. Gerek görülmesi halinde, bu süre Tarafların yazılı mutabakatıyla 90 güne kadar uzatılabilir.

MADDE 31

Hususilik kuralı

İadesi yapılmış olan bir kişi, aşağıda belirtilen durumlar haricinde tutuklanamaz, hakkında takibat yapılamaz, hakkında ceza verilemez veya verilmiş bir hüküm infaz edilemez, üçüncü bir devlete nakledilemez yahut tesliminden önce işlediği başka bir suçtan ötürü kişisel özgürlüğünden mahrum bırakılamaz:

a) Talep Edilen Taraf, kendisine yapılan talebe rıza gösterdiğinde. Bu durumda, Talep Eden Taraf, böylesi bir rızanın verilmesi yönünde karar alırken gerekli olan ve işbu Anlaşmanın 25. maddesinde belirtilen bilgi ve evrakları Talep Edilen Tarafa sunar.

b) Bu kişi, teslim edildiği devletin sınırlarını nihai tahliyesinden sonra fırsatı varken 30 gün içerisinde terk etmemiş yahut ayrıldıktan sonra bu devlet sınırlarına tekrar dönmüşse. İadesi yapılmış olan kişiyi, Talep Eden Tarafın sınırlarını özgür bir şekilde terk etmekten alıkoyan, kişinin kendi kontrolünün ötesindeki sebepler istisnadır.

MADDE 32

Eşyaların teslimi

1. Suçlunun iadesine onay verilmesi halinde, Talep Edilen Tarafın uygulanabilir kanunlarının elverdiği ölçüde ve üçüncü şahısların hakları gözetilerek, Talep Edilen Tarafın sınırlarında bulunan, suçtan dolayı elde edilmiş olan veya ceza yargılaması için delil niteliği taşıyan eşyalar Talep Eden Tarafa verilir. Eşyalar, suçlunun iadesi ölüm veya aranılan kişinin kaçmış olması gibi sebeplerden ötürü yerine getirilemese dahi teslim edilir.

2. Talep Edilen Taraf, başka bir yargılama gerekli olabileceği düşünülen ve işbu maddenin 1. paragrafında bahsedilen eşyaların teslimini geçici olarak erteleyebilir.

3. Talep Edilen Tarafın uygulanabilir kanunlarının gerektirmesi yahut üçüncü şahısların haklarının korunması adına gerek görülmesi halinde, bu şekilde teslim olunan tüm eşyalar, bu yargılamanın tamamlanması sonrasında talep edilmesi halinde Talep Edilen Tarafa karşılıksızca ve mümkün olan en kısa süre içerisinde geri verilir.

MADDE 33

Transit geçiş

1. Taraflardan her biri, işbu Anlaşmanın 25. maddesinde belirtilen gerekli evrak ve bilgiler ile suçlunun iadesi hakkındaki kararın bir nüshasıyla beraber diğer tarafın talebi üzerine, üçüncü bir devlete iadesi yapılacak kişinin sınırlarından transit geçişine izin verir.

2. Tarafların yetkili makamları, her bir davada transit geçişin türü, rotası ve diğer koşulları üzerinde karara varır.

3. Transit geçiş havadan gerçekleştiriliyor ve diğer tarafın sınırları üzerinde herhangi bir iniş beklenmiyorsa işbu maddenin 1. paragrafında belirtilen izne, gerek duyulmaz.

4. Hava aracının beklenmeyen bir iniş yapması halinde, işbu maddenin 1. paragrafına uygun olarak hazırlanmış transit geçiş talebi sunulur. Sınırlarına inişin gerçekleştiği Taraf, transit talebi alınmadan önce, şahsa eşlik eden görevlinin talebi üzerine, işbu maddenin 1. paragrafına uygun olarak hazırlanmış transit geçiş talebi sunulana kadar şahsı iade edilmek üzere 24 saat gözaltında tutabilir. Ayrıca, şahsın iade edilmek üzere tutuklanması, bu tarafın kanunlarına uygun olarak gerçekleştirilir.

5. Böylesi bir transit geçiş talebi, işbu Anlaşmanın 23. maddesinin 1 ve 2. paragraflarında belirtilen durumlar halinde geri çevrilebilir.

MADDE 34

Bilgi alışverişi

Taraflar, iadesi yapılmış kişiler hakkında başlatılan ceza yargılamalarının sonuçları, bu kişilerin firarları ve bu kişilerin üçüncü bir devlete yeniden iadelerinin sonuçları hakkında bilgi alışverişinde bulunur. Buna ek olarak, talep edilmesi halinde, Taraflar, iadesi yapılan kişiye karşı ceza yargılamasını sonlandıran nihai kararın bir nüshasını da birbirine iletirler.

MADDE 35

Masraflar

1. Talep Edilen Taraf, iade talebinden kaynaklanan kendi yargı alanındaki tüm muhakeme masraflarını karşılar.

2. Talep Edilen Taraf, iadesi aranan kişinin tutuklanması ve gözaltına alınması yahut eşyanın el konulması ve nakliyle bağlantılı olarak kendi sınırlarında doğan masrafları karşılar.

3. Eşyanın el konulması ve nakliyle bağlantılı masrafların aşırı düzeyde olması halinde, Tarafların Merkezi Makamları bu masrafların dağıtımı amacıyla istişarede bulunurlar.

4. Talep Eden Taraf, işbu Anlaşmanın 32. maddesinin 3. paragrafı kapsamında, eşyanın Talep Edilen Tarafa geri verilmesiyle ilgili masrafları karşılar.

5. Talep Eden Taraf, iadesi istenen kişinin Talep Edilen Tarafın sınırlarından taşınmasıyla ve transit geçişle alakalı masrafları karşılar.

BÖLÜM IV
NİHAİ HÜKÜMLER

MADDE 36
İstişare ve uyuşmazlıkların çözümü

1. Tarafların Merkezi Makamları, ikisinden herhangi birinin talebiyle işbu Anlaşmanın yorumlanması ve uygulanması hakkında danışır.

2. İşbu Anlaşmanın yorumlanması ve uygulanmasından doğan ve üzerinde uyuşmazlık yaşanan konular diplomatik görüşmeler yoluyla çözülür.

MADDE 37
Anlaşma üzerinde yapılacak değişiklikler

Akit Tarafların karşılıklı rızasıyla, işbu Anlaşmaya ilave hükümler eklenebilir veya ayrı bir protokol yapmak suretiyle değişiklikler yapılabilir. İlaveler ve değişiklikler işbu Anlaşmanın 38. maddesinde belirtilen usullere uygun olarak yürürlüğe girer.

MADDE 38

Anlaşmanın yürürlüğe girmesi ve fesih

1. Tarafların, işbu Anlaşmanın yürürlüğe girebilmesi için kendi ilgili iç yasal düzenlemelerinin uygun hale getirildiğini birbirine diplomatik kanallar yoluyla bildirdikleri son tarihten itibaren 30 gün sonra İşbu Anlaşma yürürlüğe girer.

2. Mevcut Anlaşma, taraflardan herhangi birinin diplomatik kanallar vasıtasıyla işbu Anlaşmanın feshedilmesine dair niyetini yazılı bir şekilde diğer tarafa tebliğ etmesinden 180 gün sonra feshedilir.

3. İşbu Anlaşmanın feshi, işbu maddenin 2. paragrafında belirtilen tebligatın ulaştığı tarihten önce alınmış herhangi bir adli yardımlaşma veya iade talebinin yerine getirilmemesi için bir dayanak oluşturmaz.

Ankara'da, 1 Aralık 2014 tarihinde, iki suret olarak, Türkçe, Rusça ve İngilizce dillerinde ve her bir metin aynı etkide olmak üzere düzenlenmiştir. İşbu Anlaşmanın yorumlanmasında farklılık olması halinde, İngilizce dilinde hazırlanmış metin kullanılacaktır.

TÜRKİYE CUMHURİYETİ ADINA	RUSYA FEDERASYONU ADINA
Bekir BOZDAĞ	Aleksandr KONOVALOV
ADALET BAKANI	ADALET BAKANI

[TRANSLATION IN FRENCH – TRADUCTION EN FRANÇAIS]

TRAITÉ ENTRE LA RÉPUBLIQUE TURQUE ET LA FÉDÉRATION DE RUSSIE RELATIF À L'ENTRAIDE JUDICIAIRE EN MATIÈRE PÉNALE ET À L'EXTRADITION

La République turque et la Fédération de Russie (ci-après dénommées « Parties »),

Désireuses de promouvoir les liens d'amitié qui les unissent et d'organiser l'entraide judiciaire en matière pénale et l'extradition sur la base des principes de souveraineté nationale, d'égalité des droits et de non-ingérence dans les affaires intérieures des Parties,

En vue de faciliter l'application entre les Parties de la Convention européenne d'extradition du 13 décembre 1957 et de la Convention européenne d'entraide judiciaire en matière pénale du 20 avril 1959,

Ont décidé de conclure le présent Traité relatif à l'entraide judiciaire en matière pénale et à l'extradition et sont convenues de ce qui suit :

CHAPITRE PREMIER. DISPOSITIONS GÉNÉRALES

Article premier. Autorités centrales et autorités compétentes

1. Les Parties désignent des autorités centrales pour assurer une coopération efficace dans le cadre du présent Traité.

2. Aux fins de l'entraide judiciaire, l'autorité centrale de la Partie turque est le Ministère de la justice de la République turque. Aux fins de l'entraide judiciaire, les autorités centrales de la Partie russe sont :

   Le Ministère de la justice de la Fédération de Russie en ce qui concerne les procédures des tribunaux de la Fédération de Russie, ainsi que l'application des dispositions de l'article 2 du présent Traité ;

   Le bureau du Procureur général pour toute autre matière relative à l'octroi de l'entraide judiciaire.

3. Aux fins d'extradition, l'autorité centrale est, pour la Partie turque, le Ministère de la justice de la République turque et, pour la Partie russe, le bureau du Procureur général de la Fédération de Russie.

4. Les autorités compétentes sont les autorités des Parties qui participent à la mise en œuvre du présent Traité.

5. Les autorités centrales des Parties communiquent directement ou, si nécessaire, par la voie diplomatique.

6. Les Parties se notifient dans les meilleurs délais, par la voie diplomatique, tout changement apporté à leurs autorités centrales et à leurs compétences.

7. Les autorités centrales des Parties transmettent et reçoivent directement toutes les demandes d'entraide judiciaire visées par le présent Traité et les réponses qui y sont apportées.

Article 2. Échange de renseignements

Les autorités centrales des Parties se fournissent mutuellement, sur demande, des renseignements sur leur législation en vigueur ou abrogée ainsi que sur leurs pratiques judiciaires concernant les questions juridiques qui font l'objet du présent Traité.

Article 3. Langues

Les demandes d'entraide judiciaire ou d'extradition, les pièces à l'appui de ces demandes et les renseignements complémentaires transmis conformément au présent Traité sont accompagnés d'une traduction certifiée dans la langue de la Partie requise.

Article 4. Validité des documents

1. Les documents transmis en vertu du présent Traité et certifiés par le cachet officiel de l'autorité compétente ou de l'autorité centrale de la Partie qui les transmet sont admissibles comme preuve sans nécessiter d'autre autorisation ni aucune autre forme de certification.

À la demande de la Partie requérante, les documents transmis dans le cadre du présent Traité peuvent être certifiés sous toute autre forme, comme indiqué dans la demande, à condition que cela ne soit pas contraire à la législation de la Partie requise.

2. Aux fins du présent Traité, les documents qui sont reconnus comme officiels sur le territoire d'une Partie sont reconnus comme tels sur le territoire de l'autre Partie.

Article 5. Confidentialité et limites de l'utilisation des renseignements

1. La Partie requise, à la demande de l'autorité centrale de la Partie requérante, assure, conformément à sa législation, la confidentialité de la demande d'entraide judiciaire, de sa teneur et de toute action entreprise pour l'exécution de la demande, sauf dans les cas où il est nécessaire de rompre la confidentialité pour exécuter la demande.

Si l'exécution de la demande rend nécessaire la suppression de cette limitation, la Partie requise demande par écrit l'autorisation de la Partie requérante, sans laquelle la demande ne sera pas exécutée.

2. La Partie requérante n'utilise ni les renseignements ni les preuves obtenus en vertu du présent Traité à des fins autres que celles indiquées dans la demande d'entraide judiciaire sans l'autorisation préalable de la Partie requise.

3. Dans les cas où la Partie requérante a besoin de divulguer et d'utiliser tout ou partie des renseignements ou des preuves à des fins autres que celles indiquées dans la demande, elle doit demander le consentement de la Partie requise, qui peut soit accepter soit refuser, totalement ou partiellement, cette autorisation.

CHAPITRE II. ENTRAIDE JUDICIAIRE EN MATIÈRE PÉNALE

Article 6. Obligation d'entraide judiciaire

1. Les Parties s'engagent à s'accorder l'entraide judiciaire en matière d'enquêtes, de poursuites et d'autres actes de procédure en matière pénale (ci-après dénommée « entraide judiciaire ») conformément aux dispositions du présent Traité.

2. La Partie requise peut accorder une aide judiciaire si l'infraction pour laquelle la demande a été reçue n'est pas pénalement punissable en vertu de sa législation.

3. Le présent Traité a pour objet l'octroi d'une aide judiciaire par une Partie à l'autre Partie. Ses dispositions ne confèrent pas à une personne physique ou morale le droit d'obtenir ou d'exclure un élément de preuve ou d'empêcher l'exécution d'une demande.

4. Le présent Traité n'accorde pas aux autorités compétentes d'une Partie le droit d'exercer sur le territoire de l'autre Partie des pouvoirs qui relèvent exclusivement de la compétence de cette autre Partie.

5. Le présent Traité s'applique aux demandes d'entraide judiciaire présentées après la date de son entrée en vigueur, même si les actes ou omissions auxquels elle se rapporte ont eu lieu avant cette date.

Article 7. Champ d'application

L'entraide judiciaire comprend notamment :

1) La remise de documents ;

2) Le recueil de témoignages et de dépositions de personnes et l'obtention d'autres preuves ;

3) La localisation ou l'identification de personnes et d'objets ;

4) L'invitation de témoins, de victimes et d'experts à comparaître volontairement devant l'autorité compétente de la Partie requérante ;

5) Le transfèrement temporaire de personnes détenues ou purgeant une peine d'emprisonnement afin de participer à une procédure pénale sur le territoire de la Partie requérante en tant que témoins et victimes ou aux fins d'autres procédures pénales indiquées dans la demande ;

6) L'adoption de mesures de recherche, de confiscation et de restitution des produits du crime et des instruments du crime ;

7) Le transfert de documents, d'objets et d'autres éléments de preuves ;

8) L'octroi aux personnes visées dans la demande des autorités compétentes de la Partie requérante, de l'autorisation d'assister à l'exécution de la demande ;

9) L'exécution des demandes de poursuites pénales à l'égard des ressortissants de la Partie requise et des apatrides résidant sur son territoire de façon permanente ;

10) Les perquisitions et les saisies ;

11) Toute autre forme d'entraide judiciaire compatible avec les objectifs du présent Traité et qui n'est pas incompatible avec la législation de la Partie requérante.

Article 8. Forme et contenu des demandes

1. Les demandes d'entraide judiciaire sont formulées par écrit.

2. La Partie requise reçoit immédiatement la demande pour exécution dès sa remise par télécopie, courrier électronique ou tout autre type de communication de ce type et l'original de la demande est soumis sans délai par la Partie requérante. La Partie requise n'informe la Partie requérante des résultats de l'exécution de la demande qu'à la condition qu'elle en reçoive l'original.

3. Les demandes d'entraide comportent :

a) Le nom de l'autorité compétente requérante ;

b) L'indication de l'objectif de la demande et une description de l'aide demandée ;

c) Une description de l'acte à propos duquel l'enquête ou la procédure est menée, sa qualification juridique, des extraits des textes de lois pertinents de la Partie requérante nécessaires à l'exécution de la demande, les noms complets des suspects, des accusés ou des condamnés ; des indications sur leur domicile ou leur résidence, leur nationalité et leur profession et, si possible, les lieux et dates de naissance et les noms des parents, et pour les personnes morales le titre, l'adresse légale et effective ;

d) Si cela est utile, une indication du montant des dommages subis du fait de l'infraction ;

e) Les raisons de l'utilisation et une description de toute procédure particulière que la Partie requérante souhaite voir suivie dans l'exécution de la demande ;

f) Les données permettant d'identifier les témoins ou les victimes ;

g) La spécification du délai dans lequel la Partie requérante souhaiterait qu'il soit donné suite à sa demande ;

h) Les noms et adresses complets et, si possible, les numéros de téléphone des personnes qui doivent être informées, et leur lien avec l'enquête ou la procédure en cours ;

i) Des indications sur l'emplacement et la description du lieu où l'inspection et la perquisition sont requises, et des objets à saisir ;

j) Les questions à poser afin de recueillir des preuves dans la Partie requise ;

k) Si les autorités compétentes de la Partie requérante indiquent que la présence des personnes qu'elles ont désignées est souhaitée, leurs noms complets et leurs désignations officielles ainsi que les motifs de leur présence ;

l) La nécessité, le cas échéant, de préserver la confidentialité de la demande, de son contenu et/ou de toute action entreprise dans le cadre de la demande ;

m) Toute autre information qui pourrait se révéler utile à la Partie requise pour l'exécution de la demande.

4. Si la Partie requise estime que les renseignements contenus dans la demande sont insuffisants pour son exécution, elle pourra demander un complément d'information.

Article 9. Exécution d'une demande

1. Les demandes d'entraide judiciaire sont exécutées conformément à la législation de la Partie requise et aux dispositions du présent Traité. Toutefois, à la demande de la Partie requérante, sa législation pourra être appliquée dans la mesure où elle n'est pas contraire à celle de la Partie requise.

2. Les autorités centrales des Parties exécutent directement la demande d'entraide judiciaire ou la transmettent à l'autorité compétente pour exécution. Si une autorité centrale transmet la demande d'exécution à une autorité compétente, elle prend toutes les dispositions utiles pour que cette dernière exécute ladite demande de manière rapide et appropriée.

3. Si la Partie requérante demande que les personnes indiquées par ses autorités compétentes soient présentes lors de l'exécution d'une demande, la Partie requise informera la Partie requérante de sa décision. En cas de décision favorable, la Partie requérante sera informée au préalable de la date et du lieu d'exécution de la demande.

4. L'autorité centrale de la Partie requise envoie, après l'exécution de la demande, les renseignements et les documents concernant l'exécution de la demande à l'autorité centrale de la Partie requérante.

5. En cas d'impossibilité d'exécuter la demande, l'autorité centrale de la Partie requise informe l'autorité centrale de la Partie requérante de ce fait, ainsi que des raisons empêchant l'exécution de la demande.

Article 10. Refus ou report de l'entraide judiciaire

1. Les demandes d'entraide judiciaire peuvent être refusées si :
   a) La Partie requise estime que l'exécution de la demande pourrait porter atteinte à sa souveraineté, à sa sécurité, à l'ordre public ou à d'autres intérêts essentiels ;
   b) La Partie requise a de sérieux motifs de croire que la demande a été présentée en vue de poursuivre la personne en raison de sa race, de son genre, de sa religion, de sa nationalité, de son origine ethnique ou de ses opinions politiques, ou qu'il pourrait être porté atteinte à la situation de cette personne pour l'une de ces raisons ;
   c) L'exécution de la demande est considérée par la Partie requise comme incompatible avec sa législation et les dispositions du présent Traité ;
   d) La demande porte sur une infraction au regard de la loi militaire mais non au regard de la loi pénale ordinaire ;
   e) La demande concerne une infraction pour laquelle la personne accusée d'une infraction pénale dans la Partie requérante a été condamnée ou acquittée dans la Partie requise en relation avec la même infraction, ou pour laquelle le délai de prescription s'est écoulé conformément aux lois de la Partie requise.

2. Le secret bancaire ou la confidentialité des données fiscales ne peut être invoqué comme un motif absolu de refus d'accorder l'entraide judiciaire.

3. La Partie requise peut différer ou refuser l'exécution de la demande d'entraide judiciaire si son exécution risque de nuire ou d'entraver une enquête en cours ou des poursuites sur son territoire.

4. Avant d'opposer un refus définitif à une demande d'entraide ou de différer son exécution, la Partie requise examine si elle ne pourrait pas y consentir sous certaines conditions. Si la Partie requérante souscrit à ces conditions, elle sera tenue de les observer.

5. Si la Partie requise décide de différer l'exécution d'une demande ou de refuser d'y faire droit, elle en informe la Partie requérante dans les plus brefs délais par l'intermédiaire de son autorité centrale et motive sa décision.

Article 11. Comparution de témoins, de victimes et d'experts, et sauf-conduit

1. Si la Partie requérante soumet une demande de comparution personnelle pour produire des éléments de preuve, réaliser une expertise ou pour d'autres mesures procédurales sur son territoire, la Partie requise informe cette personne de l'invitation à comparaître devant les autorités compétentes de la Partie requérante.

2. La demande de comparution contient des renseignements sur les conditions et les exigences relatives à la couverture des coûts et des frais liés à la comparution de la personne citée, ainsi que la liste des garanties qui seront fournies à la personne en vertu des paragraphes 5 et 6 du présent article.

3. Les invitations visées au paragraphe 1 ne contiennent pas de menace de recourir à des mesures coercitives ou à des sanctions en cas de non-comparution de la personne sur le territoire de la Partie requérante.

4. La personne convoquée prendra la décision de se présenter volontairement. L'autorité centrale de la Partie requise informe sans délai l'autorité centrale de la Partie requérante de la réponse de l'intéressé.

5. Une personne présente devant l'autorité compétente de la Partie requérante, quelle que soit sa nationalité, ne peut être poursuivie, détenue ou soumise à quelque autre restriction de liberté personnelle sur le territoire de cette Partie pour quelque acte ou condamnation que ce soit, qui est antérieur à son départ du territoire de la Partie requise.

6. La personne convoquée ne peut être contrainte de témoigner pour une affaire autre que celle indiquée dans la demande.

7. La personne convoquée perd le droit à l'inviolabilité prévu au présent article si, étant libre de quitter le territoire de la Partie requérante, elle ne l'a pas fait dans un délai de 15 jours après qu'il lui a été notifié par écrit que sa présence n'était plus requise par l'autorité compétente concernée ou si, ayant quitté ce territoire, elle y est retournée volontairement.

Article 12. Transfèrement temporaire de détenus
(y compris ceux qui purgent une peine d'emprisonnement)

1. Une personne détenue (y compris une personne qui purge une peine d'emprisonnement), quelle que soit sa nationalité, dont la comparution personnelle en tant que témoin ou victime ou pour prêter son concours à d'autres procédures indiquées dans la demande est demandée par la Partie requérante, peut être transférée temporairement sur le territoire de la Partie requérante, à condition d'être renvoyée dans le délai fixé par la Partie requise et sous réserve des paragraphes 5 et 6 de l'article 11 du présent Traité, dans la mesure où ces dispositions sont applicables.

La durée initiale du transfèrement de la personne n'excède pas 90 jours. À la demande de l'autorité centrale de la Partie requérante, fondée sur des motifs substantiels, la durée du séjour de la personne transférée peut être prolongée par l'autorité centrale de la Partie requise.

L'ordre et les conditions de transfèrement et de retour de la personne sont coordonnés par les autorités centrales des Parties.

2. Le transfèrement peut être refusé :

a) Si la personne détenue n'y consent pas ;

b) Si sa présence est nécessaire dans une procédure pénale en cours sur le territoire de la Partie requise ;

c) Si son transfèrement est susceptible de prolonger sa détention ;

d) S'il existe d'autres motifs valables de ne pas transférer la personne sur le territoire de la Partie requérante.

3. La personne transférée reste en détention sur le territoire de la Partie requérante sur la base et en vertu de sa législation et dans la mesure où la décision de l'autorité compétente de la Partie requérante de la maintenir en détention est en vigueur. En cas de libération de la personne détenue sur décision de la Partie requise, la Partie requérante applique les dispositions des paragraphes 5 et 6 de l'article 11 et de l'article 21 du présent Traité à l'égard de cette personne.

4. La période de détention de la personne en dehors du territoire de la Partie requise est considérée comme faisant partie de sa détention.

5. Si la personne détenue ne consent pas à comparaître devant la Partie requérante, elle ne peut, de ce fait, faire l'objet d'aucune mesure de contrainte ou de sanction.

Article 13. Protection de la personne comparaissant sur demande ou transférée sur le territoire de la Partie requérante

Si nécessaire, la Partie requérante assure la protection de la personne qui comparaît sur demande ou qui est transférée sur son territoire, conformément aux articles 11 et 12 du présent Traité.

Article 14. Remise d'actes

1. La Partie requise procède à la remise d'actes accompagnés d'une traduction certifiée établie dans sa langue selon les modalités prévues par sa propre législation.

2. La Partie requérante transmet une demande de remise d'acte relatif à une réponse ou à une comparution sur le territoire de la Partie requérante dans un délai raisonnable, avant la réponse ou la comparution prévue, normalement au plus tard 60 jours avant la date prévue pour la comparution.

3. L'adresse connue du destinataire et la nature de l'acte sont indiquées dans la demande de remise d'actes.

4. L'exécution de cette demande est confirmée par le document de remise indiquant la date et la signature du destinataire ou par la déclaration de l'autorité compétente de la Partie requise, confirmant le fait, la date et le moyen de remise des actes.

5. La Partie requérante est informée sans délai de la remise des actes ou de l'impossibilité de les remettre.

Article 15. Demande de poursuites pénales

1. Sur demande et conformément à sa législation, chaque Partie s'engage à poursuivre ses ressortissants et les apatrides ayant une résidence permanente sur son territoire qui ont commis une infraction relevant de la compétence de l'autre Partie.

Dès réception de ladite demande, la Partie requise transmet le dossier reçu à ses autorités compétentes afin qu'elles prennent la décision d'engager des poursuites pénales conformément à la législation de cette Partie.

2. Les demandes de poursuites pénales contiennent les renseignements suivants :

a) Le nom de l'autorité compétente requérante ;

b) Le nom complet de la personne qui est soupçonnée d'avoir commis un crime, sa nationalité et, dans la mesure du possible, des renseignements sur son domicile ou son lieu de résidence, une description de son apparence, une photographie, ses empreintes digitales ou toute autre donnée nécessaire à son identification ;

c) Une description et la classification juridique de l'acte pour lequel la demande de poursuites est transmise ;

d) Une indication précise, dans la mesure du possible, de l'heure et du lieu de l'infraction ;

e) Si nécessaire, une demande de restitution des documents originaux et des objets de preuve matérielle.

3. Les documents suivants sont fournis à l'appui de la demande de poursuites pénales :

a) Les dossiers d'enquête ou des copies certifiées de ceux-ci, y compris les éléments de preuve disponibles ;

b) Le texte de la législation pénale applicable et, si nécessaire, des autres lois de la Partie requérante qui sont essentielles pour les poursuites ;

c) Le cas échéant, dans la mesure du possible, des données sur le montant des dommages ;

d) Les demandes des victimes pour l'engagement de poursuites pénales, si cela est requis conformément à la législation de la Partie requise.

4. En vue de garantir les droits légitimes des tiers, la Partie requise, après avoir accompli les actes de procédure, restitue, à la demande de la Partie requérante, les documents originaux et les éléments de preuves matérielles.

5. La Partie requise notifie à la Partie requérante les mesures prises dans le cadre de la demande formulée par cette dernière, le résultat des poursuites pénales et lui transmet une copie du jugement définitif.

6. Lorsqu'une demande a été reçue, qu'une décision d'une autorité judiciaire de la Partie requise a été rendue contre la personne visée par la demande et que ladite décision est entrée en vigueur, les autorités compétentes de la Partie requérante ne peuvent pas poursuivre ladite personne pour la même infraction.

7. Lorsque la Partie requise a pris la décision de ne pas faire droit à la demande ou de clore l'affaire ou qu'un accord à l'amiable a été conclu pour ne pas engager de procédure, les dossiers et les éléments de preuves matérielles transférés par la Partie requérante lui sont restitués sans délai.

Article 16. Recueil de témoignages sur le territoire de la Partie requise

1. La Partie requise recueille sur son territoire des témoignages et des avis d'experts ou produit les documents, objets et éléments de preuves indiqués dans la demande et les transmet à la Partie requérante.

2. Les personnes indiquées par la Partie requérante qui sont présentes lors de l'exécution de la demande sont autorisées à formuler des questions qui peuvent être posées à la personne concernée par l'intermédiaire du représentant de l'autorité compétente de la Partie requise.

3. La Partie requérante respecte toute condition imposée par la Partie requise en ce qui concerne les documents et objets qui peuvent lui être remis, y compris les conditions relatives à la protection des intérêts des tiers dans lesdits documents et objets.

4. Si la Partie requise en fait la demande, la Partie requérante restitue, dès que possible, les originaux des documents et objets qui lui ont été remis conformément au paragraphe 1 du présent article.

Article 17. Transmission de renseignements, de documents et d'objets

1. La Partie requise fournit à la Partie requérante des copies des documents et des renseignements des autorités gouvernementales qui, conformément à sa législation, sont accessibles au public.

2. La Partie requise peut, sous réserve de sa législation, fournir à la Partie requérante les renseignements, les documents et les objets en la possession d'une autorité gouvernementale, mais qui ne sont pas publics, dans la même mesure et dans les mêmes conditions que s'ils étaient disponibles pour ses propres autorités répressives et judiciaires.

3. Chaque Partie peut fournir à l'autre Partie les renseignements ou documents qui, selon elle, pourraient être utilisés dans le cadre de poursuites pénales contre des personnes physiques ou morales ou pour l'ouverture de procédures pertinentes à l'égard de personnes morales en lien avec la commission d'infractions par des personnes physiques.

Article 18. Perquisitions et saisies

1. Dans la mesure où sa législation le permet, la Partie requise procède aux perquisitions, aux saisies et à la livraison de documents et d'objets à la Partie requérante qui sont pertinents pour une enquête ou d'autres procédures en rapport avec l'affaire pénale pendante dans la Partie requérante, à condition que la demande contienne des renseignements suffisants pour justifier ladite action conformément à la législation de la Partie requise.

2. La Partie requise fournit les renseignements demandés par la Partie requérante concernant le résultat d'une perquisition, le lieu et les circonstances de la saisie ainsi que la garde ultérieure des documents et objets saisis.

3. La Partie requérante respecte les conditions imposées par la Partie requise en ce qui concerne les documents et objets saisis qui lui sont remis.

Article 19. Localisation ou identification de personnes ou d'objets

Les autorités compétentes de la Partie requise prennent toutes les dispositions utiles, conformément à sa législation, pour établir l'emplacement et l'identité des personnes et des objets mentionnés dans la demande.

Article 20. Mise en œuvre de mesures de recherche, de blocage, de confiscation et de restitution des produits du crime et des instruments du crime

1. Les Parties, conformément à leur législation, se prêtent mutuellement assistance pour localiser, geler, bloquer et confisquer les produits et instruments du crime.

Aux fins du présent Traité, l'expression « produits du crime » désigne les fonds monétaires ou autres biens reçus à la suite d'un crime, les revenus et autres avantages tirés de ces produits, ou les biens en lesquels les produits du crime ont été convertis ou transformés, ou les biens auxquels les produits du crime ont été adjoints.

2. Sur demande, la Partie requise s'efforce d'établir si des produits du crime ou des instruments du crime se trouvent sur son territoire, et informe la Partie requérante des résultats de ses investigations. Lorsqu'elle présente sa demande, la Partie requérante fait connaître à la Partie requise les raisons qui la portent à croire que lesdits produits ou instruments pourraient se trouver sur son territoire.

3. Lorsque, en application du paragraphe 2 du présent article, des produits ou instruments du crime présumés sont découverts, la Partie requise donne suite, sur demande, à une ordonnance restrictive rendue par une autorité compétente de la Partie requérante ou prend les mesures permises par sa législation pour empêcher toute négociation, toute cession ou toute aliénation de ces produits ou instruments du crime présumés, en attendant qu'ils aient fait l'objet d'une décision définitive de la part d'un tribunal de la Partie requérante ou de la Partie requise.

4. La Partie requise, dans la mesure où son droit le permet, donne effet à une décision définitive rendue par une autorité compétente de la Partie requérante concernant la saisie ou la confiscation des produits ou des instruments du crime.

5. Dans l'application du présent article, les droits des tiers de bonne foi sont respectés conformément à la législation de la Partie requise.

6. À la demande de la Partie requérante, la Partie requise peut, dans la mesure où sa législation le permet et selon les modalités et conditions convenues par les autorités centrales des Parties, transférer les produits ou instruments du crime à la Partie requérante.

7. Les dispositions du présent article ne portent pas atteinte aux droits et obligations des Parties découlant d'autres accords internationaux multilatéraux auxquels elles sont parties.

Article 21. Frais

1. La Partie requise prend en charge les dépenses régulières engagées pour l'exécution de la demande d'entraide judiciaire, à l'exception de celles qui sont à la charge de la Partie requérante :

a) Les frais liés au voyage des personnes à destination et en provenance de son territoire conformément aux articles 11 et 12 du présent Traité et à leur présence sur ce territoire, ainsi que les autres paiements dus à ces personnes ;

b) Les frais et honoraires des experts ;

c) Les frais liés au voyage et à la présence des personnes indiquées par les autorités compétentes de la Partie requérante lors de l'exécution de la demande conformément au paragraphe 3 de l'article 9 du présent Traité ;

d) Les frais liés au passage des objets transmis du territoire de la Partie requise au territoire de la Partie requérante et inversement.

2. Si les dépenses liées à la fourniture de l'entraide judiciaire nécessitent des dépenses importantes ou de nature extraordinaire, les autorités centrales des Parties se consultent pour déterminer les conditions dans lesquelles l'aide demandée peut être fournie, ainsi que l'ordre de règlement des frais.

CHAPITRE III. EXTRADITION

Article 22. Obligation d'extrader

1. Dans le cadre des dispositions du présent Traité, les Parties s'engagent à se livrer réciproquement, sur demande, les personnes qui se trouvent sur leur territoire et qui sont recherchées par la Partie requérante aux fins de procédures pénales ou de l'exécution d'une peine pour des infractions donnant lieu à extradition.

2. L'extradition aux fins de procédures pénales est accordée uniquement pour les infractions punies d'une peine d'emprisonnement d'au moins 12 mois ou d'une peine plus sévère en vertu de la législation des deux Parties.

3. L'extradition d'une personne aux fins de l'exécution d'une peine n'est accordée que pour les infractions punies d'une peine d'emprisonnement et dans le cas où la personne recherchée a été condamnée à une peine d'emprisonnement d'au moins quatre mois à purger ou à une peine plus sévère en vertu de la législation des deux Parties.

4. Si la demande d'extradition vise plusieurs infractions distinctes punies chacune d'une peine d'emprisonnement par la législation des deux Parties, mais dont certaines ne remplissent pas les conditions définies aux paragraphes 2 et 3 du présent article, la Partie requise peut également accorder l'extradition pour ces dernières infractions.

5. Les différences de terminologie juridique ne font pas obstacle à l'exécution de la demande d'extradition, si l'acte pour lequel l'extradition est demandée est un acte pénal tel que défini dans le droit applicable des deux Parties.

6. Si l'infraction a été commise hors du territoire de la Partie requérante, l'extradition est accordée dans les cas où la législation de la Partie requise prévoit de punir une infraction commise hors de son territoire dans des circonstances similaires.

7. Le présent Traité s'applique aux demandes d'extradition formulées dès la date de son entrée en vigueur, même si elles concernent des infractions commises avant cette date.

Article 23. Refus d'extradition

1. L'extradition n'est pas accordée si :
   a) L'acte pour lequel l'extradition est demandée n'est pas une infraction donnant lieu à extradition en vertu du présent Traité ;
   b) La personne recherchée est un ressortissant de la Partie requise ;
   c) Aucunes poursuites pénales ne peuvent être engagées ou le jugement ne peut plus être exécuté pour cause de prescription ou pour un autre motif prévu dans la législation de la Partie requise ;
   d) La personne recherchée fait l'objet de poursuites pénales, d'un procès en cours, d'un jugement définitif ou d'un non-lieu prononcé par l'autorité compétente de la Partie requise pour la même infraction que celle pour laquelle l'extradition est demandée ;
   e) La Partie requise a de sérieux motifs de croire que la demande d'extradition a été présentée en vue de poursuivre ou de punir une personne en raison de sa race, de son sexe, de sa religion, de sa citoyenneté, de son origine ethnique ou par rapport à ses opinions politiques ou à d'autres convictions ;

f) La Partie requise estime que l'extradition de la personne est susceptible de porter atteinte à sa souveraineté, à sa sécurité, à son ordre public ou à d'autres intérêts essentiels ;

g) L'infraction pour laquelle l'extradition est demandée est punie de mort selon la législation applicable de la Partie requérante, à moins que cette Partie ne présente des assurances suffisantes, de l'avis de la Partie requise, à l'effet que la personne dont l'extradition est demandée ne risque pas la peine de mort.

2. Toute demande d'extradition peut être rejetée si l'infraction pour laquelle elle est demandée, conformément au droit applicable de la Partie requise, a été commise entièrement ou partiellement sur le territoire de cette Partie.

3. Si la Partie requise n'extrade pas la personne recherchée conformément à l'alinéa b) du paragraphe 1 ou au paragraphe 2 du présent article, elle remet, à la demande de la Partie requérante, tous les éléments reçus à ses autorités compétentes pour qu'elles envisagent d'engager des poursuites pénales contre cette personne conformément à sa législation. Pour ce faire, les fichiers, les renseignements et autres éléments de preuve relatif à l'infraction sont soumis par la Partie requérante à la Partie requise. Tous les éléments de l'affaire, reçus dans le cadre de l'enquête menée dans la Partie requérante, peuvent être utilisés dans le cadre de la procédure pénale dans la Partie requise. La Partie requérante est informée des résultats de cet examen et des procédures pénales.

La Partie requérante n'utilise pas les témoins, les déclarations ou les objets fournis conformément au présent Traité pour effectuer des enquêtes ou des actes de procédure autres que ceux spécifiés dans la demande, à moins que l'autorité centrale de la Partie requise n'y consente.

Article 24. Arrestation provisoire

1. En cas d'urgence, l'autorité centrale de la Partie requérante peut demander l'arrestation provisoire de la personne recherchée. L'autorité centrale de la Partie requise statue sur la question conformément à sa législation.

2. La demande d'arrestation provisoire indique qu'il existe un mandat d'arrêt ou une condamnation définitive contre la personne recherchée et que l'extradition va être demandée. Elle précise également l'infraction pour laquelle l'extradition sera demandée ainsi que le moment et le lieu où ladite infraction a été commise. Dans la mesure du possible, il est donné une description de la personne recherchée.

3. La demande d'arrestation provisoire est envoyée à l'autorité centrale de la Partie requise soit par la voie diplomatique, soit directement par la poste ou par télécopie, soit par l'intermédiaire de l'Organisation internationale de police criminelle (INTERPOL), soit par tout autre moyen permettant de fournir une déposition écrite ou acceptée par la Partie requise.

4. La Partie requérante est informée de la suite donnée à sa demande dans les plus brefs délais.

5. L'arrestation provisoire peut prendre fin si, dans un délai de 18 jours après l'arrestation, la Partie requise n'a pas reçu la demande d'extradition et le mandat d'arrêt ou la condamnation définitive concernant la personne recherchée. L'arrestation provisoire ne peut en aucun cas se prolonger au-delà de 40 jours à compter de la date de l'arrestation. La possibilité de libération provisoire à tout moment n'est pas exclue, mais la Partie requise prend toutes les mesures qu'elle juge nécessaires pour empêcher la fuite de la personne recherchée.

6. La remise en liberté ne fait pas obstacle à une nouvelle arrestation et à l'extradition si la demande à cet effet est reçue ultérieurement.

Article 25. Demandes et documents à l'appui

1. La demande d'extradition est faite par écrit et envoyée par l'autorité centrale de l'une des Parties à l'autorité centrale de l'autre Partie. Elle contient le nom de l'autorité compétente de la Partie requérante, le nom complet de la personne recherchée, sa nationalité et sa description physique, dans la mesure du possible, des renseignements sur sa résidence ou son domicile et est accompagnée d'une photographie et des empreintes digitales de la personne recherchée, si possible.

2. Une demande d'extradition présentée aux fins de toute procédure pénale est accompagnée d'une copie certifiée conforme au mandat d'arrêt, d'un exposé de l'acte constitutif de l'infraction et du texte intégral des articles pertinents du droit applicable à l'infraction, ainsi que du délai de prescription. Si l'infraction a entraîné un dommage pécuniaire, le montant du dommage est indiqué de manière aussi précise que possible.

3. Une demande présentée aux fins de l'exécution d'une peine est accompagnée d'une copie certifiée conforme au jugement définitif et du texte intégral des articles pertinents du droit applicable à l'infraction, ainsi que du délai de prescription et d'une indication de la durée de la peine purgée.

4. La Partie requise reçoit immédiatement la demande d'extradition dès sa remise par télécopie, courrier électronique ou tout autre type de communication de ce type et l'original de la demande est soumis sans délai par la Partie requérante.

Article 26. Complément d'information

1. Si une demande d'extradition ne contient pas tous les renseignements nécessaires, la Partie requise peut demander qu'un complément d'information soit fourni. Pour ce faire, la Partie requise peut fixer un délai n'excédant pas 30 jours. Dans des cas exceptionnels, le délai indiqué peut être prolongé avec l'accord des autorités centrales des Parties, pour une durée n'excédant pas 30 jours.

2. Si la personne visée par la demande d'extradition est en détention et que le complément d'information fourni n'est pas jugé suffisant ou n'a pas été reçu dans le délai prévu au paragraphe 1 du présent article, la personne peut être remise en liberté. Cette remise en liberté n'empêche pas la Partie requérante de présenter une nouvelle demande d'extradition de cette personne et de la placer en détention.

3. Lorsque la personne est remise en liberté en application du paragraphe 2 du présent article, la Partie requise en avertit dès que possible la Partie requérante.

Article 27. Concours de demandes

Si plusieurs États demandent l'extradition de la même personne, soit pour la même infraction, soit pour des infractions différentes, la Partie requise décide vers lequel de ces États la personne doit être extradée en prenant en considération toutes les circonstances, notamment la gravité et le lieu de l'infraction, les dates des demandes, les traités d'extradition, la nationalité et le lieu de résidence principal de la personne recherchée pour extradition.

Article 28. Notification de la décision relative à la demande

1. La Partie requise communique sa décision relative à l'extradition à la Partie requérante.

2. Les motifs de tout refus total ou partiel de la demande d'extradition sont communiqués à la Partie requérante.

Article 29. Remise d'une personne

1. S'il est fait droit à la demande, les autorités compétentes des Parties conviennent de la date et du lieu de la remise de la personne. La Partie requise informe la Partie requérante de la durée pendant laquelle cette personne a été détenue en vertu de la demande d'extradition, afin que cette durée soit prise en considération dans la détermination de la durée totale d'incarcération de cette personne.

2. Si l'extradition est accordée, la Partie requérante reçoit la personne remise dans un délai de 30 jours à compter de la date de la notification de cette décision. Si aucune prise en charge par la Partie requérante n'a lieu dans ce délai, cette personne est remise en liberté.

3. Si des circonstances indépendantes de sa volonté empêchent une Partie de remettre ou d'emmener la personne à extrader, elle en informe l'autre Partie et le délai de remise peut être prolongé de 15 jours au maximum. Si aucune remise n'a lieu dans le délai fixé, la personne est libérée.

4. Si le transport de la personne faisant l'objet de l'extradition vers le territoire de la Partie requérante peut présenter un risque pour sa vie ou sa santé, la remise est reportée jusqu'à ce que, selon l'autorité centrale de la Partie requise, son état de santé permette d'effectuer cette remise.

Article 30. Remise reportée ou conditionnelle

1. La Partie requise, après avoir statué sur la demande d'extradition, peut reporter la remise de la personne recherchée afin d'engager des procédures contre cette personne ou, si la personne a déjà été condamnée, afin qu'elle purge sa peine sur le territoire de cette Partie pour une infraction autre que celle pour laquelle l'extradition est demandée.

2. Si le report de l'extradition prévu au paragraphe 1 du présent article risque d'entraîner un délai ou de nuire à l'enquête sur un crime, la Partie requise peut remettre la personne recherchée à la Partie requérante pour une durée maximale de 90 jours. La personne ainsi remise est maintenue en détention sur le territoire de la Partie requérante et renvoyée sur le territoire de la Partie requise après l'accomplissement des actes de procédure la concernant, conformément aux conditions convenues par les Parties. Si nécessaire, ce délai peut être prolongé par accord écrit des Parties jusqu'à 90 jours.

Article 31. Règle de la spécialité

Une personne extradée ne peut être placée en détention, poursuivie, punie, soumise à l'exécution d'une sentence, ni transférée vers un pays tiers, ni soumise à aucune restriction de sa liberté personnelle pour une infraction commise avant sa remise, et qui est autre que celle qui a donné lieu à l'extradition, sauf :

a) Lorsque la Partie requise donne son consentement. Dans ce cas, la Partie requérante soumet à la Partie requise les renseignements et les documents visés à l'article 25 du présent Traité, qui sont nécessaires pour prendre la décision d'accorder ce consentement ;

b) Lorsque cette personne, ayant eu la possibilité de quitter le territoire de la Partie à laquelle elle a été remise, ne l'a pas fait dans les 30 jours qui suivent sa libération définitive, ou, ayant quitté ce territoire, elle y est retournée. Il n'est pas tenu compte du délai pendant lequel la personne extradée ne peut quitter librement le territoire de la Partie requérante pour des raisons indépendantes de sa volonté.

Article 32. Remise d'objets

1. S'il est fait droit à la demande d'extradition, dans la mesure où la législation de la Partie requise le permet et en prenant dûment en considération les droits des tiers, les objets trouvés sur le territoire de la Partie requise, dont l'acquisition est le résultat de l'infraction commise ou qui peuvent constituer des éléments de preuve dans le cadre d'une procédure pénale sont remis à la Partie requérante. Les objets peuvent être remis même si l'extradition ne peut être réalisée en raison du décès ou de l'évasion de la personne recherchée.

2. La Partie requise peut reporter temporairement la remise des objets mentionnés au paragraphe 1 du présent article si elle estime que ceux-ci sont nécessaires dans d'autres procédures.

3. Lorsque la législation applicable de la Partie requise ou les droits de tiers l'exigent, les objets ainsi remis sont retournés à la Partie requise sans frais, le plus rapidement possible une fois la procédure achevée, si cette Partie le demande.

Article 33. Transit

1. Chaque Partie peut, si l'autre Partie fait une demande à cet effet en y joignant les documents et renseignements nécessaires visés à l'article 25 du présent Traité ainsi qu'une copie de la décision d'extradition, permettre qu'une personne devant être extradée de cette Partie vers un État tiers transite par son territoire.

2. Les autorités compétentes des Parties conviennent du type, de l'itinéraire et des autres conditions de transit dans chaque cas.

3. L'autorisation visée au paragraphe 1 du présent article n'est pas requise si ce transport en transit est effectué par voie aérienne et qu'aucun atterrissage sur le territoire de l'autre Partie n'est prévu.

4. En cas d'atterrissage imprévu d'un aéronef, la demande de transit faite conformément au paragraphe 1 du présent article est présentée. Avant la réception de la demande de transit, la Partie sur le territoire de laquelle l'atterrissage a eu lieu peut détenir la personne faisant l'objet d'une extradition pendant 24 heures, à la demande de l'officier qui escorte cette personne, jusqu'à ce que la demande de transit, faite conformément au paragraphe 1 du présent article, soit reçue. La détention ultérieure de la personne faisant l'objet de l'extradition est effectuée conformément à la législation de cette Partie.

5. Cette demande de transit peut être rejetée dans les cas prévus aux paragraphes 1 et 2 de l'article 23 du présent Traité.

Article 34. Communication de renseignements

Les Parties échangent des renseignements sur les résultats des procédures pénales engagées contre des personnes extradées, sur leur évasion, ainsi que sur la réextradition de la personne vers un État tiers. En outre, sur demande, les Parties se transmettent mutuellement la copie de la décision finale concluant la procédure pénale contre la personne extradée.

Article 35. Frais

1. La Partie requise prend à sa charge les frais de toute procédure découlant d'une demande d'extradition engagée sur son territoire.
2. La Partie requise prend à sa charge les frais afférents sur son territoire à l'arrestation et à la détention de la personne visée par une procédure d'extradition, ou à la saisie et à la cession de biens.
3. Si les frais liés à la saisie et à la cession de biens ont un caractère extrême, les autorités centrales des Parties organisent des consultations en vue de leur répartition.
4. La Partie requérante prend à sa charge les frais de restitution des biens à la Partie requise en application du paragraphe 3 de l'article 32 du présent Traité.
5. La Partie requérante prend à sa charge les frais du transport de la personne dont l'extradition est consentie hors du territoire de la Partie requise, y compris les frais de transit.

CHAPITRE IV. DISPOSITIONS FINALES

Article 36. Consultations et règlement des différends

1. Les autorités centrales des Parties se consultent, à l'initiative de l'une ou de l'autre, au sujet de l'interprétation ou de l'application du présent Traité.
2. Les questions litigieuses découlant de l'interprétation et de l'application du présent Traité sont réglées par voie de négociations diplomatiques.

Article 37. Amendements du présent Traité

Des dispositions supplémentaires peuvent être insérées dans le présent Traité ou des amendements peuvent y être apportés par un protocole distinct, avec le consentement mutuel des Parties contractantes. Les ajouts et les amendements entrent en vigueur selon les procédures prévues à l'article 38 du présent Traité.

Article 38. Entrée en vigueur et dénonciation

1. Le présent Traité entre en vigueur 30 jours après la dernière date à laquelle les Parties se sont notifié, par la voie diplomatique, l'accomplissement de leurs formalités respectives nécessaires à l'entrée en vigueur du présent Traité.
2. Le présent Traité prend fin 180 jours après la date à laquelle l'une des Parties a reçu par la voie diplomatique une notification écrite de l'autre Partie de son intention de le dénoncer.

3. La dénonciation du présent Traité ne peut être une cause de non-exécution d'une demande d'entraide judiciaire ou d'extradition reçue avant la date de réception de la notification visée au paragraphe 2 du présent article.

FAIT à Ankara, le 1er décembre 2014, en double exemplaire en langues turque, russe et anglaise, tous les textes faisant également foi. En cas de divergence d'interprétation, le texte anglais prévaut.

Pour la République turque :

BEKIR BOZDAĞ
Ministre de la justice

Pour la Fédération de Russie :

ALEKSANDR KONOVALOV
Ministre de la justice

No. 54790

Poland
and
Russian Federation

Agreement between the Government of the Republic of Poland and the Government of the Russian Federation on cooperation in the field of culture, science and education. Warsaw, 25 August 1993

Entry into force: *15 December 1993 by notification, in accordance with article 30*

Authentic texts: *Polish and Russian*

Registration with the Secretariat of the United Nations: *Poland, 1 November 2017*

Pologne
et
Fédération de Russie

Accord entre le Gouvernement de la République de Pologne et le Gouvernement de la Fédération de Russie sur la coopération dans les domaines de la culture, de la science et de l'éducation. Varsovie, 25 août 1993

Entrée en vigueur : *15 décembre 1993 par notification, conformément à l'article 30*

Textes authentiques : *polonais et russe*

Enregistrement au Secrétariat de l'Organisation des Nations Unies : *Pologne, 1er novembre 2017*

[TEXT IN POLISH – TEXTE EN POLONAIS]

UMOWA MIĘDZY RZĄDEM RZECZYPOSPOLITEJ POLSKIEJ A RZĄDEM FEDERACJI ROSYJSKIEJ O WSPÓŁPRACY W DZIEDZINIE KULTURY, NAUKI I OŚWIATY

Rząd Rzeczypospolitej Polskiej i Rząd Federacji Rosyjskiej zwane dalej Stronami,

kierując się zasadami i celami Aktu Końcowego Konferencji Bezpieczeństwa i Współpracy w Europie, Dokumentami Końcowymi Spotkania Madryckiego i Wiedeńskiego, postanowieniami Paryskiej Karty Nowej Europy i Dokumentu Sympozjum Krakowskiego na temat dziedzictwa kulturalnego,

uwzględniając postanowienia Europejskiej Konwencji Kulturalnej z 1954r.,

kierując się postanowieniami Traktatu między Rzecząpospolitą Polską a Federacją Rosyjską o przyjaznej i dobrosąsiedzkiej współpracy z 22 maja 1992 roku,

rozwijając postanowienia Deklaracji o współpracy kulturalnej, naukowej i oświatowej między Rządem Rzeczypospolitej Polskiej a Rządem Federacji Rosyjskiej z dnia 22 maja 1992 roku,

opierając się na wielowiekowych tradycjach powiązań kulturalnych pomiędzy narodami obu Państw i ich wkładzie do cywilizacji ogólnoświatowej,

biorąc pod uwagę przemiany społeczno-polityczne, gospodarcze i socjalne w obydwu Państwach,

w celu wspierania wzajemnie korzystnej współpracy i wymiany między instytucjami kulturalnymi, naukowymi i oświatowymi oraz nadania szczególnego znaczenia bezpośrednim kontaktom międzyludzkim,

uzgodniły co następuje:

ARTYKUŁ 1

Strony będą popierać rozwój dwustronnej współpracy kulturalnej i wymiany na wzajemnie korzystnych zasadach. Każda ze Stron będzie podejmować wysiłki mające na celu popularyzację osiągnięć artystycznych i kulturalnych drugiej Strony, zapewniając swobodny dostęp do nich swoich obywateli, wspierając kontakty państwowe, społeczne i prywatne.

ARTYKUŁ 2

Strony będą z odpowiednim wyprzedzeniem informować się o międzynarodowych konferencjach, konkursach, festiwalach i innych imprezach w dziedzinie kultury i sztuki, które odbywają się w ich Państwach.

ARTYKUŁ 3

Strony będą popierać nawiązywanie bezpośrednich kontaktów i wymianę grup operowych, baletowych i teatralnych i innych zespołów artystycznych i solistów.

Będą one udzielały pomocy w realizacji wymiany zawodowych zespołów operowych, teatralnych i innych chórów i orkiestr oraz zespołów folklorystycznych, na zasadach komercyjnych.

ARTYKUŁ 4

Strony będą sprzyjać wymianie wystaw między muzeami, galeriami, bibliotekami i archiwami, udzielając wystawom gwarancji rządowych, łącznie z odpowiedzialnością finansową i ubezpieczeniem, oraz wspierać będą wymianę pracowników merytorycznych tych instytucji.

ARTYKUŁ 5

Strony będą popierać współpracę w dziedzinie kinematografii i w tym celu podpiszą odrębne Porozumienie o współpracy i wspólnej realizacji filmów. Będą one przyczyniać się do popularyzacji sztuki filmowej swoich krajów przez wymianę filmów na zasadach handlowych i niehandlowych oraz przez organizację tygodni filmów drugiej Strony.

Odpowiednie instytucje będą zapraszać się do udziału w festiwalach organizowanych w kraju drugiej Strony oraz będą popierać bezpośrednie kontakty między twórcami filmowymi i przedstawicielami kinematografii obu krajów.

ARTYKUŁ 6

Strony będą popierać rozwój bezpośrednich kontaktów i współpracę organizacji twórczych, fundacji i instytucji kulturalnych.

ARTYKUŁ 7

Strony będą sprzyjać wzajemnemu przekazywaniu doświadczeń w dziedzinie rozwoju kultury, sztuki i literatury przez organizowanie konferencji i innych spotkań naukowych oraz przez wymianę specjalistów i wspólną działalność naukowo-badawczą.

ARTYKUŁ 8

Strony będą udzielać pomocy w działalności Ośrodka Informacji i Kultury Polskiej w Rosji oraz Rosyjskiego Ośrodka Nauki i Kultury w Polsce. Działalność ta będzie regulowana odrębnym porozumieniem międzyrządowym.

ARTYKUŁ 9

Strony będą podejmować wysiłki na rzecz zachowania zabytków kulturalno-historycznych i innych obiektów kultury materialnej i duchowej jednej Strony na terytorium Drugiej. Przedmiotem szczególnej uwagi będzie zachowanie pomników i miejsc pamięci, związanych z historią dwóch narodów i zapewnienie do nich swobodnego dostępu.

ARTYKUŁ 10

Strony zobowiązują się do podejmowania działań w celu zapobieżenia bezprawnemu wwozowi i wywozowi i przekazywaniu własności dóbr kultury każdej ze Stron. Zgodnie ze swym ustawodawstwem wewnętrznym i zobowiązaniami międzynarodowymi, Strony zapewnią współdziałanie kompetentnych organów państwowych, wymianę informacji i podejmowanie działań związanych z przywróceniem słusznych praw do własności dóbr kultury oraz do ich zwrotu w przypadku bezprawnego wywozu lub wwozu na terytoria swoich krajów.

ARTYKUŁ 11

Strony będą współdziałać na rzecz ujawniania, scalania, ochrony prawnej i materialnej, wprowadzania do obrotu kulturalnego i zwrotu znajdujących się na ich terytorium dóbr kultury związanych z historycznym i kulturalnym dziedzictwem narodów drugiej Strony, włącznie ze zbiorami artystycznymi, bibliotecznymi i archiwalnymi, które zaginęły, zostały bezprawnie wywiezione lub w inny nielegalny sposób znalazły się na jej terytorium.

Prace te będą koordynowane przez specjalnych pełnomocników rządowych, którzy podpiszą odpowiednie porozumienia.

ARTYKUŁ 12

Biorąc pod uwagę, że znajomość języka polskiego i rosyjskiego jest ważnym czynnikiem współpracy, Strony będą popierać naukę i upowszechnianie języka polskiego w Rosji, jak i języka rosyjskiego w Polsce.

Strony będą stwarzać dogodne warunki dla nauki języka ojczystego obywatelom polskiego pochodzenia w Rosji i obywatelom pochodzenia rosyjskiego w Polsce, przez włączenie szkół polskojęzycznych i rosyjskojęzycznych do struktur szkolnictwa Polski i Rosji.

ARTYKUŁ 13

Strony będą popierać działalność mającą na celu zachowanie i rozwój tożsamości narodowej, kulturalnej, religijnej i językowej Polaków zamieszkałych w Rosji oraz przedstawicieli narodów i grup etnicznych Federacji Rosyjskiej, zamieszkałych w Polsce.

W tym celu będą one popierać zachowanie powiązań kulturalnych mniejszości z ich ojczyzną etniczną, zachowanie tradycji, zapewniając możliwość swobodnych kontaktów, w tym podróży do etnicznej ojczyzny. Strony będą udzielać wszechstronnego poparcia dla działalności organizacji społeczno-kulturalnych mniejszości narodowych i w ramach wewnętrznego ustawodawstwa umożliwią im otrzymywanie pomocy materialnej z etnicznej ojczyzny.

ARTYKUŁ 14

Strony będą wspierać wymianę naukowców, wykładowców, studentów i uczniów w celu kształcenia, uzupełniania wiedzy i specjalizacji oraz prowadzenia wspólnych badań naukowych, udziału w sympozjach, konferencjach i innych zgromadzeniach naukowych, będących przedmiotem wspólnego zainteresowania.

ARTYKUŁ 15

Strony będą sprzyjać rozwojowi bezpośrednich kontaktów i współpracy pomiędzy szkołami wyższymi, średnimi i zawodowymi, instytucjami i organizacjami naukowymi, kultury i sztuki na podstawie zawartych między nimi umów, porozumień i programów.

Strony popierać będą również współpracę między uczelniami artystycznymi.

ARTYKUŁ 16

Strony będą sprzyjać rozwojowi współpracy w dziedzinie szkolenia zawodowego i podwyższania kwalifikacji kadr.

ARTYKUŁ 17

Strony będą sprzyjać nawiązywaniu bezpośrednich kontaktów między organizacjami i instytucjami Rzeczypospolitej Polskiej i Federacji Rosyjskiej zajmującymi się sprawami nauczania, wychowania i rehabilitacji dzieci z zaburzeniami rozwojowymi i dzieci niepełnosprawnych.

ARTYKUŁ 18

Strony będą współpracować w dziedzinie rozwoju kształcenia pozaszkolnego.

ARTYKUŁ 19

Strony będą współdziałać w dziedzinie ochrony praw dzieci i nieletnich zgodnie z Konwencją Organizacji Narodów Zjednoczonych o prawach dziecka z 1989r.

ARTYKUŁ 20

Strony przeprowadzą rozmowy w celu zawarcia porozumienia między Rządem Rzeczypospolitej Polskiej i Rządem Federacji Rosyjskiej o wzajemnym uznaniu równoważności dokumentów o wykształceniu, stopniach i tytułach naukowych.

W okresie do zawarcia nowego porozumienia pozostają w mocy analogiczne uzgodnienia, a zwłaszcza Porozumienie z dnia 10 maja 1974 roku.

ARTYKUŁ 21

Strony będą popierać rozwój współpracy między instytucjami naukowymi obu krajów.

ARTYKUŁ 22

Uwzględniając swoje ustawodawstwo państwowe, Strony będą popierać wzajemnie korzystną współpracę, w dziedzinie prasy i środków masowego przekazu, przez zawieranie bezpośrednich porozumień między odpowiednimi instytucjami i organizacjami zawodowymi dziennikarzy, wspólne wydawnictwa, wymianę specjalistów, sprzyjanie wystąpieniom w środkach masowego przekazu jednej Strony przedstawicieli kultury i nauki drugiej Strony, organizowanie wystaw książek, wzajemny udział w międzynarodowych targach książki odbywających się na terytorium ich Państw.

Strony będą popierać bezpośrednią współpracę między polskimi i rosyjskimi stacjami telewizyjnymi i radiowymi, a także odpowiednimi instytucjami. Formy i warunki będą omówione w bezpośrednich porozumieniach między nimi.

ARTYKUŁ 23

Strony będą sprzyjać dalszemu rozwojowi współpracy między instytucjami archiwalnymi obu krajów w takich podstawowych dziedzinach jak wymiana informacji, specjalistów, kopii dokumentów archiwalnych, pomoc badaczom w ich pracy w archiwach, wydawanie wspólnych zbiorów dokumentów, zwrot dokumentów na podstawie odrębnych porozumień.

ARTYKUŁ 24

Strony będą współpracować w dziedzinie praw autorskich i pokrewnych. Tryb i warunki takiej współpracy określa odrębne porozumienie.

ARTYKUŁ 25

Strony będą realizować współpracę w dziedzinie ochrony zdrowia i nauk medycznych na podstawie bezpośrednich porozumień.

ARTYKUŁ 26

Strony będą popierać współpracę w dziedzinie kultury fizycznej i sportu oraz przyczyniać się do bezpośrednich kontaktów między sportowcami, trenerami, działaczami, drużynami i organizacjami sportowymi swych krajów.

ARTYKUŁ 27

Strony będą rozwijać współpracę między państwowymi organizacjami i instytucjami, odpowiadającymi za sprawy młodzieży oraz popierać bezpośrednie kontakty między organizacjami młodzieżowymi i młodzieżą obu krajów.

ARTYKUŁ 28

Strony będą popierać rozwój wymiany turystycznej w celu wzajemnego zapoznania się z kulturą i nauką obu krajów.

ARTYKUŁ 29

Strony będą realizować współpracę i wymianę w dziedzinie kultury, nauki i oświaty na zasadach wzajemności.

Konkretne warunki finansowe będą uzgadniane w bezpośrednich porozumieniach i programach współpracy między odpowiednimi instytucjami i resortami w ramach ich kompetencji i zgodnie z ustawodawstwem każdego kraju.

ARTYKUŁ 30

Niniejsza Umowa wejdzie w życie w dniu ostatniego pisemnego zawiadomienia potwierdzającego spełnienie odpowiednich wymogów wewnętrznych, niezbędnych dla jej wejścia w życie.

Niniejsza Umowa zostaje zawarta na okres pięciu lat i automatycznie ulega przedłużaniu na kolejne okresy pięcioletnie, jeżeli żadna ze Stron nie wypowie jej w drodze notyfikacji, na sześć miesięcy przed upływem danego okresu.

Sporządzono w Warszawie, dnia 25 sierpnia 1993 roku, w dwóch egzemplarzach w językach polskim i rosyjskim, przy czym obydwa teksty mają jednakową moc.

Z UPOWAŻNIENIA RZĄDU RZECZYPOSPOLITEJ POLSKIEJ

Z UPOWAŻNIENIA RZĄDU FEDERACJI ROSYJSKIEJ

[TEXT IN RUSSIAN – TEXTE EN RUSSE]

СОГЛАШЕНИЕ

МЕЖДУ ПРАВИТЕЛЬСТВОМ РЕСПУБЛИКИ ПОЛЬША И ПРАВИТЕЛЬСТВОМ РОССИЙСКОЙ ФЕДЕРАЦИИ О СОТРУДНИЧЕСТВЕ В ОБЛАСТИ КУЛЬТУРЫ, НАУКИ И ОБРАЗОВАНИЯ

Правительство Республики Польша и Правительство Российской Федерации, далее именуемые Сторонами,

руководствуясь принципами и целями хельсинкского Заключительного акта Совещания по безопасности и сотрудничеству в Европе, Итоговых документов Мадридской и Венской встреч, положениями Парижской хартии для новой Европы и Документа Краковского симпозиума по культурному наследию,

принимая во внимание положения Европейской культурной конвенции 1954 года,

исходя из положений Договора между Республикой Польша и Российской Федерацией о дружественном и добрососедском сотрудничестве от 22 мая 1992 года,

в развитие положений Декларации о сотрудничестве в области культуры, науки и образования между Правительством Республики Польша и Правительством Российской Федерации от 22 мая 1992 года,

опираясь на многовековые традиции культурных связей между народами обеих стран и их вклад в мировую цивилизацию,

принимая во внимание общественно-политические, экономические и социальные перемены в обеих странах,

с целью поощрения взаимовыгодного сотрудничества и обмена между культурными, научными и образовательными учреждениями, а также придавая особое значение непосредственным контактам между людьми,

согласились о нижеследующем:

СТАТЬЯ 1

Стороны будут поощрять развитие двустороннего культурного сотрудничества и обмена на взаимовыгодной основе. Каждая из Сторон будет прилагать усилия для популяризации художественных и культурных ценностей другой Стороны, обеспечивая широкий доступ своих граждан к ним, поощряя государственные, общественные и частные контакты.

СТАТЬЯ 2

Стороны будут своевременно информировать друг друга о международных конференциях, конкурсах, фестивалях и других мероприятиях в области культуры и искусства, которые проводятся в их странах.

СТАТЬЯ 3

Стороны будут поощрять установление прямых контактов и взаимный обмен оперными, балетными и театральными труппами и другими исполнительскими коллективами и солистами.

Они будут оказывать содействие в осуществлении обмена профессиональными оперными, театральными и другими труппами, хорами и оркестрами, фольклорными коллективами на коммерческой основе.

СТАТЬЯ 4

Стороны будут содействовать развитию обмена выставками между музеями, библиотеками, архивами, принимая меры к обеспечению правительственных гарантий, включая финансовую ответственность и страхование в отношении таких выставок, а также поощрять обмены специалистами этих учреждений.

СТАТЬЯ 5

Стороны будут содействовать сотрудничеству в области кинематографии и с этой целью подпишут Соглашение о сотрудничестве и совместном производстве фильмов. Они будут способствовать популяризации киноискусства своих стран путем обмена фильмами на коммерческой и некоммерческой основе, а также проведения недель фильмов другой Стороны.

Соответствующие учреждения будут приглашать друг друга для участия в фестивалях, проводимых другой Стороной и поощрять развитие прямых контактов между деятелями киноискусства и представителями кинематографии обеих стран.

СТАТЬЯ 6

Стороны будут поощрять развитие прямых контактов и сотрудничества между творческими организациями, фондами и культурными институтами.

СТАТЬЯ 7

Стороны будут содействовать взаимному обмену опытом в области развития культуры, искусства и литературы путем организации конференций и других научных форумов, а также посредством взаимного обмена специалистами и совместной научно-исследовательской деятельности.

СТАТЬЯ 8

Стороны будут оказывать помощь в осуществлении деятельности Польского центра информации и культуры в России и Российского центра науки и культуры в Польше, которая будет регулироваться отдельным межправительственным соглашением.

СТАТЬЯ 9

Стороны будут прилагать усилия к сохранению культурно-исторических памятников и других объектов материальной и духовной культуры одной Стороны на территории другой Стороны. Предметом особого внимания станет сохранение памятников и памятных мест, связанных с историей двух народов и обеспечение к ним свободного доступа.

СТАТЬЯ 10

Стороны обязуются принимать меры по предотвращению незаконного ввоза, вывоза и передачи собственности на культурные ценности каждой из Сторон. В соответствии со своим внутренним законодательством и международными обязательствами. Стороны обеспечат взаимодействие компетентных государственных органов Сторон в обмене информацией и принятии мер, связанных с восстановлением законных прав собственности на культурные ценности, возвращении их по принадлежности при незаконном вывозе и ввозе на территории своих стран.

СТАТЬЯ 11

Стороны будут сотрудничать с целью выявления, сохранения в целостности, правовой и материальной защиты, введения в культурный оборот и возвращения находящихся на их территории культурных ценностей, связанных с историческим и культурным наследием народов другой Стороны, включая художественные, библиотечные и архивные фонды, пропавшие, незаконно вывезенные или оказавшиеся иным незаконным образом на территории другой Стороны.

Эту работу будут координировать специальные уполномоченные правительств, которые подпишут соответствующие соглашения.

СТАТЬЯ 12

Учитывая, что знание польского и русского языков является важным фактором сотрудничества. Стороны будут поощрять изучение и распространение как польского языка в России, так и русского языка в Польше.

Стороны будут содействовать созданию благоприятных условий для изучения родного языка гражданами польского происхождения в России и гражданами русского происхождения в Польше путем включения польско- и русскоязычных школ в образовательные системы Польши и России.

СТАТЬЯ 13

Стороны будут поддерживать деятельность, направленную на сохранение и развитие национальной, культурной, религиозной, языковой самобытности поляков, проживающих в России, а также представителей народов и этнических групп Российской Федерации, проживающих в Польше. В этих целях они будут содействовать поддержанию культурных связей меньшинств со своей этнической родиной, сохранению их традиций, обеспечивая возможность свободных контактов, в том числе поездок на этническую родину. Они будут оказывать всестороннюю поддержку деятельности общественно-культурных организаций национальных меньшинств, а также предоставят им, в рамках внутреннего законодательства, возможность получения материальной помощи с этнической родины.

СТАТЬЯ 14

Стороны будут поощрять взаимный обмен научными работниками, преподавателями, студентами и учащимися для обучения и специализации, а также проведения совместных научных исследований, участия в симпозиумах, конференциях и других научных форумах, представляющих взаимный интерес.

СТАТЬЯ 15

Стороны будут способствовать развитию прямых связей и сотрудничества между высшими, средними и профессиональными учебными заведениями, учреждениями и организациями науки, культуры и искусства на основе заключенных между ними договоров, соглашений и программ.

Стороны будут также поддерживать сотрудничество между художественными высшими учебными заведениями.

СТАТЬЯ 16

Стороны будут оказывать содействие развитию сотрудничества в области профессиональной подготовки и переподготовки кадров.

СТАТЬЯ 17

Стороны будут содействовать установлению прямых связей между организациями и учреждениями Республики Польша и Российской Федерации, занимающимися вопросами обучения, воспитания и реабилитации детей с аномалией в развитии и детей-инвалидов.

СТАТЬЯ 18

Стороны будут сотрудничать в области развития внешкольного образования.

СТАТЬЯ 19

Стороны будут взаимодействовать в области охраны прав детей и несовершеннолетних в соответствии с Конвенцией Организации Объединенных Наций о правах ребенка 1989 года.

СТАТЬЯ 20

Стороны проведут переговоры с целью заключения Соглашения между Правительством Республики Польша и Правительством Российской Федерации о взаимном признании и эквивалентности документов о полученном образовании, ученых степеней и званий.

В период до заключения нового соглашения остаются в силе ранее подписанные аналогичные договоренности, а именно Соглашение от 10 мая 1974 года.

СТАТЬЯ 21

Стороны будут содействовать развитию сотрудничества между научными учреждениями обеих стран.

СТАТЬЯ 22

С учетом национального законодательства, Стороны на взаимовыгодных условиях будут поощрять сотрудничество в области печати и средств массовой информации, в частности, путем заключения прямых соглашений между соответствующими учреждениями и профессиональными организациями журналистов, совместного производства печатной продукции, обмена специалистами, содействия выступлению в средствах массовой информации одной Стороны деятелей культуры и науки другой Стороны, организации книжных выставок, взаимного участия в международных книжных ярмарках, проводимых на территории их государств.

Стороны будут поддерживать прямое сотрудничество между российскими и польскими телевизионными и радиокомпаниями, а также соответствующими организациями, формы и условия которого могут быть оговорены в прямых соглашениях между ними.

СТАТЬЯ 23

Стороны будут способствовать дальнейшему развитию сотрудничества между архивными учреждениями двух стран по таким основным направлениям, как обмен информацией, специалистами, копиями архивных документов, содействие исследователям в их работе в архивах, издание совместных документальных сборников, возвращение документов на основе специальных договоренностей.

СТАТЬЯ 24

Стороны будут сотрудничать в сфере авторских и смежных прав. Порядок и условия такого сотрудничества определяются отдельным соглашением.

СТАТЬЯ 25

Стороны будут осуществлять сотрудничество в области здравоохранения и медицинских наук на основе прямых соглашений.

СТАТЬЯ 26

Стороны будут поддерживать развитие сотрудничества в области физической культуры и спорта, а также поощрять прямые связи между спортсменами, тренерами, спортивными руководителями, командами и организациями своих стран.

СТАТЬЯ 27

Стороны будут развивать сотрудничество между государственными организациями и учреждениями, отвечающими за молодежные вопросы, а также поощрять прямые контакты между молодежными организациями и молодыми людьми обеих стран.

СТАТЬЯ 28

Стороны будут содействовать развитию туристических обменов с целью взаимного ознакомления с культурой и наукой обеих стран.

СТАТЬЯ 29

Стороны будут осуществлять сотрудничество и обмен в области культуры, науки и образования на основе взаимности.

Конкретные финансовые условия будут оговариваться в прямых соглашениях и программах сотрудничества между соответствующими учреждениями и ведомствами в рамках их компетенции и в соответствии с законодательством каждой страны.

СТАТЬЯ 30

Настоящее Соглашение вступает в силу с даты последнего письменного уведомления, подтверждающего выполнение соответствующих внутригосударственных процедур, необходимых для его вступления в силу.

Настоящее Соглашение заключается сроком на пять лет и автоматически продлевается на последующие пятилетние периоды, если одна из Сторон не уведомит в письменном виде другую Сторону не менее, чем за шесть месяцев до истечения очередного срока о своем намерении прекратить его действие.

Совершено в Варшаве "25" августа 1993 года в двух экземплярах, каждый на польском и русском языках, причем оба текста имеют одинаковую силу.

ЗА ПРАВИТЕЛЬСТВО РЕСПУБЛИКИ ПОЛЬША	ЗА ПРАВИТЕЛЬСТВО РОССИЙСКОЙ ФЕДЕРАЦИИ

[TRANSLATION IN ENGLISH – TRADUCTION EN ANGLAIS]

AGREEMENT BETWEEN THE GOVERNMENT OF THE REPUBLIC OF POLAND AND THE GOVERNMENT OF THE RUSSIAN FEDERATION ON COOPERATION IN THE FIELD OF CULTURE, SCIENCE AND EDUCATION

The Government of the Republic of Poland and the Government of the Russian Federation, hereinafter referred to as the Parties,

Guided by the purposes and principles of the Final Act of the Conference on Security and Cooperation in Europe, the Concluding Documents of the Madrid Meeting and the Vienna Meeting, the provisions of the Charter of Paris for a New Europe and the Document of the Cracow Symposium on the cultural heritage of the CSCE Participating States,

Taking into account the provisions of the European Cultural Convention of 1954,

Bearing in mind the provisions of the Treaty between the Republic of Poland and the Russian Federation on friendly and good-neighbourly cooperation of 22 May 1992,

Further to the provisions of the declaration on cooperation in the field of culture, science and education between the Government of the Republic of Poland and the Government of the Russian Federation of 22 May 1992,

On the basis of the centuries-old traditions of cultural relations between the peoples of the two countries and their contribution to world civilization,

Taking into account the sociopolitical, economic and social changes in both countries,

In order to promote mutually beneficial cooperation and exchanges between cultural, scientific and educational institutions, while attaching special importance to direct interpersonal contact,

Have agreed as follows:

Article 1

The Parties shall encourage the development of bilateral cultural cooperation and exchanges on a mutually beneficial basis. Each Party shall endeavour to popularize the artistic and cultural treasures of the other Party by ensuring broad public access to them and encouraging State, public and private contacts.

Article 2

The Parties shall inform each other in a timely manner of international conferences, competitions, festivals and other events in the spheres of culture and the arts which are held in their countries.

Article 3

The Parties shall encourage the establishment of direct contacts and exchanges of opera, ballet and theatre groups and other performance groups and soloists.

They shall promote the exchanges of professional opera, theatre and other groups, choirs and orchestras and folklore groups on a commercial basis.

Article 4

The Parties shall promote exchanges of exhibitions among museums, libraries and archives by ensuring Government guarantees, including financial liability and insurance, in respect of such exhibitions, and shall also encourage exchanges of specialists of such institutions.

Article 5

The Parties shall promote cooperation in the field of cinematography and, to that end, shall sign an agreement on cooperation in joint film production. They shall facilitate the popularization of the cinematographic art of their own countries by exchanging films on a commercial and non-commercial basis, as well as holding film weeks for films of the other Party.

The relevant institutions shall invite each other to participate in festivals held by the other Party and shall encourage the development of direct contact between film personalities and cinematographic representatives of both countries.

Article 6

The Parties shall encourage the development of direct contact and cooperation between creative organizations, funds and cultural institutions.

Article 7

The Parties shall promote the exchanges of experience in the spheres of cultural development, art and literature by organizing conferences and other academic forums as well as exchanges of specialists and joint research activities.

Article 8

The Parties shall provide assistance for the activities of the Polish information and cultural centre in the Russian Federation and of the Russian centre for science and culture in Poland, which shall be governed by a separate intergovernmental agreement.

Article 9

The Parties shall make efforts to preserve cultural and historical monuments and other sites of material and spiritual cultural value of one Party in the territory of the other Party. Special attention shall be paid to the conservation of monuments and sites associated with the history of the two peoples and ensuring unrestricted access to them.

Article 10

The Parties undertake to adopt measures to prevent the illegal import, export and transfer of ownership of cultural treasures of each Party. In line with their domestic law and international obligations, the Parties shall ensure cooperation between competent State authorities in the exchange of information and the adoption of measures for the restoration of legal rights of ownership of cultural property and its return in the event of illegal export or import into their territories.

Article 11

The Parties shall cooperate in identifying, preserving, ensuring legal and material protection for, bringing into cultural circulation and returning cultural treasures in their territory associated with the historical and cultural heritage of the peoples of the other Party, including art, library and archival collections which have been lost, illegally exported or have otherwise illegally appeared in their territory.

This work shall be coordinated by special Government commissioners, who shall sign corresponding agreements.

Article 12

Given that knowledge of the Polish and Russian languages is an important factor in cooperation, the Parties shall encourage the study and dissemination of the Polish language in the Russian Federation and of the Russian language in Poland.

The Parties shall promote the establishment of an environment fostering the study of their native language by citizens of Polish origin in the Russian Federation and citizens of Russian origin in Poland by including Polish and Russian language schools in the educational systems of Poland and the Russian Federation.

Article 13

The Parties shall support activities aimed at preserving and developing the ethnic, cultural, religious and linguistic identity of Poles living in the Russian Federation, as well as members of the populations and ethnic groups of the Russian Federation living in Poland.

To this end, they shall promote the maintenance by minorities of cultural ties with their ethnic homelands, the preservation of their traditions and ensure the possibility of unhindered contact, including visits to ethnic homelands. They shall provide comprehensive support to the activities of social and cultural organizations of national minorities, and, within the framework of domestic law, shall accord them the possibility of receiving financial support from their ethnic homeland.

Article 14

The Parties shall encourage exchanges of academics, teachers, students and schoolchildren for training and specialized study, and also for undertaking joint academic research and participating in symposiums, conferences and other scientific forums of mutual interest.

Article 15

The Parties shall facilitate the development of direct links and cooperation between higher, secondary and vocational education institutions, and scientific, cultural and arts agencies and organizations, through treaties, agreements and programmes concluded between them.

The Parties shall also support cooperation between higher art education institutions.

Article 16

The Parties shall promote the development of cooperation in the area of vocational training and retraining.

Article 17

The Parties shall promote the establishment of direct links between the organizations and agencies of the Republic of Poland and the Russian Federation concerned with the training, education and rehabilitation of children with developmental problems and disabled children.

Article 18

The Parties shall cooperate in the development of extracurricular education.

Article 19

The Parties shall cooperate in the area of protection of the rights of children and adolescents in accordance with the Convention on the Rights of the Child of 1989.

Article 20

The Parties shall conduct negotiations with a view to concluding an agreement between the Government of the Republic of Poland and the Government of the Russian Federation on the mutual recognition and equivalence of educational diplomas, academic degrees and titles.

Pending the conclusion of a new agreement, similar agreements signed previously, specifically the Agreement of 10 May 1974, shall remain in force.

Article 21

The Parties shall promote cooperation between academic institutions of the two countries.

Article 22

Taking into account domestic law, and on mutually beneficial terms, the Parties shall encourage cooperation in the area of press and the media, in particular through the conclusion of direct agreements between relevant agencies and professional organizations of journalists, joint publication of printed materials, exchanges of specialists, promotion of coverage in the media of one Party relating to culture and science of the other Party, the organization of book exhibitions, and reciprocal participation in international book fairs held in their territories.

The Parties shall support direct cooperation between Russian and Polish television and radio companies, as well as relevant organizations, the forms and terms of which may be determined in direct agreements between them.

Article 23

The Parties shall facilitate the further development of cooperation between the archive institutions of the two countries in key areas such as exchanges of information, specialists, copies of archive documents, assistance for research workers in their archive work, issuance of joint documentary collections and the return of documents on the basis of special arrangements.

Article 24

The Parties shall cooperate in the field of copyright and related rights. The procedure and conditions for such cooperation shall be determined in a separate agreement.

Article 25

The Parties shall cooperate in the field of health care and medical science on the basis of direct agreements.

Article 26

The Parties shall support the development of cooperation in the field of physical culture and sports and shall also encourage direct contact between athletes, coaches and sports directors, teams and organizations of their countries.

Article 27

The Parties shall develop cooperation between State organizations and institutions responsible for youth issues and shall also encourage direct contacts between youth organizations and young people of the two countries.

Article 28

The Parties shall promote tourist exchanges as a means of gaining knowledge about the culture and science of each country.

Article 29

The Parties shall engage in cooperation and exchanges in culture, science and education on a basis of reciprocity.

Specific financial conditions shall be stipulated in direct agreements and programmes of cooperation between relevant institutions and departments within their areas of competence and in accordance with the legislation of each country.

Article 30

This Agreement shall enter into force from the date of the last written notification confirming completion of the relevant domestic procedures required for its entry into force.

This Agreement shall be concluded for a period of five years and shall be automatically extended for subsequent five-year periods unless one of the Parties notifies the other Party in writing, no less than six months before the expiration of such period, of its intention to terminate it.

DONE at Warsaw on 25 August 1993 in two copies, in the Polish and Russian languages, both texts being equally authentic.

For the Government of the Republic of Poland:
[KRZYSZTOF SKUBISZEWSKI]

For the Government of the Russian Federation:
[ANDREY KOZYREV]

[TRANSLATION IN FRENCH – TRADUCTION EN FRANÇAIS]

ACCORD ENTRE LE GOUVERNEMENT DE LA RÉPUBLIQUE DE POLOGNE ET LE GOUVERNEMENT DE LA FÉDÉRATION DE RUSSIE SUR LA COOPÉRATION DANS LES DOMAINES DE LA CULTURE, DE LA SCIENCE ET DE L'ÉDUCATION

Le Gouvernement de la République de Pologne et le Gouvernement de la Fédération de Russie, ci-après dénommés les Parties,

Guidés par les buts et principes énoncés dans l'Acte final de la Conférence sur la sécurité et la coopération en Europe d'Helsinki, les textes issus des réunions de Madrid et de Vienne, les dispositions de la Charte de Paris pour une nouvelle Europe et le document du Symposium de Cracovie sur le patrimoine culturel,

Tenant compte des dispositions de la Convention culturelle européenne de 1954,

Ayant à l'esprit les dispositions du Traité de coopération amicale et de bon voisinage entre la République de Pologne et la Fédération de Russie du 22 mai 1992,

Conformément aux dispositions de la Déclaration sur la coopération dans le domaine de la culture, de la science et de l'éducation entre le Gouvernement de la République de Pologne et le Gouvernement de la Fédération de Russie du 22 mai 1992,

Sur la base des traditions séculaires des relations culturelles entre les peuples des deux pays et de leur contribution à la civilisation mondiale,

Tenant compte des changements sociopolitiques, économiques et sociaux dans les deux pays,

Afin de promouvoir une coopération et des échanges mutuellement bénéfiques entre les institutions culturelles, scientifiques et éducatives, tout en accordant une importance particulière aux contacts directs entre les personnes,

Sont convenus de ce qui suit :

Article premier

Les Parties encouragent le développement de la coopération et des échanges culturels bilatéraux sur une base mutuellement avantageuse. Chaque Partie s'efforce de populariser les trésors artistiques et culturels de l'autre Partie en garantissant leur accès à un large public et en encourageant les contacts entre l'État, les acteurs publics et les acteurs privés.

Article 2

Les Parties s'informent en temps utile des conférences, concours, festivals et autres manifestations internationales dans le domaine de la culture et des arts qui se tiennent dans leurs pays.

Article 3

Les Parties encouragent la création de contacts directs et d'échanges entre groupes d'opéra, de ballet et de théâtre et autres groupes et solistes du spectacle.

Elles coopèrent en faveur de l'échange de groupes professionnels d'opéra, de théâtre et autres, de chœurs, d'orchestres et de groupes folkloriques sur une base commerciale.

Article 4

Les Parties soutiennent les échanges d'expositions entre musées, bibliothèques et archives en assurant pour ces expositions les garanties gouvernementales, notamment en ce qui concerne la responsabilité financière et l'assurance, et encouragent également les échanges de spécialistes de ces institutions.

Article 5

Les Parties encouragent la coopération dans le domaine de la cinématographie et signent à cette fin un accord de coopération et de coproduction cinématographique. Elles facilitent la popularisation de l'art cinématographique de leurs pays en échangeant des films sur une base commerciale et non commerciale, ainsi qu'en organisant des semaines cinématographiques pour les films de l'autre Partie.

Les institutions concernées s'invitent mutuellement à participer aux festivals organisés par l'autre Partie et encouragent le développement de contacts directs entre les personnalités et les représentants du cinéma des deux pays.

Article 6

Les Parties encouragent le développement de contacts directs et de la coopération entre les organisations créatives, les fonds et les institutions culturelles.

Article 7

Les Parties encouragent l'échange d'expériences dans le domaine du développement culturel, de l'art et de la littérature en organisant des conférences et des forums universitaires, ainsi que des échanges de spécialistes et des activités de recherche conjointes.

Article 8

Les Parties soutiennent les activités du centre culturel et d'information polonais en Fédération de Russie et du centre russe pour la science et la culture en Pologne, qui sont régies par un accord intergouvernemental distinct.

Article 9

Les Parties s'efforcent de préserver les monuments culturels et historiques et les autres sites ayant une valeur culturelle matérielle et spirituelle d'une Partie sur le territoire de l'autre Partie. Une attention particulière est accordée à la conservation des monuments et des sites associés à l'histoire des deux peuples et à la garantie de leur accès sans restriction.

Article 10

Les Parties s'engagent à adopter des mesures pour prévenir l'importation, l'exportation et le transfert de propriété illégaux des trésors culturels de chaque Partie. Conformément à leur droit interne et à leurs obligations internationales, les Parties assurent la collaboration de leurs autorités gouvernementales compétentes dans l'échange d'informations et l'adoption de mesures pour le rétablissement des droits légaux de propriété des trésors culturels et leur restitution à leurs propriétaires légitimes en cas d'exportation et d'importation illégales sur leurs territoires.

Article 11

Les Parties coopèrent pour identifier, préserver, assurer la protection juridique et matérielle, mettre en circulation culturelle et restituer les trésors culturels se trouvant sur leur territoire associés au patrimoine historique et culturel des peuples de l'autre Partie, y compris les collections d'art, documentaires et d'archives qui ont été perdues, exportées illégalement ou qui sont apparues illégalement sur leur territoire de toute autre manière.

Ce travail est coordonné par des commissaires spéciaux du Gouvernement, qui signeront les accords correspondants.

Article 12

La connaissance des langues polonaise et russe étant un important facteur de coopération, les Parties encouragent l'étude et la diffusion de la langue polonaise en Russie et de la langue russe en Pologne.

Les Parties agissent pour la création d'un environnement favorable à l'étude de leur langue maternelle par les citoyens d'origine polonaise en Russie et par les citoyens d'origine russe en Pologne, en incorporant des écoles de langues polonaise et de langue russe dans les systèmes éducatifs de la Pologne et de la Russie.

Article 13

Les Parties soutiennent les activités visant à préserver et à développer l'identité ethnique, culturelle, religieuse et linguistique des Polonais vivant en Russie, ainsi que des membres des populations et des groupes ethniques de la Fédération de Russie vivant en Pologne. À cette fin, elles favorisent le maintien des liens culturels des minorités avec leurs patries ethniques et la préservation de leurs traditions, en assurant la possibilité de contacts sans entrave, notamment de visites des patries ethniques. Elles apportent un soutien global aux activités des organisations sociales et culturelles des minorités nationales et, dans le cadre du droit interne, leur accordent la possibilité de recevoir un soutien financier de leur patrie ethnique.

Article 14

Les Parties encouragent les échanges d'universitaires, de professeurs, d'étudiants et d'écoliers à des fins de formation et d'études spécialisées, ainsi que pour entreprendre des activités de recherche universitaire conjointe et participer à des symposiums, conférences et autres forums scientifiques d'intérêt mutuel.

Article 15

Les Parties facilitent le développement de liens directs et la coopération entre les établissements d'enseignement supérieur, secondaire et professionnel ainsi qu'entre les agences et organisations scientifiques, culturelles et artistiques, par le biais de traités, d'accords et de programmes conclus entre ces acteurs.

Les Parties soutiennent également la coopération entre les établissements d'enseignement supérieur artistique.

Article 16

Les Parties favorisent le développement de la coopération dans le domaine de la formation professionnelle et de la formation continue.

Article 17

Les Parties favorisent la création de liens directs entre les organisations et agences de la République de Pologne et de la Fédération de Russie concernées par la formation, l'éducation et la réadaptation des enfants ayant des problèmes de développement et des enfants handicapés.

Article 18

Les Parties coopèrent dans le domaine du développement de l'éducation non formelle.

Article 19

Les Parties coopèrent dans le domaine de la protection des droits des enfants et des adolescents, conformément à la Convention relative aux droits de l'enfant des Nations Unies de 1989.

Article 20

Les Parties mènent des négociations en vue de conclure un accord entre le Gouvernement de la République de Pologne et le Gouvernement de la Fédération de Russie sur la reconnaissance mutuelle et l'équivalence des diplômes d'enseignement et des grades et titres universitaires.

En attendant la conclusion d'un nouvel accord, les accords similaires signés antérieurement, notamment l'Accord du 10 mai 1974, restent en vigueur.

Article 21

Les Parties soutiennent la coopération entre les institutions universitaires des deux pays.

Article 22

En tenant compte du droit interne, et dans des conditions mutuellement bénéfiques, les Parties encouragent la coopération dans le domaine de la presse et des médias, notamment par la conclusion d'accords directs entre les agences concernées et les organisations professionnelles de journalistes, la publication conjointe de documents imprimés, les échanges de spécialistes, la promotion de la couverture dans les médias d'une Partie de la culture et de la science de l'autre Partie, l'organisation d'expositions de livres et la participation réciproque aux foires internationales du livre organisées sur leur territoire.

Les Parties soutiennent la coopération directe entre les télévisions et radios russes et polonaises, ainsi que les organisations concernées, sous des formes et dans des conditions qui peuvent être déterminées par des accords passés directement entre ces acteurs.

Article 23

Les Parties facilitent le développement de la coopération entre les institutions chargées des archives des deux pays dans des domaines clés tels que l'échange d'informations, de spécialistes et de copies de documents d'archive, l'assistance aux chercheurs dans leurs travaux d'archivage, la création de collections documentaires communes et la restitution de documents sur la base d'arrangements spéciaux.

Article 24

Les Parties coopèrent dans les domaines des droits d'auteur et des droits voisins. La procédure et les conditions de cette coopération sont déterminées dans un accord distinct.

Article 25

Les Parties coopèrent dans le domaine des soins de santé et de la médecine sur la base d'accords directs.

Article 26

Les Parties soutiennent le développement de la coopération dans le domaine de la culture physique et des sports, et encouragent également les liens directs entre les athlètes, les entraîneurs et les directeurs sportifs, les équipes et les organisations de leurs pays.

Article 27

Les Parties développent la coopération entre les organisations et institutions publiques chargées des questions relatives à la jeunesse et encouragent également les contacts directs entre les organisations de jeunes et les jeunes des deux pays.

Article 28

Les Parties encouragent le développement des échanges touristiques comme moyen d'acquérir des connaissances sur la culture et la science de chaque pays.

Article 29

Les Parties coopèrent et font des échanges dans les domaines de la culture, de la science et de l'éducation sur une base de réciprocité.

Des conditions financières spécifiques sont fixées dans les accords directs et les programmes de coopération entre les institutions et les services concernés dans leurs domaines de compétence et conformément à la législation de chaque pays.

Article 30

Le présent Accord entre en vigueur à la date de la dernière notification écrite confirmant que les procédures internes nécessaires à son entrée en vigueur ont été accomplies.

Le présent Accord est conclu pour une période de cinq ans et est automatiquement reconduit pour des périodes de cinq ans successives, sauf si l'une des Parties notifie par écrit à l'autre Partie, au moins six mois avant l'expiration de la période, son intention de le dénoncer.

FAIT à Varsovie, le 25 août 1993, en deux exemplaires en langues polonaise et en russe, les deux textes faisant également foi.

Pour le Gouvernement de la République de Pologne :
[KRZYSZTOF SKUBISZEWSKI]

Pour le Gouvernement de la Fédération de Russie :
[ANDREI KOZYREV]